D0217906

The Islamic Challenge and the United States

The Islamic Challenge and the United States

Global Security in an Age of Uncertainty

EHSAN M. AHRARI
with
SHARON LEYLAND AHRARI

McGill-Queen's University Press
Montreal & Kingston · London · Chicago

ISBN 978-0-7735-4816-9 (cloth)
ISBN 978-0-7735-4835-0 (ePDF)
ISBN 978-0-7735-4836-7 (ePUB)

Legal deposit first quarter 2017
Bibliothèque nationale du Québec

Printed in Canada on acid-free paper that is 100% ancient forest free (100% post-consumer recycled), processed chlorine free

McGill-Queen's University Press acknowledges the support of the Canada Council for the Arts for our publishing program. We also acknowledge the financial support of the Government of Canada through the Canada Book Fund for our publishing activities.

Library and Archives Canada Cataloguing in Publication

Ahrari, Mohammed E., author
The Islamic challenge and the United States: global security in an age of uncertainty / Ehsan M. Ahrari.

Includes bibliographical references and index.
Issued in print and electronic formats.
ISBN 978-0-7735-4816-9 (cloth). – ISBN 978-0-7735-4835-0 (ePDF). – ISBN 978-0-7735-4836-7 (ePUB)

1. Islamic fundamentalism. 2. Islam – 21st century. 3. Jihad. 4. Terrorism – Religious aspects – Islam. 5. War – Religious aspects – Islam. 6. IS (Organization). 7. Security, International. 8. United States – Foreign relations – Middle East. 9. Middle East – Foreign relations – United States. I. Title.

BP166.14.F85A47 2017 297.7'2 C2016-905567-1
C2016-905568-X

This book was typeset by Marquis Interscript in 10.5/13 Sabon.

To my loving elder brother, Aziz, for his constant encouragement.
To my adoring sister, Khadija, for her unconditional love and prayers.
To my wonderful wife, Sharon, for her persistent work on this book and, above all, for her love.

With endless love and gratitude

Contents

Tables

Abbreviations

AfPak	Afghanistan-Pakistan
AIPAC	American-Israel Political Action Committee
AQAP	Al-Qaida in the Arabian Peninsula
AQI	Al-Qaida in Iraq
AQIM	Al-Qaida in the Islamic Maghreb
AQIP	Al-Qaida in Pakistan
ATC	Anti-Terrorism Centre
AUMF	Authorization to Use Military Force
BMD	ballistic missile defense
BSA	Basic Security Agreement
CENTCOM	Central Command
CIA	Central Intelligence Agency
CIS	Commonwealth of Independent States
CJTF	Combined Joint Task Force
COIN	counterinsurgency
CPA	Coalition Provisional Authority
CRRF	Collective Rapid Reaction Force
CSIS	Center for Strategic and International Studies
CSTO	Collective Security Treaty Organization
DIA	Defense Intelligence Agency
ETIM	Eastern Turkistan Islamic Movement
EU	European Union
FATA	Federally Administered Tribal Areas
FBI	Federal Bureau of Investigation
GCC	Gulf Cooperation Council
GDP	gross domestic product
GWOT	global war on terrorism

HOR	House of Representatives
HT	Hizb ut-Tahrir (Islamic Liberation Movement)
HUA	Harakat-ul-Ansar
HUJI	‘Harakat ul-Jihad al-Islami
HUM	Harakat-ul-Mujahedeen
ICBM	intercontinental ballistic missile
IDF	Israel Defense Forces
IED	improvised explosive device
IGC	Iraqi Governing Council
ILSA	Iran-Libya Sanctions Act
IMT	Islamic Movement of Turkestan
IMU	Islamic Movement of Uzbekistan
IRGC	Islamic Revolutionary Guard Corps
IRP	Islamic Renaissance Party
IRPT	Islamic Renaissance Party of Tajikistan
IS	Islamic State
ISA	Iran Sanctions Act
ISAF	International Security Assistance Force
ISG	Iraq Study Group
ISI	Inter-Services Intelligence
ISI	Islamic State of Iraq
ISIL	Islamic State of Iraq and the Levant
ISIS	Islamic State of Iraq and al-Sham
JCPOA	Joint Comprehensive Plan of Action
JI	Jamaat-e-Islami
JUI	Jamiat-e-Ulema-e-Islam
JUM	Jamiat-ul-Ulama of Pakistan
JUP	Jamiat-e-Ulema-e-Pakistan
K2	Karshi-Khanabad
LeT	Lashkar-e-Taiba
LTTE	Tamil Tigers
NATO	North Atlantic Treaty Organization
NGO	nongovernmental organization
NWFP	North-West Frontier Province
OAPEC	Organization of Arab Petroleum Exporting Countries
OBOR	One Belt, One Road
OEF	Operation Enduring Freedom
OIC	Organisation of the Islamic Congress
OPEC	Organization of Petroleum Exporting Countries
Pak-Afghan	Pakistan-Afghanistan

PLO	Palestine Liberation Organization
PNA	Pakistan National Alliance
PPP	Pakistan Peoples Party
PRC	People's Republic of China
Q	Qaid
RAW	Research and Analysis Wing
SCO	Shanghai Cooperation Organization
SF	Special Forces
SLV	satellite launch vehicle
SOFA	status of forces agreement
SSP	Sipah-e-Sahaba Pakistan
TNSM	Tehrik-e-Nifaz-Shariat-e-Mohammadi
TTP	Tehrik-e-Taliban-e-Pakistan
UAE	United Arab Emirates
UAR	United Arab Republic
UK	United Kingdom
UN	United Nations
UNSC	United Nations Security Council
UNSCR	United Nations Security Council Resolution
US	United States
USSR	Union of Soviet Socialist Republics
WMD	weapons of mass destruction
YPG	Yekîneyên Parastina Gel (People's Protection Units)

Preface

The original title of this book was *The Islamic Challenge and the Great Powers*. I later changed it to focus entirely on the United States (except in chapter 7), because the global jihadists' main fight is with the lone superpower. The Russians reportedly ended the Chechen insurgency successfully in 2009, and China was successful in suppressing the independent movement in its Xinjiang province. Thus, the global jihadists' fight with Russia and China has not yet begun.

For the global jihadists, defeating the United States is the most challenging part of their struggle. The chatter about the so-called demise or decline of the United States as a superpower is limited chiefly to armchair scholarship inside the United States. I am sure that the global jihadists have neither time for, nor interest in, acquainting themselves with those discussions. They are too busy fighting their war and trying to figure out ways to defeat the "global crusader." They see American troops in Afghanistan, American aircraft carriers and other US naval ships lurking in the Persian Gulf and around the Horn of Africa, and US military jets flying in and out of Iraq and countries of the Persian Gulf. They have long concluded that current regional state systems are being constantly protected by the United States.

My treatment of Islamism in this volume is not yet a common one; at least, I have not seen it anywhere else. I define Islamism as a politico-religious movement focused on the acquisition of territory, such as ISIS has done in a swathe of territories in Syria and Iraq, and then declaring those territories as part of a so-called caliphate. ISIS has given priority to that strategy everywhere in escalating its presence and influence. Even al-Qaida affiliates are trying to emulate ISIS in Africa.

I decided to write this book because I concluded that the conflict between the lone superpower and the jihadists is likely to last for quite some time, and it will likely become deadlier with the passage of time. Although al-Qaida received its global fame and attention by carrying out the horrendous terrorist attacks of 11 September 2001 on the United States, ISIS's declaration of a caliphate and its resolve to turn the Levant into an inferno are unprecedented. My fear is that the jihadist organizations and movements that come after ISIS will likely be deadlier than ISIS itself.

I also wrote this book because I was troubled (and continue to be troubled) by the simplistic and naive endeavours of the United States to deal with the Islamist challenge. I know that it will not be resolved by conducting drone wars or through the intermittent use of America's talented Special Forces. The United States has to radically alter its policies along the lines that I have suggested in this book. I am also convinced that Muslim countries have to do their fair share by transforming their own polities and, equally important, by taking a vanguard stance on the military and economic fronts of fighting this war. More to the point, the focus of this war must be on developing real antiterrorism strategies, not merely using shortsighted counterterrorism tactics mislabelled as antiterrorism strategy.

My definite conclusion is that, despite the United States' simplistic propaganda campaign to "win the hearts and minds of Muslims," America will continue to lose that propaganda war because anti-American sentiments are constantly being fuelled by the policies that the United States has implemented in a number of Muslim/Arab countries. Most important, the United States has to recognize the similarities between the cosmic nature of its own war and that of the jihadists. America's cosmic war is driven by its exercise of secular fundamentalism, which is no less absolutist and demonizing of the jihadists than is the jihadists' own conduct of jihad against the United States. I am making no attempt to create moral equivalency here. I am merely emphasizing that thousands of people have died because of the wars carried out in the name of jihad or for the victory of secular fundamentalism.

Acknowledgments

I would like to thank my acquisitions editor, Jacqueline Mason, who tirelessly guided me through the arduous review process; my outstanding copy editor, Ellie Barton, for her tenacity and unfaltering attention to detail; the managing editor, Ryan Van Huijstee, who ensured that I had what I needed and that I stayed on track; and Elena Goranescu, production manager, and her team, especially the designer, Will Brown, for the clever and eye-catching book cover.

Although the peer review process was a gruelling one, I am grateful to the anonymous reviewers contracted by McGill-Queen's University Press. They all provided guidance and constructive feedback. However, I would especially like to thank the third reviewer, whose critique introduced me to the thought-provoking work of Professor William T. Cavanaugh.

I have used Cavanaugh's brilliant discussion in his book *The Myth of Religious Violence: Secular Ideology and the Roots of Modern Conflict*, and Mark Juergensmeyer's concept of "cosmic war," in developing my own analysis. Cavanaugh's use of "secular fundamentalism" as the driving force behind America's version of cosmic war served as vital food for thought for this study. I also greatly benefited from Cavanaugh's generous willingness to answer a number of my questions, especially about how to develop my thinking regarding the future of these cosmic wars. I cannot thank him enough.

Last, but not least, I am grateful to my loving wife, Sharon. She has been my "first-line" editor and has spent countless hours labouring over my often cumbersome and arcane prose. Her critical eye for detail in an effort to submit the initial manuscript with all of the i's dotted and the t's crossed was incredibly helpful to me. I can honestly say that this book would not have been completed without her help. However, the responsibility for any errors remains mine alone.

The Islamic Challenge
and the United States

1

Introduction and the General Premise of the Study

A SYNOPSIS OF THE STUDY

This book deals with the conflict between the United States and the Islamists. To be precise, it is about the conflict between what certain militant Islamists say Islam demands or requires and the liberal philosophy that underpins and justifies the American state. According to William T. Cavanaugh, professor of theology at DePaul University, Americans are "accustomed to dividing life into separate religious and secular spheres." They have been "habituated to think that devotion to one's religion is fine within limits, while public patriotic devotion to one's nation is generally a good thing." Americans are "appalled at violence on behalf of religion," but they "generally accept the necessity and even the virtue of killing for one's country."[1] When translating this cultural value into policies, the US administration accepts that killing for one's country is sometimes warranted. Violence in the name of religion, on the other hand, is demonized by various American scholars: Cavanaugh, in another essay, argues that religion has a strong tendency to push the believer toward absolutism, an extreme position that justifies religious violence.[2]

According to Roxanne Euben, this "Enlightenment narrative" – that is, the separation of religion and state – envisions Islamic fundamentalism as the "irrational other." In this view, proponents of Enlightenment are "the voices of modernity, freedom, liberation, happiness, reason, nobility, and even natural passion," whereas the "irrational" Islamists are tied to "all that came before: tyranny, servility to dogma, self-abnegation, superstition, and false religion." On the basis of these frames of reference, "understanding Muslim hostility toward America ... does not require careful scrutiny of

America's historical dealings with the Muslim world."[3] Indeed, the belief "that religion causes violence ... can be used to blind us in the West to our own forms of fanaticism and violence."[4] Even those analysts who recognize the similarities between violence perpetrated in the name of a religion and violence enacted by a secular state still think that "actors labelled religious are peculiarly prone to violence in ways that secular actors are not." Mark Juergensmeyer is one of those scholars who acknowledge that many US politicians and commentators have elevated the war on terrorism "above the mundane – 'like all images of cosmic war, all-encompassing, absolutizing, and demonizing' – but he attributes the problem to the 'role of religion' and the way it has 'problematized the conflict.'"[5]

What emerges from the preceding is that the conflict between the United States and the various Islamist groups is also a conflict between forces of democracy and secularism (the United States and the West, even though the focus of this study is the United States) and those groups who categorically reject democracy and secularism as antithetical to Islam.

Using a case study method, this study analyzes the evolution of this conflict from the colonial era to contemporary times in the Middle East – the Persian/Arabian Gulf and the Levant – and South and Central Asia. The case study method is useful in examining the fluctuating as well as immutable features of US foreign policy. For instance, the implosion of the Soviet Union and the end of the Cold War brought about a major shift in US foreign policy from a preoccupation with the Soviet Union to a focus on the visibility and rising power of the Islamist forces. The immutable aspect of America's foreign policy is what Cavanaugh calls the sanctification of violence, especially evident in America's decision to declare its "global war on terrorism" and in what Euben labels America's assessment of the Islamists as "irrational other."[6]

The case study form of analysis also will enable readers to discern how the Islamists transformed and expanded their objectives from demands for political reforms in the 1940s to regime change and acquisition of territory in the second decade of the twenty-first century. On the basis of this analysis, we can speculate about the prospects (or the lack thereof) for a potential resolution to the conflict between the United States and the Islamists.

On the Islamist side, the conflict involves the Islamists, the Salafists, and the self-styled jihadists (aka "terrorists"). It is partly ideological, partly cultural, and partly religious, especially when it comes to the

Islamists' notion of Islamic government. The jihadists support this form of government, except that they call it a caliphate.

The most obdurate issues related to the conflict between the Islamists and the United States involve the type of government, westernization, modernization, and secularism. The most explosive aspect of this conflict – and the major focus of this book – involves the jihadists and the United States. Ample attention will also be given to the prospects of resolving the aforementioned intractable issues. Further, this study will examine some of the major changes in the strategic environment of the Arab World in the aftermath of the Arab Awakening and how the United States and the Islamists are reacting to these changes.

The general outline of the Islamic government is based on what the Prophet of Islam established in Medina from the 620s to 630s. Although this city-state had limited jurisdiction, existed over 1,400 years ago, and was too rudimentary and impractical in any age, these factors have not discouraged its advocates' zeal for emulating that model even into the twenty-first century. On the issue of establishing a caliphate – a system of government ruled by a caliph (religious ruler) where the constitution is based on Shariah (Islamic) law – Islamic scholars, Islamists, and Salafists, as well as jihadists are of one mind.

From the very inception of Islam, Muslims have been highly motivated to spread their faith, even by conquering territories and maintaining political control over them. From the Umayyad dynasty (661–750) to the Ottoman dynasty (1299–1923), a number of rulers gave themselves the title of *Amir al-Mu'minin* (leader of the faithful). More often than not, that title was more symbolic than real (in that its holder was not exactly driven by the zeal of spreading Islam); nonetheless, use of the title gave those rulers some claim to be perceived by the ruled as Islamic rulers.

Struggle for political power has been central to the entire history of Islam. This assertion will be fully discussed and documented throughout this book. The so-called first great schism resulted from an acute conflict about who should be the rightful political (as well as religious) successor to the Prophet of Islam. That split remained very much alive during the rules of the successors to the first caliph, Abu Bakr, and led to a permanent division between the Sunnis and the Shias, who had radically divergent views about the basis of political succession. This division is proffered as one of the chief reasons driving the strategic competition between the Sunni kingdom of Saudi Arabia and the Shia-dominated Islamic Republic of Iran.

Another permanent feature in the world of Islam has been the resurgence or revival of religion in response to crises in political authority. In almost all instances, this revival either was aimed at or resulted in political change.[7] In various eras of their past history, different Islamic dynasties encountered challenges from new rival Muslim dynasties or from non-Muslim ones. In the case of destruction stemming from conflicts with non-Muslim rulers, the revivalist response was both vocal and militant. A prime example is Imam Ibn Taymiyya's call for Islamic renewal in response to the Mongol destruction of the Abbasid Empire in 1258. Ibn Taymiyya's target was the Mongol ruler, Khan Mahmud Ghazan. Even though Ghazan had converted to Islam, he implemented the Yasa code of Mongol law instead of following the Shariah (Islamic religious law). The non-observance of the Shariah, in Ibn Taymiyya's judgment, made Ghazan an "infidel" and a legitimate target of attack. That type of declaration – the practice of declaring other Muslims as *kafir* (infidels) and then condemning them to death on the basis of the *Takfiri* doctrine – was to cause enormous turbulence in various Muslim regions of the world.[8] Through this doctrine, Ibn Taymiyya not only condemned a ruler of his time but also deviated from most Sunni scholars in abandoning his support of the political status quo, a tradition that was to be followed in later generations by the jihadists.[9]

Taymiyya's writings emphasized the necessity of a puritanical commitment of rulers to the tenets of Islam, a theme that reemerged in the writings of Muhammad ibn 'Abd al-Wahhāb of Saudi Arabia in the eighteenth century and Sayyid Qutb of Egypt in the 1960s.[10] This resurgence of the Takfiri doctrine has driven the jihadists to an endless spree of violence in various Muslim countries from the eighteenth century through the second decade of the twenty-first century. The Takfiri doctrine also motivated jihadists in their futile endeavours to assassinate or overthrow the existing rulers of a number of Muslim states of the Arab world and Pakistan. The significance of this doctrine, for the purposes of this study, is that – despite the fact that it did not succeed in bringing about regime change anywhere – it remains at the heart of almost all jihadist movements, even today.

The roots of the Islamic challenge to the West go back to the colonial era, when a variety of ragtag Islamic individuals and groups engaged the militarily superior European colonialists in an attempt to liberate their homeland. The occupation of Islamic lands by European powers was seen by the Islamist forces as an affront to Islam itself. The failure of the second siege of Vienna of 1683 is regarded by historians to be the beginning of the decline of the Muslim civilization. The conquest of Egypt by Napoleon Bonaparte in 1798, when Muslim rulers were defeated and brought under the suzerainty of European colonialism, was further evidence of that decline.

Placing the events in their historical context, Bernard Lewis notes that "Muslim peoples, like everyone else in the world, are shaped by their history, but, unlike some others, they are keenly aware of it."[11] The victory of Napoleon's "small expeditionary force" and its occupation of "one of the heartlands of Islam was a profound shock." Muslims also never forgot that General Bonaparte was ousted from Egypt "by a small squadron of the British Royal Navy, commanded by a young admiral named Horatio Nelson."[12] The downward slide of the Ottoman Empire and the successful advancement of European countries during the Renaissance, the Reformation, and the Industrial Revolution (the latter "passed virtually unnoticed in the lands of Islam" but played a crucial role in transforming former barbarians into fledgling empires) raised a lot of questions among Islamic countries about "what went wrong."[13]

The role of Great Britain in the dismantlement of the Ottoman Empire, and the British and French agreements (the secret Sykes-Picot Agreement of 1916, officially known as the Asia Minor Agreement, depicted as a "conspiracy" in the Muslim lexicon) sowed the seeds of future intense resentment, even hatred, of the West and its "shenanigans" in Muslim countries to keep the world of Islam down and enslaved.[14] The abolition of the caliphate in 1924 caused abundant political turbulence as far east as India, where Muslims for generations had felt a powerful sense of despair stemming from the abolition of the Mogul Empire and in the aftermath of the First War of Independence of 1857 (also called the Indian Mutiny or Sepoy Mutiny).[15] South Asia's renowned Islamic mujaddid, Maulana Abul A'la Maududi, spent his entire intellectual career developing a rough blueprint for the establishment of *Hukumat-e-Ilahiyya* (an Islamic government).[16] Although he did not succeed in that endeavour, he played a major role in General Zia-ul-Haq's Islamization of Pakistan in the 1970s. These political developments, along with the US-sponsored "jihad" of Afghanistan in the 1980s, played a crucial role in transforming Pakistan into a place where jihadism, sectarianism, acute anti-Americanism, and religious obscurantism have been rampant ever since. Collectively, these problems continue to threaten the future stability, if not the survival, of that country in the second decade of the twenty-first century.

The end of European colonialism left the lands of Islam in a particularly depressed form, both politically and economically. The Islamic interpretation of that state of affairs played a crucial role in the struggle for power. In Egypt, the power struggle between the military and the Islamist party, the Muslim Brotherhood, started in 1952. Although there was no chance that the latter would emerge victorious, the struggle created a permanent schism within Egypt's polity. The long rule of dictators, from Nasser to Abdel Fattah el-Sisi, turned the largest Arab state into a highly corrupt and economically backward polity. In the 1950s and 1960s, the struggle within Egypt between the autocratic regimes and the Islamists was eclipsed by the emergence of the "Arab Cold War" between the republican (pan-Arabist or so-called modernist) groups and the monarchies' (conservative or "reactionary") forces. The relevance of Islam as a challenge to the forces of secularism inside the republican Arab states, and to the West in general, had to wait until after the 1967 Arab-Israeli war, when the pan-Arabism of earlier decades convincingly seemed to be a spent force.

As the heir-apparent of the United Kingdom, the United States emerged as the dominant power in the Middle East starting in the late 1960s. It was already one of the superpowers of the Cold War era and had established a record of asserting its power in the Middle East on two previous occasions: in 1956, when, in the aftermath of the Suez crisis, the United States dictated that the United Kingdom, France, and Israel vacate their aggression toward Egypt; and in 1957, when under the aegis of the Eisenhower Doctrine it expressed its readiness to provide economic and military assistance to any country resisting communist aggression.[17] In the 1950s and 1960s, however, America's focus of confrontation in the Middle East was the Soviet Union and Gamal Abdel Nasser of Egypt, not any geopolitical threats from jihadist forces.

It was not until the Iranian revolution of 1979 and the US-sponsored Afghan war of the 1980s that Islam entered into the calculations of the United States. Iran's Islamic revolution not only radically transformed that country from a monarchy to an Islamic republic, it also brought to the forefront the possibility of repeating that development elsewhere. All US presidents since Jimmy Carter – who was in the White House at the time of the Iranian revolution – have been determined to forestall any future Islamic revolutions carried out by violent or "revolutionary" groups in the Islamic world.

The first major military involvement of the United States in the Middle East occurred in response to the invasion and occupation of Kuwait in August 1990 by the forces of Iraqi dictator Saddam Hussein. President George H.W. Bush succeeded in creating a powerful international coalition to expel Iraqi troops from that sheikhdom. The US forces' performance in defeating the Iraqi military during the 1991 Gulf War was impressive. However, Saddam Hussein managed to stay in power largely because the Bush administration did not wish to invade and occupy Iraq. The Bush administration's decision to continue stationing American forces in Saudi Arabia as the main conduit for the military operation of the coalition forces became the chief reason for the antipathy between the head of the al-Qaida movement, Osama Bin Laden, and King Fahd bin Abdul Aziz of Saudi Arabia.

The terrorist attacks of 11 September 2001 inside the United States were watershed events for at least two reasons. First, they were depicted as the beginning of a "global jihad" by Osama Bin Laden, who was responsible as the mastermind behind those attacks.[18] Second, by declaring a "global war on terrorism" (GWOT), President George W. Bush, in reality as well as symbolically, threw down the gauntlet of military retaliation, not only against Afghanistan (where that attack was planned) but against any other Muslim country suspected of aiding and abetting a jihadist movement. Al-Qaida's use of the language of Islam and its depiction of America as an "enemy" of Islam forced the United States to be on the defensive from the outset.

Since 9/11, Washington has been adamant in its insistence that it was fighting al-Qaida as a transregional terrorist organization that was bent on altering the political status quo in the Muslim regions and, further, was grossly misrepresenting Islam, and that it (the US) had no quarrel with Islam, the religion. The declaration of al-Qaida and the counterdeclaration of the United States notwithstanding, the rules of the game for international affairs radically changed in the aftermath of the al-Qaida–sponsored attacks on US territory. The decision of the Bush administration to invade two Muslim countries in the name of fighting GWOT made the conflict between the jihadists and the lone superpower the dominant source of turbulence and instability in the Middle East and South Asia.

In the context of this study, the conflict between the Islamists and the West – especially the United States – is not theological in nature in the conventional sense of the word. However, considering that secularism as envisioned by American secular fundamentalists is arguably a form of religion, an entirely different picture of this conflict emerges. A powerful feature of secular fundamentalism in the United States holds "that the ultimate claims of religion should simply not be allowed to interfere with political and religious freedom."[19] To defend these freedoms, secular fundamentalists accept, and even advocate, going to war. Andrew Sullivan, in his essay "This Is a Religious War," writes, "What is really at issue here is the simple but immensely difficult principle of the separation of politics and religion. We are fighting not for our country as such or for our flag. We are fighting for the universal principles of our Constitution – and the possibility of free religious faith it guarantees. We are fighting for religion against one of the deepest strains in religion there is. And not only our lives but our souls are at stake."[20] The secular fundamentalist perspective envisions Islam as "dangerous and volatile because it mixes religion and politics."[21]

Islamic countries, to be sure, have no tradition of separation of politics and religion, except for Indonesia, Malaysia, and Turkey. In the case of Turkey, that reality has been steadily changing in favour of Islamism under the rule of Recep Teyyip Erdoğan, when he was prime minister, and now as that country's president. On the contrary, this separation is at the heart of America's global promotion of democracy. Similarly, secularism is an important aspect of Western-style democracy, whereas Islamists of all varieties emphatically reject that notion. Religion has been pushed into the realm of private affairs in the United States, while religion remains a central issue in the polities of almost all Muslim countries. Consequently, Islamists and America's political leaders and cultural pundits have remained on opposite (conflicting) sides of issues that are at the heart of politics, the style of governance, and the place of religion in a polity.

Resolution of such conflicts requires either fundamental changes in the nature and style of governance in most Muslim countries – changes that the existing governments are not likely to promote – or changes in the United States' secular fundamentalist-oriented perspectives. That the Islamists might change their views regarding democracy and secularism (those views are not monolithic) is are hard but not impossible to imagine. By the same token, one has to envision some willingness among Americans to question their own assumptions and to be flexible enough to accept some sort of Islamic government in Muslim countries.

In fact, despite earnestly believing that Western-style democracy is vital for the evolution of a stable and economically prosperous polity, the United States has remained highly dubious about promoting it in a number of Muslim countries for fear of bringing Islamists to power, as was the case in post-Saddam Iraq, and for fear of losing its guaranteed influence and presence in almost all Muslim countries in the post–World War II era. The gaining of power by democratically elected rulers in those Muslim countries promises to bring an end to the era of sycophant and diffident rulers who unswervingly linked their continued cooperation with the United States with a guarantee for the prolongation of their autocratic rule.

However, events related to the Arab Awakening may signal the start of an era when the attitudes of at least some Islamists – and those of the United States regarding the prospects of democracy in the world of Islam – are changing. These changes will be discussed at length in chapters 7 and 8.

In the wake of the Arab Awakening (aka the "Arab Spring") – which started in Tunisia in December 2010 and became a tsunami of political change in the Arab world resulting in the ousting of autocrats like Zine El Abidine Ben Ali of Tunisia, Muammar Qaddafi of Libya, and Hosni Mubarak of Egypt – there emerged the hope inside the Arab world that a new era of democracy was in the making. Therein arose a public chatter about how democracy was likely to expel long-standing regimes from other countries of the Middle East and North Africa. Then the discussion swirled around what type of democracy predominantly Muslim countries are likely to have. The notion of "Islamic democracy" – a concept that has been derided in some quarters of the United States as an oxymoron – was bandied about. In fact, Egypt held democratic elections, and a candidate from the Muslim Brotherhood, Mohammed Morsi, won the election. However, his one-year-long misrule resulted in a military coup, and the prospects of democracy in that country – as well as elsewhere in the Arab world – were dealt a serious setback. Nevertheless, the social revolutions in the Arab/Muslim world and the reality of regime change rejuvenated the discussions of Islamic democracy, or at least some form of it, and the potential emergence of some sort of secularism in Muslim countries. Any stable emergence of these two concepts – democracy and secularism – in any Muslim country of the Middle East, North Africa, and South Asia would be iconoclastic in nature, considering that in the past these concepts have provoked increased conflict in a number of countries in those regions.[22]

One of the most noteworthy developments related to the Arab Awakening was that Tunisia emerged as a democratic secular Islamic republic, something no one would have envisaged.[23] The second remarkable outcome of the Arab Awakening as a regime-changing social force was that al-Qaida's notion of jihad suffered a serious setback. However, it may have been the reality of regime change related to the Arab Awakening in three or four Arab countries that, in a perverse way, also contributed to the emergence of the Islamic State (IS / ISIS / ISIL) in Iraq. It was the serious challenge to the Iraqi government posed by ISIS, a newly transformed jihadist entity, that made the United States make a *volte-face* to its original decision to get out of that country in 2011 without signing a status of forces agreement (SOFA). That agreement would have enabled a large US force presence in Iraq. Nevertheless, the chief blame for the resurgence of ISIS as a jihadist force must be placed squarely on the intensely sectarian, bigoted policies of the former prime minister of Iraq, Nouri al-Maliki.

THE ISLAMIC CHALLENGE AND THE UNITED STATES: A GEOPOLITICAL OVERVIEW

Islamists of all varieties envisage the United States as the superpower that is attempting to dominate their polities by supporting pro-Western autocratic rulers, by endeavouring to transform ("pollute" might be more apt here) their culture by inserting highly westernized modernization, and by making sure that the establishment of an independent Palestine is pushed way into the future when Israel's policy of incessant expansion of illegal settlements will leave virtually no chance for the Palestinians to live in a genuinely independent homeland. Needless to say, on this last-mentioned issue, both Hasan al-Banna (an Islamist) and Osama Bin Laden (a jihadist) were of one mind.[24]

For the United States – the lone superpower and the only global proselytizer of Western secular democracy – the prospect of Islamic government emerged as a great challenge that it should defeat. This challenge became one of the top issues of America's foreign policy in the aftermath of the terrorist attacks on its territory in 2001. Although the United States insists that it has no quarrel with Islam as a religion, its determination since 9/11 to defeat those groups (Islamists and jihadists) who wish to establish an Islamic caliphate globally or an Islamic government in one or more countries places it in direct conflict with the Islamists' religious and political aspirations. In almost all Western countries, one regularly hears discussions about "political Islam" as if it were something quite separate from Islam, the religion. Such a spurious distinction might be used to convey the notion that Islam, the religion, has nothing to do with politics. However, that type of discussion has nothing to do with Islam; for Islamists of all varieties – and for many Muslims – there is no distinction between Islam as a religion and Islam as a political force. The challenge that the United States has taken upon itself vis-à-vis Islamist forces is therefore of massive proportion.

The United States' assertion of leadership in the Middle East can be traced to the Suez crisis of 1956; this event, which undermined the interests of US allies, turned out to be of great significance from the standpoint of its strategic presence and interests in that region.[25] It replaced Great Britain as the dominant Western power around 1970. The Arab world was recovering from the "Arab Cold War" that was "fought" between the republican camp, under the leadership of Egypt's President Nasser, and the monarchical camp led by King Faisal bin Abdel Aziz of Saudi Arabia.[26] The defeat of Arab forces by Israel in the 1967 war and the death of Nasser in 1970 brought an end to that Cold War. No other leader of Nasser's calibre emerged in the Arab world to replace him. In fact, the overwhelming defeat of the Arab forces in the 1967 war and Nasser's death in 1970 initiated an era when pan-Arabism was no longer envisioned as an ideology that would glorify the Arab world either by unifying it or by resolving the Arab-Israeli conflict. Arabs remained hopelessly divided. Wittingly or unwittingly, they were on a quest to find an ideology that would unify them or make them believe that indeed there was some light at the end of the dark tunnel through which they were passing in the aftermath of a humiliating war.

The American strategic agenda toward the Middle East went through major changes between the 1950s and the 1970s. The United States clearly emerged as the chief backer of Israel, both in terms of equipping it with sophisticated weapons and providing it with massive economic assistance. At the same time, the United States managed to maintain considerable clout with a number of major Arab states, who perceived it as an actor that could muster its influence to resolve the Arab-Israeli conflict. That very idea motivated President Anwar Sadat of Egypt to break close military ties with the USSR in the aftermath of the 1973 Arab-Israeli war and establish strong diplomatic relations with the United States.[27] This decision created an environment where a serious attempt could be made to resolve the Arab-Israeli conflict. The success of the administration of President Jimmy Carter in presiding over the Camp David negotiations between Egypt and Israel in 1979 – as controversial and divisive as that agreement turned out to be in the Arab world – proved the point that no great power other than the United States had the clout to be a peacemaker between the Arabs and the Jews.

In the context of developments that either affected the global distribution of power or altered the course of events in the last century, the Islamic revolution of 1979 in Iran stands out as pivotal. It brought about an end to the tyrannical reign of Mohammad Reza Pahlavi, the Shah of Iran and one of America's staunchest allies. The success of the Islamist forces in ousting the Shah dealt a major blow to America's prestige and dominance in the Persian Gulf. Within ten years of the Iranian revolution, the mujahedeen (religious fighters) scored a major victory in Afghanistan when they brought about a humiliating departure of the Soviet Union from that country (1989). Thus the presence and prestige of both superpowers were negatively affected. In both instances, Islamist forces emerged victorious. Those realities sowed the seeds of the mega conflict that became acute in the first decade of the twenty-first century involving the Islamist groups – the descendants of those who had played a crucial role in defeating the Soviet Union in Afghanistan as well as those who had ousted the Shah.

One of the major achievements of the United States in any Muslim country has to be its success in using the Islamic doctrine of jihad to defeat the Soviet Union, which had invaded and occupied Afghanistan in December 1979. In the US military campaign in Afghanistan in the 1980s, which turned out to be the last epic battle of the Cold War, Pakistan, along with Saudi Arabia, played a crucial role. It was the peak of irony that the first epic battle of the post–9/11 era in 2001 was fought once again in Afghanistan, with Pakistan serving as the "frontline" state supporting the United States in both instances. That battle was in response to a series of attacks conducted by al-Qaida jihadists on 11 September 2001 on the US homeland. However, there were two noteworthy differences in the US invasion of Afghanistan in 2001. First, the lone superpower had become the target of the jihad perpetrated by al-Qaida and the Taliban. Second, Saudi Arabia did not play any visible role in that battle.

As a result of its invasion of Afghanistan in November 2001, the United States succeeded in dismantling the Taliban regime. That regime had provided al-Qaida sanctuary and safe haven from where, according to Chinese and Russian assertions, it conducted "regional jihad" in Central Asia, Xinjiang, and Chechnya. However, the defeat of the Taliban turned out to be the outcome of just one battle. The remnants of al-Qaida and the Taliban continued to challenge the sustained presence of the US and NATO forces (aka, the International Security Assistance Force [ISAF]) even after the assassination of Osama Bin Laden in May 2011 at the hands of US Special Forces. And the battle for the future of Afghanistan seems interminable.

Pakistan involvement in Afghanistan, especially since the Soviet withdrawal in 1989, has aimed to ensure that Afghanistan remains friendly to Pakistan and, at the same time, does not develop friendly ties with India. Because of the historical animosity between these two South Asian neighbours, Pakistan has remained convinced that any Indian presence in Afghanistan would lead to anti-Pakistan activities through cooperation between the Indian and the Afghan security forces. Such cooperation, Pakistan believes, has been responsible for the sustained anti-Pakistan insurgency in Baluchistan.[28] To counteract the Indo-Afghan security nexus, Pakistan has consistently underscored the notion of strategic depth. For that purpose, Afghanistan has become a convenient place, especially since it is militarily weaker than Pakistan and, thus, would not be able to deny Pakistani military presence inside its borders should there be a war with India.

India not only understands the significance of Pakistan's conception of strategic depth and Afghanistan's potential role in it but, without making public declarations about countering it, is doing precisely that by maintaining a high-profile diplomatic and economic presence in Afghanistan. Pakistan, in turn, is suspected to have relied on jihadist forces – mainly the Haqqani group – to periodically attack the Indian diplomatic buildings and personnel in Afghanistan. In the post–9/11 environment, and in the wake of the mounting US-India diplomatic friendship, both the United States and India have been voluble in criticizing Pakistan's alleged use of jihadist forces in attacking India. In that sense, Pakistan's policies have promoted instability in Afghanistan to ensure that no "anti-Pakistan" government survives in Afghanistan. This heightened political instability favours the forces of al-Qaida and the Taliban, who fully utilize the argument that Islam continues to be under attack by the forces of the United States and the West. Thus the Islamist forces remain very much at the centre of this battle.

The US invasion of Afghanistan decimated various Central Asian jihadist groups that had taken refuge in that country. Since 2001, most of the remainder of those forces either have gone back to their native regions or are reported to have been residing in the Pak-Afghanistan border, where they are being attacked by the Pakistan Army or by the ISAF. Still, one hears frequent reports of the presence of those groups, albeit in small numbers.[29] The stability of the Central Asian states is difficult to assess because there is no widespread coverage by global media of the security situations inside their borders.

In the post–Cold War years, the development of events in the Middle East and in South Asia defied the rules of engagement that had governed the behaviour of nation states in previous decades. The emergence of Islam as a political force – whether as an important element of the foreign policies of Iran, Pakistan, and Saudi Arabia, or as manifested through the activities of jihadist and Islamist forces – created new types of challenges for the United States. Islamist groups not only defy the United States, but their defiance is becoming increasingly ominous in the form of mounting threats to the stability and even the survival of a number of important US allies and friends in the Middle East and South Asia. For Iran, this defiance has emerged in the form of policies that promote its dominance in its immediate neighbourhood as well as in the Levant. That reality is perceived by the United States as being aimed at eroding its own pre-eminence in the region. During the Cold War years, the United States learned to accept the Soviet Union as its equal, and moved away from the policy of containment to a more sophisticated framework of détente.[30] From the 1950s through the 1980s, the United States accepted the proposition that it, along with the Soviet Union, would co-manage global affairs as two superpowers. By contrast, in the post–Cold War years, in dealing with a major Islamist country like Iran, the chief motivation driving American foreign policy has been either to weaken the Iranian government by developing a web of powerful economic sanction regimes that would prevent that country from developing nuclear weapons (a charge that Iran continues to deny categorically) or to pursue covert or not-so-covert policies aimed at bringing about regime change. This policy did not change during the administration of Barack Obama, even though he started his presidency by publicly offering to seek a rapprochement with the Islamic Republic. The conclusion of the US-Iran nuclear deal – officially known as the Joint Comprehensive Plan of Action (JCPOA), reached between Iran and the P5+1 nations (US, UK, France, China, Russia, and Germany) in Vienna on 14 July 2015 – has provided a semblance of legitimacy to the Islamic Republic.[31] The United States and Iran reportedly are coordinating their military activities against the Islamic State in the Iraqi theatre of operations, while continuing to disagree about the survival of the Assad regime. Outside of these two theatres of operation, both Washington and Tehran continue to issue antagonistic statements on a number of strategic issues of mutual concern in and around the Middle East.[32]

In other Middle Eastern countries, as well as in Pakistan and Afghanistan, the Islamic perspective remains a major force in the policies of existing governments as well as a sustained challenge to those governments. Even if a number of Middle Eastern and South Asian countries become democracies, the Islamist parties will likely escalate their presence by participating in popular elections. There are at least two chief concerns for the United States on this issue. First, it remains apprehensive that, once an Islamist party captures power through the ballot box, it may change the rules and attempt to establish its own dictatorship.[33] Second, even if the Islamists were to adhere to the principles of democracy once they become part of the government, they would likely be assertive in pursuing their respective national interests when dealing with the United States. The capture of power by the Muslim Brotherhood in Egypt through a democratic election in June 2012 and then its miserable performance once in office may not have surprised those in Washington, who already had low esteem for the affinities of the Islamists toward democracy. However, the Islamists' attitude toward democracy in Tunisia was a major surprise to every cynic in Washington. The fact that the Ennahda Party in Tunisia "agreed to surrender power to a politically neutral caretaker government that steered the country through the successful 2014 elections" was a source of amazement and gratification for the United States.[34] Still, one can state with certainty that it will be a long time before the United States will get used to dealing with the Islamic democrats of the post–Arab Spring Middle East.

The nonstate Islamists (aka the jihadists) of the Middle East, South and Central Asia, and North Africa pose a special challenge to the United States. They envision it as "anti-Islamic" and condemn all Muslim countries that cooperate with the lone superpower as equally "anti-Islamic." The jihadists' recipe for dealing with the United States and its Muslim friends is the same: all of them ought to be destroyed. By the same token, the United States has sustained a policy of eradication of Islamists. During the presidency of George W. Bush, that was the most crucial (if not the sole) aim of his global war on terrorism. Indeed, the American tradition of secular fundamentalism may have played a role in the thinking of those Department of Defense officials who wanted to name the US invasion of Afghanistan in 2001 as "Operation Infinite Justice." When it was pointed out to them that the notion of infinite justice in Islam is associated only with God, they dropped that phrase in favour of the less controversial "Operation Enduring Freedom."[35] President George W. Bush's reference to his war on terrorism as a "crusade," although it "passed almost unnoticed by Americans, rang alarm bells in Europe. It raised fears that the terrorist attacks could spark a 'clash of civilizations' between Christians and Muslims." Even though Bush immediately reacted by appearing at an Islamic centre in Washington and telling Muslims and the world that "the face of terror is not the true faith of Islam," and "that's not what Islam is all about," one cannot help but wonder what his true feeling was.[36]

During the tenure of President Barack Obama, the United States has substantially followed the same objective but with slightly nuanced modus operandi, as has been witnessed by his administration's high reliance on the use of counterterrorism drone attacks in Pakistan, Yemen, and Somalia.[37]

One of the chief problems that the United States encounters is that, even though it has not declared a war against Islam – a point that it persistently attempts to make – there is a general perception in the Muslim world at large that America's "global war on terrorism" is merely a euphemism for its war against Islam. This is an important point because, as the old adage goes, reality almost invariably is what it is perceived to be. Such a perception in the world of Islam also gives al-Qaida and ISIS a palpable advantage against the lone superpower and other great powers. Those entities have been exploiting that perception by keeping Iraq and Syria as highly unstable countries. Afghanistan also has remained a heated battleground between the American-dominated ISAF and the Taliban forces.

The United States' claim that it is not at war with Islam appears less believable when one examines its great apprehension regarding the notion of Islamic government or democratically elected Islamist groups. As long as one of the chief purposes of its foreign policy is to minimize the chances of the capture of power by Islamist groups – even through the use of the ballot box – the United States will remain vulnerable to charges by the Muslim world that it perceives Islam as a threat. Such a perception may be the chief reason why the United States will continue to face tremendous challenges in its interactions with the world of Islam.

The post–Cold War and post–9/11 world is characterized by a unipolar global order where the military might of the United States remains unchallenged. Events since the toppling of the government of Saddam Hussein in Iraq in 2003 have proven that having unchallenged military prowess was no guarantee that the United States would succeed even in sustaining its hegemony over Iraq. Perhaps President Obama understood the limits of America's power too well when he withdrew American forces from Iraq toward the end of 2011. Similarly, the United States' decision to significantly reduce its forces in Afghanistan was driven by Obama's perception of limitation of power. He concluded that the best option would be to help the government of President Ashraf Ghani reach some sort of a political power-sharing agreement with the Taliban. However, toward the beginning of 2016, the chances of such an agreement emerging were slim at best.

To summarize, the Arab Awakening affected the United States in the following ways. First, the original anticipation that democracy would take hold in the Arab world did not materialize, except in the case of Tunisia. However, even in that country, fears about the rise of terrorism are high because of its proximity to Libya and Egypt, where ISIS is mounting its presence. Second, the authoritarian rulers of the Arab world did next to nothing about altering their style of governance or democratizing their systems. Third, the sabotage of democracy and the return of authoritarian rule in Egypt in July 2013 has proven demoralizing to the forces of change elsewhere in the Arab world. Fourth, the capabilities of the United States to manage or influence events in the Middle East have palpably waned. Fifth, the emergence of ISIS in Iraq and Syria and its growing popularity in a number of Arab and Muslim countries have become a source of grave concern to the United States and its Muslim and European allies and friends. At the same time, al-Qaida's affiliates have escalated their terrorist activities in different countries of the Middle East, South Asia, and Africa. Chapters 7 and 8 will examine these issues in detail.

Table 1.1 highlights the major Islamic actors and what they want, and what this intricate conflict is all about.

Table 1.1 The nature of the Islamic challenge: A thematic outline

The Islamists	• From the perspective of Islamic scholars and Salafists (generally referred to as Islamists in this study), the challenge is underpinned by anti-westernism and anti-Americanism. The Islamists perceive the United States as a modern suppressor because of its unwavering support of Muslim autocrats (from the American perspective, its support of autocrats reflects its commitment to political stability and avoidance of chaos that a potential regime change would bring in any Muslim country). • The conflict between the United States and the Islamists is not necessarily violent in nature, but it could become violent if a dictator is ousted and the United States continues to support that dictator. President Barack Obama's quick decision to abandon the support of Hosni Mubarak in the wake of intensified demands for Mubarak to step down demonstrated America's eagerness to bring about a major policy change in order to avoid its loss of influence in Egypt. The military coup, which brought an end to democracy and the return of a military dictatorship, lessened America's influence in the country, despite the fact that the Obama administration continued to supply its usual military assistance. • The Islamic challenge also involves forces of anti-modernism (a form of anti-westernism): The Islamist perspective is that, since modernization is a part of westernization, its introduction in a Muslim country constitutes an "invasion" of Western values, which are fundamentally anti-Islamic (or at least un-Islamic) in nature. For this reason, Islamists reject Western democracy and secularism, issues that have been consistently promoted by the United States in the Muslim world. • The obduracy and intractability of these issues make future cooperation between the United States and the Islamists quite difficult, if not nearly impossible.
The jihadists	• The Islamic challenge also involves the jihadists (terrorists), who are bent on waging a global "jihad" against the United States. • This aspect of the conflict – a substantial theme in this book – is couched in geostrategic terms that will determine which of these two actors, the United States or the terrorists, are likely to emerge as victorious.
Arab Awakening	• The Arab Awakening has complicated the conflict between the Islamists and the lone superpower for the following reasons: • The Arab Awakening has escalated political instability in countries where long-standing autocrats have abruptly fallen or are likely to fall (Egypt, Tunisia, Libya, Yemen, and Syria). • In Tunisia and Egypt, the Islamists won the democratic elections. The heartening part of political development in Tunisia was that the Islamists (Ennahda), after winning elections for a transitional Constitutional Assembly in 2011, agreed to transfer power to the secular Nida' Tunis party on 26 October 2014. However, Tunisia remains a country to watch because of its geographic proximity to Libya and Egypt, where ISIS is steadily increasing its presence. In addition, the hardline Salafists are still very much alive and present in Tunisia, threatening the future continuance of a secular democratic government. • One of the most significant developments of the post–Arab Awakening era is the emergence of the Islamic State and the establishment of a so-called caliphate in the territories captured in Iraq and Syria.

DEFINITIONAL CLARIFICATIONS

A few observations are in order regarding the use of the term *Islamists* in this book. Labels are important, because they delineate a verbal portrait of things, actors, or phenomena. Journalistic usage lumps all varieties of Islamic activists under this label. In this book, for analytical clarity, the phrase *Islamic challenge* subsumes Islamists, Salafists, and jihadists. The US government does not pay much, if any, attention to distinctions among these various groups and uses a catchall term – *terrorists* – to refer to them. However, in this book, the terminology will respect the distinctions among the different groups as much as possible.

Islamists and Salafists are committed to the establishment of an Islamic government based on the Shariah; however, they do not necessarily prefer a violent path.[38] They are concerned with the following issues: the form of government (democracy or theocracy, or some sort of Islamic democracy); modernization (which type of modernization – Western or Islamic);[39] and secularism (outright rejection of it or the possibility of some accommodation). Conflicts in this latter category must be resolved by Muslim scholars and political leaders first before any notion of accommodation with the West – most specifically with the United States – on the other issues may be achieved. Such accommodation is not likely to emerge in the next several decades, if at all.

The self-styled *jihadists*, or terrorists, are committed to implementing their understanding of the doctrines of Takfiri and militant jihad to deal with the governments in their respective countries as well as with the United States. The modifier "self-styled" reflects the position in this book that they are not genuine jihadists, a position discussed in depth in chapters 2 and 3. The challenge posed by the self-styled jihadists is primarily geopolitical in nature: their goal is to oust Muslim autocrats and establish a caliphate. Although this study will address the aforementioned issues of conflict between the United States and the Islamists, *the geostrategic nature of the conflict between Islam and the United States is at the heart of this book.*

The term *Islamism* (*Islamiyyun*) underscores the role of Islam as a political power, no matter which group is using it. An excellent definition is provided by Mehdi Mozaffari. Islamism, he writes, "is a religious ideology with a holistic interpretation of Islam whose final aim is the conquest of the world by all means."[40] Islamism encompasses the spectrum of Sunni and Shia sects as well the Wahhabi schools.

Regarding a holistic perspective, Mozaffari states that even though all Islamists – including Mohammad ibn 'Abd al-Wahhāb of Saudi Arabia, Sayyid Qutb of Egypt, Abul A'la Maududi of Pakistan, Ayatollah Rouhollah Khomeini of Iran, and Hassan al-Turabi of Sudan – "are selective when choosing religious principles from the original sources of Islam," there is no contradiction here. The Islamists insist "that their set of selected elements is, in reality the 'true' Islam and ... that this 'true' Islam is holistic and embraces all aspects of Muslims' life in eternity." More to the point, "this holism is based on the absolute indivisibility of the trinity *Dîn* (religion), *Dunya* (way of life) and *Dawla* (government). This indivisibility is supposed to be permanent and eternal. Its ultimate goal boils down to the fulfillment of this mentioned triad on a global scale."[41] From the perspective of this definition, the dynamic of the Islamic challenge to the United States is ideological as well as geostrategic. The Islamists of all varieties – but especially the jihadists – are dedicated to the goal of ousting pro-US governments from their respective countries, and of eliminating US presence and influence from them. The most significant aspect of the definition as used in this study is that Islamism is "the ideologically-motivated political instrumentalization of a primarily legalistic interpretation of Islam." According to this understanding of Islamism, jihadists "acquire territory for a particular motive and based on a particular ideological understanding of Islam."[42]

Although the phrase "the world of Islam" is used in this book to include the Muslim countries of Southeast Asia, South Asia, Central Asia, the Middle East, North Africa, the trans-Sahel region, the Horn of Africa, the North Caucasus, and Xinjiang, only the countries of South Asia, Central Asia, and the Middle East are the subject of specific chapters.

Finally, this book is called *The Islamic Challenge*, rather than the Islamist challenge, for a reason. The primary challenge for the United States comes from the jihadists, who treat Islam both as a religion and as a political force. The jihadists challenge the status of the United States both as a hegemon and as an almost messianic promoter of secularism and democracy throughout the world. From their perspective, their ultimate victory (which they invariably depict as a victory of Islam) would be not only to dismantle the pro-US regimes in the Middle East and other Muslim countries, but also to force the United States to retreat from all Muslim regions of the world. Their secondary objective is to bring about the conversion of

Christians in the American population, as well as in all the Christian states of Europe, Asia, and Africa. These objectives have been highlighted by ISIS through incessant global propaganda campaigns in social media.

PLAN OF THE BOOK

Each chapter in this book is a case study of the dynamics of the struggle between Islam and the United States in a different region of the world. The focus of inquiry on different countries and regions will underscore (a) how this conflict evolved from the Islamist perspective during the colonial era and in the aftermath of World War II, the Cold War, 9/11, and the Arab Awakening; and (b) how the United States has responded to the Islamists' changing demands from the creation of an Islamic government in the 1940s to the threats related to regime change from self-styled jihadists like al-Qaida, its various affiliates (starting in the 1990s), and ISIS's declaration of the establishment of a caliphate (starting in June 2014).

Chapter 1 provides an overview of the book, and chapter 2 establishes the modalities of the Islamic challenge by focusing on the activities of the Islamists. These individuals and groups attempted without success to establish Islamic governments that would restore the former glory of Islam. The jihadists, the successors to the Islamists, also wanted to establish Islamist governments or the caliphate. However, they had a radically different approach toward that objective: the incessant use of violence and the implementation of the Takfiri doctrine.

Chapter 3 analyzes the concept of jihad. As much as it has been in the limelight and under scrutiny in the West since the 11 September 2001 terrorist attacks on the United States, there does not seem to be a clear understanding of this doctrine, especially regarding the circumstances under which it is declared and the identification of a proper authority to declare it. This chapter will present a comprehensive explanation of this doctrine. The militant version of jihad is the chief focus of this book, since it remains the greatest challenge to the continued dominance of the United States in the world of Islam.

Chapter 4 outlines the United States' endeavours to establish a dominant presence in the Middle East during the Cold War years, and its attempts to escalate its dominance since 9/11. Even though the jihadists attacked US embassies, personnel, and assets in the 1990s, it was al-Qaida's attack on the lone superpower that unleashed the United States' global war on terrorism. However, the real confrontation between the jihadists and the US forces took place when the United States was militarily occupying Iraq. This chapter initiates the thesis that Islamism – the ideologically motivated use of Islam as a political force and the acquisition of territory to promote a particular understanding of Islam – owes its origin to the chaos that emerged as a result of the withdrawal of US occupation forces from Iraq. This thesis is pursued in the remaining chapters of the book.

Chapter 5 deals with Pakistan and Afghanistan. The significance of Pakistan in this book stems from the fact that Islamization (i.e., the use of Islamic theology throughout the political arena) was carried out as a matter of policy by Zulfiqar Ali Bhutto and General Zia-ul-Haq in the 1970s. The United States entered this Islamic milieu with its own highly ambitious agenda of using the Islamic doctrine of militant jihad to defeat and expel the Soviet Union from Afghanistan. Another aspect of this chapter is the transformation of Afghanistan – from a country where the Taliban ruled from 1996 through October 2001 – into a fledgling democracy. Afghanistan is a place where the government of President Ashraf Ghani remains fragile. It is also a country where the opium trade is booming. As such, it remains a place where the enemies of political stability and democracy endure. That the remnants of al-Qaida and the Taliban are constantly enhancing their presence and influence in Afghanistan is an ongoing challenge for the United States. The jihadist groups of Pakistan – especially the Tehrik-e-Taliban-e-Pakistan (TTP) – remain important players.

Chapter 6 examines Iran's foreign policy toward the United States, especially in the aftermath of that superpower's invasion of Iraq in 2003. The Islamic Republic of Iran and the United States bore long-term antagonism toward each other. As a country where an Islamist regime ousted America's presence and dominance, Iran was poised to pursue policies that would hasten the ouster of the United States from Iraq and minimize its influence in Lebanon. An argument can be made that Iran's attempts to destabilize American-occupied Iraq, in conjunction with the heightened violence perpetrated by the Shia and Sunni insurgent groups, convinced the United States that its best strategy was to seek an early exit from that country. This chapter also discusses the successful conclusion of the US-Iran nuclear deal on 14 July 2015, Iran's role in stabilizing the government of Prime Minister Haider al-Abadi in Iraq, and Iran's resolute military support of the regime of President Bashar al-Assad of Syria since the

March 2011 inception of a civil war to oust him from power. While the United States and Iran are involved in fighting ISIS in Iraq, they remain on opposite sides regarding the ongoing civil war in Syria.

Chapter 7 covers Central Asia, a region where the struggle between the autocratic regimes and the jihadist forces has not even begun in earnest. These forces were active between 1997 and 2001. The US invasion of Afghanistan and its dismantling of the Taliban regime was a major blow to the organizational structure, proactivism, and morale of the jihadist forces. However, toward the beginning of 2016, all indications are that these forces continue to flourish and maintain their underground activities. They also appear to be biding their time in the wake of continued unrest in Uzbekistan, Kyrgyzstan, and Tajikistan.

Chapter 8 concludes the book with a comprehensive analysis of the themes and theses of the preceding chapters. An important aspect of this analysis is a futuristic examination of the Islamic challenge. Important topics include the emergence of ISIS, the establishment of the caliphate, conflicts between ISIS and al-Qaida, and the future dynamics of US-Iran relations and their implications for the overall involvement of the United States in the world of Islam. The chapter ends with a discussion of the dynamics of Islamism versus secular fundamentalism, and the prospects of any rapprochement between the two in the coming decades.

2

The Nature of the Islamic Challenge: When the Islamists (Moderates) Failed

SYNOPSIS

This chapter examines the postcolonial history of the Arab states and South Asia in order to comprehend why two of Islam's greatest features – peace and moderation, frequently iterated in the Holy Qur'an – have been sidelined and marginalized and why, especially since the 1990s, the doctrine of militant jihad has been excessively implemented by the self-styled jihadists. The focus of inquiry here will be the aspirations and agendas of the Islamists and the causes of their failure.

Historically, the Islamists as politico-religious groups had their own confrontational agenda in dealing with the Western countries that went to Islamic countries to subjugate them. The colonization of Muslim countries, more than any other catastrophic experience since the burning of Baghdad by the Mongols in 1258, not only traumatized Islamic leaders of all varieties, but also marked the beginning of an era of political instability and economic backwardness of those countries and the resultant quest for solutions to these ostensibly obdurate ailments. The Islamist antipathy toward the West was further intensified by the Franco-British legacy of colluding to bring about the end of the Ottoman Empire.

The general question of what went wrong has its roots in this particular experience of Muslims: Why does there seems to be no end to their downward slide and its related humiliation? While Islamic modernists wanted Muslim countries to adopt westernization and the values that came with it to reverse this slide, more traditional Islamist thinkers envisaged the West as largely responsible for the backwardness and enslavement of their polities. They had their own definite views about dealing with the West, a crucial aspect of which was aimed at retaining Islamic purity and establishing an Islamic government. A vital feature of Islamist thinking was that Muslims had been at the peak of their achievement when they adhered to the *straight path*, and their decline was the outcome of their subversion of Islam.

The United States, the power that inherited the British primacy of the Middle East, has come into conflict with Islamists of all persuasions because, first, as the most industrially advanced and most militarily powerful nation, it represented the best and the worst of the West. The best trait of the United States, from the Islamists' perspective, was its technological advancement, while its worst features were its staunch commitment to promoting Western-style democracy and the attendant doctrine of secularism, and its profound proclivity to exercise its strategic influence inside various Muslim countries. Second, in the 1990s, and especially in the post–9/11 era, the United States was perceived as the chief supporter of the autocratic regimes of the Middle East, North Africa, and South Asia that were regarded as un-Islamic or anti-Islamic by the jihadists, who became highly proactive, voluble, and visible during that period. Their aspirations to overthrow those regimes clashed with the US determination to sustain the political status quo in those countries.

The anti-westernism of the world of Islam was nurtured during the colonial era, but the Islamists (and later the jihadists) were mistaken in making the West chiefly responsible for the political instability and the general economic underdevelopment of their polities – or civilizational decline,[1] to use the grander Huntingtonian phrase – during the postcolonial era. The brunt of that responsibility falls on the shoulders of the authoritarian rulers, who purposely lowered the scholastic quality of religious schools and used the resultant poorly trained Islamic scholars to legitimize their rule. Such a tradition also enabled self-appointed "experts" on Islam to lead populist Islamist movements and to emphasize militant jihad as the only way to bring about political change.

THE QUEST FOR ANSWERS

Of the three Judaic religions of the world – Judaism, Christianity, and Islam – the most political religion is Islam. The Prophet of Islam, aside from being the messenger of God, was also a ruler – the ruler of a tiny city-state – but a ruler nonetheless. His mission was to spread the message of God in the world. As such, he wrote letters to the Byzantine and Sassanid emperors inviting them either to convert to the true faith of Islam or to be conquered. During the era of the four caliphs who succeeded the Prophet – known as the *Rashidun* – and those who came after, spreading the message of Islam continued to be a chief objective. There were, to be sure, no forced conversions. However, the environment in the conquered territories facilitated the spread of Islam because it was the faith of the new rulers.

Islam, undeniably, does not subscribe to the Christian proposition "Render unto Caesar the things that are Caesar's, and unto God the things that are God's." The Qur'an declares, "His are all things in the heavens and on earth."[2] In the realm of governance, Islam offers its adherents an "Islamic government." Even though it is inchoate and imprecise, and there is no consensus about the exact nature of an Islamic government, it has never lost its relevance and potency; indeed, since the Islamic revolution in Iran, an Islamic form of government has been envisioned as an achievable reality. Islamic government is generally understood to be what the Prophet of Islam had created in the city of Mecca in 629. However, in almost all Muslim countries, the proposition of establishing an Islamic government or caliphate (*khilafah*) is envisaged as the Islamic version of utopia – something that is desired in principle but not actively pursued by a great majority of the believers.

Under dynastic rule, which succeeded the rule of the fourth caliph (Ali, who was assassinated in 661), Islam, as a religion, remained at the centre of Islamic polities. Various Muslim rulers, as a matter of tradition, called themselves "caliphs" and "defenders of the faith." During the Renaissance and the Enlightenment, when the conflict between church and state in Christian Europe was resolved in favour of secularism, Muslims did not even consider separating religion and government. That idea did not enter into the arena of public debate in the Muslim world until the dying days of the last Muslim dynasty, the Ottoman Empire.

The abolition of the Ottoman sultanate in 1922 was a major blow to the Muslim perception of a glorious past. The end of the caliphate, the nadir of Muslim despair, had been in the making for the past several centuries. Long before its dissolution, the Ottoman state had been derisively described as the "sick man of Europe" by the European powers. However, for Muslims at large, its very existence symbolized their presence in the corridors of the great powers of that time, and its dismantlement created a great sense of loss. Its dissolution carried a powerful symbolic message that Muslims would not play an important role in world affairs for a long time to come.

Furthermore, the caliphate was dismantled at a time when Western Europeans had won World War I and occupied most of the Islamic world. No greater tribute could have been paid to the ostensible superiority of Western cultural- and modernization-related achievements than Mustafa Kemal Atatürk's decision to abandon his Islamic heritage and to change the Muslim nature of the Turkish state to a Western one. His other measures included the implementation of the "Hat Law" outlawing the wearing of turban and fez (1925), the shift of calendars from the Muslim to the Christian era (1925), the adoption of Swiss and Italian penal codes (1926), the adoption of the Latin alphabet (1928), and the proclamation of Turkey as a secular state.[3] Atatürk's measures, revolutionary though they may have appeared to the West, had their origins in a series of measures from the days of Sultan Selim III (1789–1807), who was long regarded as the "father of Ottoman-Turkish Westernization."[4]

Following Atatürk's example, Reza Khan, the founder of the Pahlavi rule, decided to take Iran on the road to modernization by paying little regard to the Islamic nature of his country. Both Atatürk and Reza Khan, by deciding to abandon the Islamic traditions of their respective polities, blamed Islam, at least tacitly or indirectly, for the technological backwardness and economic underdevelopment of their countries. Reza Khan's son, Mohammad Reza Pahlavi, launched a campaign aimed at consolidating his power as well as silencing and marginalizing the political opposition.[5] Then in 1963, he introduced his own massive westernization program under the rubric of "White Revolution" (*Enghelab-e Sefid*).

More important than its association with any one example, the phrase "Muslim despair" describes the endless anguish experienced by Muslims in their struggle to come to grips with the decline of their civilization. This decline created deep wounds in the Muslim frame of reference and in the Muslim spirit. They were subjugated by Western colonial powers who drew artificial boundaries and created equally artificial entities, called nation states, as they occupied them. Once they departed, these boundary lines became sanctified borders. The colonial powers also implanted the notion of national sovereignty among the ruling elites who succeeded them. Since that time, these notions – nationalism related to nation states and national sovereignty versus the sovereignty of God – have emerged as additional issues of conflict among Islamists of all colourations.

Muslim despair also signifies an overall quest among Muslims, especially among their intelligentsia, for a blueprint or a grand strategy that will enable one or more Muslim states to emerge as a great power. The Qur'an asserts, "You are the best of peoples ever raised up for mankind."[6] Under the banner of Islam, Arabs emerged from obscure tribal warriors to world-class empire builders. Even though this tradition was taken over by the Ottomans and by other non-Arab Muslims in later years, in all of these instances, empire building was done under the banner of Islam. But that glory appears to have eluded the Muslim *ummah* since then.

The onslaught of colonialism brought about modernization, westernization, and secularization. Western political analyses of the 1950s and 1960s dealing with modernization in "developing" societies argued that "wherever the modernization process has had an impact, it has contributed to secularization, both social and political."[7] A classic study on the modernization of the Middle East published in 1958 "gave concrete specifics of [the] declining role of religion as people became more 'modern' and less 'traditional.'"[8] Another scholarly consensus was that "especially in the political realm, 'the general forces of secularization of culture and society' would reduce the 'effectiveness' of religion."[9] Thus, modernization, westernization, and secularization were regarded as antidotes for reducing the role and influence of religion by Western intellectuals, who were also advising and influencing the development-related policies of major Western governments. The Islamists categorically rejected these perspectives; their counternarrative was that Islam must play a central role in the development of their polities. The efforts by modernizing elites of that era – Nasser of Egypt, Reza Pahlavi of Iran, Habib Bourguiba of Tunisia, Ahmed Ben Bella of Algeria, etc. – to follow the West's recipe for modernization caused conflict with Islamist forces.

One powerful effect of westernization is that the "Islamic institutions were replaced by Western institutions and the sacred law (Shari'a) [was] superseded by secular legislation."[10] El Fadl, one of the world's leading scholars of Islamic law, argues that the greatest damage to Islam was done by the Western-appointed, secular military rulers of the postcolonial era. They nationalized the Shariah schools, thereby severely narrowing the role of the Shariah, and replaced Shariah law with "Western-based secular legal systems." The governments also initiated "the dual policy of enforcing poor educational standards and paying low wages [to the jurists]." Such important subjects as "jurisprudential theory, legal maxims, legal precedents, hermeneutics, rhetoric, procedural theory, or any of the kind of subjects normally encountered in schools of law" that contributed to the education and reputation of powerful jurists of the past were deliberately eliminated from the curricula. By "dumbing down" the curricula of religious schools, the governments ensured that the schools did not train jurists or legal experts of high calibre who could question the authority (or, to be precise, the autocratic governing styles) of the rulers on the basis of Islamic *fiqh* (jurisprudence). Consequently, the corps of *ulama* (religious scholars) that emerged from those schools was no longer of the quality of the precolonial era. In their reduced role, they became "more like Western-styled ministers, who functioned at the margins of the society as religious advisers without being able to influence social or political policy in any meaningful way."[11] The autocratic rulers wanted the ulama to legitimize their rule, and only secondarily to perform such roles as give Friday sermons or serve as judges in Muslim personal law courts.

To these observations, one must add El Fadl's perceptive explanation of why the Arab world became the victim of jihadists. Fadl observes that the modernists (like Muhammad 'Abduh, Rashid Rida, Jamal al-Din al-Afghani, Muhammad Iqbal, and Fazlur Rahman) who attempted "to stem the disaster [related to the Muslim decline] by promoting liberal programs for Shari'a reform" and "to reinterpret Islamic law in order to make it more responsive to modern challenges" were by and large "scholars and jurists who did not lead mass movements."[12] This "vacuum in religious authority that they were working to address was quickly filled by popular movements led by men who had neither the training nor the education of the liberal jurists," but who "reduced the Islamic heritage to the least common denominator." These leaders of the popular Islamists (the jihadists) – the "self-proclaimed and self-taught jurists" (the autodidacts) – emerged as voluble spokesmen for Islam. This "vacuum in authority meant not so much that *no one* could authoritatively speak for Islam, but that virtually *every* Muslim with a modest knowledge of the Qur'an and the traditions of the Prophet was suddenly considered qualified to speak for Islamic tradition and Shari'a law." Frequently, "these self-proclaimed experts were engineers [Bin Laden], medical doctors [Ayman al-Zawahiri] and physical scientists." The cumulative result of these developments was that Islamic law as well as the religion itself became "ripe for pietistic fictions and crass generalizations, rather than a technical discipline of complex interpretive practices and sophisticated methodologies of social and textual analysis."[13] The Shariah – which, despite its remarkable diversity and pluralism, represents the unified Muslim identity – was exploited by the leaders of popular movements, the jihadists, in order to mobilize the masses and "to win significant popular support."[14]

The post-1952 history of Egypt exemplified these tensions within Islam. Sheikh Hasan al-Banna, founder and leader of the Muslim Brotherhood, blamed his country's traditional religious establishment (al-Azhar University), as well as the Egyptian military under President Gamal Abdel Nasser, for Egypt's humiliating enslavement by the West. However, the "real enemy" of Islam and Egypt, in al-Banna's view, was the United States. Al-Banna stated that the "capitalist" United States was using its "technical and economic aid programs to pervert the political independence of the countries aided and to establish this 'commercial dominance' by 'glutting the local markets.'"[15] The West in general, al-Banna stated, "surely seeks to humiliate us, to occupy our lands and begin destroying Islam by annulling its laws and abolishing its traditions. In doing this, the West acts under the guidance of the Church."[16] The solution to this mega problem, according to al-Banna, was for Egypt to reject "the way of the West" and "be restored to Islam."[17] His Brotherhood lost that struggle because it was crushed by Nasser and brutally suppressed by his successors.

In British India, Muslims suffered the trauma associated with the dissolution of the Mogul Empire and the emergence of British rule in their country. Then, their hopes for an ostensible Muslim unity under the Ottoman caliphate were shattered with the dissolution of the Ottoman Empire and the creation of Turkey as a republic in 1924. Fissures began to emerge within the Muslim community between coreligionists who identified with Indian nationalism for the future and those who insisted on finding ways to restore lost glory, or at least to sustain the Muslim community with all its political rights and privileges of the past. Maulana Abul A'la Maududi, an Islamist scholar of global repute, played a crucial role in formulating and strengthening the latter perspective. He blamed "the machinations of

Westernized Turkish nationalists" and "the betrayal of Islam by Arab nationalists – who had rebelled against the Ottomans in collusion with Europeans," for the demise of the caliphate; the Muslim-Hindu competition for power in British India, he believed, was the greatest challenge of the 1930s and 1940s. The solution to that challenge, in Maududi's thinking, had to emerge from Islamic revivalism "that could compete with both traditional Muslim identity and secular nationalism."[18] For Muslims to regain power, they must follow the "true teachings of Islam," which would make them "immune to the lure of Western thought as it was reflected in Indian nationalism."[19] This revival, he believed, should begin at the individual level. Maududi wrote extensively on the subject of revival, in the process borrowing generously, but without acknowledgment, from Western writings. He was convinced that Islam had to be reinterpreted through the implementation of *tajdid* (renewal). It was through *tajdid*, he believed, that Islam could compete with the West and its version of modernization.

Abul A'la Maududi's views of the West may best be described by the word "ambivalence." His was a more nuanced perspective than the outright and intense hatred of the West held by other Islamists like Sayyid Qutb of Egypt. Maududi was anti-Western in that he regarded the West as "an evil force determined to destroy Islam;" however, he did not endorse a "blanket rejection" of it.[20] He was intrigued by the Western notion of modernization, a concept that he wanted to internalize (or, to be precise, Islamize) for Islamic revival. However, when Maududi emerged as a politician in Pakistan, his previous commitment to *tajdid* was not evident in his public role; consequently, the richness of his Islamic thinking did not become a driving force for the modernization and political stability of Pakistan.[21]

What emerges from the preceding is an incessant but futile quest on the part of Islamists and modernists for an Islamic government – one that would be perceived by Muslims as representative of "true Islam" and a model for good governance, and that would reverse the backwardness and downward slide of the Muslim world. That quest was not shared by the authoritarian rulers; on the contrary, they perceived such Islamist debates, discussions, and related activities as an attempt to overthrow their rule and to replace it with some form of Islamic government. The response of the powers that be was a ruthless suppression of such thinking and incarceration of those advocating it. Thus, these debates were never allowed to flourish in the acutely nondemocratic and autocratic environments of Muslim countries. Equally important, the uncompromising nature of Islamist ideology meant that the Islamists were not inclined to seek common ground with the reigning autocrats about the achievement of their sacred goal.

This state of affairs produced different results in different countries. In Saudi Arabia, there emerged a compact between the Islamists and the rulers that heavily favoured the former. In Egypt, a series of showdowns between the autocrats and Islamists culminated in the crushing of the Muslim Brotherhood by the military rulers. In Tunisia, the dictatorial regimes of Habib Bourguiba and then of Zine El Abidine Ben Ali succeeded in crushing Islamist opposition and in ruling the country for several decades. In Iran, the autocratic rule of Mohammad Reza lasted until its ouster by the Islamic revolution in 1979. In prepartitioned British India, the Muslim minority's fear of becoming sidelined and marginalized by an overwhelmingly large and better-educated Hindu majority once the British colonialists left the country drove them to secure their religious identity and their Islamic civilization through the pursuit of "the two-nation theory." That discordant theory, under the leadership of a British-educated Bohra Muslim leader, Mohammad Ali Jinnah, resulted in partition of British India into separate states – India and Pakistan. Postpartitioned India steadfastly pursued its destiny as a Hindu-dominated, but secular and democratic state. Pakistan's own history, on the contrary, was marked by the sabotage of democracy by its army through intermittent coups d'état and a steady escalation in Islamization of its polity. Consequently, in the second decade of the twenty-first century, Islamists as well as jihadists continue to violently clash with civil and military authorities, and the future of a stable democracy in Pakistan remains questionable. Thus, there is no Muslim state where the Islamists have any clue as to what the cure is for the sustained decline of Muslim civilization.

The blame for the absence of peaceful political change and moderation should be placed squarely on the shoulders of the autocratic rulers. These rulers, as a matter of general practice, loathed quality education and its most crucial features – the promotion of critical thinking, original ideas, innovations, and creativity – that might also lead to demands for political change from their citizenry. The resultant massive, systematic dumbing down of education not only affected secular educational institutions and their curricula but also their Islamic counterparts. The reduced standards of modern education impaired the capacity of Muslim polities to train bright and state-of-the-art doctors, engineers, architects, scientists, and other professionals who could compete with their counterparts in the West and also prepare generations of highly educated and skilled young people.

In religious education, the lack of intellectual rigour produced ill-to-half-educated religious scholars who could retain employment only by becoming chief instruments of the autocrats' own impetus to remain in power. This vicious cycle of mutual support created economically backward and religiously obscurantist polities, where the only avenues for political change were through the use of violence, which the semi-educated or, at best, autodidactic jihadist leaders were to adopt. Avenues for peaceful change through an emphasis on Islamic moderation thus were never given a chance in most Muslim polities. The failure of the Islamists brought forward the self-styled jihadists, who would seek the same objectives but through an entirely different modus operandi.

ENTER THE SELF-STYLED JIHADISTS

The cacophony of Islamist ideas about altering the nature of government and their sustained inability to do so made militant jihad a highly feasible option. Even regarding jihad, there are two powerful debates taking place inside the world of Islam and among Muslims residing in the West. The first one is about redefining the conditions under which jihad may be declared and who is to declare it. (This issue will be taken up in the next chapter.) The second debate is about modernizing Muslim countries in order to ensure their place in the rank and file of powerful nations, as well as about the issue of democracy. The Islamists want nothing to do with democracy. Indeed, a major Islamist thinker, Abu Muhammad Asim Al-Maqdisi – following in the footsteps of some of the major Islamist thinkers of the immediate past, such as Maulana Abul A'la Maududi, Sayyid Qutb, and Hasan al-Banna – depicts democracy as a polytheistic "religion" that Allah warns against. In that capacity, he argues, it is totally unacceptable to Islam, which is the final religion of God. By linking the doctrine of *al wala' wal bara'* (loyalty to God and Islam and disavowal of everything else) with that of *takfir* (the concept of declaring some Muslims "apostates" or "unbelievers"), Al-Maqdisi freely declares all Muslim rulers as "infidels" who thus must be eliminated.[22]

For Muslims at large, however, the notion of religious freedom, which is an essential ingredient of Western-style democracy, remains very much alive (see table 2.1). Indeed, uniquely Islamic versions of democracy have been implemented in a number of countries. In the functioning democracies of Iraq and Palestine, for example, there is no separation of religion and politics; Islam remains a central force in both polities. Turkey, under the administrations of Recep Teyyip Erdoğan, as prime minister and then president, increasingly appears to be an Islamic democracy. Indonesia, a country with the largest Muslim population, has been democratic for more than a decade. Thus, a pertinent question is whether there is such a thing called "Islamic democracy." Under such a system, elections are held periodically and the governors are responsive to the governed. But in such a system, Islam remains a central force. Still, the chief litmus test of a democratic system is whether it tolerates the practices of religious minorities without interference or intimidation from public or private quarters.

As important as the potential evolution of Islamic democracy remains for the world of Islam, the doctrine of militant jihad and its related objective of establishing an Islamic government received its biggest endorsement and boost in two neighbouring countries, Afghanistan and Iran. During the US-sponsored Afghan war of the 1980s, the jihadist forces witnessed the defeat of a superpower. They gave full credit for that victory to their own zeal to wage jihad. In Iran, the Islamic revolution established an Islamic republic around the same time. Even though the latter was not an outcome of jihad, in the self-congratulatory lexicon and the exhilarated frame of mind that then prevailed regarding these two developments, regime change in Iran was seen as another victory for Islam. These events glorified the notion of jihad, especially among those who had tasted victory over a superpower in Afghanistan. They were ready to wage mini-jihads against the tyrants and autocrats in their own respective homelands in the Middle East and Africa, thereby starting a process of confrontation with the United States that culminated in the terrorist attacks on 11 September 2001.

The terrorist attacks on the United States were al-Qaida's declaration of war on the lone superpower. In turn, President George W. Bush

Table 2.1 Muslim support for democracy and religious freedom

Region	*Median % of Muslims who:*	
	Prefer democracy over strong leader	*Say religious freedom is a good thing*
Sub-Saharan Africa	72	94
Southeast Asia	64	93
Southern Eastern Europe	58	95
Middle East–North Africa	55	85
Central Asia	52	92
South Asia	45	97

Sources: Data for Southeast Asia, Southern Eastern Europe, the Middle East, Central Asia, and South Asia are from Pew Research Center, "The World's Muslims." Data for all African countries, except Niger, are from Pew Research Center, "Tolerance and Tension."

declared a global war on terrorism (GWOT) and on 7 October 2001 launched a military operation against the Taliban regime in Afghanistan. The immediate objective, in the atmosphere of anger inside the United States, was to punish the terrorists. Any long-term search for causes of conflict brewing between American and transnational Islamists, or comprehension of Islam as the defining feature of this conflict, was expected to come later. However, before even stabilizing post-Taliban Afghanistan, the United States decided to enlarge the scope of its war on terrorism by invading Iraq on 17 March 2003. The objective was to topple the regime of Saddam Hussein.[23] The United States also cooperated with the governments of the Philippines and Georgia to launch military operations against Muslim insurgents in those countries. China and Russia found unprecedented openings in Bush's global war on terrorism to suppress and, indeed, to eradicate Muslim secessionists in the Xinjiang province and in Chechnya and other Muslim republics of Russia's North Caucasus. Cumulatively, these developments resulted in the deaths of thousands of Americans and hundreds of thousands of people in Afghanistan, Iraq, the Philippines, Indonesia, North Caucasus, and Xinjiang. Through these global "antiterrorist" campaigns, George W. Bush, wittingly or unwittingly, provided Bin Laden's highfaluting phrase "global jihad" with direly needed substance, at least from the latter's perspective.

In the post–9/11 era, the United States is challenged by Islamist forces in all Muslim regions of the globe – the Middle East, South Asia, Southeast Asia, Central Asia, and North Africa. The toughest part of this challenge is that it presents an aggregated politico-religious perspective that is nearly impossible to disaggregate. For instance, the notion of Islamic government is part of the political legacy of Islam; however, since some form of it was implemented by the Prophet of Islam, its contemporary advocates (both the Islamists and the jihadists) steadfastly claim its pursuit as their religious obligation (*fard al-kifayah*). Thus, a number of jihadist groups continue to pose a sustained threat to the political survival of various regimes in those regions and are determined to replace them with their versions of Islamic governments. There are four direct parties to this post–Cold War mega conflict. The first party is Islam (the religion) and the Islamist forces who are challenging the legitimacy of various governments by labelling them as "anti-Islamic" or "un-Islamic," thereby keeping the internal political environments of those countries charged. The second party comprises the jihadists who are waging their "jihad" against the United States. The third party is the United States as the lone superpower and as the natural leader of the West, because of its politico-economic dominance and its awesome military prowess. The fourth direct party is the world of Islam or the Muslim world, an umbrella phrase that is used in this study to underscore the commonality of Islam as a political and religious force.

Al-Qaida deliberately used the doctrine of jihad to assign longevity, if not permanence, to its war against the United States. That doctrine was also used to assign universal comprehension of the struggle among Muslims, in the sense that even Muslims who disagreed with the war would grasp the underlying rationale. This is an important point because, from al-Qaida's perspective, as long as Muslims understand the essence of the struggle, they will serve as potential sympathizers, even if they do nothing to join the ranks of al-Qaida and other Islamist groups.

Since the 9/11 attacks on its territory, the United States has become embroiled in major struggles not only in the Middle East but also in Muslim countries of East Asia, South Asia, Central Asia, and different parts of Africa (North and West Africa, the trans-Sahel region, and the Horn). The very notion of a global war on terrorism is so inextricably linked to the world of Islam that its reverberations have been felt in the form of increased activism of Islamist groups in different regions of the world. Al-Qaida was largely responsible for universalizing its fight with the United States, especially by couching it in the lexicon of Islam. That strategy made its war against the United States a "war without borders."[24]

Given the totally unmatched "hard power" (generally defined as military power to achieve national objectives) between the superpower and the transnational jihadist group, such a strategy is, indeed, brilliant.[25] The assumption on the part of al-Qaida seems to be that if it gains popularity and support from Muslims the world over, it will be able to shrink considerably the United States' presence – the area and the ease of operations of its military – around the globe. Thus, al-Qaida envisions all Muslim areas of the world as battlefields of the present and future where it will continue to confront the United States. A related strategy may be to force the United States and its allies to spread their forces all over the globe, thereby exposing them where al-Qaida has a better chance to strike. As Bruce Riedel speculated in 2007,

> Bin Laden's goals remain the same, as does his basic strategy. He seeks to, as he puts it, "provoke and bait" the United States into "bleeding wars" throughout the Islamic world; he wants to bankrupt the country much as he helped bankrupt, he claims, the Soviet Union in Afghanistan in the 1980s. The demoralized "far enemy" would then go home, allowing al Qaida to focus on destroying its "near enemies," Israel and the "corrupt" regimes of Egypt, Jordan, Pakistan, and Saudi Arabia. The U.S. occupation of Iraq helped move his plan along, and bin Laden has worked hard to turn it into a trap for Washington. Now he may be scheming to extend his strategy by exploiting or even triggering a war between the United States and Iran.[26]

For the purpose of getting the United States involved in "bleeding wars," another theoretician of al-Qaida, Abu Bakr al-Naji (a pseudonym), advocates the concept of "imperial overstretch" to weaken the superpower and then to strike a fatal blow.[27] Imperial overstretch, according to Kennedy, is a situation in which the costs of waging wars outweigh the benefits of conquering extensive territories. The problem becomes acute when a great power enters a period of relative economic decline.[28] Given that in the twenty-first century the United States has had to absorb the enormous costs of waging two wars – in Iraq and Afghanistan – while its economy was in a downturn, it is not easy to dismiss the relevance of al-Naji's argument.[29] Possibly the growing international debate over America's reported decline has been studied by the jihadists, especially since the assassination of Bin Laden by the US Special Forces in May 2011. On the other hand, viewing their activities in a number of troubled countries of the Middle East, Africa, and South Asia, one can surmise that they are too busy creating mayhem to indulge in anything else (the operations of the jihadists will be taken up in chapter 3).

In their zeal to create mayhem and instability, al-Qaida's suicide bombers have been very effective. One has to keep in mind that these suicide bombers are driven by their willingness – indeed, their eagerness – to kill themselves while attempting to blow up their enemies. The notion of deterrence is thus rendered meaningless in the United States' handling of terrorism. Deterrence – the concept that was central to the buildup of nuclear weapons – was based on the rationale that both sides would avoid all acts that triggered wars, especially the use of nuclear weapons, because of the enormously destructive nature of nuclear conflagrations. That thinking was also based on the notion that all nation states operate in accordance with the code "live and let live."[30] However, al-Qaida is a nonstate entity, and its suicide bombers (who are invariably described as "martyrs" by that organization) made all deterrence-related rationales irrelevant to the fight with the United States. They believed that their willingness to sacrifice themselves for their cause would ultimately force their enemies to retreat, especially since human life is cherished in the Western value system.[31]

The fact of the matter is that life is cherished and valued in all cultures, especially in the culture of Islam. The Holy Qur'an forbids suicide in no uncertain terms: "O ye who believe! ... [do not] kill (or destroy) yourselves, for verily Allah hath been Merciful to you. And whoever does this aggressively and unjustly, We will soon cast him into fire."[32] However, al-Qaida departed from the conventional Islamic regard and, indeed, respect for human life, and adopted the view that sacrificing one's life in the struggle between Islam and the "infidels" is a noble service for the glory of Islam, a blessing, and an act performed to please God. Needless to say, that notion is subject to varied interpretations and is a source of huge contention among Muslim scholars. For instance, Sayyid Muhammad Tantawi, the former grand mufti of Egypt, declared that suicide bombing was forbidden in Islam and condemned its use against Israel, whereas Yusuf al-Qaradawi, another major Egyptian Islamist scholar, endorsed "defensive" suicide bombing against Israeli targets, labelling them "legitimate" targets.[33]

Although some simplistic studies have attempted to associate suicide bombings with various Qur'anic verses, the fact of the matter is that this practice was frequently exercised by the Tamil Tigers (LTTE), an ethno-nationalist entity; by Hamas, a nationalist organization; and by the PKK, which is Marxist in orientation. Another temptation in the West is to depict suicide bombers as demented individuals. On the contrary, systematic studies have demonstrated that two factors motivate suicide bombers: personal crisis and commitment. Personal crisis refers to pain suffered by a suicide bomber as a result of enemy action. A well-known example is the so-called black widows, Chechen women whose husbands fell victim to violence perpetrated by the Russian security forces. Commitment refers to the devotion or allegiance of a suicide bomber to an organization or a cause sponsoring such an action. A 2005 study done by Robert Pape, for example, found that 95 per cent of suicide attacks worldwide were initiated by organizations. An organization will follow this strategy as long as it serves its purpose. In order to promote a "culture of death," such organizations systematically glorify suicide missions. Evidence of this practice is present in all the organizations mentioned above. Studies concur that the suicide bombers do not manifest any special traits underscoring any psychological problem.[34]

CLOSING OBSERVATIONS

The failure of the Islamists to bring about the kind of change they desired had a lot to do with the anachronistic nature of their aspirations as well as the sustenance of autocratic rule in most Muslim countries after the demise of European colonialism. Western modernization is based on scientific progress and technological breakthroughs, both of which are ineluctable products of rationality-based educational systems that have prevailed in the West since at least 1760 – the year that is generally referred to as the beginning of the Industrial Revolution. The Islamists, by contrast, hearkened back to the Islamic golden age, which began in the mid-eighth century and "lasted roughly 500 years." To Muslim scholars, this golden age was "proof that there's no conflict between Islam and science. What started as a movement to translate the scientific and philosophical texts of ancient Greece and India led to a remarkable flowering of science, philosophy, and theology. The golden age emerged in Baghdad in the 8th century, spread to Cairo, Damascus, and other Middle Eastern cities, and later flourished in Andalusian Spain."[35]

But what caused the Muslim decline? A definite and straightforward answer may not exist, because there appear to be many underlying causes. However, one can develop a broad understanding of it by considering the following. First, the congenital preference for obscurantism on the part of autocratic rulers in Muslim polities – especially in the aftermath of the end of European colonialism – choked all opportunities for the evolution of scientific thinking. Second, to this syndrome, one has to add the historical role of semi-educated ulama of the state-controlled religious schools. Generation after generation, these religious scholars spent their energy declaring any scientific technological advancement or serious challenge to political authority to be "un-Islamic." Third, to this pile of general decay the Western colonial masters made their own contribution by promoting, encouraging, and in some instances handpicking autocrats and tyrants to ensure that the postcolonial Arab world did not become hostile to Western economic interests and dominance by becoming democratic and, thereby, independently minded.[36] These developments created an environment in most Muslim polities where questioning political authority and striving to bring about political and economic reforms were declared to be "treason." As a general rule, those autocrats were not enthusiastic about promoting Western scientific education, fearing that such curricula would also nurture critical and original thinking, traits that are progenitors of demands for democracy. Thus, any radical transformation of political and economic decay and obscurantism could be achieved only through the use of violence. However, the perpetrators of violent political struggle – the jihadists – used violence not to democratize, secularize, or modernize their polities or make them scientifically advanced. On the contrary, their recipe was to drag their polities as close to the governmental model that prevailed in the Arabian Peninsula in the seventh century. And their tool was the militant doctrine of jihad. The next chapter will take a closer look at this issue.

3

Jihad: The Unsheathed Weapon

SYNOPSIS

This chapter aims to explain the intricacies underlying the doctrine of jihad by examining its religious basis and its interpretations in the writings of Ibn Taymiyya and other Islamist theoreticians of the nineteenth and twentieth centuries. Even though the self-styled jihadists have been eager to act on the violent aspect of it, the doctrine of jihad is much more nuanced than that. In the context of this book, it is important to note that the United States drew on the doctrine of jihad to oust the Soviet occupiers from Afghanistan in the 1980s. However, in the 1990s, the United States itself became a major target of Islamist groups – most notably al-Qaida – that started labelling their fight against the lone superpower as jihad.

Among Islamist groups, the chief controversy underlying jihad is, Who (which entity) should declare it? and what circumstances would justify its declaration? A Muslim organization like the Organisation of Islamic Cooperation (OIC – the name was changed from Organisation of the Islamic Congress on 28 June 2011) might come close to being considered a legitimate entity to declare jihad, since a number of Muslim countries are members. However, it has never considered declaring jihad against the United States or the West. About the only other country that might lay claim to declaring it is Saudi Arabia, which is the birthplace of Islam, but Saudi Arabia would not consider taking such a measure. In the final analysis, given that Sunni Islam does not have a singular authority – à la the Catholic pope who speaks for the entire Catholic Church – the legitimacy of any authority to declare jihad will remain surrounded in considerable controversy.

Two important aspects of this chapter need to be highlighted here. First is the issue of attacking the "near enemy" (*adou al-qareeb*) versus the "far enemy" (*adou al-bayeed*). Following the preference of the originator of this concept, an Egyptian named Muhammad Abd al-Salam Faraj, al-Qaida at first focused on the "near enemy" by carrying out regional jihads around Afghanistan from the late 1990s to 2000. In 2001, it shifted its focus to the far enemy by attacking the United States. ISIS similarly expanded its attacks from the near enemy to the far enemy. It attacked the near enemy by capturing swathes of territories in Iraq and Syria, and then creating the caliphate in those territories in June 2014. However, under mounting air attacks by the United States, France, and Russia on the caliphate, ISIS, without fanfare, carried out terrorist attacks on the far enemies in Paris in November 2015 and Brussels in March 2016. In addition, there have been several ISIS-inspired attacks in a number of Western and Arab countries.[1] Second, this chapter deals with the strategic and operational aspects of carrying out global jihad. In this context, the writings of Abu Bakr al-Naji and Abu Mus'ab al-Suri became significant, especially when ISIS emerged as a nemesis of al-Qaida and used social media to create a global presence.

The chapter concludes by comparing the impressive capabilities of the Arab Awakening to bring about regime change in Tunisia, Egypt, and Libya with the inability – indeed the miserable failure – of the Islamists to use jihad to oust the autocrats of their respective countries. Still, it will be argued that one cannot dismiss jihad as a weapon for radically altering the political status quo in the Arab world.

THE MEANING OF JIHAD IN SACRED WRITINGS AND EARLY THEOLOGY

The doctrine of jihad is as old as Islam. It has been invoked many times in both religious and political struggles throughout the history of Islam. There are several important points one must keep in mind in seeking to understand the role and meaning of jihad. First, even though the Prophet of Islam never declared jihad (at least not using that word), every battle that he fought could be described as jihad. The Prophet Muhammad participated in twenty-seven recorded battles and deputized an additional fifty-nine. In later generations, when a Muslim dynasty or a Muslim ruler was involved in a military skirmish with non-Muslim forces, the name of jihad was invoked, thereby implying that that ruler was defending Islam in the same manner as the Prophet of Islam. Second, since jihad is a multifaceted doctrine – it has several meanings – different observers or specialists have been able to emphasize one or another meaning as the sole interpretation, thereby confusing laypersons regarding its true meaning. Third, the Sunni and Shia notion of jihad is very similar, except that the Twelver Shias (followers of twelve imams, which is the faith of the majority of the populace in Iran) believe that they may wage jihad only under the leadership of the rightful imam. However, when attacked, they may wage jihad under the leadership of *ulama* (religious scholars, plural of *alim*), who are regarded as the representatives of the hidden imam. Finally, to comprehend the current use of jihad by al-Qaida and other Islamists as the basis of "war" against the United States and other great powers, a nuanced understanding of the doctrine of jihad is essential.

The root of jihad is *juhuda*, which means "struggle" or "exerting oneself." Its meaning emerges from the two original sacred texts of Islam, the Qur'an and the Hadith (the statements and traditions of Prophet Muhammad regarding what transpired during his lifetime). All six canonical collections *ahadith* (singular Hadith) of Sunni Islam – Sahih Bukhari, Sahih Muslim, Sunan al-Tirmidhi, Sunan Abu Dawood, Sunan al-Sughra, and Sunan Ibn Majah – assign primacy to jihad. It is written in the Abu Dawood that jihad is a force until the Day of Resurrection.[2]

Islam is a religion whose followers had to fight for survival from its very inception. Those were the days when wars settled threats to survival, and Islam was no exception. Permission to wage jihad was granted by Allah to the Prophet of Islam after his migration from Mecca to Medina. At first, the purpose of jihad was to enhance the security of the small fledgling Islamic community. Later, especially in the last ten years of the Prophet's life, jihad was aimed at expanding Muslim control of hostile territory and gaining adherents. The great battles fought by the Prophet and narrated in the Qur'an – Badr, 624; Uhud, 625; Khandaq, 627; and Hunain, 630 – underscore God's testing of the strength of the faith of the believers. The victory of the Battle of Badr was followed by a defeat in the Battle of Uhud, in which the Prophet's uncle Hamza ibn 'Abdul-Muttalib (described in the lexicon of Islam as "prince of martyrs") died, and the Prophet himself narrowly escaped. After the death of the Prophet in 632, Muslims pursued an aggressive campaign of conquest without necessarily using the term jihad.[3]

In the Qur'an, the concept of jihad, if not the term itself, can be interpreted as legitimizing the conquest of the non-Muslim world. Sura At-Tauba (Sura 9) deals with the issue of jihad at length without using the word. Sura 9:5 (the "verse of the sword") states, "Then, when the sacred months have passed, slay the idolaters wherever ye find them, and take them (captive), and besiege them, and prepare for them each ambush. But if they repent and establish worship and pay the jizya (non-Muslim tax), then leave their way free. Lo! Allah is Forgiving, Merciful." This verse was interpreted by later Muslim jurists as a declaration of universal jihad against all non-Muslims.

The term *jihad* and two related terms – *jahidu* (which appears thirty-three times in the Qur'an) and *qatilu* (which appears in 167 verses) – mean warfare. The purpose of *qatilu* is to wage war against non-Muslims to subdue them, and then force them to pay *jizya* (a protective tax). *Jahidu*, on the other hand, is defensive in nature. For instance, the Qur'an (22:39–40) states, "To those against whom war is made, permission is given (to fight), because they are wronged." Verse 2:190 categorically forbids aggression: "And fight (*qatilu*) in the way of Allah those who fight you. But do not transgress limits; For God loveth not aggressors." Thus, jihad is enjoined against those who fight Muslims or who have committed wrongs against Muslims. These verses have been used by Islamists to legitimize violence in defence of Islam in response to the historical injustices that the West has perpetrated through colonialism, and through the subjugation of Muslims in Palestine, Xinjiang, Chechnya, Kashmir, southern Philippines, southern Thailand, and elsewhere. The jihadists' depiction of their use of violence as a means of protecting Islam strikes a sympathetic chord inside the world of Islam at large.

There is little doubt that fighting and dying for Allah is an important, *though not the sole*, aspect of jihad. This clear-cut understanding has driven Muslims to fight for Islam when they considered their religion to be threatened. This reality came to the attention of the West in a huge way only after the 9/11 terrorist attacks on the United States. However, America should have been neither shocked nor surprised to encounter this reality in 2001, given that it won a gigantic victory over the Soviet Union in Afghanistan in the late 1980s by purposely resurrecting the doctrine of militant jihad. In doing so, President Ronald Reagan described the Soviet Union as the "focus of evil." As such, at least in the minds of Americans, it was a legitimate target of jihad. What shocked the United States was that it, too, had become, in the minds of Islamists, a legitimate target of jihad. Americans in general, and secular fundamentalists in particular, believed that their political system, which represented democracy, equality, and human rights, fully qualified the United States to be envisioned as a moral force. Obviously, the Islamists strongly disagreed with this characterization of the lone superpower.

Aside from its significance as an Islamic doctrine that is frequently pronounced in the Qur'an and in numerous ahadith, jihad owes its prominence to one of Islam's greatest theologians, Taqi al-Din Ahmad Ibn Taymiyya (1263–1328). For him, the chief trait of Islam was its refusal to separate religion from politics. He was also probably the greatest champion of Islamism – the ideologically motivated use of the religion as a political force. Some of his contributions are highly relevant to this study.[4]

First, Ibn Taymiyya was committed to a strict, literal understanding of the Qur'an and the ahadith. He noted, "The most reliable speech is the book of God and the best guidance is the guidance of Mohammad." In the tradition of the *sulafa* (pious ancestors, singular *salafi*), he believed that God's message could be disseminated without obstruction by ensuring that political power remained in the hands of a Muslim ruler. Second, Ibn Taymiyya's commitment to jihad was total. "Know that Jihad is the finest thing in this world and the next," he wrote, "and to neglect it is to lose this world and the next ... This means: either victory and triumph or martyrdom and paradise." Third, Ibn Taymiyya was strongly opposed to the Shia sect of Islam as well as to the Sufi tradition of Ibn al-Arabi, the greatest Sufi master.

Finally, for Ibn Taymiyya, the ultimate proof of the commitment of a Muslim to Islam was manifested in complete devotion to the Shariah. The failure or unwillingness of any Muslim to demonstrate this commitment meant that he or she was an apostate, not a "true" Muslim. Punishment for apostasy, in the judgment of Ibn Taymiyya, was death. This principle applied to rulers as well: when a ruler failed to enforce the Shariah, he stopped being a Muslim and forfeited the right to rule. Taymiyya therefore declared jihad against the Mongol rulers. Even though they had converted to Islam, they were still using the Yasa code (laws created by Genghis Khan), instead of the Shariah. In Taymiyya's view, they were living in a state of *Jahiliyya* (pre-Islamic era of ignorance). He wrote, "Everyone who is with them (Mongols) in the state over which they rule has to be regarded as belonging to the most evil class of men." This innovative way of declaring a Muslim *kafir* (infidel) – also known as *takfir* – would be adopted by a number of Islamist scholars of the nineteenth and twentieth centuries. Ibn Taymiyya's influence on later Islamist thinkers will be taken up in the next section.

The militant notions of jihad undeniably have their origins in the original sources of Islam – in the Qur'an and the six ahadith. All four Sunni *Mazahib* (plural of *Mazhab*, meaning religious school) also reiterate these same notions. But that is not the definitive word on the meaning of jihad. It also includes the act of peaceful striving, a concept described as *sughra* (lesser jihad), and jihad *kubra* (greater jihad), the inner struggle that pulls an individual between good and evil. Some sources cite a Hadith to make that point, but other sources deny the authenticity of that Hadith.

Still, the debate over the meaning of jihad continues. A well-known Pakistani-Canadian Islamic scholar, Muhammad Tahir-ul-Qadri, has consistently rejected the militant interpretations of jihad and insisted on its peaceful meaning. In a speech at the US Institute of Peace in 2010, he said that the terrorists "misinterpret Islamic jihad to radicalize ... Muslims in general ... They also supply radical and extremist meanings to some of the verses of the Qur'an and traditions of the holy prophet ... They take jihad meaning out of context." Given his vast knowledge of Islam and the Qur'an, he is quoted at length here.

> There are, in total, 36 verses of the holy Qur'an, where the word jihad and its derivatives such as jahada, jaahada, yujahid or yujahiduna have been used, including the commandment of jihad. Out of these 36 verses, 31 verses have absolutely no mention of fighting anywhere, neither in the text nor context. There are three ways of deriving the meaning or significance of a particular command in a verse. You understand [a] certain commandment, teaching or prohibition either from the text of a verse, or its context, or historical context – what were the circumstances when this commandment was revealed, on what date, in which year, and the particular situation, and what was the historical background of the text, context or historical background in which 31 verses out of 36 do not make any direct or indirect mention of the commandments of jihad, not even the defensive war, or a fair or lawful war. There is absolutely no mention of fighting or combating ... It must, therefore, be made clear that

> the term "jihad" does not denote or connote any kind of fighting, combating, torturing or killing. On the contrary, it means extreme exertion, effort, and struggle for a good cause.[5]

Regardless of this controversy, three points should be kept in mind in the context of this study. First, there is no single interpretation of jihad. It covers the entire gamut of interpretation from a personal level to that of the whole Muslim community (*ummah*). Second, it engages individuals in the classic tug-and-pull of doing good or evil. Third, it includes the militant notion of fighting and killing the enemies of God. Those who call themselves jihadists on the sole basis of the militant interpretation are referred to in this study as "self-styled" jihadists because their notion of jihad is illegitimate. Islam does not condone the blind use of violence and killing. Finally, and most important, jihad can be peaceful or violent, depending on which interpretation of jihad an individual or group selects, and how they decide to act on it. The militant version of jihad is the focus here, since it remains the utmost, and a relentless, challenge to the continued dominance of the United States in different regions of the world.

THE EVOLUTION OF JIHADIST THINKING

Ibn Taymiyya's religious interpretations acquired a new significance when they were adopted by Muhammad ibn 'Abd al-Wahhāb of Saudi Arabia in the eighteenth century, and Hasan al-Banna and Sayyid Qutb of Egypt in the twentieth century.[6] It is this resurgence of the Takfiri doctrine – the necessity of a puritanical commitment of rulers to the tenets of Islam – that has driven the jihadists to an endless spree of violence in various Muslim countries from the eighteenth century through the second decade of the twenty-first century. This doctrine has also fuelled jihadists in their futile endeavours to assassinate or overthrow the existing rulers of a number of Muslim states of the Arab world and Pakistan. The significance of this doctrine, for the purposes of this study, is that – despite its failure to bring about a regime change anywhere – it remains at the heart of almost all jihadist movements, even today.

The notion of jihad evolved in the religious schools of Saudi Arabia in the eighteenth and nineteenth centuries. Muhammad ibn 'Abd al-Wahhāb (1703–1792), a religious cleric who was influenced by the precepts of Ibn Taymiyya in his advocacy of puritanical militancy, succeeded in selling his ideology to Muhammad bin Saud, whose main interest was to expand his rule on the Arabian Peninsula. They signed a pact in 1744 whose purpose, from the viewpoint of 'Abd al-Wahhāb, was to wage "Jihad against all who deviated from his understanding of *tauhid* [tawhid or oneness of God]." From the perspective of the Saudi ruler, the pact became the basis of legitimacy of the Saudi dynasty as it went through a number of ups and downs in reestablishing or expanding that rule and in its battles with other neighbouring rulers, even the Ottoman Empire. Muhammad bin Saud's only concern was that 'Abd al-Wahhāb would prevent him from taxing the people of al-Durriya. However, the latter assured the Saudi ruler that "the forthcoming Jihad would yield booty far in excess of that tax." Thus the association between them was highly symbiotic in nature.[7]

'Abd al-Wahhāb emphasized the doctrine of Tawhid, which is also at the core of the Qur'an and the teachings of the Prophet of Islam. *Tawhid* literally means "asserting oneness," and it stems from the Arabic verb *wahada* (to unify or to consolidate). When it is used in reference to God (Allah), it describes "the belief that Allah is One, without partner in His dominion (*Rububiyah*), One without similitude in His essence and attributes (*Asma' was-Sifat*), and One without rival in His divinity and in worship (*Uluhiyah/Ibadah*)." These three aspects of Tawhid "overlap and are inseparable to such a degree that whoever omits any one aspect has failed to complete the requirement of Tawhid." Any act of omission is depicted as *shirk* (sharing) or "the association of partners with Allah," which is idolatry.[8]

The doctrine of Tawhid is central to Islamic belief and is one of the foremost requirements of being and remaining a Muslim. The chief point of divergence is that, following the tradition established by Ibn Taymiyya, the Wahhabis have assigned themselves the right to judge who is a *muahid* (a believer in Tawhid) and who is a *mushrik* (an apostate, idolater, pagan, or a disbeliever in the Oneness of Allah). This ideology was known for its rigidity in defining who was not Muslim (i.e., anyone who did not subscribe to Wahhabism) and for the ruthlessness of adherents in dealing with those deemed *mushrikin* (plural of *mushrik*), that is, all non-Wahhabis. The blood of *mushrikin* "could legitimately be shed, their property was forfeit, and their women and children could be enslaved."[9] These precepts are derided as "Wahhabism" by critics, while those who accept them call themselves *muahid* (Unitarians) or *sulafa* (followers of the pious ancestors of the days of the Prophet of Islam).

The acceptance of 'Abd al-Wahhāb's interpretation of Tawhid, *shirk* (polytheism), and jihad by Saudi rulers has had enormous implications, driving them to proclaim jihad against those who disagreed with these doctrines. Even to this day, the Saudi dynasty discreetly operates to promote those doctrines, claiming to be a protector of Muslim interests. A similar ruthlessness has driven al-Qaida and other jihadist organizations in their campaigns of bloodletting in Iraq and other Arab countries, as well as in Indonesia and the Philippines, in the post–9/11 era.

Ibn Taymiyya's staunch rejection of the separation of politics and religion in Islam was reiterated by Hasan al-Banna (1906–1949) of Egypt, a school teacher who founded the Muslim Brotherhood. While strongly opposing Western-oriented pan-Arabism, Hasan al-Banna championed pan-Islamic nationalism, "insisting that Islam and nationalism were complementary, especially when the latter operated within the parameter of the Islamic truth, since, for the Muslim Brethren, Islam was of course both religion and state."[10] In a message to his followers of the Brotherhood in 1943, al-Banna wrote: "When asked what it is for which you call, reply that it is Islam, the message of Muhammad, the religion that contains within it government, and has one of its obligations freedom. If you are told that you are political, answer that Islam admits no such distinction. If you are accused of being revolutionaries, say, 'We are voices for right and for peace in which we dearly believe, and of which we are proud.'"[11] The Muslim Brotherhood played a pioneering role in enhancing the role of Islam in the liberation of Egypt in 1952 and survived the repressive policies of presidents Gamal Abdel Nasser, Anwar Sadat, and Hosni Mubarak. Although it was banned in September 2013 and declared a "terrorist group" that December by the army, the organization remains very much alive as an underground Islamist party under the military reign of General Abdel Fattah el-Sisi, and it awaits the time when it will be allowed to participate in elections, if and when they are again held. The Muslim Brotherhood has served as an ideological template for a number of Islamist parties in Muslim countries, even outside the Arab world.

Abul A'la Maududi (1903–1979) of Pakistan was another major theoretician of militant global jihad, but instead of declaring the Pakistani government an illegitimate entity, he worked inside the political system of that country to Islamize it in the 1970s. Perhaps for that reason, his writings are not well known in the West. His work garnered the admiration of General Zia-ul-Haq and influenced his official campaign to Islamize Pakistan in the 1980s. Maududi provided a unique definition of Islam, Muslim, and jihad:

> Islam is not merely a religious creed or compound name for a few forms of worship, but a comprehensive system which envisages to annihilate all tyrannical and evil systems in the world and enforces its own programme of reform which it deems best for the well-being of mankind ... Islam is a revolutionary ideology and programme which seeks to alter the social order of the whole world and rebuild it in conformity with its own tenets and ideals. "Muslim" is the title of that International Revolutionary Party organized by Islam to carry into effect its revolutionary programme. And "Jihad" refers to that revolutionary struggle and utmost exertion which the Islamic Party brings into play to achieve this objective.[12]

As a revolutionary ideology, "Islam shuns the use of current vocabulary and adopts a terminology of its own, so that its own revolutionary ideals may be distinguished from common ideals." Maududi goes on to explain that

> Islam purposely rejected the word *harb* ... [or] "war" and used the word "Jihad" which is synonymous with "struggle," though more forceful and wider in connotation ... Islam wishes to destroy all states and governments anywhere on the face of the earth which are opposed to the ideology and programme of Islam regardless of the country or the Nation which rules it. The purpose of Islam is to set up a state on the basis of its own ideology and programme, regardless of which nation assumes the role of the standard-bearer of Islam or the rule of which nation is undermined in the process of the establishment of an ideological Islamic State.[13]

Through such authoritative statements, Maududi affected the thinking of another renowned Islamist, Sayyid Qutb.

While Maududi was pragmatic in his overall approach, Sayyid Qutb (1906–1966) clashed head on with the intensely authoritarian regime of Gamal Abdel Nasser of Egypt in the 1960s. Qutb developed his anti-Western (US) views as a young student visitor to Greely, Colorado, in the late 1940s. The conservative environment of the town contributed to his loneliness. He also claimed that the United States sent a female "agent" to seduce him on board a ship when he was returning home.[14] He became a harsh critic of the Western lifestyle – the intermingling of sexes, the seductive appearance of Western women, the secular culture, and the proclivities for instant gratification. His political views of the United States were further poisoned when the *New York Times*, in reporting Hasan al-Banna's death, called him a "terrorist." Qutb was infuriated by this despicable depiction of a righteous and a noble man by "a nation of sinners."[15] Back in Egypt, he became immersed in anti-government activities. The Nasser regime, envisioning Islamists and jihadists as the chief threats to its survival, brutalized them. Qutb was arrested in 1954 and spent ten years in an Egyptian prison, where he fully developed his jihadist ideology. The dungeons of Egypt thus became nurturing grounds for militant jihad.

Upon his release from prison in 1964, Qutb published his book, *Ma'alim fil-Tariq* (Milestones), which has served as a highly influential instruction manual for contemporary Islamist/jihadist movements. Upholding the steadfastness of Ibn Taymiyya, Qutb refused to bend or to compromise. And he went even further, accusing modern Muslim governments that did not adhere to Islamic rule (by observing the Shariah) to be practitioners of Jahiliyya. That charge has become the basis of conflict in almost all contemporary Muslim countries. This idea of overthrowing "un-Islamic" rulers became a popular notion among the cadre of Islamists who opposed them purely on theological grounds, or at least on the basis of their interpretations of Islam. Thus Qutb became one of the foremost contemporary intellectual architects of militant jihad.

Sayyid Qutb endorsed the discussion of Jahiliyya in Sayyed Abul Hasan Ali Nadwi's book, *Islam and the World: The Rise and Decline of Muslims and Its Effect on Mankind*. In the foreword to the second edition, Qutb notes with approval Nadwi's description of Jahiliyya as a condition of spiritual and moral relapse of Muslims worldwide since they lost their global leadership.[16] Jahiliyya is not a temporal condition, Qutb writes. Rather, it is a spiritual and intellectual condition that arises when false values replace those that God grants. This is a weighty observation because it makes Jahiliyya a constantly recurring condition that Islamist groups must not only confront but defeat and destroy. In his early writings, Qutb used the term *Jahiliyya* to describe "barbarianism" rather than "ignorance," and he treated it as a social or ethical problem. By 1964, however, he had fully developed his thinking on this concept, and, most likely influenced by the writings of Maududi and Nadwi, he presented Jahiliyya as a theological problem and as a "definitional opposite of Islam."

Qutb's full explanation of the meaning of Jahiliyya comes to us from his *Fi Zilal al-Qur'an* (In the shade of the Qur'an):

> *Jahiliyya* ... is not a period of time but a condition, a condition which existed yesterday, exists today, and will exist tomorrow. [*Jahiliyya*] ... stands over against Islam and contradicts it. People – in any time and any place – are either governed by God's shari'a – entirely without any reservations – accepting it and submitting to it, in which case they are following God's religion, or they are governed by a shari'a invented by humans, in whatever form, and accept it. In that case they are in *jahiliyya* and are following the religion of those who govern by that shari'a, and are by no means following the religion of God. Whoever does not desire the rule (*hukm*) of God desires the rule of *jahiliyya*, and whoever rejects the shari'a of God accepts the shari'a of *jahiliyya* and lives in *jahiliyya*.[17]

Qutb argued that the failure of contemporary Muslim polities to implement Shariah has left them in a state of ignorance (Jahiliyya) under the rule of illegitimate governments. Thus, it is the obligation of all Muslims to rebel against governments and, indeed, to work to overthrow them. The alternative to these illegitimate governments, according to Qutb, is the establishment of an Islamic government, thereby ending, once and for all, the age of Jahiliyya. The combined tradition of Ibn Taymiyya's belief, Qutb's notion of Jahiliyya, and Maududi's view that Islam should destroy all ideologies that are opposed to it accounts for the durableness of jihad in the thinking of those who are waging it against the West today.

Indeed, the doctrine of jihad has endured despite its lack of political success. Perhaps because the concept of jihad was unsuccessfully used to overthrow the Nasser regime in the 1950s, it did not emerge as a basis for political change for the entire Middle East. It was never a factor in the "Arab Cold War" that was fought between the monarchical and republican Arab regimes from 1954 to 1967.[18] Nor did it emerge during the global Cold War as a force for change that captured the attention of major powers. When a number of Muslim countries – like Indonesia and Pakistan, along with Egypt – became independent, Qutb became hopeful about the establishment of Islamic governments. However, these governments disappointed him by moving in a secular rather than an Islamist direction.

Muhammad Abd al-Salam Faraj (1954–1982), a young theoretician and a follower of Sayyid Qutb who led the Islamic jihad in Egypt, is best known for his original thinking on the near enemy versus the far enemy and his categorical preference for attacking and defeating the near enemy: "To fight an enemy who is near is more important than to fight an enemy who is far." Muslims must concentrate on establishing "the Rule of God's Religion in our own country first, and to make the Word of God supreme ... There is no doubt that the first battlefield for *jihad* is the extermination of these infidel leaders and to replace them by a complete Islamic Order. From here we should start."[19] The Muslim rulers, in his view, were "in apostasy from Islam," and they should be punished more severely than those who were by origin infidels; in short, such rulers should be killed. The jihadists implemented that thinking in 1981 when they attacked and killed President Anwar Sadat of Egypt.

Another major theoretician of the ilk of Faraj was Abdullah Yusuf Azzam (1941–1989). In the tradition of Taymiyya, 'Abd al-Wahhāb, Maududi, and Qutb, he assigned high significance to jihad. "One of the most important lost obligations," he wrote, "is the forgotten obligation of fighting [jihad]. Because it is absent from the present condition of the Muslims, they have become as rubbish of the flood waters." Even though Azzam, as a Palestinian, was totally committed to fighting for the liberation of his native land, in the 1980s he assigned primacy to fighting in Afghanistan over fighting in Palestine. He states, "It is our opinion that we should begin with Afghanistan before Palestine, not because Afghanistan is more important than Palestine," but because of the intensity of the battles being fought in Afghanistan under the Islamic flag with the aim of creating an Islamic state.[20] In his book *Defense of the Muslim Lands*, Azzam made the following points regarding jihad:

> One: Jihad by your person is *Fard Ayn* [individual duty] upon every Muslim in the earth.
>
> Two: No permission for one from another for Jihad and no permission from the parents for the child.

Three: Jihad by your wealth is *Fard Ayn* and it is *Harram* [forbidden] to make savings while the jihad is in need of the Muslim's money.
Four: Neglecting the Jihad is like abandoning fasting and praying, more than that, neglecting the Jihad is worse in these days.[21]

Given Azzam's preoccupation with the war in Afghanistan that was in progress in the 1980s, jihad was uppermost in his mind. He quotes Ibn Taymiyya regarding defensive jihad, which is to be waged in order to repel aggression on Muslim lands and to protect the religion and what is sacred. "Jihad becomes *Fard Ayn* if the enemy attacks one of the borders of the Muslims, and it becomes *Fard Ayn* upon those close by. For those who are far away, it is *Fard Kifaya* [community duty], if their assistance is not required."[22] The following quotation from Azzam seems to speak for the jihadists on the battlefields of Afghanistan, Palestine, and Iraq: "Love of Jihad has taken over my life, my soul, my sensations, my heart and my emotions. If preparing [for jihad] is terrorism, then we are terrorists. If defending our honor is extremism, then we are extremists. If jihad against our enemies is fundamentalism, then we are fundamentalists." [23]

JIHAD IMPLEMENTED

The Wahhabi notion of jihad as a force for political change tested its metal in the 1980s against another "anti-Islamic" entity, the Soviet Union. The United States played a crucial role in reviving the military doctrine of jihad in Pakistan and using it to bring about the defeat and ouster of the Soviet Union from Afghanistan. It was the nexus among the United States, Pakistan, and Saudi Arabia that implemented jihad against the Soviet occupiers. As a communist country, the Soviet Union was a perfect candidate to be depicted as a force against God and His religion, Islam. It had invaded and occupied a Muslim country (*Dar al-Islam*), established a puppet regime, and tormented and brutalized the Afghan opposition, all the while claiming that it had entered Afghanistan upon the "invitation" of the Afghan government. In fighting the Soviet Union, the jihadists fully implemented the principles of *fard al-ayn* and *fard al-kifayah* as legitimate doctrines of Islam. A Hollywood screenwriter could not have written a better script for uniting the Afghan people to liberate their Islamic homeland and to defend their religion. Chapter 5 examines this topic in more detail.

The 1978–79 Islamic revolution of Iran also played a pivotal role in providing a high degree of relevance to jihad as a doctrine for political change. Although that revolution was not carried out as jihad, it did bring about the establishment of an Islamic government. And from the vantage point of the Sunni Islamists and jihadists, the precedent of ousting a tyrant and replacing him with an Islamic government was a model that was perfectly suited in the Middle East and elsewhere in the world of Islam. In fact, in the late 1980s, Ayatollah Rouhollah Khomeini threatened to export the Islamic revolution to neighbouring states of the Persian Gulf.[24]

In the context of what jihad is supposed to achieve, the Islamic revolution of Iran is regarded as a watershed event in the contemporary history of the world of Islam for a number of reasons. First, it succeeded in ousting the brutal regime of Mohammad Reza Pahlavi (aka the Shah of Iran), who was determined to westernize his country. In the view of Iran's religious community of Shia Islam, the Shah appeared largely heedless of the implications of modernization for Iran as a Muslim country. For his part, the Shah never really understood the significance of Islam inside his country. Nor did he anticipate the enormity of power that Islam was capable of unleashing. That power came to the fore when the leadership of the various political groups that played a crucial role in finally overthrowing the Shah in 1979 was immediately taken over by the late Ayatollah Rouhollah Khomeini. For Khomeini, this success was long in coming, given that he had been involved in his religio-political struggle against the Shah since 1964.

Second, the success of the revolution in ousting a perceived "un-Islamic" and pro-Western regime was remarkable because it achieved what the Sunni Islamist groups (jihadists who had not yet become a major threat to existing governments) could not, despite their constant clashes with the autocratic rulers.

Third, the very occurrence of a revolution in a country like imperial Iran signalled to the Sunni Islamists – that is, to the jihadists who would become highly visible in the 1990s – that all regimes in the world of Islam were vulnerable to a similar modus operandi for the establishment of an Islamic government.

Fourth, the Iranian revolution occurred at a time when Islam was being viewed as a solution to the suffering of the Middle Eastern masses. Because the revolution radically altered the shape of political power in Iran, it seemed logical to hope that a similar transformation could happen in other Muslim countries, especially in the sheikhdoms of the Persian Gulf. A major question of that time was whether the radical and revolutionary brand of Islam could develop a different way of thinking about modernization. No reasonably persuasive answers emerged then, and, needless to say, the same question remains even more relevant in the twenty-first century.

Finally, the Islamic revolution symbolically assured Muslims at large that the establishment of an Islamic government through cataclysmic change (jihad) lay well within the realm of possibility.

After watching the fall of the Shah of Iran, the United States had a very different perspective about the potential recurrence of that phenomenon elsewhere in the region. The Islamic regime, to be sure, was stridently anti-American. But Washington perceived the loss of that friendly regime as a major blow to the system of US dominance that had been intact since Great Britain ended its hegemony in the Persian Gulf in 1970. As one of the reigning superpowers, the United States was in no mood to idly sit by and watch the repeat of the Islamic revolution in the Gulf emirates, especially Saudi Arabia, one of the most vital suppliers of oil to Western Europe and Japan. These regions were too crucial to American global hegemony and dominance. In 1980, therefore, it proceeded to establish the Combined Joint Task Force, which in January 1983 became a full-blown regional command, the US Central Command (CENTCOM).

But the time was not ripe in the 1980s for the Islamic revolution to become a regional phenomenon. The Arab states of the Persian Gulf – Saudi Arabia, Bahrain, Kuwait, the United Arab Emirates (UAE), Oman, and Qatar – as a purely defensive maneuver, created the Gulf Cooperation Council (GCC). The real purpose of that organization was to forestall the chances of an Islamic revolution inside their borders; however, the member states did not wish to antagonize Iran by declaring so. Instead, the public speeches and documents released at the time of the GCC's inception emphasized mutual economic interests as important factors underlying its creation. Besides, the GCC rulers were fully aware that, if their security and existence were threatened by Iran or the Soviet Union – which was occupying Afghanistan at the time – the United States would instantly come to their rescue.

What is important to underscore here is that the era 1979–89 was unique in that both superpowers experienced defeats in their dealings with Islam. In Afghanistan – largely because of American resolve and its military and financial backing, the equally ardent political and theological backing of Pakistan and Saudi Arabia, and the zealotry of hundreds of thousands of mujahedeen to wage militant jihad against the occupation of that country – the Soviet Union was defeated. That humiliating defeat was also a major victory for the three countries that had backed the mujahedeen. The Soviet Union lasted only two years after its withdrawal from Afghanistan in 1989. Similarly, the end of the monarchy in Iran in 1979 was a defeat for the United States, especially after the arrest and internment of American diplomatic staff for 441 days.[25] The Iranian hostage crisis and, indirectly, the Islamic revolution were two of the most significant events that contributed to the defeat of President Jimmy Carter in the presidential election of 1980.

However, for the Islamist groups and the jihadist forces, both the Iranian revolution and the expulsion of the communist superpower from Afghanistan were nothing short of significant victories for Islam. Even though the Islamic revolution was a Shia phenomenon, the establishment of an Islamic government was a groundbreaking development from the perspectives of Muslims around the globe. For the first time since the dissolution of the caliphate and the end of the Ottoman Empire in Turkey in the early 1920s, Muslims realized that the concept of Islamic government could once again become a reality.

Aside from establishing an Islamic government, the Khomeini revolution was also characterized by its intense rhetoric of anti-Americanism. No one can forget Khomeini's condemnation of the United States in the quintessentially Islamic phrase, the "Great Satan." The world media broadcast the ululating crowds in the streets of all major cities of Iran chanting *marg bar Amrika* (death to America). Although the vitriolic barrages cast upon the United States were largely in response to Iran's experience with America's installation of a puppet regime in 1953 (and America's supporting it for twenty years), the Iranian revolution became a template for Sunni Islamists that they believed could be implemented in other Muslim countries, albeit in an altered form. The Khomeini revolution clearly established the basis of anti-Americanism in the late 1970s and early 1980s. In the 1990s, the Afghan mujahedeen created their own template of anti-Americanism under which al-Qaida could function as a jihadist organization.

But why hate the United States? After all, it played a decisive role in the liberation of Afghanistan from Soviet occupation. The answer to this question is quite complicated and requires an analysis of the United States' involvement in the world of Islam during the last three decades of the twentieth century and the first decade of the twenty-first century.

The involvement of the United States in Afghanistan in the 1980s was part of its intricate global strategy to defeat the Soviet Union. During that era, it confronted the former communist superpower in South America, Africa, and Asia for the same reason. Except in the case of Afghanistan, the United States purposely based its strategy to defeat the Soviet Union on one of Islam's major doctrines, jihad. For the United States, it was a proxy war. No American troops were involved, but Soviet troops were. They had occupied Afghanistan and fought the US-supported Afghan mujahedeen. However, when the Soviet Union was defeated, the Afghan mujahedeen never gave credit to the United States for that victory. To them, it was the victory of jihad and a reminder of the Battle of Badr of 624 when angels of God helped Muslims win against the *kuffar* (plural of *kafir*). God was glorified once again when Afghanistan was liberated. As the mujahedeen saw it, the victory had nothing to do with the support, military wherewithal, or huge amounts of money that the United States had invested in that struggle.

Nor did the Saudi and Pakistani allies of the United States in that war expend any effort in giving credit to the United States; they were too busy emphasizing their own respective perspectives on the victory. One cannot help but be impressed by how magnificently Saudi Arabia maneuvered its support of the Afghan mujahedeen to enhance its strategic interests, not just in the Arab world, but also in the Muslim world at large. The Saudi role in bringing about the defeat of the Soviet Union boosted its prestige in the Arab world both as a centre of Sunni Islamic orthodoxy and as a supporter of a military action that restored the sovereignty of a Muslim country to its rightful heirs, the people of Afghanistan. The Sunni world was expected to recognize that Saudi Arabia was as much of a supporter of Muslim causes as Shia Iran had become under the banner of the Islamic revolution. The Iranian revolutionary leaders, too, were expected to notice this Saudi role and to recognize the Saudi monarch's Islamic credentials. Moreover, support of the Afghan jihad placed the Saudi monarchy on the "right" side of its chief patron, the United States, which was also attempting to defeat the Soviet Union – an actor envisaged in the world of Islam as a force of atheism. No matter the outcome of the Afghan war, the Saudis had little to lose. Had the mujahedeen been defeated, the battlefield of Afghanistan was far enough away from the Arabian Peninsula for the monarchy not to suffer the deleterious spillover effects. As it was, the victorious campaign provided the kingdom an enormous amount of prestige and clout. The power of Saudi petrodollars was also invested in that struggle with great zest. Indeed, Saudi Arabia's collusion with the United States and Pakistan became an important basis for creating a long-standing – if not permanent – legacy for its role as a major Arab power in the 1980s and onward.

Pakistan envisioned its own support of the mujahedeen as the ultimate validation of the Islamization campaign that the regime of General Zia-ul-Haq had implemented in that country in the 1970s. However, Pakistan may not have been as much motivated by jihad as by the prospects of replacing the Soviet Union in Afghanistan with a government that unequivocally favoured Islamabad over New Delhi. Pakistan was determined never to let a pro-Indian government capture political power in Afghanistan, which was regarded as a place that provided coveted "strategic depth" for Pakistan in its incessant strategic competition with India.[26]

What is important to note here is that the US involvement in the liberation of Afghanistan did not enable the United States to be perceived as a friend of Muslims. The fact of the matter is that the United States did not get involved in Afghanistan to bring victory to Islam. On the contrary, it used the doctrine of militant jihad to defeat an adversary, which was America's chief objective throughout the course of the Cold War. Once it achieved that purpose, it folded up its tent and went home. Other highly intricate strategic objectives were awaiting the attention of American decision makers. They had bigger fish to fry than spending any more time attempting to stabilize Afghanistan or pursuing the de-Islamization of Pakistan.

When one examines the general course of America's foreign policy in the Middle East, which is predominantly Muslim, it becomes obvious that it was not driven by motives of either favouring or opposing Islam or, for that matter, any other religion. However, given the strong and sustained US commitment to the security and survival of Israel, the Islamists may make a strong case that it favoured the Jewish state over Muslim countries. This is an important point, for the Arab-Israeli conflict – despite the signing of the Camp David Accords in 1978 and the Jordanian-Israeli peace agreement of 1994 – has remained a core Muslim issue from Malaysia to Morocco. During the Cold War years, the Islamic nature of the Palestinian conflict was least emphasized within the Islamic power corridors of the world. Thus Muslims viewed Israel's occupation of the Golan Heights in 1967 as a conflict between Israel and Syria rather than a "Muslim issue." However, when the Cold War was over – and especially since the United States itself used Islam to attain its purpose of defeating the Soviet Union – the Islamic nature of the Palestinian conflict not only became quite apparent, but it was incessantly depicted in those terms by the propaganda machines of the Arab states and Islamist websites worldwide.

A NEW WORLD ORDER?

When the implosion of the Soviet Union in December 1991 brought an end to the Cold War, the next question was what conflict would replace it. Samuel Huntington was one of the first thinkers to start a major controversy about this in his book *The Clash of Civilizations*. Huntington wrote, "It is my hypothesis that the fundamental source of conflict in this new world will not be primarily ideological or primarily economic. The great divisions among humankind and the dominating source of conflict will be cultural. Nation states will remain the most powerful actors in world affairs, but the principal conflicts of global politics will occur between nations and groups of different civilizations. The clash of civilizations will dominate global politics. The fault lines between civilizations will be the battle lines of the future."[27] After discussing the ideological incompatibility between the Islamic world and the West, he posited that the next major conflict would be between Islam and the model of modernity presented by the West. Huntington's argument was highly contentious, but the second phrase of his title – *and the Remaking of World Order* – was more portentous. The post–Cold War order was supposed to be US-centric, since the United States remained the lone superpower. However, what idea, force, or country would challenge the new order? And how much violence would it take to dislodge the US-dominated order? No clear-cut answers were expected to emerge soon after the end of the Cold War.

Francis Fukuyama, in the highly touted hyperbolic essay "The End of History?," proposed that "what we may be witnessing is not just the end of the Cold War, or the passing of a particular period of post-war history, but the end of history as such: that is, the end point of mankind's ideological evolution and the universalization of Western liberal democracy as the final form of human government."[28] As controversial as that essay was, it captured the attention of strategic thinkers everywhere who were groping for answers. To most global observers, the triumph of liberal democracy was apparent in the fact that the United States – the arch practitioner and promoter of liberal democracy – was still around, while the Soviet Union – the antithesis of liberal democracy – had imploded. But the notion of the "end of history" sounded like nothing more than a tongue-in-cheek observation that had no basis in fact. There were, to be sure, a number of ideologies still around. Besides, for the global triumphant promulgation of liberal democracy, the question was whether the United States would promote it with zeal or wait for its natural occurrence in various nondemocratic countries. Most of Africa, almost all of the Middle East, and a number of countries of East Asia and South America were not democratic at the end of the Cold War. And no fast-paced version of democratization was expected to ensue as evidence of a global triumph of liberal democracy.

The post–Cold War era created a sanguine feeling within the United States that no power would be able to challenge it as the Soviet Union had done. The implosion of the communist superpower transformed the bipolar global power arrangement into a unipolar one. There was even a suggestion of "the unipolar moment": "There is but one first-rate power and no prospect in the immediate future of any power to rival it ... [The United States] is the only country with the military, diplomatic, political and economic assets to be a decisive player in any conflict in whatever part of the world it chooses to involve itself."[29] Indeed, when Saddam Hussein invaded Kuwait in 1990, the United States, by masterfully utilizing its practice of multilateralism of the Cold War years, put together an international coalition of Western and Arab forces to beat back his invasion. The awe-inspiring performance of the US military during the 1991 Gulf War left no doubt in the minds of its adversaries that it had, indeed, emerged as the sole superpower.

Even those who did not buy into the proposition of the unipolar moment were still of the view that, with the implosion of the Soviet Union, America's dominance of the global arena was substantial. Given that reality, the debates were about which types of policies – multilateral and consensus-based or unilateral ones – would become the hallmark of its foreign policy. As much as American and European strategic thinkers wanted Washington to follow the consensus-oriented model that President George H.W. Bush used in order to build an international coalition to vacate Saddam Hussein's invasion of Kuwait, the United States also had a record of unilateral action in such places as Vietnam, Grenada, and Panama. In opting for a multilateral approach to the Gulf War, the US administration knew that Japan and the European countries did not want Washington to take military action against Iraq. The Gulf War not exactly popular in the Middle East either, where Iraq enjoyed considerable sympathy. The decimation of Iraqi military power was viewed by a number of moderate as well as radical groups as really aimed at ensuring Israel's qualitative military edge over the Arabs, a subject that had created quite a bit of resentment in that region toward the United States. Another issue of debate related to the new international order was whether the United States would lead it or whether it would be organized under the auspices of the United Nations. However, given that the United States is a "profoundly nationalistic society with deeply unilateral attitudes," it was highly questionable that it would "accept decisive U.N. influence on its own policymaking."[30]

President Bush was his usual modest self in describing his vision of what the new world order should be in his *National Security Strategy* document issued in August 1991:

> In the emerging post–Cold War world, international relations promise to be more complicated, more volatile and less predictable ... We cannot be the world's policeman with responsibility for solving all the world's security problems. But we remain the country to whom others turn when in distress. This faith in us creates burdens, certainly, and in the Gulf we showed that American leadership must include mobilizing the world community to share the danger and risk. But the failure of others to bear their burden would not excuse us. In the end, we are answerable

> to our own interests and our own conscience – to our ideals and to history – for what we do with the power we have. In the 1990s, as for much of this century, there is no substitute for American leadership. Our responsibility, even in a new era, is pivotal and inescapable.[31]

However, for the Islamists, Fukuyama's elucidation of the universalization of liberal democracy was totally alien, irrelevant, and indeed, "un-Islamic." As discussed in chapter 2, al-Maqdisi, a major Islamist and a mentor to Abu Musab al-Zarqawi, the founder of al-Qaida in Iraq (AQI), warned against democracy: "You should be aware of the origins of the evil word of *democracy* ... [The] literal translation of this word ... is *the people's judgment*, or *the people's authority* or *the people's legislation* ... it is not Allah's judgment ... So, the democracy is on one side a polytheism and on the other side a disbelief in Allah that contradicts with monotheism [Islam]."[32] Democracy establishes the sovereignty of the people, whereas sovereignty, according to the Islamists' interpretation of Islam, belongs only to God. For Islamists of all varieties, the end of history was to come on the Day of Judgment, when Islam would become the universal religion. Their "success" in defeating the Soviet Union in Afghanistan had given them a confidence similar to what the United States was manifesting as the sole superpower – except that the bases for America's confidence were tangible and real, stemming from its military prowess in tandem with its status as one of the primary global economic powers, whereas the Islamists' confidence was rooted in absolute faith in the invincibility of Islam. The intangible aspects of these variables were of no concern to them.

FROM REGIONAL TO GLOBAL JIHAD: ISLAMISM RUNNING RAMPANT

When Osama Bin Laden approached King Fahd in 1990, asking permission to let him deploy his jihadist fighters against the well-equipped professional army of Saddam Hussein, he was confident that his fighters would win that battle. Bin Laden got the "biggest shock of his entire life" when King Fahd politely denied his request. That shock played a major role in transforming his feelings of ambivalence toward the king into animosity. Bin Laden started sending the king a series of letters whose tone was increasingly threatening.[33]

King Fahd's decision to allow the US-led international coalition forces to use Saudi territory as the chief stationing place to liberate Kuwait was, indeed, controversial. From his point of view, it was purely a political decision to save his kingdom, since the top US civil and military officials had persuaded him that Iraq was poised to invade Saudi Arabia. However, for the jihadists, that decision was akin to defiling the birthplace of Islam. They quoted a statement of the Prophet of Islam condemning such a decision. Some of them even depicted the presence of Christian forces on Saudi soil as an "occupation" of the holy land, thereby attempting to legitimize the call of jihad against the Saudi government. In the process, the animosity between the Saudi rulers and the jihadists steadily intensified.

Even though President Bush promised King Fahd that US forces would leave Saudi Arabia after defeating Saddam Hussein, that promise was not fulfilled with the liberation of Kuwait. Soon after ousting Iraqi forces from Kuwait, the United States became preoccupied with the objective of keeping Saddam "inside the box" by narrowing the physical space allowed for his brutal forces against the Shias in southern Iraq and the Kurds in the north. The rationale was that, by wearing down Saddam's dictatorship, it might become the victim of a military coup bringing about an end to his regime. But the chances of ousting Saddam Hussein were lost when the Shiites in southern Iraq and the Kurds in the north rose up against his regime at the conclusion of Desert Storm, in response to a general call by President George H.W. Bush. Those groups expected some sort of American assistance, which never came. The goal of the Shiite rebellion was to establish a Shia-led government in Baghdad, while the Kurdish front – which was a coalition of two dominant Kurdish parties – wanted to establish an independent Kurdish state in northern Iraq. As much as the United States wanted to see an end to Saddam's regime, no one in Washington had thought through the implications of a Shia-dominated government in Iraq – especially a government supported by Iran – for US strategic interests. At the same time, the Bush administration was not exactly endorsing an independent Kurdistan, which was staunchly opposed by one of America's North Atlantic Treaty Organization (NATO) allies, Turkey. Consequently, the United States looked on in apparent frustration while Saddam brutally crushed the uprisings, thereby prolonging the duration of his rule.

The US decision to stay in Saudi Arabia was driven primarily by the intricacy and multidimensionality of America's strategic interests in the Middle East at large. Whether those interests complemented or contradicted the comparatively narrower strategic interests of Saudi Arabia was not something about which America's top national security officials spent a lot of hours pondering. However, the continued presence of American forces in Saudi Arabia intensified the animosity between the monarch and the Islamist purists (including the jihadists) in that country. The controversy was couched in the latter's claim that the presence of "Christian crusaders" defiled the birthplace of Islam, and that the Saudi regime was a willing party to that act. The theologically based, but still controversial, legitimacy of the Saudi government came under increasing attack, not only from al-Qaida, but also from a number of Wahhabi scholars inside the kingdom. The pact of 1744 between Mohammad ibn Abd al-Wahhāb and the Saudi dynasty – which was the basis of the legitimacy of that dynasty's rule – appeared to be losing its credibility among a group of Saudi religious scholars as well as a section of the population. Given that Saudi Arabia is a closed polity, it is well-nigh impossible to come up with hard data about the level of opposition inside the kingdom. But the growing violence against the government in the 1990s was an indication that the jihadist forces did not differentiate between the security forces of Saudi Arabia and the American troops stationed in their country.

Although the presence of US forces in Saudi Arabia beginning in 1991 was one of the major reasons underlying the flare-up of the conflict among Muslims – the Islamists of all varieties and the Saudi government – the conflict was still specific and narrow in scope. In order to establish a universal basis (universal to the extent that it would involve all Muslim countries) for the conflict between Islamists and the West, additional political and religious reasons needed articulation. Here, Islam's role as a political force becomes quite important. To the extent that Islamist groups opposed the Western colonization of Muslim countries, they aimed to change the status quo inside the Middle East as well as in South and Central Asia. The role of Islamist groups as anti–status quo forces was epitomized in the 1952 military coup in Egypt brought about by a coalition of military officers and the Islamic Brotherhood, a major Islamist party. However, when the leader of the coup, Gamal Abdel Nasser, refused to establish an Islamic government in Egypt – which was the reason underlying the alliance between young military officers and young Islamists – there emerged a schism between the two sides. That schism continues to divide the polities of even a contemporary Egypt.

By contrast, in Saudi Arabia, where the compact between Wahhabi Islamists and Saudi rulers was the foundation of government, Islamists not only remained part and parcel of the government, but they also supported the status quo. Even the emergence of Saudi Arabia as a major ally of the United States from the 1940s through the 1980s did not negatively affect its legitimacy in the eyes of Islamist forces. The 1990s, however, marked the beginning of an entirely different era. The perspectives of jihadists of Saudi origin were heavily coloured by their military experience in Afghanistan. The militant Islamic zeal that had fuelled their fight against the communist superpower was not only very fresh, but it was looking for other outlets, causes, and targets. Those jihadists viewed the presence of US forces in Saudi Arabia as an occupation and as a symbol of offending Islam. They were willing to apply a similar modus operandi in order to oust the United States from Saudi Arabia.

A significant debate among jihadists is the use of jihad as a tool or rationale for attacking the "near enemy" (*adou al-qareeb*) as opposed to the "far enemy" (*adou al-bayeed*).[34] As previously discussed in this chapter, this concept was first raised by Faraj in his essay *The Neglected Duty* (1981), and it remains a powerful source of tension and schism among the jihadists in the second decade of the twenty-first century.

"Near enemy" described the pro-Western Arab regimes bordering Israel; these "cordon" states attempted to deny the jihadists any opportunity to launch attacks on Israel because of the brutality of Israeli retaliation. Although the bordering states did not have much of a choice but to forestall jihadist attacks on Israel, this policy made these Arab states targets of the jihadists. The phrase "far enemy" included the United States as well as Israel, even though it was located in the heart of the Levant, because US military support secured Israel's survival. The conventional practice of referring to the United States as far enemy went through a mutation after its invasion and occupation of Afghanistan and Iran. Then it was also referred to as near enemy.

Faraj's stated preference for attacking the near enemy was based on his rationale that the creation of Israel in 1948 was made possible as a result of the dissolution of the caliphate in 1924. Thus, for the reestablishment of the caliphate, destruction of Israel should be the foremost objective of the jihadists. Faraj's advocacy for attacking the near enemy was rejuvenated by Abdullah Azzam, who, after the Afghan jihad of the 1980s, wanted to refocus on fighting the near enemy with the goal of liberating Jerusalem. The subgroup of so-called global jihadists – whose most famous members were Bin Laden and al-Zawahiri – had a definite preference for attacking the far enemy (the United States); however, they did not want to create the impression that their commitment to the liberation of Jerusalem was any less.

The jihadists viewed their involvement in the Afghan war of the 1980s as an exception to their preference for fighting the near enemies. The Soviet Union was attacked because it occupied a Muslim country. That act made the defence of Afghanistan the *fard al-kifayah* (legal obligation of the entire ummah), according to the traditional Islamic doctrine. In the 1990s, despite the fact that al-Qaida was accusing the United States, the European Union, NATO, and even the United Nations of committing crimes against Muslims, its focus was on fighting the near enemy. In 1996, Bin Laden, through his "Declaration of Jihad against the Americans Occupying the Land of the Two Holy Sanctuaries," targeted the American forces, but only those that were stationed in Saudi Arabia in order to repel Saddam Hussein's troops from Kuwait.

By 1997, al-Qaida's attitude toward global jihad was steadily evolving through a series of statements issued by Bin Laden himself. In a famous interview with Peter Arnett, he stated, "Our main problem is the US government while the Saudi regime is but a branch or an agent of the US."[35] Bin Laden's 1998 "Declaration of Jihad against Americans Occupying the Land of the Two Holy Mosques" was significant for its abandonment of the traditional resolve of the jihadists to fight the near enemy and for its new focus on direct confrontation with the far enemy, the United States. He declared,

> No one argues today about three facts that are known to everyone; we will list them, in order to remind everyone:
>
> First, for over seven years the United States has been occupying the lands of Islam in the holiest of places, the Arabian Peninsula, plundering its riches, dictating to its rulers, humiliating its people, terrorizing its neighbors, and turning its bases in the Peninsula into a spearhead through which to fight the neighboring Muslim peoples.
>
> Second, despite the great devastation inflicted on the Iraqi people by the Crusader-Zionist alliance, and despite the

> huge number of those killed, which has exceeded 1 million … despite all this, the Americans are once against trying to repeat the horrific massacres, as though they are not content with the protracted blockade imposed after the ferocious war or the fragmentation and devastation. So here they come to annihilate what is left of this people and to humiliate their Muslim neighbors.
>
> Third, if the Americans' aims behind these wars are religious and economic, the aim is also to serve the Jews' petty state and divert attention from its occupation of Jerusalem and murder of Muslims there. The best proof of this is their eagerness to destroy Iraq, the strongest neighboring Arab state, and their endeavor to fragment all the states of the region such as Iraq, Saudi Arabia, Egypt, and Sudan into paper statelets and through their disunion and weakness to guarantee Israel's survival and the continuation of the brutal crusade occupation of the Peninsula.[36]

On the basis of these "crimes," Bin Laden declared, "the ruling to kill the Americans and their allies – civilians and military – is an individual duty for every Muslim who can do it in any country in which it is possible to do it, in order to liberate the al-Aqsa Mosque and the holy mosque from their grip, and in order for their armies to move out of all the lands of Islam, defeated and unable to threaten any Muslim …This is in accordance with the words of Almighty God, 'and fight the pagans all together as they fight you all together,' and 'fight them until there is no more tumult or oppression, and there prevail justice and faith in God.'"[37]

In expanding the scope of jihad, al-Qaida adopted the doctrine of Takfir, the notion that unbelievers should be eliminated and that modernism should be shunned as a threat to Islam. However, al-Qaida's approach to this doctrine has been highly selective. For instance, al-Qaida has skilfully used the tools of modernization and globalization – the Internet and international banking transactions – to disseminate its message and to finance its destructive activities throughout the world. At the same time, it denounces modernization as a part of a Western "plot" to subjugate Muslims. The delusion on the part of "Arab Afghans" that it was they who had defeated the Soviet Union, and not the United States with its resolute backing and supply of weapons, may also have motivated their attack on the lone superpower.

Al-Qaida's attack on the United States on 11 September 2001 was its declaration of global jihad. One may be tempted to interpret it as al-Qaida's journey on the road to committing suicide. However, that interpretation would be simplistic. Al-Qaida seemed to have calculated that, if it explained its basis for jihad against the United States in politico-religious terms, its campaign would endure. Muslim grievances against the United States had been on the rise since the end of the Cold War. Throughout the 1990s, al-Qaida intensified those grievances by using its global propaganda machine and launching limited but frequent attacks on US assets and personnel. However, they were also aware that it was difficult to make a clear-cut case that the United States was the "enemy" of Islam, after what it had done to liberate Kuwait, and then Bosnia and Kosovo, when it had come to the rescue of the Muslims. Furthermore, not all jihadist thinkers agreed with Bin Laden about attacking the far enemy. Somehow, Bin Laden needed to transform Muslim grievances into rage. That rage would materialize if al-Qaida provoked the United States into getting involved in Muslim regions by first attacking it on its own soil.

Provoking the United States into military action defied conventional wisdom, given America's impressive record of fighting and annihilating its enemy. The jihadists had seen the dynamic "warfighting" strategies of the United States in action in Afghanistan in the 1980s, in the Gulf War in 1991, and in Yugoslavia in 1999 as part of the NATO-led military operation. But they were unconstrained by the fear of being annihilated. What the jihadists were not too sure about was how the lone superpower would react to a terrorist attack. Would it limit its response to defensive actions, or would it initiate an offensive response? And if the United States were to take offensive action against the alleged perpetrators, how far would it go? The United States had no previous record of invading a Muslim country. Its military actions in Kuwait were primarily aimed at ousting Iraq's invading forces. Would it topple the regime whence the terrorist attack was initiated, or would it go beyond one country and take down other regimes? Military action against the offending regime would cause a lot of bloodshed, but no matter; the jihadists were more than happy to die for their cause.

Regardless of what actual thinking went into the decision to attack the lone superpower on 11 September 2001, these attacks started a new and bloody era when the United States and the jihadists were to adopt a strategy of mutual annihilation. The concepts that were part of the vocabulary of policy makers and scholars of international relations in the Cold War era – such as balance of power, balance of terror (related to nuclear weapons), mutual assured destruction (MAD), MAD versus NUTS (nuclear utilization target selection), nuclear deterrence, minimum nuclear deterrence, credible nuclear deterrence, counterforce versus countervalue, détente, and so on – were shelved, at least temporarily. Instead, the world has become familiar with such notions as suicide bombing, IED (improvised explosive device) warfare, flying IED warfare (IEDs installed on drones), drone warfare, and counterinsurgency operations between the low-tech ragtag Islamist forces and the heavily equipped high-tech forces of the United States.

The decision to strike the United States on its own territory was a risk of immense proportion. However, describing it as a "risk" implies that jihadists follow the Western definition of rationality. Their own calculation was rational in the sense that in their jihad against "un-Islamic" forces, nothing is more precious than to fight and die for Islam. Still, what might have surprised al-Qaida was the severity and swiftness of the US military invasion of Afghanistan. As a result, al-Qaida as an organization was nearly destroyed. It would have suffered an even worse fate if the United States had maintained its relentless attacks to destroy it. However, the Bush administration handed al-Qaida direly needed respite by not following through with its military actions in Afghanistan. Instead, it diverted its attention to Iraq. Al-Qaida could not have wished for better circumstances to be able to continue its fight with the lone superpower.

IDEOLOGICAL TENSIONS WITHIN THE GLOBAL JIHADIST MOVEMENT

In the post–9/11 era, when the administration of President George W. Bush invaded and occupied two Muslim countries, Afghanistan and Iraq, it became much easier for the jihadists to couch their fight against the United States (the far enemy) as a war against Islam. Strategic thinkers of the global jihadist movement therefore expected these developments to reduce the ideological tensions among jihadists over the near enemy versus the far enemy, and put disagreements over Bin Laden's 1998 declaration on the backburner. After all, the Bush administration not only invaded a Muslim country but also stayed there as an occupying force. The jihadists' ebullience related to the highly favourable environment was expressed by one prominent thinker, Mus'ab al-Suri: "Praise God, the enemy's military attack now has put us within the borders of the same map, it is called 'The middle area of operations' (*mantiqat al-'amaliyyat al-wusta*) and in practice, it includes most of the states and countries of the Arab and Islamic world."[38]

However, the schism among jihadists over Bin Laden's 1998 declaration persisted. The most vitriolic and well-publicized attack on al-Qaida's change in strategy came in 2008 from al-Jihad of Egypt, the organization to which Ayman al-Zawahiri, Bin Laden's deputy, belonged. The former head of al-Jihad, Sayyid Imam al-Sharif, condemned al-Zawahiri and Bin Laden's decision to attack the United States as an action based on "criminal principles."[39]

By definition, all jihadists are also Salafists, but not all Salafists are jihadists. According to historian Brynjar Lia, the conflicts within what he calls the Salafist-jihadist movement may be understood along a "continuum or spectrum." At one extreme "are hard line Salafist purists for whom doctrinal purity is of quintessential importance, even if it means fighting side battles, alienating allies and shattering any semblance of a common front against the 'Zionist-Crusader' enemy. At the other extreme are hard line jihadists, who are primarily military strategists, and whose main preoccupation is political outcome, not doctrinal purity."[40] Abu Musab al-Zarqawi, emir of al-Qaida in Iraq (AQI), a hardline jihadist doctrinaire, was dedicated to the proposition of fighting local apostasy (near enemy), which he felt would take a long time. He did not change his mind even after pledging allegiance to Bin Laden in 2004. This dispute between the two was never resolved, and AQI and al-Qaida Central (AQ Central) continued their mutual ties as a matter of "strategic convenience rather than doctrinal agreement." The feebleness of that relationship "became increasingly apparent when Zarqawi ignored instructions from Al Qaeda to cease attacks against civilian and Shi'a cultural targets, which could not easily be interpreted as strikes against the far enemy."[41]

It is also possible that, when the United States occupied Iraq in 2003, the influence of AQ Central had already been shattered as a result of the 2001 US invasion of Afghanistan. A large number of its senior leaders either had been killed or were hiding. Since the chief thrust of US military operations was in Iraq, the ideological predilections of AQI's leadership determined the dynamics of the operations.

Al-Zarqawi was a doctrinally righteous jihadist. His "war-fighting strategy was about the art of dying heroically on the battlefield"; his frame of reference had no room for pragmatism in attaining the supreme goal – the establishment a caliphate. He hated the Shias and "disparagingly dismissed" Sunni religious leaders "as 'Sufis doomed to perdition.'" Increasingly, he saw his campaign "as a global epic struggle, heroic, devout and pure, devoid of petty politics and dishonorable compromises."[42] Thus, when al-Zawahiri wrote a letter to al-Zarqawi in 2005 pointing out that the latter's brutal and public killing of the Shias did not serve the greater cause and urging him to "avoid any action that the masses do not understand or approve," the chances of al-Zarqawi's acceptance of the elder leader's advice were nonexistent. Al-Zawahiri also wanted al-Zarqawi to seek political unity by consulting "all leaders of opinion and influence."[43] The strategic differences between al-Zawahiri and al-Zarqawi were never resolved. The death of al-Zarqawi at the hand of US forces in June 2006 proved that doctrine-driven jihadists have a tough road ahead of them.

STRATEGIC AND OPERATIONAL ASPECTS: THE MAKING OF GLOBAL JIHAD

In the post–9/11 era, militant jihad became an ideology whose purpose was to bring about political change in the world of Islam. A generation of Islamists, who were a little younger than those of the Osama Bin Laden generation, and even considerably younger ones, started to focus on the development of the operational theories of jihad.

The dismantlement of al-Qaida as an organization after the US invasion of Afghanistan spawned a variety of trends that are far from being formalized. The US *9/11 Commission Report* popularized the thesis that al-Qaida, although pretty much destroyed as an organization, has become a highly adaptable movement or ideology: "Al Qaeda and other groups are popularly described as being all over the world, adaptable, resilient, needing little higher-level organization, and capable of anything ... an omnipotent hydra of destruction."[44] Between 2002 and 2014, al-Qaida emerged as a franchise, willing to lend its name to various regional jihadist groups. AQ Central made commitment to its strategic priority of attacking the United States a condition of establishing relationships with new affiliates, which has kept the strategy very much alive. A disadvantage of franchising, from al-Qaida's perspective, is that leaders of different affiliates may insist on maintaining operational independence, causing harm to AQ Central's strategy by pursuing their narrower goals.

One must also keep in mind the flare-up of the previously discussed strategist-doctrinarian divide within the Salafist community. It was the unresolved nature of this divide between al-Zawahiri of AQ Central and al-Zarqawi of al-Qaida in Iraq (AQI) that came to a head when the AQI transformed into the Islamic State of Iraq (ISI). ISIS's zealous commitment to establishing a caliphate drove the two jihadist organizations further apart. AQ's Central Command issued a statement on 3 February 2014 declaring that ISIS "is not a branch of the al-Qaeda group ... does not have an organizational relationship with it and [al-Qaeda] is not the group responsible for their actions." That occasion marked "the first time the leadership has formally repudiated an affiliate."[45]

The predilection for an acute commitment to ideological purity is very much alive in al-Qaida's regional affiliates. No one knows when this doctrinarism is likely to show its deleterious effects on the performance and continued effectiveness (from al-Qaida's perspective) of an affiliate whose leader decides to emulate al-Zarqawi's example. Perhaps this possibility, and the passing of a major corps of senior al-Qaida leaders, further increases the significance of operational theorists (or military strategists) among jihadist groups.

Two Islamist theorists have made major contributions to the strategic and operational aspects of jihad: Abu Mus'ab al-Suri, a native of Syria; and Abu Bakr al-Naji, whose nationality is unknown, since the name itself is considered a pseudonym. Future Islamists will likely follow their work closely and make their own contributions as well. In this way, the jihadists' war against the United States will likely become even more intricate than it is today.

In terms of insight, vision, and brilliance, al-Suri was decades ahead of any Islamists of his generation (he was reportedly born in 1958). For him, al-Qaida was "a call, a reference, a methodology." He envisioned jihad as a social movement comprising "all those who bear weapons – individuals and groups, and organizations – and wage jihad on the enemies of Islam." Al-Qaida's main goal, he argued, should be to stimulate other groups to become part and parcel of the global jihadist movement. Al-Suri understood the limitations of al-Qaida as an organization; it had no chance of winning a military victory against the United States. After al-Qaida was nearly destroyed by the American military in Afghanistan in 2001, al-Suri envisioned a jihadist movement conducted by small groups or individuals in the form of "leaderless resistance." Such a movement, in his view, would never depend on the "wisdom" or "vision" of a single leader whose death or capture would serve as a jolt or even a death blow to the movement. A leaderless resistance, on the other hand, would be almost impossible to defeat, for it would rely on the motivations, dedication, and innovative capabilities of individuals who would not be thwarted by membership in a controlling organization.[46]

Athough al-Suri is not part of the new generation of jihadists, his thinking has made him an iconoclast and a trailblazer.[47] After studying international affairs and power politics, he concluded that the Islamists not only must understand the strategic aspects of conducting jihad – where a meticulous knowledge of the dynamics of international relations becomes crucial – but also must become extremely well-versed in the operational aspects. For him, jihad was a military operation, and it should be conducted with a high degree of professionalism and without a simplistic and dogmatic commitment to theology. He seemed to be telling the current (and especially future) generations of jihadists what General George Patton told his troops (as depicted in the movie, *Patton*): "The object of war is not to die for your country; it is to make the other poor dumb bastard die for his." By studying the operational art of the United States' military, al-Suri set a precedent and left a legacy that is most assuredly to be followed by future generations of Islamists, especially those who live and study in the West.

Al-Suri was convinced that if the jihadists became expert warriors – if they underwent rigorous training in the operational and tactical aspects of warfare – they would have a better than slight chance against the prowess of the US military. Without explicitly saying so, he neither attached much significance to theological purity, nor demonstrated much knowledge of it in writing prolifically about jihadist warfare. That may be one reason why he did not emerge as a superstar in the jihadist world, which remained mired in singing the praises of such theological heavyweights as Ibn Taymiyya, Maududi, Qutb, Azzam, and al-Maqdisi. However, there is little doubt that al-Suri's reputation in the world of the Islamists and jihadists will increase immensely in the coming years. He advocated the following operational aspects of jihad:

- *Decentralized jihad*: He emphasized the significance of decentralized jihadi warfare.
- *Acquisition of weapons of mass destruction (WMD)*: He rationalized using WMD as a terror weapon.

- *Rational approach to terror campaign*: He made Western experts rethink their culturally biased perspectives that Islamists, or suicide bombers, were fanatics who acted purely out of their passionate hatred of the West.
- *Global jihad*: In 1991, al-Suri advocated the creation of a global terrorist campaign that would be based on decentralized networks.
- *Nizam la Tanzim* (system, no organization): He argued that jihad should be a virtual system, which is not driven by a conventional organization like al-Qaida. As such, the jihadist movement would be hard to fight and eradicate through the application of any amount of force.
- *Guiding principle*: He underscored the notion of self-motivation and individual judgment, which became the essence of what was later known in the West as "leaderless jihad."
- *Operational force*: Al-Suri promoted the concept of individual terror, an idea that deemphasized the then prevailing view of al-Qaida as a springboard organization that guided regional global jihad.
- *Dissemination of "Commander's intent" to the "foot soldiers"*: He promoted communication among jihadists across the globe via the Internet.
- *Ultimate objective*: He advocated a polycentric approach to the jihad movement. Let the United States chase many rainbows. The more its forces are scattered all over the globe, the higher are the chances of victory for Islamist groups.

The ultimate objective of al-Suri's approach to jihad was to create virtual terror networks and facilitate global conditions that would lead to a "war without borders." The military superiority of the United States may best be handled by forcing it to spread its military forces throughout the world of Islam. Such a situation would not only make it difficult for the lone superpower to occupy Muslim lands indefinitely, but it would also cause enormous resentment of it in Muslim countries, thereby creating an environment that would be highly conducive for its defeat and expulsion.

Al-Naji – al-Qaida's Sun Tzu – seems to follow the Chinese grandmaster's well-known aphorism, "Know thy self, know thy enemy. A thousand battles, a thousand victories." He advocates studying the national strategies of the United States and its allies in order to find weak links and fracture the Western alliance. He is confident of defeating the Jahiliyya-based regimes in the Muslim world. Jihadists should learn the art of governance from the West, he believes, so that they, too, can become proven managers of savagery (his view of Western governance). Al-Naji studied the work of such authors as Paul Kennedy, whose *Rise and Fall of the Great Powers* posits that, historically speaking, imperial overstretches and a yawning gap between economic wealth and military power were the chief causes for the decline of great powers. Al-Naji recognized the significance of that thesis. He is of the view that, even though the United States is overstretched, it has not yet reached a point of decline. Further deployment of US forces is needed beyond Afghanistan and Iraq in order to severely strain its economy and provoke social turbulence within its own borders. Such tumults would force the American giant to reconsider its policies of remaining an occupying power in Muslim lands.

Al-Naji's analysis is quite prescient. According to a report written by twenty political scientists, economists, lawyers, anthropologists, and humanitarian personnel of Brown University's Watson Institute for International Studies, the final cost of the conflicts in Iraq, Afghanistan, and Pakistan for the United States is an estimated $3.7 to $4.4 trillion. The report also estimates that the US government has already spent "between $2.3 and $2.7 trillion and will spend at least a trillion more over the next fifty years."[48] Thus, it is logical to conclude that the United States' capacity and political will to stay in Muslim lands are not indefinite. A resultant withdrawal of the United States from Muslim countries would be only the beginning of a landslide victory for the jihadists, according to al-Naji's frame of reference.

The influence of both al-Suri's and al-Naji's contributions are evident in ISIS's operational strategies. Following al-Suri's thinking, ISIS has created a virtual terror network for "communication, recruitment, financing, and terror plot coordination."[49] Christina Schori Liang, senior program advisor and senior fellow, Emerging Security Challenges Program, Geneva Centre for Security Policy, highlights the features of ISIS's cyber strategy and suggests ways to counteract it:

- The Islamic State (IS) has a sophisticated and effective communications strategy that uses online media tools to disseminate its multidimensional propaganda. It has populated social media platforms and has attracted a global network of supporters who articulate, magnify, and circulate its violent, extremist messages worldwide.
- The Islamic State is strategically recruiting young men and women worldwide, using Internet sites and online magazines, but mostly

social media tools, including Facebook, YouTube, Twitter, Instagram, and AskFM.

- The online frontline needs to be better defended. Censorship and removal of extremist content are ineffective. Current government-sponsored counternarrative and counterextremism efforts are largely inadequate in suppressing IS extremist ideology and preventing it from spreading on- and offline.
- Throughout the world there is a need to better address the roots of radicalization, which is being driven by the ideological appeal currently cultivated by extremist groups online.
- It is important to build and extend international cooperation to support the creation and dissemination of credible content and positive alternatives to counter extremist narratives on- and offline.[50]

ISIS's management of its affairs during the fledgling days of the caliphate seems to follow al-Naji's writing in its constant reliance on savagery (manifesting extreme violence, beheading, and even burning prisoners alive, as it did the captured Jordanian pilot) in dealing with "enemies, hypocrites and spies." In its daily practice of dealing with enemies, it also seems to be closely following one of the statements that al-Zarqawi made in his famous letter to al-Zawahiri: "We have told them in our many sessions with them that safety and victory are incompatible, that the tree of triumph and empowerment cannot grow tall and lofty without blood and defiance of death, that the [Islamic] nation cannot live without the aroma of martyrdom and the perfume of fragrant blood spilled on behalf of God, and that people cannot awaken from their stupor unless talk of martyrdom and martyrs fills their days and nights."[51] The fact that the United States and Russia are using their respective air power to dismantle the caliphate gives one little time to think about what the future of the caliphate might look like; there seems to be no end to destruction and mayhem around that entity.

Toward the end of the first decade of the twenty-first century, the Islamists' fight against the United States entered a markedly different phase than the preceding years. Iraq, though far from being a peaceful country, manifested evidence of being a place where democracy could evolve. On 18 December 2011, the last American military convoy left Iraq, thereby bringing an end to the seven-year American combat mission.[52] However, years after the withdrawal of the US forces, the violence perpetrated by al-Qaida–affiliated terror groups in Iraq is on the rise.[53] In the theatre of operations in Afghanistan, NATO's International Security Assistance Force (ISAF) also faced an uphill battle against the combined forces of al-Qaida and the Taliban.

President Obama's decision to redeploy American troops from Afghanistan by 2014 put the Taliban of Afghanistan on the offensive. A report published by the Center for Strategic and International Studies ominously observed: "The U.S. is slowly and steadily losing the war in Afghanistan. It is not losing the war at the military level – although such defeat is possible in coming years if the U.S. does not provide the necessary funds, advisors and partners. The U.S. is losing the war at the political level by failing to win (and merit) the support of the Congress, the American people, its allies, and the Afghans."[54] That process of slow American defeat continued as Obama's term was coming to an end. The Taliban, fully knowing what was transpiring in the United States, continued to mount their attacks inside Afghanistan. In the meantime, the hapless government of President Ashraf Ghani hoped that the United States would change its mind and plunge its forces into fighting the resurging Taliban.

The assassination of Osama Bin Laden in May 2011 created intense tensions in US-Pak relations. Washington was irate that the al-Qaida leader was found in Abbottabad, which is regarded as a bastion of the Pakistani Army. It wanted answers to numerous questions about how he got there, who in the Pakistani Army knew about his presence in that city, and who helped him acquire a safe haven. The Pakistani Army, for its part, was annoyed that the US Special Forces carried out the military operation to kill Bin Laden by keeping them totally out of the loop. Another reason for their anger was the violation of Pakistan's sovereignty. In the meantime, the United States continued its drone attacks on "high-valued targets" (a euphemism for the leaders of al-Qaida and the Pakistani Taliban inside Pakistan's borders). The ISAF attack on two Pakistani military checkpoints, which killed twenty-four soldiers on 26 November 2011, made matters worse. Outraged at the incident, on 27 November 2011 Pakistan's army closed two vital NATO supply lines and demanded the closure of the Shamsi Air Base located in the southwestern region of Baluchistan. That base was the home for US drones.[55]

Pakistan remained under increased pressure from domestic jihadist groups. However, there has been a steady evolution of democracy in Pakistan, especially when the elected government of President Asif

Ali Zardari successfully completed its term in September 2013 and handed over power to the succeeding government of Prime Minister Nawaz Sharif. The army also seems to have adopted a lower profile on national security issues. However, unambiguous evidence of civilian control of decision-making on these issues has yet to emerge.

Although the government of Saudi Arabia was reported to be cracking down on jihadist groups, the worrisome reality was that, because of the closed nature of its polity, it was very difficult for the United States to make reasonable conclusions about how potent those forces were inside the kingdom, and how effective the government really was in eradicating them or in getting them under substantial control. The worsening internal conflict in Yemen was bound to have a spillover effect on Saudi Arabia, especially as al-Qaida in the Arabian Peninsula (AQAP) was intensifying its terrorist activities inside that country. Even an increasing number of US drone attacks did not succeed in decreasing the popularity of the terrorist forces.

However, the Central Asian countries were relatively calm. Kyrgyzstan experienced political change twice – in March 2005 and in April 2010. On both occasions, two presidents were ousted from office. Uzbekistan experienced political violence in June 2005 when the government of Islam Karimov brutally suppressed demonstrations in the Andijan region, resulting in hundreds (some say thousands) of deaths.[56] No Islamist elements were allegedly involved in that incident either. The Islamist groups of Central Asia periodically launched military operations in Kyrgyzstan, Uzbekistan, and Tajikistan in the 1990s. However, toward the end of 2001, the US invasion of Afghanistan – Operation Enduring Freedom – reported to have seriously damaged the cadres that were present in large numbers there. The continued presence of US military forces in Kyrgyzstan also served to deter a high degree of proactivism by Islamist forces in Central Asia.

The Arab Awakening – which started in December 2010 in Tunisia and became an awesome force that brought down President Zine El Abideen Ben Ali of Tunisia, President Hosni Mubarak of Egypt, and Muammar Qaddafi of Libya, and promised to oust Bashar al-Assad of Syria – created a new corps of Islamists, whose ideological predilections will likely take the next several years to settle. The year 2011 was momentous in that it brought down three of the longest-serving autocrats in North Africa.[57]

The most significant outcome of the Arab Awakening is that, by successfully ousting three autocrats and promising to oust even more, it unwittingly reduced the significance of al-Qaida and its brand of jihadists. That fact, more than even the counterterrorism tactics of the Obama administration – which successfully targeted and killed al-Qaida's top leaders including Osama Bin Laden – made the Arab Awakening and the new corps of Islamists a major force for change in the Arab world. However, al-Qaida and its regional affiliates, as well as other jihadist organizations, remain alive and effective in Algeria, the countries of the trans-Sahel region and the Horn of Africa, Nigeria, Kenya, Yemen, Pakistan, and Afghanistan. The governments of those countries must succeed in governing well, and soon, if they are to have any chance of driving the Islamists from their midst.

The Arab Awakening provided a glimmer of hope that regime change, brought about by massive opposition to the unpopular regimes, might render jihad irrelevant in that region. However, that did not happen, as a democratically elected Islamic government in Egypt was overthrown by the military and a brutal dictatorship was reestablished. The fact that Libya turned into a failed state after the NATO-sponsored ouster of Qaddafi also disheartened those in the West who were hoping for the emergence of a democratic Libya. It was that Libya-related Western fear that prevented another bold Western action to oust Bashar al-Assad, when his military started its own campaign to brutally suppress the civilian uprising. Even though Tunisia remains a democratic-secular state, its continuity appears shaky, as ISIS continues to enhance its presence and influence in neighbouring Libya. The emergence of ISIS in Iraq and its declaration of a caliphate in a swathe of territories in Iraq and Syria proved to the world that jihad in the Middle East is not a thing of the past.

One of the most enduring and controversial aspects of declaring jihad is who (which entity) should be regarded as a legitimate source for its declaration and under what circumstances its pronouncement should be considered legitimate. In the contemporary era, only the Organisation of the Islamic Congress comes close to being considered as one such authority. Even then, the circumstances for declaring jihad remain highly contentious. Thus far, about the only issue on which there is some semblance of agreement is that when a Muslim country is attacked and occupied by a non-Muslim state, the declaration of jihad becomes a legitimate tool for bringing an end to that occupation.

As discussed earlier, the United States was very effective in bringing together Saudi Arabia and Pakistan to support the declaration of jihad against the Soviet Union in the 1980s, and in facilitating a global campaign to bring about the defeat and ouster of that superpower from Afghanistan. However, in the post–9/11 era, when the United States was attacked and it responded by attacking Afghanistan and then occupying it, no Muslim country was willing to endorse the concept of declaring jihad against it. One possible reason may have been that the US attack on Afghanistan was retaliatory in nature, since al-Qaida had planned and executed the 9/11 terrorist attacks from that country. But even when the Bush administration invaded Iraq in 2003 on the false premise that Saddam Hussein possessed weapons of mass destruction (WMD) and occupied that country until 2008, no Muslim country considered declaring jihad against it.

In both instances of US military invasion and occupation of Muslim countries, only the jihadist groups volubly and zealously declared jihad against the United States. However, those declarations were totally devoid of legitimacy. That reality means that the declaration of jihad may no longer be a tool that can pose a serious challenge to any Muslim or Western country in the future. That does not mean, however, that jihad will not be used as a tool to bring together disparate groups of jihadists for military operations against a country, as was witnessed in the case of the Syrian civil war.

CLOSING OBSERVATIONS

The preceding analysis has established that, even though the doctrine of jihad has a variety of meanings, the Islamists of the twentieth and twenty-first centuries (following the intellectual legacy of Ibn Taymiyya) have emphasized its militant aspect – *jihad fi sabil Allah* (fighting in the path of God) – to the exclusion of other interpretations. This doctrine succeeded in bringing about regime change in the 1980s when the United States was one of its chief sponsors and its arch financial and material backer. Since then, jihad's record as a tool for regime change has been a failure.

Jihad as an individual obligation or a community obligation was emphasized by Faraj in the 1970s and by Azzam in the 1980s; Faraj went so far as to advocate jihad as a possible sixth pillar of Islam. This idea was publicized heavily by the Islamists in the 1990s and beyond. However, whether jihad should be regarded as a sixth pillar was debated inside al-Qaida from the late 1990s to early 2001. It was the ultimate preference for attacking the *adou al-bayeed* (the far enemy) that resulted in al-Qaida–sponsored attacks inside the United States.

Al-Qaida as an entity made an indelible imprint on global history through its outrageously audacious attacks on the United States in 2001. In the aftermath of those events, the outbursts of US military and political proactivism have seriously (and probably irreparably) damaged al-Qaida's capacity to carry out a similar attack on any country.

The most significant aspect of al-Qaida's use of the doctrine of jihad has been its ability to survive as a franchise after the US invasion of Afghanistan. In this context, the contributions of al-Suri and al-Naji have been utilized by ISIS in its operational tactics and will no doubt influence the operational thinking of future Islamists. Despite al-Qaida's highly adaptive capabilities, what eventually precipitated its decline in significance was (a) its total commitment to the Takfiri doctrine, (b) its related use of intense violence against the Sunnis, and (c) most significant, the emergence of the Arab Awakening toward the end of 2010 as a tsunami of political change. Although the resulting political changes were highly disappointing in Egypt and Libya, it is hard to completely rule out a possible resurgence of something similar in the coming years whose aim would be to bring about regime change in the Arab world.

In the second decade of the twenty-first century, the world is witnessing the political turbulence and mayhem caused by jihadi-related activities of a number of al-Qaida's affiliates as well as ISIS in Africa, Yemen, and South Asia. The most serious threat to global stability is the spread of ISIS's ideology through social media and its ability to carry out "lone wolf" terrorist attacks in Europe as well as in the United States. Gone are the days, it seems, when Europeans and Americans can confidently state, "If we fight them [global jihadists] over there [in the Middle East], we won't have to worry about fighting them here."

The enormous destruction of Iraq subsequent to the US invasion there in 2003 and the massive bombings by American and Russian air forces in the continuing civil war in Syria seem to be creating a situation whereby the future of the entire Levant appears dark for several more decades. Similarly, the Saudi-sponsored civil war in Yemen has created colossal human and infrastructural losses that promise to keep the Arabian Peninsula an unstable region of the Arab world.

4

The Middle East: Where US Strategic Dominance Clashes with Islamism

SYNOPSIS

This chapter analyzes the role of Islamism (*Islamiyyun*) within the United States and regimes of the Middle East. As stated in chapter 1, the term *Islamism*, as used in this study, refers to "the ideologically-motivated political instrumentalization of a primarily legalistic interpretation of Islam."[1] The Islamists surfaced as political actors, albeit weak ones, starting in Egypt in the 1950s. Islam rose to the fore in 1979, when the Islamists ousted the regime of Mohammad Reza Pahlavi (aka the Shah) and captured power in Iran. The purpose of Islamism was to minimize dominance by Western powers, especially the United States, in Muslim countries.

The self-styled jihadists, on the basis of their particular ideological understanding of Islam, pursue the acquisition of territory. This pursuit has a palpable geostrategic focus. It is acutely anti-US and aspires to eliminate the lone superpower's presence and influence from all Muslim countries. The practitioners are committed to overthrowing the existing regimes of the Arab world and replacing them with Islamic governments with a *Din* (religion), *Dunya* (way of life), and *Dawla* (government) focus. They are driven by the *Takfiri* doctrine (a *Din* focus).

Of all the regions covered in this book, the Arab Middle East has been the hottest area of American strategic interest and involvement. Since World War II, the United States has maintained its strategic dominance and presence in the region despite contradictory policies of playing a major role in sustaining the military superiority of Israel while being unable to resolve the obdurate Palestinian conflict. The greatest problem that the United States faces in the Middle East is that, as a result of its long-standing support for Israel, it has acquired an "anti-Islamic" image. That image made it easier for al-Qaida to propagate incendiary rhetoric in the region and to confront the United States. The 1979 Islamic revolution of Iran created a situation whereby that country emerged as an acute challenger to America's dominance in the Middle East. A side-effect of Islamist Iran's role was to intensify the Saudi-Iranian regional rivalry for dominance. Although the United States and Iran negotiated a nuclear deal in 2015, the continuation of the Iran-Saudi rivalry has made it difficult for the United States to develop its own comprehensive policy of potential cooperation with Iran on the unremitting Syrian conflict, where both Washington and Tehran were fighting against ISIS. Despite America's awesome military power, which succeeded in dismantling the Taliban regime in Afghanistan in 2001 and that of Saddam Hussein in Iraq in 2003, the United States failed in its attempt to bring either of those countries into its sphere of influence on a permanent basis. Moreover, the US invasion of Iraq in 2003 created a situation whereby ISIS's practice of Islamism led to the creation of a so-called caliphate. Although that caliphate seemed to have been destroyed in June 2016, ISIS's practice of Islamism could still reemerge elsewhere in the Arab/Islamic world. In contrast with the Sunni Islamism practiced by ISIS and al-Qaida, Iran's exercise of Islamism has remained open to diplomatic negotiations with the United States and the West in general.

Political instability, violence, and civil war continue in the Levant region. Toward the end of 2010, the Arab Awakening emerged as a powerful tsunami of political change and potential establishment of democracy. It brought down the dictators in Tunisia, Egypt, and Libya. However, that great promise was shattered in Egypt, where the democratically elected Islamic government headed by a candidate of the Muslim Brotherhood Party was ousted by the army, and the country reverted into a military dictatorship. Similarly, the promise of democracy turned into a nightmare in post-Qaddafi Libya, where two rival governments were locked in a civil war with affiliated Islamist militias. This conflict, combined with the mounting presence and terrorist activities of al-Qaida in the Islamic Maghreb (AQIM) and ISIS, threatened the political stability of the entire North Africa region. In Syria, the regime of President Bashar al-Assad was plunged into a civil war for its survival. The jihadist groups played a major role in that civil war. They were supported by the United States, Saudi Arabia, and Qatar, while Iran – along with Russia – strongly backed the Assad regime.

THE STRATEGIC LANDSCAPE OF THE COLD WAR AND THE ARAB-ISRAELI CONFLICT

During World War II, President Franklin Delano Roosevelt played a crucial role in bringing about an end to a long-term tradition of isolationism of the United States and setting the stage for its emergence as one of the superpowers of the world. At the end of the war, America was ready to take its place in global politics on a permanent basis. It so happened that the new American role was perfectly suited for the superpower competition that followed.

In the post–World War II era, the United States' dominance in the Middle East was largely undisputed. Since it emerged as one of the most powerful victors from that war, both in the realms of military and economic power, it had little trouble in stepping up to the role of superpower. The Cold War competition was driving America's global and regional policies, and its main objective was to establish dominance at the expense of the Soviet Union. Washington's public rhetoric was that it was motivated by the desire to help the Arab states remain "free" and to keep them from becoming Soviet colonies à la the Eastern European countries. The Soviet Union, on the other hand, had to struggle to establish its status as the "other hegemon." Remaining true to its own favourite rhetoric of the Cold War years, it used an "anti-imperial and anti-colonial" spin to sway the republican Arab states in its camp.

Rhetoric aside, both superpowers were driven by the resolve to expand their respective spheres of influence. In this zero-sum game, political gains made by the United States anywhere in the world were envisaged by the Soviet Union as its losses, and vice versa. And both superpowers were fully determined to exploit intraregional rivalries, chicaneries, and other power plays to promote their respective hegemonies.

The Iranian oil crisis of the early 1950s was one of the first US encounters with the violent uncertainties of the Middle East and the intricate question of how to deal with them. Great Britain was the reigning hegemon, and its oil-related interests in Iran coincided with those of the United States. The vastness of these reserves necessitated that they be under the control of a compliant ruler (aka the Shah of Iran). Although American officials were not keen on the notion of a "regime change" in Iran, the turn of events and Dr Mohammad Mosaddeq's (Iranian premier at the time) flair for the dramatic made the fledgling American hegemon quite uncomfortable with the option of letting him stay in power. Mosaddeq was considered an anathema to everything that the Shah, Reza Pahlavi, represented. In the final analysis, President Dwight Eisenhower personally signed the plan to overthrow the elected premier of Iran in 1953 and to return the Shah to power. Those actions guaranteed Anglo-American dominance in Iran and the security of its oil supplies.

The 1950s was also an era when Arab countries were overthrowing the yoke of colonial rule and pan-Arabism was emerging as a major political force and a potential template for Arab unity. In fact, pan-Arabism appeared to be an idea whose time had come. The aim was to unite the Arab states, if not formally, at least by establishing political alliances. The republican Arab states were ardent promoters, and for political reasons the Arab monarchies could not denigrate it. However, in reality, the monarchies were highly apprehensive and suspicious of pan-Arabism, considering it a "plot" of the republican forces to overthrow them. Pan-Arabism did not fulfill its expected promise of unifying the Arab world, in part owing to the tradition within the Arab authoritarian culture to gather around a hero or strong man. Instead, it pitted the republican (pan-Arabist) heroes against the monarchical heroes; neither was willing to accept second place. The Middle Eastern monarchs were not about to give up power so that President Gamal Abdel Nasser of Egypt – who was fast emerging as a populist Arab hero – could use pan-Arabism for personal glory and political dominance.

During the 1950s, both superpowers were developing their patterns of dominance throughout the world and, in response, Arab states were developing their long-term foreign policy behaviour by formulating alliances or partnerships with either the United States or the Soviet Union. The confluence of interactions between the Arab states and both superpowers determined the political stability and the distribution of military power inside the Middle East. This last variable would play a crucial role in the superpowers' handling of the Arab-Israeli conflict; it also determined the outcomes of the Arab-Israeli wars of 1967 and 1973, which, in turn, continue to affect the internal dynamics of the region even to this day.

From the beginning of the Cold War, the United States, along with Great Britain and France, attempted to limit Soviet clout in the Middle East. The Tripartite Declaration of 1950 to control the flow of arms to the protagonist states of the Arab-Israeli conflict was a crucial allied endeavour to minimize the influence of the communist superpower. However, President Nasser of Egypt, seeing the bias underlying the declaration in favour of Israel, quickly maneuvered to acquire military arms from the Soviet Union. Moscow moved in for the kill, using its Czechoslovakian agent to supply arms to Nasser.

The Suez crisis of 1956 established a pattern for superpower involvement. Nasser's decision to unilaterally nationalize the Suez Canal led to the secret decision of England and France to formulate a plan not only to invade Egypt but, in the process, to oust Nasser. A reading of the public debates during that conflict shows how eager British prime minister Anthony Eden and French prime minister Guy Mollet were to regularly compare Nasser's nationalization of the Suez Canal to Hitler's behaviour in Munich, thereby insisting "that this type of Western appeasement must not be allowed to occur again."[2] But when the collective military invasion of Egypt by the United Kingdom (UK), France, and Israel took place, both the United States and the Soviet Union demanded the unconditional withdrawal of the invading forces.

The Suez crisis exemplified the clashing hegemonic ambitions of the two erstwhile powers – the UK and France – on the one hand, and the two emerging superpowers on the other. This was probably the only time when Washington and London did not see eye to eye on an issue that could have affected global peace. Israel, as much as it aspired to widen its national boundaries, participated in that military adventurism mainly to humiliate its archenemy, Nasser, who was emerging as an Arab hero. Israeli prime minister Ben-Gurion was aware that any territorial expansion resulting from the invasion of Egypt would be only temporary. The idea of reoccupation of countries that had recently won independence was unthinkable.

What drove the United States was its concern that a defeat of the Egyptian military as a result of the invasion would force Egypt and other Arab republican states to become permanent allies of the Soviet Union. This topic was hotly debated among the elite ranks of the republican Arab states as well as in Washington. Such a development would have given the communist superpower an awesome advantage in the region, since no one knew then which Arab camp – the republican or the monarchical – would eventually gain the upper hand in the ongoing Arab "Cold War." The republican Arab countries were definitely on the rhetorical offensive under the populist leadership of Nasser, while the monarchies looked nervous and on the defensive.

The United States did not have the colonial experience of Great Britain. More to the point, Eisenhower remained too skeptical of the colonial-minded successors of Winston Churchill to ask for advice. Thus, the Eisenhower administration erred on the side of caution and demanded an immediate end to the aggression followed by a quick and redeployment of forces.

The UK and France were humiliated, but Nasser's stock, contrary to Ben-Gurion's wildest expectations, rose by leaps and bounds in the Third World and among the Arab states as a result of that event. Nasser stood up to two former colonial powers – the UK and France – and those powers had to back down. It did not matter that the invading forces withdrew because of US diplomacy and not because of the chivalrous performance of the Egyptian armed forces on the battlefield; for the Arab masses, Nasser became a hero almost overnight.

Pan-Arabism also began to be viewed as an anti-monarchical force. As such, it threatened the rule of King Hussein of Jordan. The United States had to intervene in 1957 and 1958 to support the monarchy in that country. Syria's internal turbulence led to a decision on the part of its politicians to approach Nasser for the creation of the United Arab Republic under his leadership. However, the union lasted for only three years, when a coup in Syria in 1961 led to its dissolution. This development intensified friction in the already-brewing Arab Cold War between the monarchies and the republican states. Now Nasser's version of pan-Arabism was in conflict with its other strain, Ba'athism.[3]

Even though the United States sided with Nasser during the Suez crisis, it never stopped envisioning him (quite wrongly) as a pro-Soviet (though not a communist) actor, largely because of his insistence on "positive neutrality." Eisenhower's secretary of state, John Foster Dulles, regarded such a posture as both "immoral" (because he saw the struggle between the two superpowers as a clash of "good and evil") and naive (because of, in Dulles's estimation, Nasser's alleged failure to recognize the "true" nature of communism). Three other factors forced the United States to draw hasty and erroneous conclusions about the long-range consequences of developments in the Arab world. First, the entire region was going through so much turbulence in the 1950s that drawing enduring conclusions about who favoured America or the USSR was well-nigh impossible. Second, the United States was very new at dealing with Third World leaders who were not only unaccustomed to Western ways of conducting affairs, but at times showed palpable contempt toward them. Third, the general predilections of the Third World leaders of that era – who were more sympathetic to the Soviet Union and suspicious of the United States – forced the American diplomats to conclude that anyone who was not supporting America's strategic agenda of the Cold War was either an ally or a potential ally of the communist superpower. To the Americans, Nasser fit that mold: he was antipathetic toward the American strategic agenda for his region, which boiled down to opposition to the expansion of the Soviet sphere of influence and guaranteed access to oil supplies. Neither of those objectives was important to Nasser. What also troubled the United States regarding Nasser was that no leader, since the Napoleonic invasion of Egypt, had "made such an impact on the Nile Valley and the world around it."[4] Washington simply did not know how to categorize him or how to deal with him, other than wrongly labelling his political predilections and then dealing with him accordingly.

Another hasty judgment was the declaration of the Eisenhower Doctrine of 1957, whose stated purpose was to save the Middle East from the threat posed by international communism. An unstated objective of that doctrine was to contain Nasser's "radical Arab nationalism." The Americans felt that the most potent way for the Soviet Union to enhance its sphere of influence would be through economic and military assistance to radical Arab regimes. The Soviet Union had already signed agreements to that effect with Syria and Egypt. The humiliation experienced by Great Britain as a result of America's demand for the withdrawal its forces from Egypt during the Suez crisis of 1956 had created a vacuum, which, the US officials felt, would be filled by the Soviets. That frame of mind drove those in charge of US foreign policy, and the twists and turns of events in the Middle East further persuaded them that their interpretation of Soviet behaviour was very much on the mark.

From the 1950s until the 1973 Arab-Israeli War, Egypt remained centre stage in Moscow's Middle East policy. Egypt was the major Arab country to the Arab-Israeli conflict and was also in constant conflict with the United States during those years. Those were good reasons for Moscow to conclude that, by anchoring its Middle Eastern policy in Egypt, it would be able to play a major role in the region. Although the Arab masses were impressed in 1956 by the US insistence that the UK, France, and Israel withdraw their troops from Egyptian soil during the Suez crisis, they also witnessed the Soviet Union siding with Egypt in demanding the withdrawal of the invading forces. And the Eisenhower Doctrine, whose raison d'être was to mobilize the Arab states against the "communist threat," did not persuade them. The Soviet Union was not seen as a country using the pretext of an external threat to enhance its presence in the region, as was the United States. Besides, given the Soviet Union's highly valuable military and economic support of Egypt, Syria, and Iraq, and its consistent support of the Palestinian cause, all American propaganda regarding the communist threat sounded vacuous and lacked credibility in the Arab world. For them, the chief threat to their security was the State of Israel, which was also a major client of the United States.[5]

The bloody coup of 1958 in Iraq, which brought an end to the monarchy and permanently transformed that country into a republic, was further evidence for Washington regarding the march of the pan-Arab (and pro-Soviet) forces in the Arab world. The role model for that coup was Egypt's coup of 1952. The Iraqi coup was a major setback for the United States, because the new leaders abrogated the US-sponsored Baghdad Pact. In 1962, pro-Nasser forces staged a coup in North Yemen, which terminated the monarchy. However, this time, Saudi Arabia decided to take on the pan-Arabist forces on behalf of the Arab monarchies. Egypt sent its forces to the ensuing war in Yemen; however, the conflict was not resolved in favour of the pan-Arabists.

In this growing Arab Cold War, Nasser emerged as the single leader who challenged the pro-US monarchies, which he derisively called "tools of imperialism," "enemies of Arabism," and "forces of reaction." He enthusiastically used the superpower rivalry to his advantage, courting the Soviet Union for nationalistic reasons. To the Eisenhower administration, Nasser was a thorn in the side. These events, along with the fermentation of the Arab-Israeli conflict, were reasons for the steady involvement of the two superpowers in the region. While the Soviet Union sided with the Arab republican regimes – notably Egypt and Syria – the United States favoured the monarchies.

In addition, Washington's commitment to the security and survival of Israel emerged as a permanent feature of America's dominance in the area. While the Arab states failed to present a united front against Israel because of their internecine bickering, the latter concentrated on becoming a major military power. The Arab states were fully aware of that reality in the wars of 1948 and 1956, in which Israel defeated their forces. The Arab military was hampered by its dependence on unreliable sources of weapons supplies and by a poor state of preparedness. In almost all Arab countries, the military served in the role of praetorian guard. As such, it focused more on saving the regimes of dictators or monarchs than on mobilizing a professional fighting force. The Israeli armed forces, by contrast, steadily upgraded their capacity as a fighting force, ready to defend the state against Arab attacks of any magnitude. In the process, they had unfettered access to superior military wherewithal from Western sources.

The Arab-Israeli war of 1967 was a watershed event. The Arab side, in their conventional hyperbole about destroying Israel, gave the Jewish state ample reasons (reasons that were seen as "justified" only in the Western world) to launch a pre-emptive war, thereby catching the Arab military napping. By the time hostilities ended, Egypt had lost the Sinai, Jordan had lost the West Bank and East Jerusalem, and Syria had lost the Golan Heights. That war created political realties whereby Israel would not only determine the modalities of future negotiations for several ensuing decades, but also set conditions for conducting them, mostly on terms of its own liking. (Whether Israel really wanted to resolve that conflict was an entirely different issue.) The 1967 war also permanently enhanced the political clout and dominance of the United States in the Arab-Israeli conflict. Given its special relations with the Jewish state, the United States was the only actor that could persuade or put pressure on Israel for political concessions. It should be noted, however, that the Arab states long held an exaggerated view of the United States' capacity to persuade or to pressure Israel. Israel has proven on a number of occasions – during the administration of presidents Gerald Ford and George H.W. Bush – its capacity to withstand pressures coming from the White House. Israel's capacity to keep the US Congress on its side is also legendary, and that has frustrated occasional presidential pressures on Israel to offer concessions to the Arab side.

The territorial gains made by Israel, in tandem with constant American military and economic assistance, created a situation whereby the Jewish state had virtually no incentive to make substantive concessions for redeploying its troops. The Israeli hard-liners' dream of "Eretz Israel" – whose boundaries far exceeded the maps of the 1947 UN mandate – was in the process of becoming a reality. The Arab states had no other option to bring about Israeli withdrawal from the occupied territories except to work with the United States, which was experiencing the best of both worlds. America's generous military and economic assistance made it a credible ally of Israel. At the same time, Washington was perceived by the Arab countries to be holding all the cards for resolving the Arab-Israeli conflict. But the deck was stacked in Israel's favour. To ensure that its political support inside the US domestic arena remained steadfast, Israel, through the American-Israel Political Action Committee, created a solid backing in the US Congress for its refusal to withdraw from occupied territories, except under the conditions and circumstances preferred by its leaders in Jerusalem.

The lack of progress in the Arab-Israeli conflict and the continued Israeli occupation of Arab land – a position that was described as no-war-no-peace – had to be broken by another war, or so concluded presidents Anwar Sadat of Egypt and Hafez al-Assad of Syria. The result was the war of 1973 – a war that Israel calls the Yom Kippur War because it started on that Jewish holiday, and that the Egyptians refer to as the Ramadan War because it was launched during the Muslim holy month of Ramadan. It was a coordinated attack by the Egyptian and the Syrian militaries. The Egyptian armed forces surprised the Israelis by breaking through the Bar Lev Line fortifications. The initial success of the Arab drive, aside from surprising their enemies, was due to the failure of Israeli intelligence, and perhaps even to Israeli hubris about the invincibility of its military. However, since the Israeli forces were definitely better equipped and better prepared than their Arab counterparts, they broke through the Egyptian defensive lines before too long, and drove through to the western bank of the Suez Canal. On the Syrian front, they also made a speedy advance. By the conclusion of hostilities, the Israeli Army was only sixty miles from Cairo and twenty-five miles from Damascus.[6]

The United States once again proved its significance as a highly reliable ally and started providing massive military assistance to Israel, claiming that Israel's military supplies had reached a dangerously low level. US-Soviet diplomacy also came into play, Moscow's chief concern being the avoidance of a serious defeat of Egyptian forces. Soviet general secretary Leonid Brezhnev, sensing that President Nixon was delaying the pace of negotiations while providing additional military advantage to the Israeli forces, threatened unilateral military action to aid Egypt. The United States, fearing Soviet intervention, placed its forces on worldwide alert on 25 October 1973. That was the second time during the Cold War that the world came to the brink of a nuclear showdown between the two superpowers (the Cuban missile crisis of 1962 was the first).

The 1973 war was also an occasion when the Arab states demonstrated a rare but respectable unity and solidarity. Under the leadership of Saudi Arabia, the Organization of Arab Petroleum Exporting Countries imposed an oil embargo on the United States and on any European country deemed a supporter of Israel. Although the oil embargo was a short-lived phenomenon, it showed how powerful Arab unity could be if it were to emerge as a lasting reality.

The "shuttle diplomacy" of US secretary of state Henry Kissinger played a crucial role in bringing about the withdrawal of Israeli forces from Egyptian and Syrian territories. However, any meaningful resolution of that conflict had to wait for a later time.[7] Kissinger's style of diplomacy reflected his long-time intellectual fixation with two types of international order: "legitimate" and "revolutionary." According to Kissinger's early writings, "States that accepted a particular international order as legitimate were in a position to negotiate their differences." However, when "a state maintained that the international order was illegitimate, diplomacy was excluded." Kissinger described those states as "revolutionary."[8] He did not speak about these two types of order while he was flying among the capitals of various Middle Eastern countries; however, the end result of the negotiations spoke volumes about his commitment to these principles.

In Kissinger's framework, Egypt and Syria were revolutionary states; they were challenging what in their view was an illegitimate international order that had enabled Israel to emerge as a powerful military actor. In response, Israel had no real incentive to narrow its borders by giving up territories that it had acquired during the wars of 1967 and 1973. However, Israel as a "legitimate" actor of Kissinger's description (since it accrued enormous benefit from the post–Cold War order) had to negotiate the differences between the portion of territory that the Arab side wanted returned and what it was really willing to give back. A crucial precondition for that withdrawal was direct negotiations between the antagonist Arab states and Israel, leading to recognition of the latter. Kissinger's not-so-publicized, deep sympathies toward Israel seemed to justify the Jewish state's mistrust of the Arab states and a strategy of gradual withdrawal, a tactic that would ensure Israel's security.

The Kissingerian notion of managing the conflict – whereby Israel would not be forced to make major territorial concessions and the United States would sustain its diplomatic prestige in the Middle East – produced its intended results.[9] Egypt gained self-respect and a heightened prestige within the Arab world as a military actor whose participation was critical for the resolution of the Arab-Israeli conflict. Saudi Arabia emerged as a new and additional centre of Arab power and a country whose views were to be taken into consideration by the United States and other great powers. The Saudi clout in the Arab world increased significantly because of its willingness to "punish" those whose policies were adversarial to the Arab cause, and because that kingdom also played a crucial and highly nuanced role in lowering tensions by politically endorsing the American initiatives regarding those disengagements.[10] Egypt's diplomatic recognition of Israel had to wait until a later date (the Camp David Accords), but recognition from Syria did not materialize. The sole losers at the conclusion of that war were the Palestinians. The pan-Arabist leaders of the 1950s and 1960s had failed miserably to liberate their homeland, an emotional promise underlying their rhetoric of those decades. If anything, it was that fiery rhetoric, in conjunction with the bungling performance of the Arab armed forces, which enabled Israel to capture the Arab territories and to emerge, almost overnight in 1967, as the final determiner of how much Arab territory it would return, when, and under what conditions.

The 1973 Arab-Israeli war provided a much-desired psychological boost to the Arab side. However, before it became a distant memory, it had to be followed up by an iconoclastic approach for the resolution of the Arab-Israeli conflict. An Arab leader had to break the fixation of Arab public opinion created by Arab leadership from the 1940s through the 1960s that Israel did not have the right to exist as a sovereign state, and that the only solution was to drive it into the sea. President Anwar Sadat had been motivated by the need for such an approach since 1971, two years before the Arab-Israeli war of 1973. He believed that only a limited war could create a new environment for such an approach. He was realistic enough to know that the Arab forces could not defeat Israel. All they had to do was to perform respectably in order to revive the prospects of a negotiated resolution of the Arab-Israeli conflict. Sadat also came to the conclusion that only the United States had the potential to broker a negotiated solution to the Arab-Israeli conflict. He knew that the Soviet

Union had no potential to play such a role. Moreover, he was getting increasingly frustrated by the Soviet posture of delaying military supplies to the Egyptian military. Leaders in Moscow were more concerned about safeguarding the détente policy between the superpowers and did not want to jeopardize it. Consequently, Sadat took the courageous step of expelling thousands of Soviet advisors from Egypt, even before the war. This decision shook the Soviet Union into abandoning the policy of delays in supplying the Egyptian Army during the 1973 war.

The United States watched Anwar Sadat's expulsion of Soviet advisors with considerable interest. Thus, after the 1973 war, when he decided to champion negotiations for peace with Israel, he was viewed in Washington as a courageous and credible leader. Sadat knew that the Arab world would not support his audacious maneuvers toward the Jewish state. Yet, he took it upon himself to be the lone messenger for the Arab cause, which only he could define, because there was not even a semblance of support, much less an Arab consensus, regarding its specifics. But in the absence of a unified Arab front and specific proposals for resolution, Israel had little reason to offer major territorial concessions. Sadat's courageous journey to Jerusalem in 1977 diminished his country to the status of a pariah in the Arab world. To his utter dismay, Israeli prime minister Menachem Begin was not interested in considering a major departure from the conventional Israeli preferences for hanging on to occupied territory as long as it could and offering minimum concessions in return for diplomatic recognition of the Jewish state by all Arab states. The only other option left for Sadat was to rely on the United States, once again, to break new negotiating ground.

Sadat's signing of the Camp David Accords – a framework of peace between Egypt and Israel – on 22 March 1979, created a major rift within the ranks of the Arab states and set a precedent for piecemeal agreements. The major winners of this treaty were Israel and the United States; the minor winner was Egypt. It got back the Sinai, and it entered into a "cold peace" with Israel. However, the Camp David Accords – made possible because of the highly proactive role of President Jimmy Carter – decoupled Egypt from the ranks of Arab military strength. That might not have been the intent of the American president, but in the minds of Arab radicals, the agreements permanently minimized the chances of a comprehensive resolution to the Arab-Israeli conflict. They viewed the agreements as a triumph of

Israeli determination to never fully resolve the conflict – an interpretation that remains prevalent in the Arab world today.

Israel has in fact used this pattern of negotiating separate peace treaties with Arab states to maintain a commanding position at the negotiating table. Comprehensive and simultaneous peace negotiations with multiple Arab states would have put pressure on Israel to withdraw, if not completely, at least substantially from parts of the territories that it occupied as a result of the 1967 war. The Jewish state had no intention of doing that. And the most assured way of avoiding complete withdrawal was to negotiate with Egypt, Jordan, the PLO, and Syria separately, and on a piecemeal basis. Following that pattern, Israel negotiated a separate peace treaty with Jordan in 1994. Thus, there were no magnanimous winners in the Middle East.

The Camp David Accords were also unequivocal proof of what Sadat had concluded at the end of the 1973 war – that only the United States had the capability to bring about a resolution to the conflict. Even the Arab States that were bitter over the ostensibly divisive role of the United States in breaking Egypt away from their ranks developed a healthy respect for the political clout of the superpower. From the American point of view, the Camp David Accords between Egypt and Israel demonstrated that the Arab-Israeli conflict was resolvable on a piecemeal basis if both contending parties showed courage and resolve. But even a lack of resolution would not have hindered American dominance in the region, as long as the oil-producing countries continued to supply oil to the United States and its industrial allies, and as long as the Arab states did not acquire military power that threatened the survival and security of Israel.

By contrast, the Soviet Union could not achieve the same degree of significance as a hegemon in the Middle East. It had neither the strong strategic ties nor the attendant clout with Israel, and even in the Arab world, its influence may have fallen victim to the acute intra-Arab differences stemming from the Arab Cold War, which remained important from the 1950s to the 1967 Arab-Israeli war. The major military defeat of its client states – Egypt and Syria – during that war was a setback for the USSR. The Soviet Union made its mark after the 1973 war by threatening to take action in order to circumvent the decisive defeat of the Egyptian forces. It also emerged as the chief supporter of the so-called rejectionist or confrontational front – which included Iraq, Syria, Algeria, Libya, and after the Islamic revolution, Iran – and the main conduit for arms supplies for these states. However, because of the significance of the United States in the Arab and the Israeli camps, Moscow could not transform its episodic importance after the Suez conflict or even after the 1973 war into lasting strategic gains. Sadat's calculation in the early 1970s about the importance of the United States in bringing about a political resolution to the Arab-Israeli conflict, his iconoclastic lone-ranger diplomatic trip to Jerusalem in 1977, and the US role in concluding the Camp David Accords had a cumulative effect in decisively assigning the USSR a secondary status in that region.

IRAN STRIKES BACK: THE FIRST MAJOR VICTORY FOR THE ISLAMISTS

The American dominance in the Middle East was seriously eroded for the first time in the post–World War II era as a result of the Iranian revolution of 1978–79. What is important in the context of this study is that the Islamist forces were responsible for that erosion. Islam did not have a major political visibility until then. In the 1950s and 1960s, the Islamist forces did pose a challenge to the dictatorship of Gamal Abdel Nasser in Egypt, but Nasser, riding the tidal wave of populism and pan-Arabism, brutally suppressed them. The Islamists were confined to his notorious dungeons where they spent all their time immersing themselves in the militant doctrine of jihad and making plans to oust the "Pharaoh." In the public sphere, Islam was mentioned only as an afterthought when the economic underdevelopment and political backwardness of the Arab polities of that era were discussed.

Islam became a topic of discussion during the 1950s and 1960s when the indigenous modernizing elites, emulating Western polities, imposed secularism. Western experts told Middle Easterners that their nirvana (if not their political epiphany) would come only when they succeeded in adopting the Western notion of modernization. That included, *inter alia*, westernization (rejecting traditional, parochial, and tribal values), secularization (removing Islam from the public domain and limiting its role to private affairs), and institutionalization (creating modern institutions that would implement distributive and redistributive state policies).[11] In their zeal to emulate Western polities, Muslim rulers never paused to comprehend the historical reasons that secularism had not become a permanent source of instability and political violence in the West. As Munir Shafiq, a Palestinian scholar on the subject notes:

> The modern state in Europe emerged out of a bitter struggle against absolutist monarchical regimes and against the hegemony of the Catholic Church. The result of this encounter was a compromise, a historical reconciliation, between the state and the church. While the church was prohibited from transforming itself into a political party, it reserved the right to support a political party, or a political candidate, of its choice. The church was also granted freedom to conduct its proselytizing activities in the society and to establish educational, social and economic institutions. On its part the church acceded that the people had the right to freedom of faith, including the freedom not to believe.[12]

By contrast, secularist authorities in the Muslim world did not (and could not) agree "to any settlement with Islam and its institutions"; instead, they sought "to eliminate Islamic rivals or at least subdue them through a process known as 'drying of the springs.'" It is worth noting that these same secular authorities did not deal with the Christian church in the same manner. They left the church "completely independent and fully in charge of its endowments and schools."[13] This simmering conflict regarding Islam has not been resolved in the Muslim world at large.

No Muslim government could have imagined that Islam would emerge as a major force until the Iranian revolution toppled one of the most powerful clients of the United States. That iconoclastic development created additional realities that were highly disquieting for that superpower. First, the revolution not only ended the dominance of the United States in Iran, but it also increased the likelihood of turbulent political changes in the rest of the Persian Gulf. Second, given that the US-Soviet rivalry was then very much alive in the region, the United States had to come up with contingency plans to forestall further erosion of its dominance. Finally, the establishment of an Islamic government in Iran instantly transformed the Islamist forces into a force that could threaten the political dominance of both superpowers. The militant doctrine of jihad was already being implemented in Afghanistan through the US-Saudi-Pakistani alliance (chapter 5), and that successful campaign would enable the Islamist forces to similarly challenge the United States in the future.

The United States' maneuverings in the Persian Gulf region after the Islamic revolution were desperate attempts to forestall the repeat of that event in neighbouring states. The Shah epitomized the era of American foreign policy when relying on loyal dictators was very much the norm. There was Anastasio Somoza of Nicaragua, Ferdinand Marcos of the Philippines, and others. Even Saddam Hussein was preferred by President Ronald Reagan as the "lesser of the two evils" during the Iran-Iraq War. The Shah personally dealt with all US presidents from Harry Truman to Jimmy Carter. He became America's gendarme in the Persian Gulf when President Nixon decided to identify regional proxies in 1970. He played that role faithfully as an ardent anti-communist ally during the height of the Cold War. In return, America sold him state-of-the-art weaponry at top price. The Shah even built nuclear plants with US assistance. The end of his regime heightened concern inside Washington about the strategic implications for the United States. Then there was the Soviet invasion and occupation of Afghanistan, which also shocked President Jimmy Carter.

President Carter, in an unprecedented, explicit statement of US foreign policy, expressed his administration's resolve to defend the states in the region. "An attempt by any outside force to gain control of the Persian Gulf region will be regarded as an assault on the vital interests of the United States," he stated. "It will be repelled by any means necessary, including military force." In a clear warning to Iran not to attempt to export its revolution to the Arab sheikhdoms, Carter made explicit his determination "to protect the Strait of Hormuz and strengthen our key friends in the region."[14] Washington was ready not only to project its military power in the region, but also to station armed forces there to forestall any shenanigans from adversarial sources. The United States eventually established the US Central Command (CENTCOM), whose chief purpose was to avert any future implosion of friendly monarchies in the Persian Gulf region. The Soviet Union was warned not to trifle with America's dominance in the Persian Gulf and, by extension, in the entire Middle East.

It is interesting to imagine what would have happened in Afghanistan, Pakistan, and Iran toward the end of the 1980s if the United States had stayed in the region after the expulsion of the Soviet Union from Afghanistan. Possibly the superpower could have worked toward the development of democracy in both Pakistan and Afghanistan. Another possibility is that the United States might have worked to soften the militant edge of jihad – which it had so eagerly promoted and implemented in its proxy war against the Soviet Union in the 1980s. However, it could also be argued that, even if the United States had maintained a visible presence in Afghanistan and Pakistan, it would not have earnestly pushed for democracy in those two countries. After all, it did not place ample pressure on General Pervez Musharraf for the achievement of that objective, even in the post–9/11 era.

Most likely the United States did not stay to fill the power vacuum left by the withdrawal of the Soviet Union because, by that time, it was becoming increasingly clear that something major was going to happen to the communist superpower. Consequently, Washington was engrossed in interpreting events leading to the implosion of the Soviet Union and in developing its own responses to this momentous development. The iconoclastic changes that President Mikhail Gorbachev introduced under the rubrics of *Perestroika* and *Glasnost* pointed to potentially unprecedented results inside that country. When the Soviet Union imploded in December 1991, the other global issues on the United States' strategic agenda receded in significance, and the grand issue of managing the globe as the lone superpower became top priority. In the meantime, the jihadists were developing their own agenda. Throughout the 1990s, their forces focused attention on attacking US diplomatic and military personnel, military platforms, and even embassies. Toward the end of the 1990s, the lone superpower was fully aware of their growing animosity, but it took the al-Qaida-sponsored attacks on its East African embassies in August 1998 to push Washington's concern to the level of alarm that it warranted. Still, if the analyses presented in a number of books on the events leading to the 9/11 attacks on the United States are correct, one gets a persuasive picture that the top US officials did not anticipate, nor did they find credible, the then seemingly alarmist analyses by some of the intelligence sources that the Islamists were planning to launch attacks on the homeland by operating inside the United States.[15]

ISLAMISM: CHALLENGING THE LONE SUPERPOWER AND KHADIM AL-HARAMAIN AL-SHARIFAIN

In the post–Cold War era, American dominance in the world of Islam should have remained unchallenged. The implosion of the Soviet Union left the United States with no competition in that part of the globe. The Islamic Republic of Iran, although an important actor in the Middle East, was barely a middle power.[16] However, the Iranian revolution, along with Islamist rule over Afghanistan from the ouster of the Soviet Union in 1989 to the dismantlement of the Taliban in 2001, marked the beginning of a new era of political activism for the Islamist forces in seeking to establish their primacy throughout the Muslim world.

Events in Afghanistan in the 1990s created an environment that was to prove highly deleterious to American interests. The capture of power by the Taliban (religious students; singular *Talib*) in Afghanistan in 1996 was a great victory for Islamism. With Osama Bin Laden's return to that country in the same year, the Islamist forces were prepared to extend their geographic area of activity. In that capacity, Islamism was to become a major force in challenging the United States and Muslim regimes in different regions.

The Taliban leadership was the product of the religious schools of Pakistan, where they were taught the primacy of jihad in Islam. In fact, they envisioned their own capture of power as an exercise of jihad. Consequently, once in power, they needed little persuading about exporting jihad to the areas contiguous to Afghanistan. Al-Qaida became the chief vehicle for the propagation of regional, and then global, jihad. There have been conflicting reports that Mullah Omar, the leader of the Taliban regime, did not share Bin Laden's views on jihad. However, if he really wanted Bin Laden to abandon his jihad-related activities, he certainly did not take any harsh measures to see that his alleged preferences were carried out.[17]

While America's involvement in the liberation of Afghanistan in the 1980s did not win it friends in the world of Islam, its longstanding support of Israel in the Arab-Israeli conflict created an image – not just in the Arab world, but also in the world of Islam at large – of the United States as an "anti-Arab" country. That perception lingered throughout the Cold War years. When Islamist groups emerged as a powerful force in the strategic affairs of the Middle East, this perception mutated into America as an "anti-Islamic" force. It is very hard to pin down exactly why or how this image was formulated, since the United States also played such a complex role in the Muslim world throughout the 1990s. One possibility is that, with the demise of the Cold War, there was no other mega-conflict to capture the attention or energy of the international community. In the post–Cold War years, Europe was no longer an arena where ancient conflicts were settled by wars. In fact, in the post–Cold War years, Europe promised to evolve into a largely war-free area. The Middle East, South Asia, Central Asia, and the Muslim-dominated portions of Africa, on the contrary, surfaced as zones of conflict, violence, and instability. As the United States was busy consolidating its "victory" over the Soviet Union in the post–Cold War years, its longstanding dominant presence in the Middle East became a source of contention for Islamist and self-styled jihadist forces.

In analyzing the evolution of Islamism, one must pay special attention to the modalities of America's presence in the Persian Gulf region in the aftermath of the Gulf War of 1991. The Kuwaiti invasion by Saddam Hussein in July 1990 led to two important developments. First, the United States opted to get involved in a Muslim fight. Second, King Fahd Bin Abdul Aziz granted the Bush administration permission to station American troops in Saudi Arabia, but refused to allow Osama Bin Laden's Islamic fighters to take on the Iraqi forces in Kuwait. Symbolically speaking, the leader of a movement that was soon to become global jihad was denied permission by the *Khadim al-Haramain al-Sharifain* (protector of the two holy shrines of Islam and thus the self-styled leader of the Sunni world) to defend the birthplace of Islam. Bin Laden was confident that his large contingent of "Afghan Arabs" (Arab participants of the Afghan war), having defeated the Soviet Union, could take on any power of that era. But King Fahd did not share Bin Laden's confidence or his optimism. He was more concerned about preventing Saudi Arabia from becoming the next victim of Saddam's aggression, and opted to accept American assistance. This incident ignited the conflict between the jihadists and the Saudi monarchy. Bin Laden started to send the king a series of letters whose tone became increasingly threatening.[18]

The international coalition of Western, Arab, and Muslim forces, under the leadership of the United States, played a crucial role in decisively defeating the Iraqi forces and in expelling them from Kuwait, a Muslim emirate. However, this action did not win much sympathy from the jihadists and the Islamists, who regarded Kuwait as a corrupt "anti-Islamic" monarchy bent on following the hedonistic lifestyle of the West, and a country willing to promote the American agenda by providing basing facilities for American troops on its soil. By extension of this logic, the United States, in restoring the Kuwaiti monarch to power, ensured its dominance in the region and guaranteed its supply of oil from the Arab sheikhdom.

The decision of the Bush administration to station a small but visible portion of US forces in Saudi Arabia became grounds for bitter animosity between Bin Laden and the Saudi government. The US forces were to act as deterrence against future aspirations of Saddam Hussein. But for Bin Laden, the US presence defiled holy ground. Khadim al-Haramain al-Sharifain was no longer worthy of his noble role; he would soon become a marked target of the jihadists.

The reasons for a major conflict between the United States and the jihadists were ever present. For Islamists of all varieties, the United States was a Christian power, with a profound and highly intricate global agenda of its own. From the jihadists' point of view, however, America's consistent support of Israel in the Arab-Israeli conflict made it an "anti-Islamic" power. Starting with the presidency of Lyndon B. Johnson, the United States became firmly and explicitly committed to providing Israel with a qualitative edge in military power, with the rationale that "Israel will always be militarily outnumbered with regard to the artillery, tanks, and combat aircraft that can be deployed by a coalition of Arab states. While Arab states structure their ground forces on the basis of standing active service formations that can be battle-ready with little preparation, Israel's army is organized *primarily* around reserve units, requiring at least 48 hours to reach full strength." Although a number of Arab states could also purchase US weapons (and weapons from other Western countries), these sales were deliberately packaged to ensure that no Arab state could gain an advantage over the Jewish state. Even after Egypt signed a peace treaty with Israel and became a major recipient of American military assistance, Israel maintained its military edge over that country by successfully persuading Washington that "it cannot ignore Egypt's capabilities when calculating the military balance in the region, because a change of government in Egypt could change matters [for Israel]."[19]

It should be pointed out that US weapons support was only half of the story. Israel put this support to good use by developing original military strategies, maintaining a high level of readiness, and investing heavily in military-related research and development. In addition, the influx of European immigrants from the 1950s through the 1970s and the development of an educated labour force spurred the growth of a technologically oriented economy. Compare these factors to the Arab states, which were seriously lacking in weapons trades, education, and technical know-how. The cumulative result was Israel's emergence as a major regional power.

America's persistent commitment to the security and survival of Israel was never based on its alleged animosity toward Islam. But that is how it was spun by the Islamists and jihadists in the mosques, streets, and coffeehouses in the world of Islam in the 1990s. They were becoming increasingly focused on ousting the lone superpower from Saudi Arabia. As America emerged as the new "focus of evil," the Islamist and jihadist forces gathered under the banner of al-Qaida – a jihadist organization formed to fight the Soviet Union under the doctrine of jihad – and under the lead of Islamist organizations in different global Muslim regions.

Bin Laden became the driving force for this new focus, the fountainhead of Islamism, and a "new Saladin" for the self-styled jihadists. As a modern-day Saladin (Salahuddin Ayyubi, the Kurdish warrior of Islam, brought Jerusalem under Muslim control in 1187), he was expected to settle all the real as well as the imaginary scores with the West. No matter that establishing a global caliphate in the twenty-first century was well-nigh impossible; Bin Laden had no state power on his side, and the lone superpower was applying a major thrust of its military might to eliminate him. To the West, Bin Laden epitomized violence, mayhem, and evil; it was an urgent matter that he be either captured or killed.

As previously stated in this chapter, Osama Bin Laden's growing opposition to the Saudi government and the latter's refusal to expel American forces from its territory in the 1990s were two visible reasons for the growing rift between Saudi Arabia and al-Qaida. If those were the only reasons, however, then the Saudi rulers would have found a way to resolve them, especially when the United States finally pulled its troops from the kingdom in 2003. But the animosity had deeper roots: the jihadists of Bin Laden's generation, especially the so-called Afghan Arabs, questioned the very legitimacy of Saudi rule (the 1745 pact between the Saudi ruler and the leader of what is now known as Wahhabism) and its commitment to Islamic puritanism.

The conflict between the Saudi monarchy and al-Qaida and other jihadist groups stemmed from the highly complex role acquired by the kingdom in the 1960s and al-Qaida's emergence as the lead organization of the self-proclaimed "global jihad" in the 1990s. Starting in the late 1960s and early 1970s, the Saudi commitment to Wahhabism came face to face with the kingdom's growing responsibilities in regional and global politics, economics, and balance of power–related activities. Given the enormity of its oil reserves, Saudi Arabia emerged as a major supplier of Western states and as the leader of moderate oil states belonging to the Organization of Petroleum Exporting Countries (OPEC). In the aftermath of the Arab-Israeli war of 1973, Saudi Arabia imposed a short-duration oil embargo on the United States and other staunch European supporters of Israel, and played a crucial behind-the-scenes role in negotiating the withdrawal of Egyptian and Israeli forces. At least twice since then, the Saudi monarchy has offered plans – the Fahd Plan of 1982 and the Crown Prince Abdullah Plan of 2002 – for a comprehensive resolution of the Arab-Israeli conflict.[20] Although these plans did not lead to diplomatic breakthroughs, they signalled the Saudi government's resolve to remain at the forefront of the Arab nations in seeking a peaceful solution. In the late 1990s and 2000s, when the Palestinian conflict increasingly received the attention of the Islamists, Saudi Arabia burnished its credentials as a key player in potentially resolving one of the core conflicts in the Middle East and in the world of Islam.

Saudi Arabia also played a leading role in attempts to persuade Saddam Hussein not to invade Kuwait. When the Iraqi dictator defied all diplomatic attempts to avert a military crisis, however, the kingdom did not take much persuading by US officials to allow America the use of its territory to launch major offensive actions against Iraq. After all, Saudi leaders were uncertain about the real intent of Saddam Hussein, whose forces remained just a few miles from the Saudi border.

After the expulsion of Saddam's forces from Kuwait, Saudi Arabia could not simply ask the United States to leave its territory, although the Saudi rulers may well have wanted to. As a major Arab state, Saudi Arabia had to respond to its regional and international responsibilities. The United States was using its continued presence inside Saudi Arabia to weaken Saddam's regime through surveillance operations on Iraq in compliance with the UNSCR 688. Besides, by keeping the Saddam regime under pressure, the United States also ensured the security of the Saudi regime. Such were the intricacies associated with Saudi Arabia's maintaining its role as an important regional actor and as America's major ally.

The jihadist forces, however, were quite indifferent, if not oblivious, to these complications. Better yet, to them such intricacies were illegitimate and anti-Islamic. All that mattered to them was that Saudi Arabia was cooperating with the United States, which they had viewed since the early 1990s as the "archenemy" of Islam. The Saudi rulers, for their part, either did not recognize the seriousness of the rift or chose to ignore it. But for Bin Laden, the seeds of suspicion and doubt about the "tainted" Islamic credentials of the Saudi monarchy were sprouting fast. In his frame of reference, the Saudi autocrats had abrogated the religious pact; they were being sustained in power by continued support from the United States. Washington was using that support to prolong its stay in the birthplace of Islam, an act that Bin Laden continually referred to as "defiling the land of the Holy Prophet."

What the Islamists and jihadists did not recognize was that Saudi Arabia was driven by regime survival. The pragmatism that prompted the Saudi rulers to grant the American-led international coalition forces use of the kingdom as a launching pad against Saddam Hussein in 1990 was no different from the pragmatism that had driven Muhammad bin Saud to sign a pact with Muhammad ibn 'Abd al-Wahhāb in 1745. Again, in 1865, Saudi rulers cooperated with a major "infidel" of the time, Great Britain, by signing a "treaty of cooperation and friendship" in exchange for handsome financial rewards and the promise to be left alone in their attempt to consolidate the grip of Wahhabi Islam on the Arabian Peninsula. Likewise, Saud Bin Abdel Aziz (aka Ibn Saud), who unified Saudi Arabia in 1932, pursued the survival of his rule for the rest of his life. In February 1945, for example, he met with President Franklin D. Roosevelt on board the USS *Quincy* to sign an agreement that guaranteed oil supplies to the United States and its allies in return for a US promise to secure the monarchy. Ibn Saud's successors continued this fixation with regime survival, deftly maneuvering to ensure it under all circumstances. The regime's survival was threatened only briefly in November 1979 when Juhayman ibn Muhammad ibn Sayf al-Otaibi and his band of zealots took control of the grand mosque. The Saudi regime brutally crushed them with the help of French forces. In this context, inviting the Americans to save the monarchy was not a decision that required intricate deliberations.

The question, then, was what strategy should al-Qaida develop? Should it strike at the Saudi dynasty and try to bring an end to its rule, or should it attack the United States? Either way, al-Qaida was edging toward a major fight with America. And, in contrast to the 1950s and 1960s, in the 1990s al-Qaida had a fighting chance. No question, Islamists' attempts to bring about regime change since World War II had been a dismal failure. Not only did they fail to overthrow Nasser, but they were severely persecuted by him and, consequently, remained on the defensive. But the political environment of the 1990s was radically different from what had prevailed in Egypt (or elsewhere in the Middle East) three decades earlier. In the 1990s, the Islamists could clearly envisage ousting a Sunni regime à la Khomeini's success in terminating the Shah's rule.

The strategic environment of the Middle East in the 1990s was also radically different from the American perspective. After watching the demise of a friendly regime in Iran (through the exercise of Islamism), Washington, under no circumstance, was going to stand by and watch the Saudi regime become a victim of al-Qaida's exercise of Islamism. The lines had been drawn: whether al-Qaida decided to destabilize Saudi Arabia or to attack the United States, the end result would be the same. Either action would lead to a direct clash between the United States and the self-styled jihadist forces of al-Qaida.

It is anyone's guess to what extent the al-Qaida leadership thought through the implications of attacking the United States on its own homeland. At the same time, considering al-Qaida's jihadist frame of reference – in which believers think nothing of sacrificing their lives for the cause – that entity did not really care how far the United States would go in striking back. Another possibility is that al-Qaida was totally off the mark in anticipating the United States response; it did not expect the United States to attack and occupy Afghanistan and, later on, to bring about regime change in Iraq. However, the enormity of the chaos that resulted from the US invasion of Afghanistan and Iraq played a major role in enabling al-Qaida to widen its presence from South Asia to the Levant.

Arguably, several attempts by al-Qaida and its cohorts to bring about regime change in the late 1990s in Central Asia (the exercise of Islamism at the regional level) were merely "dry runs" for striking at the United States in 2001. In applying the Takfiri doctrine, al-Qaida attempted to overthrow existing governments in Muslim countries judged to be "un-Islamic." This is when the self-styled jihadist groups became regular practitioners of Islamism. These groups had much preparatory work to do if they were to oust the autocratic regimes of Central Asia. In addition, the secessionist movements in the Xinjiang province of China and the North Caucasus region of Russia had to achieve independence. These secessionist movements accelerated the pace of the jihadists' struggle. A number of violent attacks were carried out in Kyrgyzstan and Uzbekistan between 1998 and

2001. Even the great powers proximate to that region – China and Russia – were running scared of the growing instability in Xinjiang and Chechnya. Their response was to create the Shanghai Five (comprising Kazakhstan, Kyrgyzstan, and Tajikistan, along with China and Russia), which was enlarged to the Shanghai Cooperation Organization (SCO) in 2001 with the addition of Uzbekistan. Try as it might, the SCO could not deter the jihadist activities of the al-Qaida-linked Islamic Movement of Uzbekistan (IMU) or eradicate the secessionist movements inside China and Russia (chapter 7).

In summary, it is worth remembering that it was in Afghanistan that the last great battle of the Cold War years' "war of ideas" was fought. With the implosion of the Soviet Union, communism as an idea was also defeated, except in a handful of countries that still called themselves communist.[21] For the jihadists, it was they who played a formidable role in defeating the arch practitioner of atheism, an idea that was considered unequivocally offensive to Islam. They envisioned the defeat of the Soviet Union as a victory of Islam and jihad. Yes, Washington found it highly pragmatic to rejuvenate the feelings of militant jihad to achieve its heady objectives of defeating and ousting the Soviet Union from Afghanistan. However, America failed to extrapolate the possibilities that jihad could become a lethal weapon against its own strategic interests.

At some point between 2000 and mid-2001, the decision was made to attack the United States. The 9/11 terrorist attack marked the beginning of a new phase, a new era. It triggered a global jihad – the exercise of Islamism at the global level.[22] The United States responded by declaring its own global war on terrorism (GWOT) and invading Afghanistan – from where al-Qaida had planned and launched its attacks. The Taliban regime, from the American perspective, was guilty of providing a safe haven. The regime was dismantled and al-Qaida, as an organization, was almost destroyed. A number of al-Qaida leaders were killed, although Bin Laden and his deputy, Ayman al-Zawahiri, escaped. It appeared that al-Qaida's practice of Islamism would be either curtailed or crushed, unless the lone superpower seriously overplayed its hand. The United States was very much in an offensive mode, resolute in its war on terrorism and eradication of the al-Qaida leadership. Fortunately for that entity, President George W. Bush had a change of heart. Instead of completing the mission to destroy al-Qaida in Afghanistan, the United States decided to invade Iraq.

US INVASION OF IRAQ: A BOON FOR ISLAMISM?

Saddam Hussein's regime had been a major source of irritation for the United States since the end of the Gulf War of 1991. However, after uprooting the Iraqi forces from Kuwait, President George H.W. Bush decided not to invade Iraq and bring about regime change in that country. No Arab state that sided with the United States in that war was in favour of removing Saddam. Bush Sr, himself, did not think it was worth getting bogged down in a potential imbroglio in Iraq by invading it. The United States left Saddam in power but kept intense pressure on Iraq. It curtailed the freedom of movement of the Saddam forces in northern and southern Iraq by creating no-fly zones. "The No-Fly Zone War is considered to have ended on 19 March 2003, when 'Operation Iraqi Freedom' began and this conflict segued into the larger war." [23] George W. Bush decided to finish the job and bring an end to the Saddam regime. The United States invaded Iraq for the declared purpose of depriving Saddam Hussein of the use of weapons of mass destruction (WMD). However, finding those weapons was later discovered to be a false pretext to start the war. The real purpose was to dismantle the Iraqi military, which the United States quickly achieved. However, the US military had no "post-conflict plans." The neoconservative (neocon) architects of the invasion of Iraq had been persuaded by Iraqi expatriates of the likes of Ahmad Chalabi, president of the Iraqi National Congress, that an invasion of that country would be a "cakewalk," that the Iraqi military would walk away from the fight and even welcome the American forces. The neocons inside the Bush administration included Vice President Dick Cheney, Paul Wolfowitz (former deputy secretary of defense), "Scooter" Libby (former chief of staff and national security adviser to Cheney), Douglas Feith (former undersecretary of defense for policy), and Elliott Abrams (assistant to the president and deputy national security adviser for global democracy strategy). The list of neocons outside the Bush administration included Richard Perle (former chairman of the National Defense Policy Board, a man also known as "the Prince of Darkness" for his hardline position on national security issues), Irvin Kristol (founding editor of the *National Interest and Public Interest*, and known as the "godfather" of the archconservative movement), his son William Kristol (chairman of the Project New American Century [PNAC] and editor of the archconservative *Weekly Standard*), and Robert Kagan (a cofounder of

PNAC and a columnist for the *Washington Post*).[24] Even though former secretary of defense Donald Rumsfeld was not a neocon, he was in complete agreement with the national security-related perspectives promoted by these neocons.

In the absence of a post-conflict plan, enormous chaos followed the toppling of the Iraqi government.[25] Then, the Coalition Provisional Authority (CPA; the official title of the US occupation forces), headed by L. Paul (Jerry) Bremer, made two major decisions – to dissolve the Iraqi Army and disband the Ba'ath Party (also known as "de-Ba'athification") – that inadvertently widened the insurgent movement in Iraq.

As the security situation worsened and the terrorist activities of the insurgents and global jihadist forces escalated, the international community of nations showed no interest in coming to America's rescue. Right after the US invasion of Iraq, thirty-eight countries formed a coalition, supplying 25,000 troops. The number of coalition partners dwindled to twenty-five countries and the troop size to 15,000. Moreover, most of the coalition forces were stationed in relatively peaceful southern Iraq and engaged "primarily in training, support, and [a] reconstruction mission." As casualties mounted and the war became increasingly unpopular, a number of coalition partners started pulling their troops from Iraq. Italy started the withdrawal of forces (3,000 troops) in 2005, followed by Washington's "staunchest partners," Ukraine and Bulgaria. Britain later followed suit by reducing its troops from 7,000 to 5,500.[26] Toward the end of 2006, Iraq had become a major quagmire for the United States. Both American and global media ceaselessly compared it with the Vietnam imbroglio, which had resulted in America's defeat in 1974. It appeared that the United States had overplayed its hand by invading Iraq, a miscalculation that turned into a boon for al-Qaida's practice of Islamism – especially the use of regional jihad to oust pro-US regimes and the declaration of global jihad to weaken the lone superpower. The assumption was that a potential weakening of the United States would significantly improve the chances of bringing about regime change through the use of regional jihad.

The United States was never meant to be an occupying power. It had very limited experience with colonialism. Yes, it had a long history of kicking up dust in Latin America, which it long regarded as its "backyard" – a policy that Latin Americans derided as "Yankee imperialism." It was a colonial power in the Philippines for a short time. However, America does not have a long legacy of being a colonial power à la Great Britain, the Netherlands, France, or other former colonial countries of Europe.

The United States became an occupying power in Vietnam for a brief period of time; however, it did so under the general rubric of fighting communism, which remained its chief fixation during the Cold War era. The "domino theory" became a guiding principle of America's secular religion – to save East Asia from the "yellow peril." But by the late 1960s, there was little support for that adventure among the American populace, especially among the young draftees who were fighting and dying in the rice fields of Vietnam. It soon became clear to the Americans that their country was nothing but a bully in Vietnam, attempting to deprive an agrarian, but proud, nation of its intense desire to unify, just because one part of it was communist. Interestingly enough, those opposing the American occupation of South Vietnam did not care about the fact that the entire episode was an integral part of America's mega-struggle with global communism, at least, that was how it was packaged by the US government. As the 1960s came to a close, a majority of the American people wanted their country to get out of Vietnam, even at the risk of experiencing embarrassing defeat.

For about fifteen years after its humiliating exit from South Vietnam, America stayed home. The "Vietnam Syndrome" became a major source of paranoia against foreign involvement. It would not send its troops to far-off places to occupy foreign lands again until the Middle Eastern brute, Saddam Hussein, invaded Kuwait in 1990. As previously mentioned, even in fighting the Gulf War of 1991, President George H.W. Bush took special care to end America's involvement after the international coalition succeeded in booting the Iraqi invaders out of Kuwait. It was the Vietnam imbroglio that forced America to define its military mission narrowly for the Kuwaiti operation and to get out of the theatre of war after its completion. Yes, some American forces remained behind in Saudi Arabia, but not as occupying forces – although Bin Laden claimed as much in his readiness to find an insult to Islam.

However, in the post–9/11 era, the United States was ready to occupy Muslim lands. It kept its troops in Afghanistan after it ousted the Taliban from power. This military action did not create serious problems, since it was generally regarded as a defensive move.

However, the US invasion of Iraq served as fuel for global jihad from the Islamist-point of view. Needless to say, that perspective received sympathetic ears in the Muslim world.

In the 1990s, only Afghanistan was the focal point of regional turbulence in the name of regional jihad. In the first decade of the twenty-first century, both Afghanistan and Iraq became gathering places of global jihad. Afghanistan remained a country where the forces of regional jihad were gathering strength and constantly confronting NATO's International Security Assistance Force (ISAF), which had taken charge of establishing security and conducting "nation building" operations. Before invading Iraq, President George W. Bush stated that, under Saddam Hussein, that country had become the focus of global terrorism. That statement was not true then. Ironically, it was only after the toppling of the Iraqi dictator that Bush's observation became a reality, and Iraq became a country where al-Qaida established a highly visible presence.

The secretive nature of the Iraqi insurgency made it difficult to determine its constituent groups. Still, the general understanding was that it comprised Iraqi Ba'athists, pan-Arabists, Islamists, and plain irate Iraqis. The insurgency drew its chief strength from the fact that, as previously noted, Jerry Bremer abolished the Iraqi Army and the Ba'ath Party with the stroke of a pen in May 2003. Thus, a considerable amount of military knowledge, especially about the use of improvised explosive devices (IEDs), was readily available to the insurgents.[27] There were also speculations that Saddam Hussein, as a backup plan, stored large quantities of small arms all over Iraq in case of a US invasion. According to such rumours, he intended to fight a real battle with the US troops in the streets and back alleys of Iraq. If that, indeed, was part of Saddam's plan, then he succeeded (even though he was captured in December 2003 by American forces) when the Iraqi insurgency – which also comprised an unknown but large number of self-styled global jihadists – became so powerful between 2005 and 2007 that there were serious recommendations inside the United States to withdraw US forces from Iraq.

The overall purpose of the insurgency was to bring about the expulsion of foreign occupiers from Iraq. Specifically, however, the Ba'athists and pan-Arabists were fighting for the creation of a nationalist government that would be very much in harmony with conventional pan-Arabist perspectives. The jihadists were resolutely fighting for the establishment of a caliphate that would glorify Islam.

Another reason why the insurgency became a major force was that it received strong political support from Sunni Iraqis who envisioned the dismantlement of Saddam's regime as a permanent loss of their political power. The overall pro-Shia posture of US officials in Iraq also gave every reason for the Sunnis to fight in order to regain at least their fair share of political power. The demographic realities of Iraqi politics in the immediate aftermath of the toppling of the Saddam regime forced the Americans to maintain a pro-Shia policy posture. Since the Shias comprised 65 percent of the Iraqi population, they knew that they would become the ruling group once democracy was introduced into their country. Thus, they had every reason to cooperate with the United States. In an ironic way, the Iraqi Shias and the American forces developed a symbiotic relationship, which further persuaded the Sunnis that the Americans did not have their best interests at heart.

The jihadist forces had the best opportunity to bring about the ouster of the US forces from Iraq between 2005 and 2007. That would have provided the kind of victory that those forces claimed after the ouster of the Soviet Union from Afghanistan in 1989. In fact, the *Iraq Study Group Report*, which was issued in December 2006, recommended the redeployment of US forces as part of its "way ahead" proposal.[28] However, the Sunni-led Sahwa (Awakening) movement came to its rescue. The genesis of that movement goes back to 2005 when a number of Sunni tribal leaders (sheikhs) of the al-Anbar province of western Iraq started promoting the fateful idea of forming alliances with the US occupation forces against al-Qaida. Its members were originally known as Concerned Local Citizens, but they later renamed themselves the Sons of Iraq. In 2006, these sheikhs publicly broke from al-Qaida and started cooperating with the US military for the explicit purpose of expelling that organization from al-Anbar, a task that "had eluded the U.S. forces for [the previous] four hard fought years."[29]

The decision of the leaders of the Sahwa movement to cooperate with the United States was based on their Machiavellian calculations regarding the stylistic differences between al-Qaida and the US forces and their reading of the prospect of a long-term al-Qaida versus US military presence inside Iraq. By 2006, al-Qaida-related violence appeared unbeatable, whereas the US presence in Iraq was increasingly perceived to be of short duration. Inside the United States, a heated debate was brewing about the withdrawal of American forces from Iraq. These two developments significantly influenced the strategic calculations of the leaders of al-Anbar. If al-Qaida were to remain as powerful an entity over the next few years as it was around 2006, it would replace the tribal sheikhs as managers of conflict and providers of economic security and social welfare inside al-Anbar and other Sunni-dominated areas. The US military, due to the battering that it was receiving at the hands of al-Qaida and other insurgents, decisively looked like an entity that would not stay in Iraq for long. In that capacity, it was no longer perceived as threatening to the political and social status of the tribal sheikhs. Thus it was not at all difficult for the sheikhs to conclude that a nexus, if not a full-fledged alliance, should be formulated with the US forces. Al-Qaida's brutal implementation of its own version of the Shariah laws in al-Anbar was another – probably the most – critical tipping point for the Sahwa movement's decision to cooperate with the United States.

The deployment of more troops as part of the surge strategy made it easier for the United States to cooperate with the Sahwa movement. It also made it easier to implement the COIN strategy of "clear, hold, and build," whereby the US military "cleared" a community from the control of al-Qaida and other insurgents and stayed ("hold") in that community long enough for the Iraqi law-enforcement authorities to "build" a peaceful community. The Sahwa movement and surge strategy resulted in a serious setback for the Islamists in Iraq.

Viewing this entire episode from the side of the jihadists, they made three major mistakes. First, the jihadist ideology alienated its chief basis of support – the Sunni tribal leaders – who knew how the Iraqi social system really worked and who could have contributed to the success of the jihadists had they only shown a willingness for compromise and power-sharing. However, that notion was totally alien to the jihadists. Second, they also alienated the Sunni populace by repeatedly announcing that they would establish an Islamic caliphate. The Iraqis, in general, hated the American occupiers and wanted to be rid of them. They may not have had a clear idea about the type of government they wanted for themselves; however, they did not want to live in a theological state of the type that al-Qaida promised to impose on them. The third mistake made by al-Qaida was the imposition of the Takfiri blueprint of passing judgment. Essentially, anyone who did not agree with the worldview expounded by the Takfiri doctrine was a *kafir* (infidel) and should be killed. Consequently, the stakes for the non-Takfiri populace were quite high, and people did not require much reflection about taking countermeasures. The Takfiris had to be destroyed before they could eradicate the non-Takfiris, who comprised the majority of the Sunni population of Iraq. It was this particular issue more than anything else that drove the Sahwa movement toward cooperation with the US military. If the Iraqis of al-Anbar and other Sunni provinces had had to determine how to rid themselves of al-Qaida, it would have taken them a long time to come up with a workable strategy. But a strategy of cooperating with the US occupier, who was not going to stay in Iraq for long, could be implemented in short order.

When United States finally withdrew all of its troops at the end of 2011, the future of Iraq looked bleak. The legendary sectarian divides between the Shias and the Sunnis, and the Arabs and the Kurds, were very much alive, and al-Qaida in Iraq appeared determined to take advantage of the absence of the American forces' deterring role by letting loose a campaign of mass murder of the Shias in an attempt to destabilize Iraq. Inside Iraq, there ensued a debate whether Prime Minister Nouri al-Maliki was overstepping his authority by going after the Sunni leaders under trumped up charges in order to assassinate them. Saudi Arabia and Iran were supporting Ayad Allawi (leader of the secularist al-Iraqiya party) and al-Maliki, respectively. One perspective was that such tensions were to be expected under a democratic Iraq. However, the other – and a disconcerting view – was that al-Maliki might be emulating Saddam Hussein's heavy-handed treatment of his perceived opponents by attempting to eliminate them, and that the Saudi-Iranian rivalry might seriously undermine the evolution of Iraq as a stable and democratic place.[30]

PROGNOSIS FOR THE TWENTY-FIRST CENTURY

The Arab Awakening that began in December 2010 created mixed results for the United States. The ouster of tyrants from Tunisia, Egypt, and Libya was expected to bring a democratic form of government to those countries. However, these democracies had a heavy Islamist tone about which the Obama administration felt guardedly optimistic at best and ambivalent at worst. This new breed of Islamists was unlike those who represented al-Qaida and its like-minded organizations; they were interested in dealing with the United States, but on their own terms. To Washington, what that meant was not quite apparent. However, the Obama administration did not expect the new governments in the post–Arab Awakening Middle East to show the same diffidence toward the United States as the autocratic regimes had done.

The United States resolved to deal with them differently. But the long-term nature of that "different" treatment was hard to imagine because the domestic environments in Egypt, Libya, and Tunisia were in a state of flux. The Obama administration demonstrated a marked flexibility by encouraging the swift departure of Hosni Mubarak from the presidency of Egypt. Then it sustained a policy of dealing with the Muslim Brotherhood as it emerged as the major Islamist party of the post-Mubarak era and captured the presidency in the first-ever democratic elections held in Egypt. Sadly, democracy only lasted for a little more than a year. The Egyptian Army ousted President Mohammad Morsi in a coup in July 2013 and incarcerated him, thereby bringing an end to democracy.

The reasons underlying the failure of the Muslim Brotherhood are many; however, the three most significant reasons are worth mentioning here. First, the Muslim Brotherhood failed to transition from an opposition party to a ruling one. As a ruling party, it was incumbent upon the leaders to spell out their "vision and program in plain language." They seemed to have failed miserably in that regard. Second, the perceived incompetence of the government of Mohammad Morsi to resolve Egypt's escalating economic problems, when added to its grab for power, made it an easy target of a large number of Egyptians who were highly suspicious of the ultimate objectives of the Brotherhood from the day it captured the presidency. Third, the Brotherhood was operating in a revolutionary environment when the "deep state" – that is, the former regime's "security agencies and their allies in the media and wider civil society" – was still very much intact. That deep state had huge vested economic interests that faced a highly uncertain future under a democratic Egypt. Thus, the army was eagerly waiting for an opening to oust the government headed by the Brotherhood, for which it had a powerful legacy of hatred and an equally long desire to destroy. The highly inept performance of the government, in confluence with its rising unpopularity, made the coup of July 2013 considerably easier.[31]

After the overthrow of the Morsi government, although the military junta spoke about the return of democracy, not many believed that it would be in a hurry to fulfill its promise of reviving it. The United States' strong ambivalence toward the establishment of a democratic government headed by an Islamist party became apparent when it decided not to call the military's ouster of an elected president a coup. If the Obama administration had declared the ouster of Morsi a coup, US laws would have instantly put an end to all economic and military assistance to Egypt, which was not in the interest of the United States. The Obama administration expressed mild displeasure with the Egyptian Army about its sabotage of democracy and issued lukewarm, periodic statements about the return of democracy. The chief reason underlying the US reluctance to take harsh action against the military dictators of Egypt was the fear of jeopardizing the long-standing Egypt-Israeli peace treaty (the Camp David Accords).

The transformation of post-Qaddafi Libya into a failed state did not surprise many observers. The Libyan dictator, during his long and brutal rule, did not allow that country to become a "normal" state with multiple centres of power or institutions, which are allowed even in other dictatorships. At the end of his regime, two rival governments eventually took control of different parts of the country. The eastern region is controlled by a secular alliance, the House of Representatives, based in Tobruk. This nationalist-leaning and internationally recognized parliament-based government has the backing of the Libyan National Army and that of Saudi Arabia, Egypt, and the UAE. The western region of Libya is controlled by the Tripoli-based General National Congress, a parliament-based government backed by hardline Islamist militias, Turkey, Qatar, and Sudan. As the rivalry among the aforementioned Middle Eastern states continues to undermine the chances for the emergence of a stable and peaceful state, "the poison in Libya" is "seeping out across a great swathe of the Sahel, Africa's scrublands south of the Sahara desert, from Mali in the west, through Niger and northern Nigeria, eastwards on to Sudan and Somalia, and even as far as Egypt's Sinai desert abutting Israel."[32] ISIS is increasing its presence in the central part of Libya and attacking the country's major oil terminals. Al-Qaida has had a longer presence in Libya, through its North African affiliate, AQIM. In the absence of a general reconciliation between the two rival governments, the two terrorist entities – ISIS and al-Qaida – are expected to do their utmost to ruin any chances of the emergence of a unified Libya.

Yemen, depicted as the newest failed state,[33] was also steadily edging toward a total collapse. The Saudi-backed civil war turned into a quagmire for that country, and the United States and a number of Western countries closed their embassies. The Obama administration was supplying intelligence and logistical support to Saudi Arabia, thereby raising criticism that it might be accused of committing "war crimes."[34] The US drone strikes against al-Qaida in the Arabian Peninsula (AQAP) succeeded in killing a few leaders; however, al-Qaida's presence and influence in Yemen were very much on the rise. Yemen, along with Syria, were countries where the Saudi-Iranian strategic rivalry continued to show its dreadful face and its attendant ferocious effects. Under these circumstances, ISIS and AQAP were very much poised to exploit the conflict to bring about "the collapse of government authority to gain new recruits and allies and expand their territorial control."[35] In other words, Islamism, as described in this book, was highly proactive in regions of the Middle East.

Thus, although the United States withdrew from Iraq in December 2011, the invasion of that country started the process of Islamism, and the devastating activities of the jihadist groups in the Middle East and North Africa have been on the rise.

CLOSING OBSERVATIONS

In the post–World War II era, the United States did not face much of a challenge in establishing its strategic dominance in the Middle East. Back in the 1950s, it demonstrated a highly discerning assessment of how important it was to establish good ties with the Arabs by supporting Nasser in the 1956 Suez crisis. Nasser did not turn out to be a friend of the United States; however, American recognition of the then emerging significance of Arab nations did not go unnoticed by the Arab monarchies. They sought the friendship of the United States during the Arab Cold War. But the most significant aspect of American maneuvering was its decision to become a staunch friend of Israel, while also keeping most of the Arab states in its camp. As a result, even though the Arab-Israeli conflict remained largely unresolved (except for the peace treaties between Egypt and Israel and between Jordan and Israel), the strategic dominance of the United States was not at all negatively affected.

The United States' primary role in negotiations leading to the Camp David Accords immensely added to its prestige. But the Bush administration's principal role in the 1991 Gulf War was even more noteworthy because it happened when the Soviet Union was about to implode. Through the 1991 Gulf War, the United States established, once and for all, that it would not tolerate any challenge to the political status quo of the Middle East.

The United States' invasion of Iraq was another momentous development for a variety of reasons. First, it provided a unique opportunity for the jihadist groups to confront the lone superpower and possibly to bring about its ouster. Second, the violent activities of the Islamists and other nationalistic Iraqi forces against the US troops convinced the United States that, despite its awesome military power, it was not going to occupy any Muslim countries. Third, the Sahwa movement of the Iraqi Sunnis came to the rescue of the US military, which the latter deftly exploited to stabilize Iraq and to considerably weaken the AQI. Fourth, although it happened after the United States' redeployment of its military forces, it was in Iraq that the nearly moribund AQI not only revived itself – thanks to the highly myopic and intensely bigoted policies of Nouri al-Maliki – but also became powerful enough to defeat the predominantly Shia army of Iraq in Mosul and to declare an Islamic caliphate in the swathe of territory that it captured in Syria and Iraq. Fifth, that declaration was the beginning of the success of Islamism as defined in this book – that is, the capture of territory for a particular motive and based on a particular ideological understanding of Islam. ISIS fully exploited the chaos related to the depredations of the civil war in Syria in its attempt to manage its rudimentary caliphate. The most troubling aspect of ISIS for the United States was its growing popularity among the Muslim youth of the Middle East, North Africa, South Asia, and East Asia, as well as in some European countries and North America. ISIS's deft use of social media made its hateful propaganda campaign against the United States, the West, and Muslim governments in general appear unstoppable.

The Arab Awakening did not fulfill its original promise of bringing an end to autocratic rule in the Middle East. The great hopes of turning Egypt into a democracy were dashed when the first democratically elected president of the Muslim Brotherhood Party, Mohammad Morsi, was ousted by the military, and the military junta returned to power in that country with a vengeance. The Arab Awakening also played a crucial role in turning Syria into a hellish place, where forces backed by the United States, Russia, Iran, Saudi Arabia, and the UAE were busy playing an intricate power game to determine the shape of government of that country. Libya and Yemen became two other states where the Arab Awakening–related regime change brought nothing but chaos, bloodshed, mayhem, and instability. And AQAP and ISIS fully manipulated these atrocious conditions to promote their own versions of Islamism.

The Saudi-Iranian animosity emerged as another explosive force in Syria and Yemen. Since this antagonism was based on religious differences (Sunni versus Shia), ethnic differences (Arab versus Persian), and, above all, strategic competition for dominance in the Middle East, chances were remote that its destructive spillover effects were going to dissipate from that region in the near future.

In the highly unstable and violent Arab world, Tunisia looked like a glimmer of hope because it survived as a secular democracy, as a result of the remarkable willingness of the Islamist, democratic, and secular groups to continue cooperating in the formulation of a government. However, Tunisia's proximity to Libya and Egypt, where AQIM and ISIS were escalating their presence and influence, continued to pose a threat to the fledgling democracy.

Iran's aspirations to emerge as a new hegemon in the Middle East remained very much in conflict with the United States' own resolve to sustain its hegemonic grip over the heavily transformation-oriented environment of the post–Arab Awakening Middle East. Still, there are signs of cooperation between the two countries in their mutual interests to weaken and destroy ISIS in Iraq, and in their willingness to negotiate a political resolution to the Syrian conflict.

The United States' role in the Middle East has gone through radical changes from the post–World War II era to the post–Arab Awakening era. As a stark contrast from President George W. Bush's military invasion of Iraq, under President Barack Obama the lone superpower has become overly cautious about plunging its forces into the Syrian, Libyan, or Yemeni conflicts. Instead, it relies on drone warfare and on its powerful air force to change the dynamics of the wars in those countries in favour of its preferred forces. In Libya, it succeeded in bringing about regime change. However, the retrogression of post-Qaddafi Libya into a failed state made President Obama overly reluctant to use military force to bring about regime change in Syria, long before Russia entered that conflict in support of the Assad regime. Russia's use of air power in an all-out endeavour to destroy the anti-Assad Islamists (whom the United States, Saudi Arabia, and the UAE supported) decisively diminished their fighting capabilities. President Obama's overly guarded approach in the Syrian conflict may have provided Russia the opportunity it had been seeking since 1973 (when it was ousted from Egypt by President Anwar Sadat right before the Arab-Israeli War) to reenter the power game in the region. Until the United States makes a *volte-face* and starts supporting anti-Assad Islamists by making massive military supplies available, the protraction of the Syrian civil war not only promises to keep Assad in power for a long time, but also heightens the chances of that country's regression into another failed state.

As the nature of the conflict and volatile instability worsens in the Middle East, there is little hope that President Obama's successor will be audacious enough to enter into any conflict in the region that requires the stationing of American ground forces. It is possible that the United States will continue to use its Special Forces in future conflicts; however, like America's reliance on drone war and air power to affect conflicts in Yemen, Syria, Iraq, and various countries of Africa, these types of conflict management tools are likely to remain highly ineffective. The general expectations in the United States and the West that Muslim and/or Arab countries will take the lead in these conflicts and engage their own ground forces, especially in the conflict against ISIS in any Muslim state, are merely wishful thinking.

5

Pakistan and Afghanistan: Battlegrounds for the Jihadi Long War

SYNOPSIS

This chapter continues to pursue the role of Islamism that was initiated in the preceding one. The US-sponsored jihad against the Soviet Union brought about the ouster of that superpower from Afghanistan in 1989. It also created a powerful zeal among the "Afghan Arabs" (the Arab jihadist participants in that war), as well as other self-styled jihadist groups, to wage jihads in their respective countries later on. Ironically, it was the pursuit of global Islamism that motivated al-Qaida to launch the 11 September 2001 attacks on the United States. The thesis here is that Pakistan's role in the US-sponsored jihad in Afghanistan, along with the systematic campaigns of civilian and military rulers (Zulfiqar Ali Bhutto and General Zia-ul-Haq) to Islamize Pakistan, made powerful contributions to the emergence of that country as a highly volatile state. The legacy of the US-sponsored jihad in Afghanistan and the Islamization of Pakistan continue to traumatize both countries, where the jihadists have emerged as the chief threat to governmental stability. This chapter presents a detailed analysis of why the jihadists and Islamism – and the resolve of those groups to capture power through the acquisition of territory – remain serious challenges in Pakistan and Afghanistan in the post–9/11 era.

This chapter contains a historical overview of Islamization in Pakistan and examines how the Islamized Pakistan played a critical role in serving as a conduit for American-sponsored "jihad" against the Soviet Union in the 1980s. The historical analysis should provide readers with a better understanding of why these two states continue to pose serious challenges to the United States. As mentioned previously, Islamization is an umbrella phrase that describes a multifaceted process whereby the state started a campaign of identifying itself with "true" Islam, which was a euphemism for Islamic orthodoxy promoted by Saudi Arabia. Second, Islamization created an environment where religiosity, as well as religious extremism, became the driving force in the political discourse, educational curricula, and the entire functioning of the government and its major institutions. Third, the sectarian differences between the Sunnis and the Shias were encouraged in Pakistan, some say purposely promoted. Fourth, a policy of excluding non-Muslims from top government jobs was instituted. Finally, the worst aspect of Islamization was that it became a fig leaf for the military regime of Zia-ul-Haq to entrench its rule under the pretext of promoting religious orthodoxy.

After the ouster of the Soviet Union from Afghanistan, the United States lost interest in shaping the power structure and governance in Afghanistan. However, Pakistan continued to affect the power play between several warring groups inside Afghanistan and was primarily responsible for bringing the Taliban to power in September 1996. Pakistan's madrassas (religious schools) played a prominent role in educating the Taliban in the Wahhabi version of Islam, which assigned primacy to the role of jihad. Pakistan's Islamization also radically altered domestic politics, with the participation of Islamist parties making the politics highly volatile.

The military of Pakistan also remained a dominant player through their sabotage of democracy and declaration of martial law in 1958, 1971, 1977–88, and 1999–2008. An Islamized Pakistan continued to envision Afghanistan as a source of "strategic depth" in its highly explosive and enduring strategic rivalry with India. In its pursuit of strategic depth, Pakistan was not going to allow the government in Kabul to become a friend of India, a relationship that Islamabad depicted as "anti-Pakistan" in nature. This Pakistani policy has also been behind its powerful security states' differentiation between "good terrorists" and "bad terrorists." Good terrorists were those groups who were used or given permission to conduct frequent terrorist attacks on the Indian-administered Kashmir and on the Afghan government. They were left alone when Pakistan launched its antiterror operation, Zarb-e-Azb, against the bad terrorists. The latter group included those terrorists who attacked Pakistani citizens and government assets. This Pakistani policy, and the fact that Osama Bin

Laden was eventually discovered hiding in that country, caused mounting frictions between Islamabad and Washington. In this sense, the jihadists of Pakistan and Afghanistan continue to challenge the United States.

PAKISTAN

The story of Pakistan is a story of a noble idea gone wrong. It was a country created for Muslims of the Indian subcontinent. As such, it could accommodate only about 12–15 per cent of the Muslims of prepartitioned India in the western and eastern extremes, known as West and East Pakistan. As the religion of the majority of the people, Islam was expected to play a crucial role in Pakistan's politics. After Pakistan's creation, Islamist parties promoted the proposition that, as an Islamic state, Pakistan should conduct its public affairs strictly according to Islam and accept the sovereignty of Allah's laws. Islamists actively sought to establish the Shariah (Muslim religious law) as the basis for criminal and civil laws. Even the Muslim League, the party that played a crucial role in the creation of Pakistan, got into the act of Islamizing the state. That was viewed as a way of creating a niche and a new identity for Pakistan, an identity that would also serve as a link with the larger world of Islam. However, as much as the Muslim League used the phrase "Islamic state," its leaders had no concept of what that meant in a contemporary context. There were too many exceedingly intricate issues to be resolved for Pakistan to undergo a process of Islamization.

First and foremost was the issue of sovereignty, which, according to the Islamist interpretation, belongs to God. At least initially, the Constitution Assembly Resolution of 1949 attempted to resolve that issue by declaring that sovereignty does belong to God, but that it has been delegated to the state to be "exercised within the limits prescribed by Him as a sacred trust."[1] However, the politicians only passed this resolution to stave off strong criticism from the Islamist parties that the government was not serious about Islamizing Pakistan. The governments's intentions became evident when the country's first prime minster, Liaquat Ali Khan, stated that Pakistan would not become a theocracy. The Islamists were not happy to be informed of that position, but they were appeased by other declarations that a non-Muslim could not become a president or prime minister.

Pakistan had its first experience of military intervention in politics in 1958 when General Ayub Khan ousted the civilian government and declared martial law. General Ayub's overall perception of the Islamist parties was quite negative. He abrogated the constitution of 1956, which the Islamists, particularly the Jamaat-e-Islami party, had hailed as a victory in their endeavours to Islamize Pakistan. He also brought to the fore modernist Islamic scholars, such as Fazlur Rahman and Khalifa Abdul Hakim, in discussing the role of Islam in Pakistan politics, a development that other religious scholars viewed as a major setback in their efforts to make Islam centre stage.

In response, Jamaat-e-Islami's proactivism escalated during the rule of General Ayub. The leader of the party, Maulana Abul A'la Maududi, was a domineering religio-political figure whose sustained opposition to Ayub's secular perspectives captured national attention. Maududi insisted on an Islamic constitution and Shariah law as the basis of governance in Pakistan. The party strongly opposed the constitution of 1962, a document that General Ayub promoted, because, *inter alia*, the title did not include the word "Islamic" (which was part of the title of the 1958 constitution). Ayub was forced to yield to the Islamists' demands and add "Islamic" to the constitution. Jamaat went so far as to present a unified front with secularist parties in its opposition to Ayub Khan. Accusing the Jamaat of fomenting political instability, Ayub banned the party in 1964 as an unlawful organization. He even arrested Ayub in 1964 and again in 1967; however, the party continued its operations.

As much as the Jamaat-e-Islami party couched its fight with the Ayub regime in the context of Islam, General Ayub was equally adamant in questioning the genuineness of Maududi's intentions. In his memoir, *Friends, Not Masters*, Ayub depicted Maududi's criticism of him and his regime as a facade: "The true intention was to re-establish the supremacy of the *ulema* [religious scholars] and to reassert their right to lead the community [of Muslims]."[2] He continued to keep the religious clerics out of the power game and even proposed to revise the curricula of the madrassas to include modern education. The religious parties opposed Ayub's proposed curricular reforms but "lacked the domestic support to successfully confront him."[3]

The post-Ayub elections of 1970 witnessed an impressive return of democracy in Pakistan. Two secular parties – Zulfiqar Ali Bhutto's Pakistan Peoples Party (PPP) in the then West Pakistan and Sheikh

Mujibur Rahman's Awami League in East Pakistan – scored sweeping victories in those regions. Islamist parties performed poorly. Jamaat-e-Islami won four seats, Jamiat-e-Ulema-e-Islam (JUI) won seven seats, and Jamiat-e-Ulema-e-Pakistan (JUP) won seven seats.[4] If one was looking for evidence that the Islamist parties and their perspectives on Islamization were popular in Pakistan, one would have been sorely disappointed. That election was, indeed, a clarion call for the popularity of secular democracy and Islamic moderation. The overwhelming victory of the Awami League in East Pakistan and the Pakistan Peoples Party in West Pakistan underscored the fact that "ethnicity, not Islam, was emerging as a unifying force within each wing."[5]

That was undeniably true. The long history of ethnic chauvinism of the Punjabis, and systematic discrimination against the Bengalis of East Pakistan had played a crucial role, not only in rejecting the "six-point formula" aimed at making East Pakistan an autonomous region, but also in sustaining the hegemony of West Pakistan over the East. The Islamist parties did not comprehend the intensity of the feelings of oppression in the East and its determination to become autonomous (if not free) of West Pakistan's dominance and all the inequities that accompanied it. For the Islamist parties, the unifying power of Islam was sufficient to keep the nation from splitting into two countries. However, when Pakistan broke up as a result of the Indian military invasion of East Pakistan in 1971, it became clear that "Islam could no longer be a bond between the two parts of Pakistan."[6]

Bhutto's Expedient Islamic Agenda

In the post-Bangladesh Pakistan, Islam was to emerge a stronger force in the arena of domestic politics than it had been at any previous point. When Zulfiqar Ali Bhutto emerged as a major political leader, his personal vision of where he wanted to take the country and his political perspectives clashed with the Islamist parties. Bhutto – like most Third World leaders of that era – was a devout socialist. He envisaged socialism, if not as a panacea for the social and economic ills of Pakistan, then undeniably as a major tool in the struggle to remedy those maladies. His socialist views, which were expressed in his attempt to nationalize private enterprise, alienated the private sector as well as the Islamists.

In the 1970s, the Islamist parties not only collided with Bhutto's vision of socialism, they also rejected the rising parochialism of proponents of the Sindhudesh movement – the demand of the Sindhis for an autonomous state along the same lines as had been enunciated in the so-called six-point formula of the East Pakistani leader, Sheikh Mujibur Rahman. As he was attempting to widen his power base, Bhutto had to decide which group he should take on directly, which group to co-opt, when to compromise, and how far he should go in offering any compromise. He was a strong opponent of Sindhi nationalism, which he saw as an obstacle in the way of his emergence as a national leader. However, since he himself was a Sindhi, he had no reason to be threatened by it. Besides, Sindhi nationalism could easily be neutralized by the more powerful Punjabi front and by the rising levels of politicization on the part of the Muhajir (Muslim migrants from India) community. That left Bhutto with the conundrum of how to deal with the Islamist parties.

The Islamists were pressing Bhutto to make the term "Islamic" in the constitution a reality in Pakistan by rejecting socialism (viewed as anti-Islamic), declaring the Ahmadiyas[7] as unbelievers (*kafir*), and introducing the teaching of the Qur'an and Arabic language in schools. As a highly astute politician, Bhutto knew that his political power was fragile, and he did not want to be seen by the Islamists as an obstacle. Therefore, he conducted a series of *coups de grâce* that anticipated and fulfilled Islamist demands. The 1973 constitution specifically declared Islam the state religion. A record number of Muslims were allowed to travel to Saudi Arabia to perform Hajj. The Arabic language and the Qur'an were introduced in schools. Ahmadiyas were declared *kafir*. Ironically, by implementing these measures, Bhutto, a person who was not even a devout Muslim, started a process of Islamization that would make Pakistan an explosive place in later years. Why did he do that?

To start, as a secular politician who took the helm of a religious country in a time of even more religious turbulence, Bhutto felt that he had no choice but to push his own Islamic agenda to convince the Islamists of his commitment to the Islamization of Pakistan. He wanted to have the Islamists on his side. At the same time, he used his support of the Islamist agenda as a safeguard against the political ambitions of the powerful and highly politicized army. He was fully aware of the evolving nexus between the Jamaat-e-Islami and the post-Ayub army on the issue of keeping Pakistan a unified country, and was looking for ways to weaken this link for his own advantage. Hence his strategy of staying a few steps ahead of the Islamists in incorporating major features of their agenda. But he did it through flip-flops.

For instance, Bhutto first talked about "scientific socialism." Regarding that concept, he said, "We have to tackle basic anomalies and no basic anomaly can be tackled without the application of the principles of scientific socialism."[8] Later on, he adopted something called "Islamic socialism," creating slogans like *roti kapda aur makan* (bread, clothing, and shelter) and *zamin kashtkaron ko* (land to the tiller). He emphasized the notions of *Islami Musawat* (Islamic egalitarianism) and *Musawat-e-Muhammadi* (Prophet Muhammad's egalitarianism). But the concept of Islamic socialism had little support in either the Islamic or the secular sectors of Pakistan. For the Islamists, the term socialism was a red flag. They regarded Bhutto's new-found devotion to Islam as a mere ploy to win elections. Similarly, the secularists groups were skeptical of a politician who was attempting to appease the Islamists by combining two mutually exclusive – at least in their opinion – issues: socialism and Islam.

The Islamist political agenda inside Pakistan was given a boost when Saudi Arabia decided to use Maududi and his Jamaat party as the conduit for financial support to promote the Wahhabi creed, an ideology very much in harmony with that of the Jamaat and other Ahle Hadith Salafist parties.[9] Bhutto responded with a rhetorical and symbolic emphasis on Islam in his public pronouncements and foreign policy. For example, he hosted the meeting of the Organization of Islamic Congress in Lahore in 1974, depicted Pakistan's fledgling nuclear program as aimed at developing an "Islamic bomb," and sought the financial backing for it from Libya's strongman, Muammar Qaddafi. Bhutto's hosting of the OIC might have been the harbinger of that organization's opposition to the government of Afghanistan, where the communist party was emerging as a visible, if not a major, player in the mid-to-late 1970s. Bhutto was quite wary of a potential coup, a nightmare that became reality with the communist coup of 1978 and the Soviet invasion of 1979. What is most important to note is that Pakistan's current obsession with "strategic depth" goes back to the days of Bhutto.

In his expedient Islamization of Pakistan, Bhutto "began turning Pakistan's back on South Asia" and looking "to the Middle East for aid, ideology, and strategic cooperation." This ominous transformation of Pakistan into a "non-Indian identity" meant that it "ceased to learn from the one state that it most resembled."[10] Whereas India emerged in the late 1990s as a prototype for economic development, Pakistan was headed toward the precipice of disaster.

What was emerging in Pakistan in the 1970s was a shortsighted, but systematic, endeavour to push that country toward Islam, for reasons driven by both politics and religion. Bhutto was a political animal, and his primary motivation was political survival. His aspirations to emerge as a strong leader clashed with even more powerful ambitions by the army to remain the most dominant actor in Pakistan. There was to be no rapprochement between the two, because rapprochement meant that one had to accept a secondary and subservient role. Bhutto had the Indian model of civilian supremacy over the armed forces in mind. He wanted to implement that model. However, he was aware that he was not going to win through political maneuvering alone. Hence Islam became a handy tool to promote his political ambitions – a mistake for three reasons.

First, portraying himself as a promoter of an Islamist agenda was not going to establish his credibility in a country where he was perceived as a shrewd secularist and opportunist. The hypocritical nature of the Islamic component of his ideology and his expediency on the issue were transparently obvious to the Islamists, who even denounced his personal and professional lifestyle as inherently anti-Islamic.[11] Given his luxurious lifestyle, Bhutto's socialist agenda appeared equally duplicitous and merely a ruse for maintaining power. Second, once he started promoting Islamization, he started down a path of no return. As Pakistan was increasingly becoming a chaotic place, no rational long-term plan regarding its future promised any type of peace and tranquility for its leaders. Third, if there was a linkage between Islamization and persuading the army to accept civilian supremacy, the army could not have accepted it, for it feared the evil genius of Bhutto. The army brass understood the deadly nature of the power game in which the winner would not remain kind to the loser.[12] And the army certainly did not wish to be on the losing side. General Zia-ul-Haq could not hide his true feelings when the news of Bhutto's hanging reached him: "The bastard's dead," he was reported to have "gleefully" told his fellow generals.[13]

The election of 1977 was significant because Islam emerged as a major force. A powerful coalition of religious and secular parties came together under the banner of the Pakistan National Alliance

(PNA) in an attempt to defeat Bhutto's PPP. The Islamic parties – such as the Jamaat-e-Islami (JI), the JUP, and the JUI – united under the leadership of Maududi. The PNA freely used such alarmist slogans as "Islam in danger" and campaigned for the promulgation of *Nizam-e-Mustapha* (system of the Prophet).

Despite the heavy use of Islamist rhetoric by the PNA, Bhutto's PPP scored an impressive victory in the 1977 elections. However, the losing side charged that the election was marred by fraud and irregularities. Consequently, it adopted the tactics of boycotting provisional elections and inciting general agitation. Employing the long-standing tactic of the Islamists of the Middle East to use sermons before the Friday prayer for political ends, the PNA vented its anger toward Bhutto, leading to a military coup launched by General Zia-ul-Haq in July 1977.

From the regimes of Ayub Khan to Zia-ul-Haq, the Army's attitude toward the Islamists went through a radical transformation from being suspicious or even contemptuous to establishing a powerful nexus, indeed, an alliance with Islamist parties, under Zia. Before the 1970s, the Pak Army, like the Indian Army, was immersed in the secular tradition of the British Army. The officer corps came largely from the upper classes, and most of them were educated in the UK or in Anglo-Indian (prepartitioned India) schools. From the 1970s onward, however, the officer corps came from the middle class and rural regions of the Punjab province, where they had been heavily inducted in religious education. The army's cooperation with Jamaat-e-Islami began in 1971, when the army and the Islamists presided over the brutal suppression of fellow citizens in East Pakistan during its struggle to break away from West Pakistan. Maududi rejected the significance of nationalism, convinced that no identity other than Islam could unite the disparate ethnic groups of Pakistan. Given the nature of the nexus between the army and Islamist parties, Bhutto's own use of the Islamic card could not give him much advantage over the army. By contrast, the army was highly receptive to the Islamization that was systematically introduced in the Command and Staff College by the government of General Zia.[14]

The regime of General Zia established a tradition whereby the Islamist parties were very much a part of the power structure. In contrast with the competition between the Islamist parties and Bhutto, under Zia the Islamists became instruments, even partners, of the dictator. As such, they promoted the same agenda – Islamization of the constitution and the entire political culture – for different political ends. The Islamist parties continued to be highly disruptive actors in the first two decades of the twenty-first century. Although they do not win significant numbers of popular votes, they manage to mar election campaigns with highly contentious rhetoric and sectarian-driven violence.

Zia's Islamization Measures

Martial law of 1977, which brought to power General Zia-ul-Haq, was also the beginning of an era of massive Islamization of Pakistan. That phenomenon was singly responsible Pakistan's emergence as a place of Islamic extremism. The policy of Islamization meant that the Shariah had to become basic law; however, as much as Pakistan was a place for Muslims, the majority of citizens were not ready to live under the Shariah. Any attempt to impose the Shariah laws was highly contentious and divisive because of the possibility that, once implemented, those laws would be interpreted to align with either the strict or liberal (in all likelihood, strict) position of the reigning government. Islamization could be carried out only by a massive revision of school curricula and by altering the objectives of educational institutions – a process fraught with risk. If the Islamization of curricula had to be carried out, it had to be done without jeopardizing modern educational objectives. But the Islamists were no experts in educational reform, and the educational experts could not have acted professionally without being labelled as "anti-Islamic" by their critics, especially if they (the experts) opted for a larger portion of modern education over Islamic education. These were only some of the issues that needed serious consideration and thorough debate – requirements that were fast disappearing from the Pakistan of the 1970s and 1980s.

One of the foremost stated objectives of Zia's martial law was promulgation of the *Nizam-e-Mustapha* (system of the Prophet of Islam), a chief promise of the PNA. That objective intensified the sectarian differences between the predominant Sunni majority and the Shia minority, since the religious order that Zia was trying to impose was based purely on Sunni Islam. However, during the days of General Zia, no attention was paid to that reality either. To implement the *Nizam-e-Mustapha*, he established a seventeen-member Islamic Ideology Council. Six members were *ulama* (religious scholars), four were Sunni, two were Shia, and the rest were also known for their commitment to Islam. The council was to recommend the best way to establish an Islamic system, focusing on the Islamic penal code, the *ushr* (trade tax), and the *zakat* (almsgiving). Until the recommendations of the council were formalized, Pakistan was to be ruled by martial law, which meant under Zia's sole rule. In the meantime, Zia continued his practice of issuing ordinances whose aim was to push Pakistan toward the observance of strict Islamic laws, for example, *hudud* punishments (forty stripes, two lashes) for drinking, and amputation of the hand for theft. In December 1978 he outlined measures to enforce *Nizam-E-Mustapha*, and in February 1979 he formalized his regime's commitment to that system. In his dedication to Islamization, Zia could not hide his contempt and utter disregard for democracy. He postponed elections twice – in 1977 and 1979 – expressing doubts about whether the political system of Pakistan was Islamic.[15]

Zia knew something about the socialization process – about acculturation and developing a new outlook and worldview, especially among children and youth. He knew that if his Islamization were to have a long-lasting (if not an everlasting) effect on Pakistan, his regime had to implement a systematic campaign of socialization in order to develop "a new generation wedded to the ideology of Pakistan and Islamism." The implementation of *Nizam-E-Mustapha* included the following measures:

- strengthening Pakistan's sense of Islamic identity as a nation through a series of symbolic and substantive measures
- changing the national dress to shalwar and khameez
- emphasizing Islam and links with the Arab Middle East and Arabic education
- renaming districts and universities – Lyallpur became Faisalabad, Islamabad University was renamed Quaid-e-Azam University, and the Open University became the Allama Iqbal Open University
- developing an "Islamic outlook" through a systematic use of the Islamic Ideology Council and the Shariah courts
- making Urdu the language of mass communication media
- censoring movies in order to eliminate "un-Islamic" activities
- requiring university students to take a course in *Islamiyat* (Islamic) studies
- revising textbooks to remove "un-Islamic" materials and to promote Islamic-Pakistani values[16]

It is possible that Zia did not see much difference between his commitment to Islam and the fact that his Islamization plans would also enhance his personal rule over Pakistan. Since Bhutto had used Islamization to safeguard his governing authority, a precedent had been set even before Zia took over the helm of the government. The chief lesson that he learned from Bhutto's version of Islamization was to ensure that the Islamist parties stayed in his corner. Bhutto's affinity for socialism and his Western education and lifestyle made him suspect among Islamists, whereas Zia's religiosity worked in his favour. He was personally a pious Muslim. He was therefore capable of implementing an all-encompassing program of Islamization. At the same time, it was quite apparent that Zia was postponing the chances of democracy for as long as possible, while cementing his personal control over Pakistan. Thus, Islamization emerged as a tool for strengthening Zia-ul-Haq's personal rule.

The Islamization of the army – even though it was done through a series of modest steps – could have become problematic, in that Islamization could negatively affect the army's professionalism. As much as Islam is a religion, the process of Islamization is the promotion of an ideology as well. What kind of system could best judge the capability of military personnel as well as their commitment to Islam? Which trait of military professionals was going to be judged superior in an Islamized polity – religiosity or professionalism? There was little doubt that the Islamization process was going to affect (most probably negatively) both the professional training and the personal outlook of military personnel. But Zia did not see it in that light. He made an interesting observation on this issue when, in an interview with Steven Cohen, he was asked, "How can Pakistanis be turned into good Muslims?" Cohen explained that Zia, privately admiring Israel as "an example of the power of faith to enhance professional competence ... firmly believed that one could be a secular scientist, soldier, or a scholar, but that a man who was truly religious would be a better professional."[17] As sincere as Zia might have been in raising the professional standards of the army by intermingling the power of faith, that earnestness was entirely lacking in the way he used the Islamist parties to postpone and sabotage all chances of the emergence of democracy in his country.

Zia relied heavily on religious schools (madrassas) to promote an extremist version of Islam. The madrassas have a powerful legacy in the Indian subcontinent.[18] In prepartitioned India, Muslim religious schools belonged to two general categories: the Farangi Mahal

School of Lucknow, and the Deobandi School. The Farangi Mahal School's curriculum, known as *Dars-e-Nizami*, was the first formal Islamic curriculum. It included courses in modern sciences and was aimed at educating students to gain employment in legal and administrative professions. It did not teach militancy or jihad. The Deobandi madrassas of India played a crucial role in formalizing Islamic education by institutionalizing the Farangi Mahal School's *Dars-e-Nizami*, except that the Deobandi version excluded the nonreligious portions of the original curriculum and emphasized purification of the belief system and rejection of Western imperialism. Still, there was no emphasis on militancy or jihad. Two characteristics of the nineteenth-century Deobandi schools played a critical role in the Islamization of Pakistan in the twentieth century. The first was a "paradoxical pattern of resistance to state authority and modernity, coupled with a selective use of new subjects, techniques and technology."[19] The second was its puritanical anti-Shia views. These two traits were readily transferred to the Deobandi schools of Pakistan, which unlike the Indian Deobandi schools, became jihadi factories and convenient instruments of Zia's Islamization process. The militancy of the madrassas reached a peak with the active nurturing of the Zia regime, which recruited Pakistani volunteers to wage jihad against the Soviet Union.

An integral aspect of Islamization was sectarianism, which has created a permanent schism in Pakistan. Sectarianism is a kind of religious racism. It was alien to South Asia, where Sunni-Shia differences had existed for centuries without erupting in major conflicts. What sectarianism did was to push that divide to an extreme, at which point the Sunnis questioned even the commitment of Shias to Islam. In its extreme manifestation, Pakistan's sectarianism does not recognize the Shias as Muslims.

Under Zia, the central government was of the view "that expansion of the role of *madrasahs* in national education would entrench Sunni identity in the public arena, just as *madrasah* graduates would help establish the place of Sunni identity in various government institutions." These students were also expected to "contain Shi'i activism. The Zia regime thus helped entrench Sunni Islam in Pakistan in order to contend with the political and geostrategic threat of Shia Islamism."[20] These madrassas served as a "Sunni wall" shielding Pakistan from Iran. Furthermore, the provincial governments – most prominently the governments of Punjab and the North-West Frontier

Province (NWFP) – helped Pakistan's intelligence agency, the Inter-Services Intelligence (ISI), organize militant Sunni groups in their respective provinces to contend with the "Shia problem."[21] The madrassas also provided training for violent Islamist groups such as the Harakat-ul-Ansar (HUA), which came into existence when Harakat-ul-Jihad al-Islami (HUJI) and Harakat-ul-Mujahedeen (HUM) merged. HUM and the Sipah-e-Sahaba Pakistan (SSP) are intensely anti-Shia terrorist groups. Both of them were heavily involved in violent attacks that terrorized Indian-administered Kashmir. Members of these organizations, and myriad similar ones, have played a crucial role in creating a "Kalashnikov culture" in Pakistan, where religious extremism is pervasive, where sectarian hatred runs rampant, and where small-arms proliferation has transformed the country into an armed camp.

The domestic aspect of Islamization would have been of limited scope, however, had it not been for the timing and nature of US involvement in Pakistan toward the end of the 1970s. The Soviet invasion of Afghanistan revived Pakistan's fear – which went as far back as the days of the British Empire – that the communist superpower was looking to fulfil its long-cherished designs of southward expansion, which included occupation of Afghanistan and Pakistan. That Soviet action also intensified America's resolve to roll back the Soviet presence from Afghanistan, largely because the communist superpower was getting too close to America's regions of hegemony.

The First Jihadi Nexus: Islamabad-Riyadh-Washington

The Islamization program of General Zia-ul-Haq, the Islamic revolution of Iran, and the US decision to use the doctrine of militant jihad to wage war against the Soviet Union's occupation of Afghanistan proved to be events of great historical coincidence.

From Zia's viewpoint, the Soviet invasion of Afghanistan could not have come at a better time. After hanging the elected prime minister (Bhutto), despite an international plea to pardon him, he was feeling isolated. By couching support for the Afghan mujahedeen's freedom struggle within the framework of jihad, Zia expected to win support (and resultant popularity) from Middle Eastern countries as well as from the West. Ironically, he was continuing Bhutto's policy of purposely establishing an ideological linkage with the Middle East. Zia's director general of the ISI, General Akhtar Abdur Rahman

Khan, who was also his confidant and close personal friend, advised him to conduct covert guerrilla warfare against the Soviet Union by supplying the Afghan "guerrillas with arms, ammunitions, money, intelligence, training, and operational advice." Zia was persuaded of the soundness of General Akhtar's military proposition with the only caveat being that the Soviets not be "goaded into a direct confrontation."[22]

From the vantage point of the United States, the traditional perspectives of jihad – fighting the enemies of Islam – were very much congruent with its strategic objectives of defeating the Soviet Union. As stated in previous chapters, President Ronald Reagan's administration fully exploited the doctrine of jihad to bring about a humiliating withdrawal of the Soviet Union. The Americans were driven by the secular notions of *realpolitik* and the balance of power. The communist superpower had to be punished for its role in America's defeat and ignominious withdrawal from South Vietnam in the previous decade.

According to the Reagan perspective, generally labelled the "Reagan Doctrine," the only way to defeat the Soviet Union was to confront its aggressive policies in different regions of the world, thereby forcing it to invest massively in military competition. This strategy was documented on the US Department of State's official website:

> Breaking with the doctrine of "Containment," established during the Truman administration – President Ronald Reagan's foreign policy was based on John Foster Dulles' "Roll-Back" strategy from the 1950s in which the United States would actively push back the influence of the Soviet Union. Reagan's policy differed, however, in the sense that he relied primarily on the overt support of those fighting Soviet dominance. This strategy was perhaps best encapsulated in NSC National Security Decision Directive 75. This 1983 directive stated that a central priority of the U.S. in its policy toward the Soviet Union would be "to contain and over time reverse Soviet expansionism," particularly in the developing world.[23]

To effectively implement this strategy, the United States used Pakistan as the chief conduit for political, financial, and military support of the mujahedeen fighters and Saudi Arabia as one of its chief allies. The main implementer of the modalities of America's involvement in Afghanistan was William Casey, director of the US Central Intelligence Agency (CIA). He was a quintessential hardliner and a Cold Warrior when it came to dealing with the communist superpower. As a devout Catholic, he saw no conflict in using Islam to defeat the Soviet Union. "It was Casey who welded the alliance among the CIA, Saudi intelligence, and Zia's Army," as well as Pakistan's ISI. "As his Muslim allies did, Casey saw the Afghan Jihad not merely as statecraft, but as an important front in a worldwide struggle between communist atheism and God's community of believers."[24]

In the back alleys of Pakistan, as well as in the mountains and valleys of Afghanistan, the mujahedeen were imbued with the idea of jihad, an idea fervently promoted by the mullahs from Pakistan and Saudi Arabia and by the pinstripe-suited CIA functionaries. There was a world of difference between the worldviews, training, and values of these individuals; however, they converged in a mission to defeat the "godless commies." This religious template with which to view and judge the modern world was zealously promoted in the form of a plan by the governmental functionaries of the world of Islam and the United States.

It was not that no one in Washington thought that the American-nurtured militant jihad would not turn against America someday. At that time, a virulently anti-American Islamic revolution was happening in Iran with the rallying cry "Death to America; death to the Great Satan." But the objective of defeating the Soviet Union then ran supreme in the American capital.

With the aim of defeating the Soviet Union in Afghanistan – a goal that was driving the top US officials as well as the Zia regime – Pakistan's Inter-Services Intelligence (ISI) got directly involved in funneling American and Arab monies to train jihadis at tribal area camps inside Afghanistan and Pakistan. The Deobandi schools located in the North-West Frontier Province (renamed Khyber Pakhtunkhwa in 2010) and Baluchistan became the vanguard of religious institutions espousing jihad. The Deobandi schools affiliated with the Haqqania faction created jihadi networks in Pakistan's major urban centres. These jihadi schools – especially those of Maulana Sami ul Haq (frequently referred to as the "Father of the Taliban") and Maulana Fazlur Rahman – later spread to Karachi and Punjab, and attracted volunteers from Central Asia, North Africa, and the Caucasus region. The schools belonging to these two Muslim clerics are significant: the Taliban movement was not only founded in these schools, but most of the commanders and leaders of the Taliban were graduates. Moreover, long after the demise of the Taliban regime, the schools continued recruiting new jihadists against diverse targets that included China, Russia, India, and the United States.

Pakistan's involvement in the Afghan war with the active support of the United States was the beginning of an era when Pakistan was to be taken seriously within the world of Islam. This had not been the case in the 1970s; although Pakistan had started a policy of deliberately identifying itself with the Middle East and the Arabs, there was no hue and cry in the Arab Muslim world over India's gleeful dismantlement of Pakistan's eastern wing in 1971. Pakistani leaders in the 1980s were either unfazed by that ostensible insult or determined to make the best of it. With US backing and active support for the implementation of militant jihad against the Soviet occupiers, Pakistan emerged as a leading nation and as a "defender of the faith." Saudi backing and heavy financial support provided the Zia regime with much-needed funding and an eagerly sought endorsement of its promotion of Islamization within the domestic arena. Now, Islamization emerged as a two-edged sword. Domestically, it was used to escalate the implementation of Sunni Islam and its most orthodox laws and to exacerbate the sectarian divide between Sunnis and Shias. In the international arena (Afghanistan), the doctrine of militant jihad would emerge as a basis for future conflict. No one planned or predicted such a role for jihad then. And no one, not even the United States, imagined the implications for the regional stability of South Asia or, indeed, for the world of Islam in general.

Another aspect of Islamization was that it was Pakistan's response, as well as that of Saudi Arabia, to the Islamic revolution taking place in neighbouring Iran. That revolution brought an end to the role of "America's Shah." In that sense, it was also the end of America's dominance in Iran and a victory for Shia Islam. As two major Sunni countries, Pakistan and Saudi Arabia could not afford to sit back and leave the ascendancy of Shia Islam unchallenged. It was lost on the West that the Afghan war was also a struggle for the victory of Sunni Islam. In the process, both Pakistan and Saudi Arabia were signalling Iran that they were not about to accept the symbolic message that Shia Islam had a superior revolutionary vision than that of Sunni Islam.[25]

The Pakistan-Saudi nexus had begun to gel even during the days of Zulfiqar Ali Bhutto, who had been pulled between dual agendas as a Third World socialist leader and a leader of a Muslim nation where the primacy of Islam was becoming an inexorable trend. However, Saudi leadership shared the skepticism of Maududi and other Islamist leaders about the credentials of Bhutto as a leader who could be trusted to promote Islamization. Indeed, the Saudis played a behind-the-scenes, yet crucial, role in attempting to defeat Bhutto's PPP in the 1977 elections. Although they did not win through use of the ballot box, the turbulent events after those elections led to Zia's launching of martial law and the ouster (and eventual hanging) of Bhutto. The process of Islamization under Zia met with the approval of the Saudi Wahhabi school of thought. In fact, the doctrine of militant jihad that the United States decided to promote so wholeheartedly in Afghanistan was an integral aspect of Saudi Wahhabi thinking.

In the promotion and intensification of sectarianism in Pakistan, the Pakistani intelligence services, along with those of Saudi Arabia and the United States, were accused of playing a critical role during the Afghan jihad. The finances from these intelligence services went to the aid of the Deobandi madrassas with the aim of entrenching Sunni identity and countering the influence of Iran. In turn, Iran started to finance the Shia madrassas of Pakistan by channeling finances and literature through its cultural centres.[26]

Finally, in the context of the Indo-Pak rivalry, Pakistan's highly visible and equally significant involvement in the American-supported jihad was expected to establish it as a valuable US ally and recipient of extensive military and economic support. Regardless of how realistic those expectations, Zia was determined to secure his country's long-term influence by ensuring that no anti-Pakistan government would be established in Afghanistan. The concept of "strategic depth" dominated his thinking then. As controversial as that concept has remained, Pakistan has never shown any evidence that it has abandoned the idea.

The short marriage of convenience between Islamization and America's strategic objectives could not save Pakistan from the deleterious effects of an ill-conceived idea based so much on violence, extremism, obscurantism, and fanaticism – all features antithetical to Islam. When the United States left the region, Pakistan was smoldering with desire to influence the highly turbulent power play between various Islamist groups. It did succeed in establishing its preferred Taliban rule, but Afghanistan remained a highly volatile place where al-Qaida and its global jihadist ideology were given sanctuary by Mullah Mohammad Omar, the spiritual leader of the Taliban. It was al-Qaida's self-styled jihadism that brought about an end to the rule of the Taliban, when the United States invaded Afghanistan in response to al-Qaida–sponsored terrorist attacks carried out on US territory on 11 September 2001.

In the meantime, the legacy of Zia's Islamism turned against Pakistan in the form of intensified Shia-Sunni murderous attacks that dismantled numerous mosques of both sects and resulted in the deaths of scores of Muslims. Sunni fanaticism increasingly manifested the Takfiri ideology of killing the followers of Sufi Islam. Even the shrines of major Muslim Sufis became the targets of mounting Wahhabi fanaticism. Al-Qaida and Pakistan's homegrown Islamist groups were transforming Pakistan into a shell state.[27]

Musharraf: Reaping the Jihadi Whirlwind

Pakistani Army leaders did not realize how potentially deleterious Islamization could become until Pakistan came under the rule of yet another dictator, General Pervez Musharraf. Musharraf ousted democracy in October 1999. Like Zia, he promised to bring democracy back to Pakistan. Like Zia, he kept breaking his promises and showed the same zeal to stay in power as his military predecessor.

However, the rule of Pervez Musharraf was starkly different from that of Zia in the context of Islam. In the days of Zia, Islam became a powerful force in the Pakistani polity. In the days of Musharraf, Islam's power and centrality continued to grow, but political developments in Afghanistan – involving the self-styled jihadists of that country – would bring about a dramatic turn of events that would transform the Pakistani Islamists into jihadists who turned against Musharraf. Eventually, as we will see, the Tehrik-e-Taliban-e-Pakistan (TTP, aka Pakistan's Taliban) would turn against its democratically elected government in a bid to capture power.

Before invading Afghanistan for the purpose of dismantling the Taliban regime and killing or capturing Osama Bin Laden and his cohorts, the United States forced Musharraf to radically alter his position by abandoning his country's staunch support of the

Taliban regime of Afghanistan and becoming an active participant in its invasion. As horrible as the 9/11 terrorist attacks on the United States were, from the viewpoint of Pakistani citizens, siding with the United States was not a promising option. They remembered only too well how the United States had used their country in the 1980s, only to leave after the Soviet Union had been defeated as a result of the active participation of Afghan and Pakistani mujahedeen and those from other Muslim countries.

However, given that Pakistan was under his dictatorship, General Musharraf, alone, decided to ignore the wishes of his people and to side with the United States in its invasion of Afghanistan. More accurately, Musharraf was given an ultimatum by the United States to either join its so-called global war on terrorism (GWOT) or face the consequences. Those consequences included targeting Pakistan to either snatch or neutralize its nuclear weapons. That was America's application of Bush's slogan, "Either you are with us or you are with the terrorists," to Pakistan. According to Musharraf, the then deputy secretary of state, Richard Armitage, told Pakistan that if it "chose the terrorists, then [it] should be prepared to be bombed back to the Stone Age."[28] Armitage denied making such a threat. Pakistan did become a frontline partner of the United States in its campaign to dismantle the Taliban regime, but it did so under duress. The mutuality of purpose and enthusiasm that had been the hallmark of Pakistan's involvement in the US-sponsored Afghan war of the 1980s was markedly absent in that country's participation in George W. Bush's war on terrorism.

In the 2001 military campaign, Pakistan's self-styled jihadists were hostile to Musharraf's willingness to fight and destroy the Taliban of Afghanistan and their al-Qaida brethren. The level of hostility between the government and the Islamists was unprecedented. While Musharraf tried to convey to Washington how indispensable he was to the stability of Pakistan, he himself became the target of assassination by the Islamists. Nevertheless, he persevered in his dealings with the Islamist parties to consolidate his rule. The rigged elections of 2002 were a classic example of how Musharraf's deceitful use of the Islamists came back to haunt him. As Ahmed Rashid observed, "By rigging the elections, Musharraf had for the first time unleashed the Islamic extremist genie within the Pakistan state and handed it political power in two provinces [North-West Frontier Province and Baluchistan] ... The rigged elections had only widened the political divide, further polarized society, and encouraged the extremists." The Islamist parties were equally duplicitous; for instance, "the MMA [Muttahida Majlis-e-Amal] acted as cheerleader for the army while opposing its policy of alliance with the United States."[29] The Lal Masjid (Red Mosque) massacre of July 2007 created a near civil war situation when the jihadists declared a war against the army, which, they were convinced, had become an "agent" of the American "infidels." Even the emergence of Lal Masjid as a major centre of jihadist activism was an outcome of the ISI's and the Army's use of it as a stopping place for jihadists who were on their way to commit terrorist acts in Indian-administered Kashmir. The mosque was located only two miles from the presidential residence and a half-mile from ISI headquarters. In fact, the two leaders of the conflict involving that mosque – Maulana Abdul Aziz Ghazi and his younger brother Maulana Abdul Rashid Ghazi – "had long-standing links to the ISI and the military."[30]

In the post–9/11 era, the ideological template used by most jihadist groups in Pakistan was the Takfiri one. Through that template they gave themselves the "right" and the "authority" to declare as "infidels" anyone (even Muslims) who disagreed with their use of terror and mayhem as an integral part of so-called jihad. They consistently applied this template to the regime of Pervez Musharraf in the post–9/11 era. The Takfiri traits of Wahhabism were fast spreading in a country whose dominant *madhab* (Islamic school of thought) was Hanafi Islam.[31]

While he was being labelled an "infidel" by the Islamists, Musharraf came under tremendous pressure from the United States. No matter how much Musharraf cooperated with the United States in its war on terrorism, the US administration believed that he was not doing enough. The litmus test of his sincerity was that al-Qaida's top leader was alive and was believed to be hiding in the Federally Administered Tribal Areas/North-West Frontier Province (FATA/NWFP). Given that understanding, the Americans expected Musharraf to launch an all-out war in those regions and clean them out. Not much attention was paid to how realistic that expectation really was – whether Musharraf or any other Pakistani official could carry out such an operation, or whether the Pakistani Army would be willing to kill massive numbers of its own citizens just to please the United States.

Musharraf played a deadly game in dealing with the United States and the Islamists. Periodically, the Pakistani Army would capture one or more terrorists and hand them over to the United States. However, Musharraf maintained a strong political nexus between the Muslim League (Qaid or Q), which was his party, so to speak, and Muttahida Majlis-e-Amal (MMA; United Action Front), an amalgamation of Islamist parties. That alliance was in power in Baluchistan and in the NWFP after the elections in 2002. For the United States and world consumption, the Musharraf regime was fully geared toward promoting Islamic moderation. However, the domestic reality was that Musharraf was very much involved not only in maintaining strong ties with the MMA but in using those ties to his advantage. Although he paid lip service to reforming the curriculum of the madrassas, no major changes ensued from his alleged resolve.

The chief problem with General Musharraf's cooperation with the United States was that Washington and Islamabad had radically different strategic agendas. Pakistan under Musharraf did not want to destroy either the Islamist groups or the Tehrik-e-Taliban-e-Pakistan. They served a useful purpose in his intricate balancing act of remaining in power while not antagonizing the United States. The United States, on the other hand, wanted Pakistan to clamp down hard on the Islamists and later on the TTP, which also had complicated linkages with the Taliban of Afghanistan. Neither of these entities (the TTP or the Taliban of Afghanistan) was subservient to the other. They had widely different agendas. The chief point of convergence between them was that both were intensely anti-American. The Bush administration wanted Pakistan to control the border movements of the jihadists on both sides of the Pak-Afghan border, as the jihadists roaming this territory were legendary for their powerful tradition of lawlessness. Pakistan, for its part, found control of this long border a logistical nightmare. More to the point, if Pakistan were to gain complete control of that border, it would lose an important tool in remaining a major player in America's GWOT.

Musharraf wanted to prolong his rule, to stabilize Pakistan by co-opting the Islamist parties and sabotaging the emergence of democracy in his native land à la the Zia regime. Despite his promise to eradicate extremism, Musharraf followed the policies of Zia by empowering the ulama "to counter his secular, civilian opposition." Mullahs had never been as powerful as they became during his regime, when they controlled "two of four provincial governments" and influenced "national politics through their presence in the National Assembly." Musharraf also left untouched Zia's

Islamization measures, which were a "primary source of religious extremism and sectarian conflict."[32]

Moreover, Musharraf wanted to resolve the Kashmir issue, which was quite important to him, given that he had been so visibly involved in planning and conducting the 1999 Kargil War that brought India and Pakistan to the brink of a major war. In the post–9/11 antiterrorist environment, Pakistan's long tradition of destabilizing Indian-administered Kashmir came under intense criticism from Washington, which did not see any difference between the terrorist attacks on its own territory and the ones carried out by the Pakistani-sponsored Islamists in Indian-administered Kashmir. An ideal scenario for Musharraf would have been the active involvement of the United States in resolving the Kashmir issue. However, that possibility was out of the question because of India's staunch opposition to US involvement. India was afraid that US involvement in negotiations over Kashmir would benefit Pakistan. In fact, the issue was so strongly opposed by India that the United States declared it a matter of policy not to get involved. The US-India strategic partnership, which germinated in the waning days of the Clinton presidency, was in full bloom under George W. Bush – a development that was highly disconcerting for Musharraf.

In the post–9/11 era, the entire involvement of the United States in Afghanistan and elsewhere was about winning the war on terrorism. As much as Pakistan's own polity had become a simmering cauldron because of the growing influence and violent activism of Islamist and jihadist groups, Musharraf's strategic agenda included resolving the Kashmir issue, modernizing the fighting capabilities of Pakistan's military in response to India's massive military modernization, and asserting Pakistan's influence in Afghanistan. However, because of the growing US-India strategic partnership, he encountered a virtual no-win situation on all those issues. With the warming of US-India strategic relations, he found Washington even telling him where to station his forces – not facing the Indian Army but on the Afghan borders so that those borders would be secured from the insurgent/terrorist activities initiated from the Pakistani territory against the International Security Assistance Force (ISAF) fighting the Taliban inside Afghanistan.

One of the greatest sources of concern for General Musharraf between 2003 and 2007 was the rising potency of the TTP, a heavily Punjabi version of the Taliban movement, which, though it was no different from the Taliban of Afghanistan, was quite independent of them. Another group was the Tehrik-e-Nifaz-e-Shariat-e-Mohammadi (TNSM). Both the TTP and the TNSM were committed to the transformation of Pakistan into a Taliban-like state and to the imposition of the Shariah. They saw the United States as a major enemy of Islam, and they were committed to defeating the US-led forces fighting the Taliban of Afghanistan. The pro-US stance of the Musharraf regime became the *quod ad bellum* (cause of the fight) between these jihadist groups and the Pakistani government, in a manner very similar to the development of antagonism between the Saudi government and al-Qaida. Such groups continue to pose the greatest threats to the stability of both Pakistan and Afghanistan.

The Wahhabization of the Pakistani polity in the FATA/NWFP dislodged the traditional role of both the elders and the jirga system, a system of decision-making in Afghanistan in which leaders made decisions on the basis of the Islamic principle of consensus. These traditional models had played a crucial role in the past in negotiations and conflict resolution with the government. The resulting modus vivendi allowed a great deal of autonomy in those regions, as long as they did not question the legitimacy of the government in Islamabad. The new jihadist groups were excessively influenced by the Wahhabism of the Deobandi madrassas. What was different about them was that they were more zealous about imposing the Shariah and waging jihad than even al-Qaida. The transformation of the hardline Islamist groups into jihadist ones appeared irreversible.

The spirit of Islamization that the Islamist parties and General Zia so zealously nurtured in the 1970s emerged as an untamable monster under the rule of General Musharraf, and that monster turned against his regime. Even though Musharraf played the same game of manipulating the Islamists to stay in power, as Zia had done by supporting the United States' war on Soviet-occupied Afghanistan, the circumstances of that war were markedly different. Zia supported the United States under the banner of "jihad," whereas Musharraf waged war against Taliban-ruled Afghanistan in support of the United States, thereby becoming a legitimate "enemy" of Islam from the perspective of the jihadists.

The only expert on the Islamist movement who was partially correct in foretelling the emergence of such groups was Olivier Roy, in his analysis of the Afghan mujahedeen of the 1980s. That movement, he observed, embodied the widespread shift in the Muslim world from a "political and revolutionary Islam to a conservative brand of fundamentalism." He called it "neofundamentalism." The members of these groups were "from the intelligentsia" and received their education in "an autodidactic way or through the 'missionary' institutes established by the Wahhabis, the Ahl-i Hadith, [and] the Pakistani Jama'at." These "self-proclaimed mullahs" zealously promoted the "Islamic state, political activism, [and] millenarianism (instead of revolution) claiming that Islam and only Islam will solve all problems ... They want[ed] to reshape and unite the Sunni Muslim ummah within the framework of a purified Islam, while getting rid of national, traditional, and cultural accretions." They represented, stated Roy, "a new, universal model of the 'Islamic militant' from Algeria to Pakistan with the same looks, gestures, references – and vacuity of thought."[33] Where Roy might be on shaky ground is that it is too early to tell whether the neofundamentalists are really uninterested in an Islamic revolution. For instance, the establishment of Islamic governments in Pakistan and Afghanistan may be only the first step toward the exportation of that model to Central Asian states. In the march of Islamism, the jihadists were resolved to capture political power and acquire territory.

As previously noted, even though the TTP was not part of the Afghani Taliban movement, it supported them morally and materially against the NATO forces. That – and the fact that the TTP and the TNSM were virulently anti-American – were the chief reasons why Washington put unrelenting pressure on Musharraf to clamp down on the TTP. But Musharraf was faced with the proverbial choice between a rock and a hard place. He did not want to take harsh action against the TTP or other Islamist groups, since they were of much use to him in his covert exploits in Indian-administered Kashmir. The MMA – the Islamic alliance – was an ally of Muslim League-Q, a pro-Musharraf party in Baluchistan and the NWFP.

The Lal Masjid massacre of July 2007 may have been the beginning of the end of Musharraf's rule. Ironically, in the domestic arena, he relied on simultaneously riding two horses – seeking the support, on the one hand, of urban and enlightened Pakistanis who were strongly opposed to the Talibanization of their country, and on the other, of the Islamist parties, on whose support Musharraf had relied from the very beginning. He was reluctant to reform the jihadist madrassas because he did not want to turn the Islamist parties against him. But the jihadists' takeover of the Lal Masjid increased pressure on him to retaliate. When he did, the jihadists became his sworn enemy. The several assassination attempts on his life were conclusive evidence. During his last two years in office, he became increasingly reliant on Washington's support – another indicator that his days in office were numbered.

When Benazir Bhutto, the erstwhile corruption diva of Pakistani politics, showed her resolve to bring democracy back to Pakistan by returning and running for office in late 2007, the Bush administration forced General Musharraf to negotiate a deal for her return to office. Musharraf, who hated everything that civilian politicians in his country stood for, had to swallow his pride. From Washington's point of view, this restoration of democracy has saved Pakistan from the death grip of the Islamists.

When Benazir Bhutto was assassinated in December 2009, Pakistan appeared to be heading toward a hellish future. Islamization – a process started largely to exploit Islam for selfish political purposes within domestic politics in the 1970s, but used to defeat the Soviet Union in the 1980s – became a force destroying anything and everything it envisaged as the "enemy." When Musharraf was forced to resign in August 2008 and become a private citizen, it was the end of only one episode in the continuing saga of Pakistan's struggle with Islamization. That saga continued with its customary ominous fury and attendant calamitous changes and tragedies, and with the United States very much present. But by 2009, the United States was determined to finish the war that George W. Bush started in 2001 when he invaded Afghanistan with the explicit purpose of dismantling the Taliban regime and eradicating al-Qaida. The new American president, Barack Obama, called the Afghan war "the right war." It appeared that the history of America's involvement in a Muslim country was about to repeat itself. This time, that involvement was to be in two Muslim countries – Afghanistan and Pakistan.

Under Barack Obama, US-Pakistan relations were dramatically different than they were under his predecessor. First, the Afghan war was depicted by the global media as "Obama's war" (in the manner Iraq was labelled as "Bush's war"); however, from the beginning, the new administration decided that it could not win without Pakistan playing a major supportive role. But billing that strategy as the Afghanistan-Pakistan (AfPak) strategy did not please Pakistan. Second, unlike Bush, Obama expressed his resolve to take unilateral action inside Pakistan – including limited military operations – in order to win the Afghan war. That was a clear ultimatum to the Pakistani Army that the only way to avoid such US action was by kowtowing to its demands. That characteristic alone unambiguously signalled the beginning of a new contentious era of US-Pak relations. Third, without making public statements to that effect, President Obama made clear to the Pakistani military leaders his suspicions that Pakistan was playing a duplicitous role in its dealings with Washington. In this regard, the role of the ISI would become a major irritant between Islamabad and Washington. Fourth, Pakistan's continued use of the jihadist card inside Afghanistan to target India's diplomatic personnel and assets caused major conflict with the Americans. It became obvious to Pakistan that the US-India strategic partnership was the driving force behind America's support of the growing Indian presence in Afghanistan, which Pakistan viewed as a major threat to its own security. Finally, under these circumstances, Pakistan was in no mood to fulfill growing American demands to launch major military actions against the jihadist groups inside its own borders or against the Haqqani group that used Pakistan and Afghan territory to launch terrorist attacks on India and the ISAF. Pakistan also ignored US demands to deploy a major part of its forces on the Afghan-Pak border, as opposed to their usual stationing on the Indo-Pak borders. Its long-standing policy of "India-centrism" was Pakistan's chief driving force for that decision.

Pakistan did allow the United States to launch increased drone attacks against al-Qaida and the Taliban leaders from inside its borders, while denying it publicly.[34] Such cooperation apparently did not measure up to the Obama administration's high standards. Still, in 2009 the United States agreed to provide $1.5 billion in economic and military assistance to Pakistan – the Kerry-Lugar-Berman Bill – over the next five years. However, that bill made US aid to Pakistan "conditional on Pakistan's military being subordinated to its elected government, and taking action against militants sheltering on its soil." If the purpose of the bill was "to counter widespread anti-American sentiment there by helping Pakistan's civilian government deliver essential services to its population," it did not succeed. Instead, the bill added to the controversy and criticism inside that country over collusion with the United States.[35]

The Obama administration proved its seriousness about taking unilateral action when, on 2 May 2011, US Special Forces flew into

Pakistan to assassinate Bin Laden, who, as it turned out, was hiding in Abbottabad, a town known for its military garrison. The Pakistani Army was furious about not being informed of that operation in advance. The United States was equally angry that the al-Qaida leader was living only a few miles away from Pakistan's top military academy. The controversy severely strained US-Pak ties. Soon after that episode, the US embassy in Kabul was attacked by the Haqqani group on 13 September 2011. Admiral Michael Mullen, then chairman of the Joint Chiefs of Staff, publicly stated that "the Haqqani network ... acts as a veritable arm of Pakistan's Inter-Services Intelligence Agency."[36] He also charged the Haqqani group with being behind the 20 June 2011 attack against the Inter-Continental Hotel in Kabul as well as the 10 September 2011 truck bomb attack, which resulted in the death of five Afghans and injured a total of ninety-six individuals, including seventy-seven US soldiers.[37] Now the American officials were not at all reluctant to state publicly what they had been saying privately to Pakistani officials during their "frank" exchanges.

As if there were no end to the worsening conflict between Islamabad and Washington, the ISAF, claiming self-defence, attacked two Pakistani Army posts in the Mohmand tribal region on 26 November 2011, killing twenty-four soldiers. The outraged Pakistan Army suspended vital NATO supply routes in its territory, and asked Washington to leave the Shamsi air base located in Baluchistan from where the US military was launching drone attacks on al-Qaida and Taliban personnel inside Pakistan. The poisoning of the political environment was underscored by the fact that only personal condolences – not an official apology – were expressed by secretary of state Hillary Clinton, secretary of defense Leon Panetta, and commander of the ISAF General John Allen.

Despite the incredibly turbulent nature of its domestic politics, Pakistan never gave up on becoming a favourite partner and ally of the United States on the same level as India. The Herculean nature of this task did not bother Pakistan's leadership. In March 2010, it succeeded in restarting strategic dialogue with the Obama administration. Three rounds of such dialogue had been conducted during the Bush administration. That the Obama administration continued to use the phrase "strategic dialogue" to describe the negotiations with Pakistan's top officials was of utmost symbolic significance, because this term was "reserved for the substantive, wide-ranging exchanges it [carried] on with important countries like China and India."[38] While the United States was eager to get Pakistan's support in fighting the Taliban in Afghanistan, Pakistan was driven by two important motives. First, it wanted to be recognized "as a de jure nuclear power with rights and responsibilities." If so recognized, Pakistan would get a waiver from the Nuclear Suppliers Group "for civil nuclear energy cooperation," a privilege accorded to India at the behest of the United States.[39] Second, Pakistan wanted to ensure that it, not India, played a vital role in determining the security environment of Afghanistan.

Pakistan knew that it had a tough row to hoe on the nuclear issue, because of the tremendously damaging role played by the father of its nuclear knowhow, Dr A.Q. Khan, in establishing a virtual Kmart of nuclear sales worldwide.[40] However, it also knew that, in the business of nuclear knowhow and nuclear proliferation, no nation could claim sainthood. Everyone, especially Washington, had a record of duplicity and double-standards.[41] In the final analysis, what might be working powerfully in favour of Pakistan was that the United States wished to get out of Afghanistan, and it knew that there could never be a stable peace in Afghanistan without the cooperation of Pakistan. Pakistan, for its part, remained a willing player with the United States, if the latter was willing to pay the price for its cooperation.

The election of Prime Minister Nawaz Sharif in June 2013 established two historical "firsts" in Pakistan. First, the former PPP-led government headed by President Asif Ali Zardari completed its terms without an attempted coup. Second, under General Musharraf's successor as Chief of Army Staff (COAS), General Ashfaq Pervez Kayani, the Pakistan Army demonstrated a palpable proclivity for staying out of politics. Despite these developments, the Army's control of and influence on Pakistan's national security policy remained unaltered. During General Kayani's tenure, especially after the election of Nawaz Sharif, it appeared that the civil-military relations in Pakistan were experiencing a period of cooperation and mutual cordiality. General Raheel Sharif (no relation to the prime minister) was handpicked by Nawaz Sharif as the new COAS.

From 2011 on, Pakistan seemed to be under the tightening grip of jihadist groups (especially the TTP), whose terror campaign against the Pakistan Army was on the rise. The TTP's continued refusal to negotiate some sort of modus vivendi with the Sharif government was a remarkable testimony to its growing Islamism-related aspirations. The Pakistani government's endeavours to start the negotiations process were not helped by periodic drone attacks that the Obama administration was carrying out to eliminate "high-valued targets" from the Afghan-Pakistan border areas. The TTP's position was that it would not negotiate as long as its leadership was targeted by US drones. More to the point, remaining consistent to its Islamism-related ambition to overthrow the Pakistani government, the TTP not only questioned the very legitimacy of the Sharif government as a "slave" of the United States, but also depicted Pakistan's constitution as illegitimate, since it was not based on the Shariah.

The tug-and-pull between the Pakistani government and the TTP continued throughout 2013 and 2014, with the terrorist groups carrying out several audacious attacks. In June 2014 the Pak Army brought about a major tactical shift in its military campaigns with the launch of Operation Zarb-e-Azb – named after one of the swords (the Azb) of the Prophet of Islam. Instead of conducting military operations against the TTP and then signing peace deals, which the latter had no intention of observing, the Army resolved "to vanquish the group and keep all conquered territory under its control." However, the Pak Army remained faithful to its old approach of not eradicating terrorist groups, just in case it had to use them against India. Furthermore, despite its propaganda campaign to the contrary, the military did not abandon its differentiation between the "bad" Taliban and the "good" Taliban. The bad Taliban included those terrorists who were determined to bring about regime change in Pakistan, that is, the TTP. And the good Taliban were terrorists who had no fight with the Pakistani government, and were largely focused on terrorizing the Indian-administered Kashmir and attacking Indian diplomatic personnel in Afghanistan. Still, quite a few positive developments resulted from Operation Zarb-e-Azb. First, it succeeded in destroying the Taliban's stronghold in northen Waziristan. Second, it severely degraded the TTP's operational capacity. Third, the Pakistan military's intelligence campaign related to Zarb-e-Azb was successful in breaking the Taliban's back in a number of major cities of that country. Still, it took the murderous attack of the TTP on the army's public school in Peshawar in December 2014, which resulted in the death of 150 children, to palpably "mobilize public opinion in favor of a continued, strong military response against the Taliban."[42]

Pakistan's security state's refusal to destroy the TTP and other terrorist groups and its unwillingness to abandon the failed policy of differentiating between the "bad" and "good" Taliban continued to haunt that country's security through deadly attacks on various civilian and military facilities throughout 2015. Relations with the United States continued to be strained, due to the general hypocrisies of Pakistan's policy toward terrorist groups and toward Afghanistan. In the last year of President Barack Obama's second term, Pakistan remained an important player in America's desire to conduct negotiations between the Taliban of Afghanistan and the government of President Ashraf Ghani. Since the successor to the late Mullah Omar, Mullah Akhtar Mansour, was supported by Pakistan, it was expected to play a crucial role in facilitating those negotiations.

AFGHANISTAN

Afghanistan has long been a magnet for conquerors to invade and try to govern it. And invade they did – from Alexander the Great in 330 BC to the United States in 2001 – but no one could govern Afghanistan and make it a peaceful place, not even its indigenous rulers (save Abdul Rahman, the "iron Amir," from 1880 to 1901). Great powers easily conquered Afghanistan, or fought to keep each other out. But like the proverbial curse inscribed in local folklore, when one power attempted to stay in Afghanistan, it paid in blood, and it paid long enough with the lives of young soldiers to realize that the price was not worth staying. In the twenty-first century, that story – like the movie *Groundhog Day* – is repeating itself.

The superpower rivalry of the Cold War years spilled over into Afghanistan when the Soviet Union decided to invade and occupy it in December 1979. Even though czarist Russia and the Soviet Union had a history of enslaving Muslim countries of the northern Caucasus and Central Asia, the Soviet invasion of Afghanistan gave birth to a plethora of analyses about what motivated the communist czars to do that. Regardless of their rationale, what was more important was that the United States – the other superpower – was not going to accept that potential expansion as a *fait accompli*. President Jimmy Carter issued a series of statements putting Moscow on notice. However, in general, his administration decided not to draw alarmist conclusions regarding Soviet intentions of expansionism.

It was under Ronald Reagan that the United States started a proactive policy of expelling the Soviet Union from Afghanistan by using Pakistan as a conduit for its military and economic assistance to the mujahedeen to wage war. A unique and unprecedented aspect of that war was that it was to be conducted by a Western power through the use of the Islamic doctrine of jihad. Saudi Arabia and Pakistan demonstrated an attitude of zealotry and ebullience in the implementation of that doctrine. The chief warriors to wage that jihad were from Afghanistan, as well as from a number of Muslim countries, thereby giving it a semblance of jihad declared by the Muslim ummah against the communist superpower.

However, the expulsion of the Soviet Union from Afghanistan in 1989 did not bring about an end to the state of warfare. After ousting the Soviet Union, the Afghan mujahedeen groups – led by Gulbuddin Hikmatyar of Hizb-e-Islam, Ahmad Shah Masood and Burhanuddin Rabbani of Jamaat-e-Islami of Afghanistan, Uzbek leader General Rashid Dostum and his "for hire" militia, Hazara leader Abdul Ali Mazari, and Ismail Khan, the warlord of Herat – turned their guns against each other. The glue that had been holding them together during their jihad was the Soviet occupation (except for Dostum, who initially backed the pro-Soviet Afghan government). When the Soviet occupation ended, the ideological differences, personal hatred of each other, and personal drive for capturing and exercising power surfaced with a vengeance, and so did the internecine warfare.

Abdul Rashid Dostum, who supported the Soviet-backed government of President Najibullah, turned against it in Mazar-e-Sharif and formed an alliance with the Tajik-dominated Jamaat-e-Islami forces of Burhanuddin Rabbani and Ahmad Shah Masood. Then he broke with them and allied himself with Gulbuddin Hikmatyar to attack Kabul from the north, while Hikmatyar's forces attacked the capital from the south. Najibullah resigned in April 1992 and Sibghatullah Mojaddedi, leader of the Afghan National Liberation, took power in Kabul. He remained in power for two months and then transferred it to Burhanuddin Rabbani.

For the next four years (1992–96), Afghanistan plunged into a civil war among the mujahedeen fighters, which destroyed most of Kabul. Tajik control of the presidency created acute resentment among the Pashtun. It was only the second time in the history of Afghanistan that the Tajiks held power at the centre.[43] However, the authority of the central government remained nominal, at best. Afghanistan's four major neighbours – Pakistan, Russia, Iran, and India – exercised their influence by backing the various warring factions. Of these four countries, three of them were facing uphill struggles in Afghanistan for different reasons. Russia was a mere shadow of the Soviet Union that it replaced. It could provide a token amount of military and economic assistance to its favoured group, but not much beyond that. Iran was engulfed in its own Islamic revolution and could concentrate only tangentially and sporadically on the power struggle going on inside Afghanistan. India was a distant power, and because it was the chief target of Pakistani maneuvers in Afghanistan, it was at a substantial disadvantage.

Pakistan, on the contrary, had an enormous advantage. It had extensive experience from its intricate involvement in Afghanistan during the jihad war against the Soviet Union. Second, it had a Pashtun population of its own, whose representatives could be used to conduct its strategic maneuvers inside Afghanistan. Third, since Pakistan was fully committed to the proposition of ensuring Pashtun control of power in Afghanistan (unlike the other three countries), it was not swimming against the powerful undercurrents in that country. Russia, India, and Iran backed Masood's Northern Alliance, while Pakistan remained committed to Hikmatyar's forces and, through him, to Pashtun rule over Afghanistan.

The United States lost interest in Afghanistan during the administration of President Bill Clinton. Washington was no longer interested in maintaining its already advantageous strategic position after the ouster and subsequent disintegration of the Soviet Union. In fact, with American interest in Pakistan waning, the erstwhile tension between Washington and Islamabad over the latter's commitment to develop nuclear weapons resurfaced during the administration of President George H.W. Bush. As long as Pakistan's role in Afghanistan had remained important to US strategic interests, the American president had seen no harm in fudging the state of Pakistan's nuclear weapons program. Once those conditions changed, Bush could no longer "misstate" the facts and certify that Pakistan was not involved in developing nuclear weapons. The Pressler Amendment (much hated in Pakistan) – banning the sale and/or transfer of US military weapons to that country – was reimposed on Pakistan in October 1990. Pakistan was reminded, once again, of the highly untrustworthy and expedient nature of America's treatment of its friends. That very lesson turned out to be one of the chief reasons that General Pervez Musharraf continued his own Machiavellian and treacherous treatment of the United States in the post–9/11 era, when George W. Bush complained that Pakistan was not doing enough to clamp down on its domestic Islamist groups or to control its highly porous borders with Afghanistan.

The power vacuum left by the sudden loss of interest and subsequent absence of the United States created a political environment perfectly suited to Pakistan's strategic interests in Afghanistan. It might not have been too worried about the potential shenanigans from Russia alone, but it certainly was apprehensive about potential strategic maneuvering between India and Iran in which Russia could do much to damage to Pakistan's interests. These three countries were staunch supporters of Ahmad Shah Masood and his Northern Alliance, whose sole aim was to overthrow the Taliban regime of Afghanistan. Saudi Arabia was very willing to help Pakistan against Iran because of its continued fear that the Iranian revolution would be exported to countries of the Persian Gulf and Arabian Peninsula, something that was also a major source of concern for the United States. Thus in the 1990s Pakistan emerged as the sole kingmaker of Afghanistan by facilitating the destruction of the remainder of the mujahedeen-led government through the new hardline Islamist upstarts, the Taliban.

Pakistani maneuvers that led to the capture of power by the Taliban had their roots in General Zia-ul-Haq's concept of creating a friendly government in Afghanistan and the vitality, if not the necessity, of having strategic depth toward India. Another important motive was the continuation of a policy to isolate Iran from Afghanistan. Even on this point, Pakistan was more concerned about a potential anti-Pakistan Iran-India nexus than the deleterious implications of Iranian maneuvers in Afghanistan. The Pakistani policy of providing assistance only to those jihadi groups willing to toe the Pakistani line – a practice that was assiduously developed during the Afghan jihadi war of the 1980s – strengthened the Taliban, whose loyalty to Pakistan was proven.

The Taliban were very much a creation of Pakistani madrassas, where they learned the Wahhabi/Salafi framework of Islamic puritanism, along with the doctrine of jihad. The Taliban movement emerged as a reaction to the mujahedeen groups, who became corrupt and remained highly unskilled as a cohesive group to govern Afghanistan. According to Ahmed Rashid, ideologically speaking, the Taliban "fitted nowhere in the Islamic spectrum of ideas and movements that had emerged in Afghanistan between 1979 and 1994." They "represented nobody but themselves and they recognized no Islam except their own."[44] Still, one can identify the Taliban's ideological template in a general way. Their ideology was a comprehensive mix of a number of traits that were part and parcel of the Deobandi schools of Pakistan, where they received Islamic education. That ideology comprised utter rejection of the Shia, even as a sect of Islam, and hatred of Iran, characteristics that all Deobandi schools of Pakistan promoted through their educational curricula. As a result of their education in those schools, the Taliban also developed a strong desire to promote Sunni Islam as a jihadi movement. The backing of jihad was a characteristic that Zia's regime not only shared with the Deobandi madrassas but actively promoted. About the only feature that the Taliban developed on their own – or a characteristic that always dominated their thinking – was Pashtun nationalism, which might have been one of the reasons that Hikmatyar never developed any real desire to cooperate with Masood (their mutual animosity was legendary). That attribute also became their chief weakness. The Taliban came to power largely as a result of the help of the Pakistani Army and its ISI. Thus, they intensified the ethnic divide within Afghanistan, and their government was viewed by other ethnic groups – especially by the Tajiks and the Shia Hazaras – as a tool of Pakistani hegemony over Afghanistan.

When the Taliban first captured power in 1996, even the United States saw them as an alternative to the chaotic situation that had prevailed during the civil war and hoped that, under their rule, Afghanistan might become a stable polity. However, the brutality that the Taliban demonstrated in torturing and then murdering Najibullah, their obscurantist practice of Islam, and especially their pathetic treatment of women elicited an intense international condemnation from which their movement would never recover. The overall modus operandi of their rule was extremely brutal. Their extreme interpretation of the Shariah, which was part of the Wahhabi but not the Hanafi tradition of Islam, might also have doomed them from the beginning. As Ahmed Rashid writes, "The Taliban's brand of Islamic fundamentalism was so extreme that it appeared to denigrate Islam's message of peace and tolerance and its capacity to live with other religious and ethnic groups."[45] To show its condemnation of the atrocious posture of the regime, the community of nations never granted the Taliban diplomatic recognition, save Pakistan, Saudi Arabia, and the UAE.[46] However, their bloody ways notwithstanding, the Taliban made Afghanistan a stable place by crushing and publicly executing the warlords, disarming the heavily armed populations, and opening the roads for smuggling, a lucrative business between Pakistan and Afghanistan.

The Taliban regime was vehemently opposed to modernization; it had "no desire to understand or adopt modern ideas of progress or economic development."[47] This characteristic would have prevented the Taliban regime from lasting for long. The world would have left it alone to fall apart on its own if not for the decision of Mullah Mohammad Omar – the supreme leader of the Taliban movement and the head of state during its rule – to establish a nexus with al-Qaida.

The Taliban–al-Qaida nexus could not have been formulated purely on the basis of Islam, because the theological differences were too divergent between Afghanistan (home of the Taliban) and Saudi Arabia (home of most Arab members of al-Qaida). As such, the Arab members of al-Qaida were the product of the Wahhabi creed, which was based on the literal translation of the Qur'an. The Taliban, on the other hand, belonged to the Hanafi sect of Islam, which was regarded as the most liberal, most decentralized, and nonhierarchical school (Mazhab). The Wahhabi school had a miniscule following in Afghanistan. In fact, the Afghans generally derided the stringent Islamic ways of the Wahhabis. However, during the Afghan jihadi war of the 1980s, Afghanistan had more than its fair share of exposure to Wahhabi Islam through the Deobandi madrassas and through generous financial assistance from Saudi Arabia, which also included the influx of Wahhabi literature. Moreover, since the Deobandi madrassas in the NWFP, Baluchistan, and other contiguous regions of Pakistan were also of Pashtun origin, their religious perspectives of jihad were the same as those of al-Qaida. Disagreements between the Taliban and al-Qaida on the issue of jihad resurfaced when Bin Laden and his Arab cohorts returned to Afghanistan after being expelled from Sudan. According to an account by an anonymous senior al-Qaida member entitled "The Afghan-Arabs," published in the *Asharq Al-Awsat* in 2005, the return of Bin Laden to Afghanistan in May 1996 "was the biggest challenge facing the Taliban movement at the time."[48] There were at least three underlying reasons. First, the term "Afghan-Arabs" underscores the ample cultural differences between the Islamists of Afghanistan and Saudi Arabia. Second, Bin Laden took it upon himself to declare jihad against the United States before the Taliban controlled Kabul. Declaring jihad from Afghanistan was the purview of Mullah Omar, the supreme leader of the Taliban. According to this narrative, Bin Laden, as a guest of the Taliban, was in no position to take action that bold in nature. That was tantamount to setting foreign policy for Afghanistan. Third, Bin Laden appeared to be obsessed with giving interviews to international media, despite being advised on behalf of Mullah Omar not to do so.

Still, the differences between the Taliban and Bin Laden over jihad might, at best, be viewed as tactical ones. That is, they disagreed not about jihad in principle but about who the right person was to declare jihad and the timing of such a declaration. Mullah Omar might not have shared Bin Laden's zealotry for regional or global jihad, but he had been fully exposed to this Islamic doctrine in the Deobandi madrassas, and fully believed in it. Perhaps because of this affinity between Omar and Bin Laden, or because of the legendary Afghan hospitality, when the Saudis wanted Omar to hand over Bin Laden to them, he declined. More to the point, he refused to hand over Bin Laden to the Americans in the aftermath of 9/11 and, in the process, was directly responsible for the destruction of his own regime.

After Bin Laden's arrival in Afghanistan in 1996, that country became the focus of America's attention because of the growing activities of al-Qaida in attacking American personnel and assets in the Persian Gulf and Africa. When the US embassies in East Africa were attacked by that Islamist group's functionaries in 1998, President Bill Clinton ordered cruise missile attacks targeting al-Qaida in Sudan and Afghanistan. It was these attacks that may have really brought the Taliban and al-Qaida together as a politico-religious entity.

The 9/11 attacks on the United States opened a new chapter for Afghanistan and Pakistan. The United States was to return to that area once again. This time, it was not as a strategic planner and financier of a war against another superpower, but as a military power determined to destroy a nonstate actor, al-Qaida, which sponsored the 9/11 attacks on US territory, and the Taliban regime, the government that provided sanctuary to that entity. As a military campaign, Operation Enduring Freedom (OEF) should have been a cakewalk for the United States. However, that old curse about Afghanistan mentioned earlier in this chapter reappeared. Despite its success in dismantling the Taliban regime, the United States could not eradicate al-Qaida. Bin Laden escaped through the mountains of Tora Bora because the US military made a critical mistake: Secretary of Defense

Donald Rumsfeld and US CENTCOM commander General Tommy Franks decided not to deploy American troops to capture the al-Qaida leader. Instead, the United States relied on two Afghan warlords of the Tora Bora region – Hazrat Ali and Haji Zaman Ghamsharik – to capture him on the Afghan side and on the Frontier Corps of Pakistan to seal the Pak-Afghan border to keep him from entering Pakistan. The US Congressional report on this failed mission concluded, "The review of existing literature, unclassified government records and interviews with central participants underlying this report removes any lingering doubts and makes it clear that Osama bin Laden was within our grasp at Tora Bora."[49]

From then on, the whereabouts of Bin Laden remained purely an issue of speculation. The US official explanation was that he was hiding in or around northern Waziristan – an area that is legendary for its political independence and autonomy from the Pakistani national government, and where anti-American feelings have remained intense. The Pakistani government denied the presence of Bin Laden anywhere in its territory. What is important about the Tora Bora event is that al-Qaida was given a new lease on life, while the Bush administration diverted its attention to another military campaign to dismantle the regime of Saddam Hussein. Between 2001 and 2008, the war in Afghanistan became merely an afterthought for the United States, thereby making that country and neighbouring Pakistan mushrooming places for Islamist forces and jihad.

In the post–9/11 era, America' war against terrorism was interpreted as a war against Islam. Osama Bin Laden harped on that theme quite consistently and effectively, and a large number of Muslims believed him. President George W. Bush invaded Afghanistan to retaliate against al-Qaida and its chief sponsors, the Taliban regime. It was expected that he would conclude that campaign by eradicating al-Qaida and the Taliban from the region and then spending resources on reconstruction within that country. Instead, Bush left those objectives in Afghanistan unfinished and went after Saddam Hussein's regime, something he wanted to do soon after he entered the White House. Perhaps it was his slow-burning rage to eliminate the man who wanted to "kill my Dad" – as he frequently stated – that led him to pursue a policy that was not in America's best interests.

The blood and gore and enormous instability and turbulence that stemmed from Bush's revenge against Saddam Hussein provoked a deeply rooted and equally intense hostility and hatred toward the United States in the world of Islam at large. According to Pew public opinion polls, America was despised throughout the world of Islam, from Indonesia to Morocco, while Bush was in the White House. In a Pew opinion survey taken in March 2004, 66 per cent of Pakistani respondents stated that the United States was overreacting to terrorism. The numbers for Jordan, Morocco, and Turkey were 76, 72, and 55 per cent, respectively. Interestingly, responses to the same query for France, Germany, and Britain were 57, 49, and 33 per cent, respectively. In the same survey, 44 per cent of Turkish respondents said that the Iraqis were worse off in post-Saddam Iraq, while 41 per cent said they were better off. The numbers for the same categories for Pakistan were 61 and 8; in Jordan, 70 and 25; and in Morocco, 48 and 37 per cent.[50]

Bush may have been sincere in insisting that his country had no quarrel with Islam. But one had only to examine the daily flow of briefings Donald Rumsfeld sent for his reading to see that they were peppered with Biblical quotes. Those briefings left little doubt that a born-again Christian president was on a crusade against the terrorists.[51] This type of retrospective debate aside, what was working against America during the Bush presidency was that the United States was occupying two lands of Islam: Iraq and Afghanistan. Iraq became a hellish place between 2003 and early 2007. In 2006, there were several powerful voices raised inside the United States urging Bush to "declare victory and get out of Iraq."[52]

Then came the Sunni protest movement against al-Qaida in Mesopotamia (AQIM) and the introduction of the "Surge" strategy by the US force commander in Iraq, General David Petraeus. Aside from inserting more troops into Iraq, the United States introduced a new counterinsurgency (COIN) doctrine. That doctrine became a success, largely because it was supported by the Sunni insurgents – also known as the Sahwa (the awakening) and the "Sons of Iraq" movement. That reality also improved the security situation inside Iraq. Still, the antipathy toward Bush and the United States remained pervasive throughout the Muslim world. It was clear that, even if he were to withdraw all US forces from Iraq, those negative feelings were not about to dissipate. A clean break from his administration was necessary before Muslims would be persuaded that the lone superpower was not fighting a war against their religion.

Obama's Long War in the "Graveyard of Empires"

President Barack H. Obama's election was generally expected to be the beginning of a new era and a stark contrast from the days of George W. Bush, when unilateralism was the chief driving force of American foreign policy, and when nations were judged on the basis of simplistic bumper-sticker-type slogans: "Either you are with us or you are with the terrorists." As the son of a Muslim father and a person who had spent four formative years of his life in Indonesia, Obama brought an enormous amount of credibility to the office. Although he was a Christian, Obama did not share the Manichean, evangelical perspectives of George W. Bush. Muslims sensed his sophisticated and respectful view of the world when they heard him speak. Bush could never convey that sense. Under Obama, the United States still occupied Iraq and Afghanistan; however, Muslims believed him when he said in his speeches in Ankara, Turkey, and Cairo, Egypt, that his country had no fight against Islam. He understood the intricacies and multidimensionalities of Islam and the Muslim world, and was not ready to formulate an instant judgment.

President Obama took several conciliatory steps soon after entering office. He sent his secretary of state, Hillary Clinton, to the largest Muslim country, Indonesia. He declared his resolve to reach a political understanding with Iran. He told Israeli prime minister Benjamin Netanyahu during their first meeting that he supported a two-state solution to the conflict between Israel and Palestine and that Israel must stop building settlements and make peace with the Palestinians.

Whereas Bush had chosen Iraq to make his definitive statement about how he wanted the Middle East to look, Obama chose the Afghan war to eradicate al-Qaida. As president, Obama was determined not to allow Afghanistan to turn into a quagmire. There was plenty for him to learn from his predecessors' approaches to the wars in Iraq and Vietnam. Before committing the 40,000 additional troops requested by General Stanley McChrystal, Obama studied Gordon Goldstein's book *Lessons in Disaster*, which detailed what had gone wrong in South Vietnam. He asked his advisors to read that book and thoroughly discuss even their private doubts about getting involved in Afghanistan.[53] Since establishing a clear "exit strategy" before getting involved in a conflict emerged as a major lesson of the "Vietnam syndrome," Obama opted to have an exit strategy and to commit only 30,000 troops to Afghanistan. He seemed to be doing all the "right" things before immersing his administration in the Afghan war. However, the Afghan war not only had its own logic but, most important, Afghanistan itself had a long legacy of creating a whirlpool-like momentum for all outside forces, thereby earning the moniker "the graveyard of empires."

One clear distinction between the way Bush got involved in Iraq and Obama committed himself to the security of Afghanistan was that Obama issued an elaborate strategy, described as the AfPak strategy. It included a combination of some new and some old features from Bush's handling of the Iraq war, especially during the last two years of his second term. One important common feature was a reliance on the COIN doctrine, which had been partially responsible for stabilizing Iraq. Obama's decision not to reinvent the wheel by implementing a new or different strategy appeared reasonable.

But the question remained whether the COIN strategy would be as successful in Afghanistan as it had been in Iraq. In Iraq, the Sunnis, as a minority, were marginalized from power by the Shia-dominated government. At the same time, they were brutalized by their previous partner, al-Qaida in Iraq. The strong desire of the Sunni groups in Iraq to fight al-Qaida to sustain their own power and influence became their chief motivation for cooperating with US forces to defeat al-Qaida. In Afghanistan, by contrast, cooperation among Sunni groups was absent. Even though the Sunnis were in the majority in Afghanistan, their ranks were divided by acute ethnic conflict between the dominant Pashtun and the minority Tajiks. President Hamid Karzai, a Pashtun, caused ample resentment among the Pashtuns by surrounding himself with the Tajik "mafia." There was also an intense rift between the predominantly Sunni Pashtun and the Hazaras, who were Shias. Then, within the Pashtun, there was powerful support for the Taliban. The Taliban were popular in Pashtun areas because of an intricate combination of fear and hatred of the American occupation forces, the hopelessly high level of corruption and ineptness of the Karzai government, abject poverty, and the seemingly uncontrollable narco-trade. Some basis had to be found for cooperation between the ISAF and the Pashtuns, or even between the ISAF and the Taliban who were willing to negotiate with the Karzai government and the Americans for the price of renouncing violence and becoming part of the government.

If President Obama had really understood the history of America's involvement in previous conflicts and the quicksand nature of any foreign involvement in Afghanistan, he would have opted for narrow objectives that could have been achieved in a short span of time. However, the objectives of his AfPak strategy were contradictory and, thereby, confusing. These objectives included:

- disrupting terrorist networks in Afghanistan, and especially Pakistan, to degrade their capacity to plan and launch international terrorist attacks;
- promoting a more capable, accountable, and effective government in Afghanistan to serve the Afghan people and to eventually function with limited international support, especially for internal security;
- developing increasingly self-reliant Afghan security forces to lead the counterinsurgency and counterterrorism fight with reduced US assistance;
- assisting efforts to enhance civilian control in Pakistan, stabilize constitutional government, and build a vibrant economy that provides opportunity for the people of Pakistan; and
- involving the international community to actively assist in addressing these objectives for Afghanistan and Pakistan, with an important leadership role for the UN.[54]

The first objective, to disrupt the capabilities of terrorist groups in Afghanistan and Pakistan to launch international terrorist attacks, was both narrow and measureable. The United States could achieve it by implementing the counterterrorism tactics of launching drone attacks (which markedly increased under the Obama administration) and by using the US Special Forces. After destroying the al-Qaida/Taliban leadership and the terrorist network, the United States could have declared victory and left the area. However, the remaining objectives of the AfPak strategy were about nation building and were destined, no matter how unwittingly, to keep the United States in Afghanistan indefinitely.

One unique feature of the AfPak strategy was that it dealt with the security of Pakistan and Afghanistan as inextricably linked, like two sides of the same coin. Second, the United States wanted Pakistan to fight its own Taliban (the TTP) and the TNSM, the two main supporters of the Taliban–al-Qaida nexus that were also involved in fighting the ISAF on the Afghan side of the border. However, Pakistan was still following its own Machiavellian strategy to deal with its jihadist groups. Even though the TTP and the TNSM became enemies of the Pakistan Army as a result of a number of operations carried out by the latter to establish its control over the FATA and NWFP regions, the army did not want to burn all its bridges by launching a campaign aimed at eradicating those groups. After all, Pakistan had an elaborate record of using those groups to destabilize Indian-administered Kashmir. Even though Pakistan's capabilities to use those groups in the Kashmir conflict were constrained, it had every intention of using them to strike at the Indian diplomatic presence in Afghanistan.

For Pakistan, the least motivating aspect of the AfPak strategy was the United States' long record of "use and abandon." The Pakistani ruling elite knew that they could – as they had done in the past – take major risks in order to help the United States stabilize Afghanistan. However, once that goal was attained, the lone superpower would once again vacate the area, leaving Pakistan to deal with the dangerous consequences of supporting American policy. It could be argued that, since the Obama administration made its intention of leaving Afghanistan clear from the outset, some sort of a rapprochement between Islamabad and Washington should have been reached about stabilizing Afghanistan with the presence and participation of Pakistan. However, diplomacy was enormously complicated because of the traditional animosity between Pakistan and India. From the point of view of the United States, India, as a major power of South Asia, had a natural and visible role in stabilizing Afghanistan. Even the Karzai government was in agreement on that issue because, as a relatively distant neighbour (since its territory is not contiguous with that of Afghanistan), India did not harbour the kind of hegemonic ambitions toward Afghanistan that Pakistan nurtured. However, any involvement of India in the security of Afghanistan was in clear violation of Pakistan's long-standing notion (or even doctrine) of strategic depth. Pakistan had always envisioned the Indian presence in its country as highly deleterious to its own security, and frequently accused India's external intelligence agency, the Research and Analysis Wing (RAW), of fomenting and promoting the insurgency in Baluchistan. The United States either did not understand Pakistan's vital security concerns, or understood but chose to ignore them because of the heady US-India strategic partnership. Whatever America's rationale was, Pakistan showed powerful resolve not to cooperate with the United

States in facilitating India's high-profile role in Afghanistan's security. That was one of the major sources of disagreement between Islamabad and Washington.

Equally important, in seeking Pakistani support to fight al-Qaida and the Taliban in Afghanistan, the United Sates wanted it to redeploy its forces from the Indo-Pak borders to the Pak-Afghan borders. Given the primacy of India-centric national security threats, which generations of the Pakistan national security establishment had nurtured, and the unresolved nature of the Kashmir conflict, there was no chance that Pakistan was going to oblige the United States by abandoning the age-old legacy of India-centricity.

The success of the Afghanistan part of the AfPak strategy and President Obama's decision to insert 30,000 more troops in Afghanistan in December 2009 (promising to withdraw them by the end of 2011) depended on the prospects of a legitimate government emerging in that country. However, those prospects got stuck in the cesspool of graft, fraud, corruption, and nepotism that was the hallmark of the government headed by President Hamid Karzai. During the Bush administration, when the United States was distracted by the war in Iraq, Bush treated Karzai as an important player and overlooked the highly corrupt nature of his rule. But President Obama – who had learned the lessons from America's disastrous experience in South Vietnam (where the illegitimacy of the South Vietnamese government was a challenge that the United States could never overcome) – insisted that Afghanistan be headed by a legitimate government free from graft. However, the Afghan presidential elections of August 2009 were marked by yet another round of ballot box stuffing and other related fraudulent practices. Consequently, the United Nations – under whose auspices the elections were held – nullified enough votes cast for Karzai that he was forced to have a runoff election. But his only opponent, Dr Abdullah Abdullah, recognizing the impossible odds of winning the runoff election, pulled out, thereby handing victory to Karzai. The extensive media coverage of electoral fraud by the Karzai campaign meant that there was no way he was going to be seen as a legitimate head of state. Yet the Obama administration was stuck with Karzai. Then it was decided in Washington that Karzai would be given a public scolding by Obama and a number of his top aides for not doing enough to clean up his administration. Karzai was left with no doubt that the Obama administration was symbolically holding its nose while dealing with him. News dispatches on the corrupt practices of the Karzai government became regular items.

US ambassador to Afghanistan Karl Eikenberry dispatched two cables to the White House in November 2009, which were promptly leaked to the press, about Karzai not behaving as an adequate strategic partner. In those cables, Eikenberry also opposed further increases in the deployment of American troops to Afghanistan. There were reports that Richard Holbrook, Obama's special envoy to South Asia, did not get along with Karzai. Another US official, Peter Galbraith, even went to the extent of stating that Karzai was unbalanced and an opium addict. The general public's overall condescension and the disdainful attitude toward Hamid Karzai by a number of prominent US officials, including President Obama, elicited a sharp response from the Afghan president. He turned the tables on the Obama administration by accusing the "West" – which was his euphemism for the Obama administration and the United Nations – of conducting a fraudulent election. He insisted that he be treated as an elected head of a sovereign state. Karzai did not take kindly to reports that US forces were threatening to put his half-brother, Ahmed Wali Karzai, on the military's "Joint Prioritized Engagement List," a euphemism for "kill or capture" list. The younger Karzai was viewed as one of the chief symptoms of the larger problems of corruption and nepotism that afflicted his brother's administration. Ahmed Wali Karzai's assassination in July 2011 underscored how fragile the Afghan government really was. Hamid Karzai's most publicized expression of anger toward the United States was his threat to join the Taliban, a statement that stunned the Obama administration.

Another prominent US official in Afghanistan, General Stanley McChrystal, had an entirely different approach toward Karzai. McChrystal, commander of the NATO forces beginning in 2009, not only treated the Afghan president with abundant respect but worked with him closely, which caused ample friction between him and Eikenberry. McChrystal was immersed in implementing the American military's COIN doctrine. That doctrine gave primacy to politics – hence the necessity for cooperation with the top political representative of that country, Hamid Karzai – and to winning the hearts and minds of the populace through a systematic campaign of nation building. McChrystal and his staff pursued this complex approach – seeking to gain the support of local civilian authorities and the

Afghan populace – with such single-mindedness that they strongly disagreed with attempts (by Eikenberry, Holbrook, and their staffs) to insert priorities that were decided in Washington. In this constant tug-and-pull between McChrystal's "nativist" and Eikenberry's Washington-driven approaches, President Obama – without publicly saying so – sided with Eikenberry. This bickering and Washington's messy way of managing its occupation of Afghanistan – which also happened in the cases of Vietnam and Iraq – were music to the ears of the Taliban and al-Qaida. That reality perfectly suited their argument that Karzai was merely a puppet and Afghanistan an occupied country to be liberated.

However, before these disagreements between Karzai and the US officials became irresolvable, a brazen sense of realism dawned in Washington. President Obama instructed his subordinates to treat Karzai with "more respect" and to regard him as a "partner" – as the legitimate chief executive of Afghanistan. Obama himself treated Karzai with more warmth and respect on his May 2010 visit to Afghanistan – a marked departure from his surprise trip to Afghanistan earlier that very month during which he reportedly lectured Karzai to clean up his government. Needless to say, the international media coverage of Obama's trips underscored the potency of the Taliban propaganda about the puppet nature of the Karzai government.

The trouble with the United States' involvement in Afghanistan was that its goals were too ambitious. The previously discussed objectives of promoting an effective government and creating a self-reliant Afghan security force were very much a part of the nation building for which the United States had neither sufficient resources nor domestic support. The global economic meltdown of 2008 also hit the lone superpower quite hard. To top it off, given the long turbulent history of Afghanistan, the chances of success for nation building in that country were slim to none.

The effectiveness of the COIN doctrine in all theatres of operation was called into serious question under the leadership of General McChrystal, whose commitment to winning the hearts and minds of Afghan civilians was criticized by American soldiers. They accused him of being more concerned about following rules of engagement that tied their hands than ensuring their safety. They were also critical of his reluctance to use air power and mortar strikes against potential civilian targets, and of restrictions on their entering the homes of Afghan civilians. As Michael Hastings, correspondent for *Rolling Stone* magazine, wrote after extensively interviewing McChrystal, his close staff, and a number of American troops, "The soldiers complain about not being allowed to use lethal force, about watching insurgents they detain be freed for lack of evidence. They want to be able to fight – like they did in Iraq, like they had in Afghanistan before McChrystal."[55] Hastings's dispatch was known more for resulting in the firing of General McChrystal by President Obama for using intemperate language about him and Vice President Joe Biden than for underscoring the real reason for his firing – McChrystal's approach was too unpopular at the White House when that *Rolling Stone* issue hit Washington. General David Petraeus took over command of the ISAF, and the United States became more focused on the counterterrorism tactics of winning the war in Afghanistan. It was apparent that the Obama administration was no longer interested in using the COIN strategy. Its slow pace of victory and resource-intensive nation-building activities were unpalatable when the US economy was facing slow growth and high unemployment.

Toward the end of President Obama's first term, the middle-to-long-range prospects of winning in Afghanistan appeared uncertain at best. To be sure, a number of tactical gains had been made, including the assassination of Bin Laden, elimination of other leaders of al-Qaida and insurgent groups in both Afghanistan and Pakistan, and reduction in the number of terrorist attacks in 2011 compared to previous years. However, there were serious questions about the economic viability of Afghanistan. According to one report, "No credible amount of aid can sustain the Afghan economy or make any form of regional development work on the necessary scale without a high degree of security and stability in virtually every critical district and city in Afghanistan, without stable and secure lines of communication in Pakistan, and without a more stable and secure Pakistan and one that puts an end to the Afghan and terrorist sanctuaries in Pakistan."[56]

During President Obama's second term in office, a number of themes have confirmed how difficult the US presence has been in Afghanistan. First, relations between Hamid Karzai and US officials (including Obama) continued to be marked by controversy and disagreement. Second, the United States' decision to recall its troops by the end of 2014 was all the proof the Taliban needed that they would emerge victorious from a conflict that had lasted more than a decade (since dismantlement of the Taliban regime in 2001).

Third, the United States' incessant focus on the "counterterrorism plus" option started to cause a lot tension between Karzai and US officials. Under that approach (which is frequently called a strategy), the United States focused on counterterrorism operations rather than on COIN-related activities. Karzai was especially infuriated with the ISAF air operations, which frequently caused civilian deaths. In addition, he wanted the US Special Forces night raids into the homes of Afghan citizens stopped. Although (from the perspective of Special Forces operations) those raids were highly effective in capturing or killing suspected terrorists, in a Muslim country, such operations were culturally offensive.

Another source of major contention between the United States and President Karzai was the former's decision to negotiate with the Taliban of Afghanistan. Since Karzai was not involved in that process, he remained highly suspicious of it. The negotiations took place in Doha, Qatar, which isolated Karzai and left him uninformed about their modalities and progress, unless decided otherwise by the United States. The negotiations became highly controversial when the representatives of the Taliban in Qatar named their office building an embassy of the Islamic Emirate of Afghanistan and hoisted their flag over it. Karzai's protestations over this development resulted in the closing of that "embassy." The negotiations, however, continued under secrecy, or so suspected the Karzai officials. If the purpose of the negotiations was to create some palpable stake for the Taliban in the governance of Afghanistan in the coming years, then Karzai had to be involved. Pakistan, although left out of the negotiations, stayed informed through its own channels of open communications with the Taliban of Afghanistan.

As an ultimate expression of disdain at the way the Obama administration had been treating him, Karzai refused to sign the Basic Security Agreement (BSA), even though it was overwhelmingly approved by the loya jirga. That agreement was aimed at keeping approximately 15,000 foreign troops stationed around the country, even after the withdrawal of most NATO forces by the end of 2014.[57] In response, the United States continued its own brinkmanship by letting the US media know that Obama was also considering a "zero option," whereby he would recall all US troops from Afghanistan toward the end of 2014. For his part, Karzai, when asked during a TV appearance before a supportive audience in Afghanistan about how his refusal to sign the agreement might result in the United

States' departure from his country, said with a smirk, "The US has come and will not go, brother. It does not go. Therefore, ask for your demands and don't worry."[58]

The election of Ashraf Ghani as the new president of Afghanistan on 21 September 2014 opened a new chapter in his country's highly turbulent ties with the United States. Unlike his predecessor, Ghani was US-educated and had spent a great deal of his professional life in the United States. He had also spent some time in Pakistan doing fieldwork on such heady topics as state building and social transformation. He had studied the role of madrassas in Pakistan and was fully aware of their influence on the evolution of jihadi culture in Afghanistan.

Ghani brought to his office a profound sense that the United State could play a positive role in Afghanistan, even as it continued to withdraw its military presence from his native land. After becoming president, he not only eagerly signed the BSA, which Karzai had steadily refused to sign, but took a bold position that the United States should consider slowing down its military withdrawal from Afghanistan. However, President Ghani was forced to accept a power-sharing agreement, brokered by US secretary of state John Kerry, with Abdullah Abdullah. Abdullah had accused the Ghani camp of election fraud and did not want to have any part in the government. As a compromise, he was offered the position of chief executive officer. This division of authority between Ghani and Abdullah promised frequent inertia and immobilism whenever those two actors failed to agree on a major policy issue. Equally disconcerting, the Taliban made it no secret that they viewed the formal conclusion of ISAF military operations as "a clear indication of their [US] defeat and disappointment." Thus, the conflict between the United States and the Taliban forces was very much alive.

Although US-Afghan relations markedly improved during the Ghani administration, the security situation inside that country was deteriorating and Pak-Afghan relations were strained. Approving President Ghani's request, President Obama announced that he would delay the US withdrawal from Afghanistan. The constant tensions that had characterized Pak-Afghan relations under Karzai eased under Ghani, at least temporarily. He made several overtures by visiting Prime Minister Nawaz Sharif and General Raheel Sharif at the Army's general headquarters. He wanted the Pakistani establishment to control the Haqqani group's terrorist attacks inside his country. Pakistan continued its duplicitous games by assuring Ghani that it was working to disrupt the infrastructure of that group. In reality, Pakistan was still dealing with the Haqqani group as a reliable tool to launch terrorist attacks on Indian diplomatic personnel and facilities inside Afghanistan. Publicly, the Pak Army complained that 80 per cent of anti-Pakistan insurgency originated from Afghanistan.[59] This type of diplomatic exchange was a clear indication that "the trust deficit between the neighbors" was descending "into the abyss."[60]

The two meetings held between Pakistan and Afghan officials and representatives of the Taliban in July and August 2015 raised hopes for some progress. However, those hopes were dashed because of bickering within the Taliban movement. Mullah Mansour's leadership was being challenged by splinter groups angered that he had hidden the news of Mullah Omar's death for two years.

China entered the dialogue by offering to host future rounds of negotiations; however, it refused to play the role of mediator. The most hopeful developments regarding the peace negotiations were the involvement of both China and the United States in pushing for a resolution, and the United States' promise to leave its forces stationed in Afghanistan until 2017. China's heightened interest in the Pak-Afghan negotiations stemmed from increased wariness about the growing activities of the Islamic Movement of Uzbekistan (IMU) terrorists in northern Afghanistan, where they were also hosting Uighur militants. Thus, China wanted to influence the Pak-Afghan dialogue to minimize the chances of any growth in the power and presence of what it called "East Turkestan terrorists."[61]

Despite these diplomatic overtures, the future of Afghanistan appeared bleak in 2016. Taliban attacks were getting more frequent and ferocious. Moreover, "Afghan government officials have become directly involved in the opium trade, expanding their competition with the Taliban ... into a struggle for control of the drug traffic and revenue." As the trade "becomes more institutionalized in Afghanistan, it has undercut years of anticorruption efforts." The United States alone has spent "more than $7 billion in the past 14 years" battling Afghanistan's poppy production.[62] To top it all, the army general John Campbell, commander of the US forces in Afghanistan, testifying before the Senate Armed Services Committee, said "that 'Afghanistan is at an inflection point' and that 2016 could be 'no better and possibly worse than 2015' if adjustments are not made." He added, "Now, more than ever, the United States should not waver in Afghanistan."[63]

CLOSING OBSERVATIONS

Pakistan and Afghanistan are extremely important countries in the context of this book. Islamization has been encouraged and nurtured in Pakistan as a state policy since the 1970s. It became a conduit for launching a US-sponsored jihad in the 1980s. That action revived the idea of jihad, at least in the minds of practitioners, as highly applicable in the context of contemporary world affairs as a tool for altering the balance of power and potentially for bringing about regime change in other Muslim countries.

General support for the promulgation of the Shariah is strong in Pakistan as a predominantly Muslim country. This fact alarms the United States. In an excellent study on Islam, militancy, and politics in Pakistan, Christine Fair, Neil Malhotra, and Jacob Shapiro found that 69 per cent of the respondents "indicated that Shariah *should* play either a 'much greater role' or a 'somewhat larger role.'" However, one has to examine closely the meaning of Shariah for Pakistanis. "Rather than evidencing support for a backward looking social order," more than 95 per cent of the respondents wanted "more Shariah because they believe[d] such a system would better provide services, justice, personal security, and diminished corruption." Pakistanis also manifested a high degree of religiosity or piety; however, that trait did not predict "increased support for Islamist militancy writ large."

A number of other noteworthy features of this study should be highlighted here. Fair, Malhotra, and Shapiro reported that the "plurality" of respondents (44.6 per cent) believed that "jihad is both a personal struggle for righteousness and protecting Muslim Ummah through war." Nearly equal numbers of respondents (one in four) indicated that "jihad is solely a personal struggle for righteousness" or that "jihad is solely protecting the Muslim Ummah through war." Both viewpoints underscore the noble aspects of jihad. The authors concluded, "Clearly a large majority of Pakistanis embrace militant dimensions of jihad *in principle*" (emphasis added). Believing in jihad in principle is entirely different from practicing its military version.

Furthermore, not all provinces of Pakistan manifest support for militant jihad. That support is "far more likely" in the Punjab and the

NWFP than in Sindh and Baluchistan, where jihad is considered "mostly as a personal struggle." And there is still some debate over "who has the proper authority to declare militant jihad be it a Muslim government or an individual or other non-state actor." Forty-three per cent of respondents believed that "the use of military force to protect a Muslim country or Muslim Ummah" was a prerogative of the state. "The next largest group (35 percent) thought that both government and non-government actors [could] do so."[64] It is also noteworthy that, as reported by the Pew Research Center, the support for Bin Laden went down in Pakistan from a high of 46 per cent in 2003 to a remarkable low of 18 per cent in 2009 and 2010.[65] This is clearly not a picture of Pakistan where Islamic extremism is even mildly popular or where a majority of the populace is supportive of militant jihad.

Nevertheless, the greatest challenge for Pakistan is its continued Islamization and the role of the Deobandi/Wahhabi forms of Islam, which actively promoted the militant doctrine of jihad in the past. From the 1980s on, the Deobandi schools of the northwestern region of Pakistan became "ideal types" for similar schools elsewhere to indoctrinate an unending number of jihadists who would not think twice before sacrificing their own lives to create instability and mayhem in a number of countries in the Arab world, Central Asia, North Caucasus, and parts of East Asia.

Pakistan in the twenty-first century has become a place where the jihadists' resolve to dismantle the existing government through their practice of Islamism appears to be on the rise (Islamism, as defined in this book, is about the acquisition of territory by jihadists for a particular motive and based on a particular understanding of Islam). The PPP-led government of Asif Ali Zardari and then the Muslim League civilian government of Nawaz Sharif appeared equally averse to taking on the jihadists. When the government of Nawaz Sharif offered to negotiate with them, they did not recognize his government as a legitimate entity. Thus, there was no basis for negotiations whereby some sort of a modus vivendi was possible. The Pak Army, in initiating Zarb-e-Azb, showed new resolve to destroy the jihadists' aspirations related to Islamism. As promising as that operation was for the defeat and possible elimination of the jihadists from Pakistan, the overall attitude of the Pak Army toward the "good" jihadists remained unchanged. The decision to allow the Haqqani group to remain intact unambiguously signalled to the world that Pakistan's attempts to defeat these jihadist forces were half-hearted. It was unfortunate that the Pakistani military leaders remained heedless of the fact that an unstable Afghanistan (which remained a target of the Haqqani group terrorists) would have deleterious spillover effects on Pakistan's own political stability.

The rising tide of Islamism in Pakistan was also aimed at eliminating the presence and influence of the United States from that country. US-Pak relations have undergone marked deterioration during the Obama presidency. During the 2008 campaign, candidate Barack Obama promised to take the war against al-Qaida to Pakistan, if necessary. As president, he did just that. During Obama's first term, the contradictions of Pakistani foreign policy under General Musharraf – telling the United States that Pakistan was fighting to eliminate jihadists from within, but continuing to cooperate with the Islamist parties in the domestic political arena and to use the Haqqani group's perpetration of terrorism in Afghanistan as a tool of foreign policy – caught up with Pakistan. Whereas President George W. Bush and his top officials had continued to do business as usual with Pakistan, despite their awareness of these contradictions, Obama made a clean break from that approach. Top Obama officials not only continued to harp on those contradictions, but they also insisted that Pak officials had better concentrate on eliminating them forthwith. When Pakistan stalled, US-Pak relations suffered.

US-Pak relations under Obama remained tense. The fact that Osama Bin Laden was found hiding in Pakistan's foremost garrison city of Abbottabad seriously undermined whatever little trust Obama had in Pakistan's earnestness about combatting terrorism within its own borders as well as in Afghanistan. Still, a substantial share of the lack of trust between the two countries must be borne by President Obama and his so-called AfPak strategy, which was supposedly assiduously put together by his top advisors. That strategy pooh-poohed Pakistan's India-related security concerns. Obama's perspective that India should play a major role in the internal security of Afghanistan showed poor judgment about how Pakistan would perceive that role. The United States did allow large security and economic assistance to Pakistan under the Kerry-Lugar-Berman Bill. However, the intrusive aspect of that aid package, designed to win the cooperation of Pakistan toward Afghanistan, did not achieve its intended outcome. The United States assumed that Pakistan would go along with Washington's conclusion that India should play a major role in America's strategic maneuvering in Afghanistan, East Asia, and particularly China. When the Obama administration leaned further toward India under its Asia Pivot strategy, Pakistan's disgruntlement toward the United States increased. Under these circumstances, Obama's AfPak strategy was doomed to fail, at least in terms of what Pakistan was expected to do to support it.

Afghanistan's distinctiveness in the context of this study stems from the fact that the US-supported jihadists succeeded in ousting the Soviet Union from that country in the 1980s. Then the mujahedeen-led government of Islamists came to power in 1991. That government lasted until 1996 when the Taliban – the self-styled jihadists – captured power. Cumulatively speaking, Islamism has an elaborate record of success in Afghanistan.

In terms of assessing Obama's legacy, Afghanistan is likely to go down as a failure. That country's security has been steadily deteriorating. The Taliban knew that the United States was on its way out. The great tragedy of Afghanistan stems from its strategic geographic location as a landlocked country contiguous to Iran, Pakistan, Turkmenistan, Uzbekistan, and Tajikistan. China, Russia, and India are not too far from there. Thus, Afghanistan is likely to remain a pawn in the traditional rivalry between Pakistan and India and between Pakistan and Iran, as it has been in past decades. Its proximity to a number of Central Asian states makes it vulnerable to a potential resurgence of historical rivalry between Russia and China, both of whom have been asserting their respective hegemonies in that region since the implosion of the USSR. In the nineteenth century, czarist Russia and the then colonial ruler of India, Great Britain, fought over it. Their legendary rivalry was well-encapsulated in the phrase "the Great Game." Soon after the creation of Pakistan, rulers of that country gravitated toward making sure that Afghanistan remained in their sphere of influence under the rubric of "strategic depth." The United States and the USSR fought their last battle of the Cold War in that country. When the war ended, Afghanistan's security continued to deteriorate, first under the mujahedeen's highly turbulent rule and then under the bloody reign of the Taliban. The historical weakness of Afghanistan also made it a favourite gathering place of the jihadist forces of al-Qaida in the1990s. Afghanistan has the unfortunate moniker of being the place from where the dreadful plan to attack the United States was hatched and launched. Consequently, Afghanistan became the battleground of the first major conflict of the post–Cold War and post–9/11 eras. It promises to remain in that capacity for at least several more decades of the twenty-first century. As much as it was hoped that the United States, after defeating the Taliban regime in 2001, would stay and build Afghanistan into a normal modern state, that did not happen. Instead, George W. Bush took his GWOT to Iraq. Not many observers stop to think that, even if Bush had stayed and tried to rebuild Afghanistan, the country may have been beyond repair given the level of poverty, underdevelopment, and corruption, and the acute dependence of farmers and bureaucrats at all levels on the opium trade. These realities make Afghanistan a place where a nexus of jihadists, global narcotics traders, international arms merchants, and human traffickers will continue to operate.

Despite the apparent failure of the United States to stabilize Afghanistan, the world should celebrate the Americans' conclusion that Afghanistan is not beyond repair and their decision to stay and stabilize it. US policy makers know how far the deadly arms of the terrorists and jihadists could reach if their ideology was allowed to mushroom in that country. Thus, America's decision to stay in Afghanistan is aimed at promoting the security of the entire community of nations. That endeavour will be successful only when the global community joins the United States. Afghanistan, it seems, is waiting to witness the resumption of the long war involving the Taliban, ISIS, and Central Asian terrorist groups who firmly believe that their ultimate victory in that war is guaranteed.

6

The Dynamics of the Islamist Challenge from Iran

SYNOPSIS

Iran is the only country where an anti-American Islamist government came to power as the result of a revolution. The protest movement against the regime of Mohammad Reza Pahlavi had been in the making since the early 1960s or even before; however, by 1978 its Islamist aspects were becoming increasingly predominant. It might not have been the intent of the anti-Pahlavi forces to establish an Islamist government, but that was what happened when the Iranian autocrat ignominiously fled and Ayatollah Rouhollah Khomeini entered the country in an unambiguous triumph of Islamism. Since then, Iran and the United States have remained adversaries. The Islamist government fired the opening salvo when it held fifty-two American diplomatic personnel hostage for 444 days – an action that affected the outcome of the 1980 US presidential election. The United States, in turn, attempted on several occasions to bring about regime change in Iran.

Since the US invasion of Iraq and the removal of Saddam Hussein's regime, the Islamic Republic of Iran remains the only major challenge to America's dominance in the Middle East. Iran's Islamist challenge to the United States in West and South Asia comes through its ongoing sectarian-based rivalry with Saudi Arabia and Pakistan. These two Sunni countries envisioned the 1979 revolution of Iran as a Shia phenomenon, and thus as a challenge to Sunni Islam, even though Ayatollah Khomeini was adamant about presenting that revolution to the rest of Muslim world as an Islamic event. The leading role of Saudi Arabia and Pakistan in the US-sponsored jihad to oust the

Soviet Union from Afghanistan in the 1980s was portrayed as a response of Sunni Islam to the communist (atheist) superpower. As such, Riyadh and Islamabad wanted to signal to the Muslim world that Sunni Islam was just as revolutionary in nature as its Shia counterpart. This evolving Shia-Sunni conflict emerged in West Asia as a spiralling rivalry between Iran and Saudi Arabia in the 1990s and beyond. Although Iran did not amplify the Shia nature of its revolution for the rest of the Islamic world, it was fully cognizant that the United States would comprehend the challenging attributes of this rivalry for its own strategic dominance in West Asia.

Iran's Islamist challenge to the United States in the Levant emerged in the 1980s in the form of a terrorist attack on the US Marine barracks and in the creation of Hezbollah. The 1983 attack on the marines was allegedly perpetrated by an Iranian-backed terrorist group, Islamic Jihad. Hezbollah, another Islamist group officially established in 1985, has become a powerful tool of Iran's foreign policy and influence against the United States and Israel.

The Islamist challenge that Iran posed to the United States after the US invasion of Iraq in 2003 became obvious right after the implosion of the Saddam regime. The US decision to transform Iraq into an Islamic democracy was going to play right into Iran's hand. Since the Shias formed more than 60 per cent of the population of that country, they would dominate the resultant democracy. Iran fully exploited that fact by supporting the Iraqi insurgency. The chief purpose of that insurgency and Iran's growing presence in the post-Saddam Iraq was to expel the American forces. The US withdrawal of its troops from Iraq in 2011 was the ultimate victory for Iran, and Iraq came fully under its influence.

The chief Islamist challenge from Iran to the United States in the twenty-first century comes from its forces in Syria, which are supporting the Assad regime. If the Assad regime falls, Iran's strategic presence and influence in the Levant will likely suffer irredeemably. Thus, Iran has been investing enormous capital and military assistance through the use of Shia militias from Iraq and Hezbollah, and especially through the use of its own Quds Force, to fight against ISIS and to boost the chances for survival of the Assad regime. Saudi Arabia and the UAE, on the other hand, have invested their respective resources in support of the anti-Assad Sunni forces seeking to bring about regime change in Syria. Consequently, Syria has become a battleground for the exercise of Shia and Sunni Islamism.

Within Iran itself, in the second decade of the twenty-first century, the Iranian government was facing a legitimacy-related challenge. As well, Iran faced a possible military conflict either with the United States and/or with Israel over Iran's nuclear program. Iran signed the nuclear agreement – the Joint Comprehensive Plan of Action – with the United States, other permanent members of the United Nations Security Council (UNSC), and Germany on 14 July 2015. Although this development considerably reduced the chances of military conflict, the legacy of conflict and suspicion, both in Tehran and in Washington, has been too long and rancorous for anyone to predict which way those ties might lead.

Iran has interacted with all great powers in a highly nuanced manner. Although Ayatollah Rouhollah Khomeini declared Iran's foreign policy to be "neither East nor West," the vagaries of global politics forced Iran to cooperate with Beijing and Moscow. Iran's ties with China and Russia are friendly in a symbiotic way. As US-Russia tensions rose due to Vladimir Putin's annexation of Crimea in March 2014, Russia's continued militarism toward Ukraine, and especially its all-out military support of Bashar al-Assad in Syria, Iran's own support of the Syrian government and cooperation with Russia has become an important development for Iran. If a political solution to the Syrian conflict emerges, Iran is likely to play a crucial role in it, along with Russia and the United States. Sino-Iranian strategic cooperation has also become paramount for both countries, as China continues to enhance its diplomatic profile in the Persian Gulf and elsewhere in the Middle East and Africa.

THE *SUI GENERIS* NATURE OF THE IRANIAN REVOLUTION

The very creation of the Islamic Republic of Iran in 1979 sowed the seeds of antagonism between that country and the United States. As a result of the Islamic revolution, America lost one of its staunchest allies in the Middle East, Mohammad Reza Pahlavi. The government dominated by the ayatollahs was stridently anti-American, as witnessed by the major role it played in the Iranian hostage crisis.

The Islamic revolution of Iran was a *sui generis* event for a variety of reasons. First and foremost, it brought about an end to an imperial government that was strongly supported by the United States. Second, it led to the establishment of an Islamic government on the basis of a brand new doctrine, *vilayat-e-faqih* (rule of the clergy). This doctrine focuses on the legitimacy of the government. Since the *Ithna'ashari* (Twelvers) Shiites give enormous importance to the descendants of the Prophet of Islam, no one else can claim that legitimacy except for the heavenly ordained line of the Twelve Imams, starting with the first Imam, Ali Ibn-e-Abu Talib, the first cousin and son-in-law of the Prophet. The last of these Imams, Muhammad al-Mahdi, went into occultation (*ghayba* or deliberate absence of undefined length). Even in occultation, according to the Twelver doctrine, only Mahdi could legitimately challenge the authority of existing governments. The Shiite clerics had the authority to serve as credible "interpreter[s] and custodian[s] of the traditions of the Imams." This practice created an "inherent tension in Shiite Iran between dynastic rulers and the clergy, with authority held by the former and legitimacy residing in the latter." Under the Pahlavi dynasty, the state took "forceful measures to subjugate and marginalize the clergy." The Islamic revolution of 1979 "was partly a backlash to this subordination of clerical power."[1]

Through the declaration of *vilayat-e-faqih*, Ayatollah Khomeini, in essence, "responded with arguments for the de jure ascent of the clergy as the political authority along with the abolition of the monarchy." Through this doctrine, he also declared that "political authority ought to be entrusted to the clerical establishment – that is, to the trustworthy custodians of the Mahdhi's traditions as well as those of the previous Imams." But in reality, Khomeini was not interested in exclusive clerical power; instead, he proposed a model that combined the clergy's legitimatizing role with that of state authoritarianism. Khomeini's vision of the *faqih* was "shaped by both the Mahdi of Shiism and the autocratic Shah of Iranian history."[2] This authoritarian feature of the Islamic government caused tension between the government and the populace, tension that has intensified in the twenty-first century as the revolution became a distant memory for the new generation of Iranians.

Third, one of the most innovative creations of the Islamic revolution was the Islamic Revolutionary Guard Corps (IRGC), a body quite separate from and independent of the conventional armed forces. Ayatollah Khomeini's decision to establish the IRGC was based on his fear that Iran's conventional army would pull a coup and overturn the Islamic Republic. The fact that the Carter administration tried to persuade the army to overthrow the then newly established revolutionary government was the chief motivating force behind Khomeini's decision to eliminate that threat. Fourth, the political message of the Islamic revolution – that it can oust a monarchy and transform a country into a republic – created a near panic situation in the Persian Gulf region, where revolutionary creeds of all sorts, especially pan-Arabism and Shia resurgence, were major threats to monarchical rule. The autocratic rulers in neighbouring West Asia shuddered at an interpretation of doctrine that gave the clergy such power. Their region was already going through turbulent times. Suddenly, in December 1979, the Soviet Union invaded Afghanistan, a Muslim country, which spawned a plethora of speculation about the Soviet Union's resolve to go beyond Afghanistan and make its presence known in the warm waters of the Persian Gulf.

As much as the Islamic Republic of Iran emphasized the Islamic nature of its revolution, the Sunni leaders of West Asia and Pakistan envisaged it as a major Shia phenomenon. Thus, one of the chief reasons that Saudi Arabia and Pakistan decided to get so visibly involved in the US attempt to dislodge the Soviet rule from Afghanistan in 1979 was to show the world of Islam at large that they, as major Sunni states, were no less revolutionary about hoisting the flag of Sunni Islam than Iran was about demonstrating the dynamism of Shia Islam.

Fear of the Iranian revolution compelled the Arab states to cooperate with, and actively support, Saddam Hussein, when he invaded Iran in 1981. America's antagonism toward Iran likewise motivated the administration of President Ronald Reagan to side with Iraq as the lesser of "two evils" in that war. Antipathy toward the Islamic Republic also motivated the United States to establish a major regional command, the US Central Command (CENTCOM), and the Arab states of the Persian Gulf to establish the Gulf Cooperation Council (GCC), an organization whose raison d'être was to promote economic and security cooperation among Arab states. As much as its members emphasized that it was not aimed at containing or isolating Iran, the fact that Iran was not allowed to become a member of the GCC spoke volumes about its original purpose.

The purpose of CENTCOM was twofold. First, it aimed to deter and discourage the Soviet Union from going beyond Afghanistan into the Persian Gulf area. The Soviet invasion and occupation of a Muslim state shattered the widely prevalent paradigm in Washington that the post–World War II order, which underscored the spheres of influence of the two superpowers, would not be challenged, much less altered. Second, the establishment of CENTCOM sent a clear message to Iran that Washington was fully prepared to take military action in the wake of the fall of another friendly Persian Gulf country. Considering that CENTCOM played a leading role in conducting the Gulf War of 1991, in invading Afghanistan in 2001, and in toppling the regime of Saddam Hussein in 2003, one can only imagine how momentous a role the Iranian revolution played in escalating the defensive as well as the offensive military capabilities of the United States.

The Saudi and Pakistani collaborative endeavours, which worked so well in expelling the Soviet Union from Afghanistan, with enormous military and economic assistance from the United States, also unleashed the Sunni jihadi forces. Those forces did not disappear simply because the Soviet Union was ousted from Afghanistan in 1989. Indeed, what the mujahedeen accomplished in defeating one superpower (the Soviet Union) and what the Islamic revolution accomplished in ousting Reza Pahlavi (America's premier ally in the Middle East) created long-lasting precedents that were to challenge the lone superpower of the post–Cold War era as well as two other great powers, China in Xinjiang and Russia in the Caucasus. The "Afghan Arabs" and just "Afghans" – the Arab fighters and those of other nationalities who volunteered to fight and defeat the "godless commies" – were to start "regional jihads" of their own in the Maghreb (North Africa) and Southeast Asia, and, after the emergence of the Central Asian republics, there as well (chapter 7). As we have seen, Pakistan and Afghanistan also became major targets of the Islamist forces (chapter 5).

The Islamic revolution of 1979–80 created an ostensibly enduring phenomenon – the Islamist challenge – that threatens the political status quo in the Muslim world at large as well as the hegemony of the United States, primarily in the Middle East and South Asia (in Pakistan and Afghanistan, next door to Iran). The *sui generis* nature of the Islamic revolution also poses internal problems of legitimacy. Iran's Green Movement of 2009 portrayed the Islamic regime as illegitimate because of the fraudulent practices implemented to keep President Mahmoud Ahmadinejad in office. Although the movement did not succeed in bringing about regime change, it might be considered a progenitor of the Arab Awakening.

FIGHTING THE "GREAT SATAN" AND DRINKING THE "POISONED CHALICE"

From the inception of the Islamic Republic, Iran relied heavily on religious rhetoric to condemn the United States as the "Great Satan" for its "exploitation" of Iran under "America's Shah." Similarly, the Soviet Union was depicted as the "little Satan." Since relations with either power were almost equally undesirable, Khomeini proclaimed neutrality by using the Qur'anic expression, *la sharaqiyya wala gharabiyya* (neither East nor West). He thereby couched in religious phraseology the popular concept of the previous two decades, "positive neutrality."

Within a year or so after the establishment of the Islamic Republic, Iraq started a war with Iran. The driving force for that war was Saddam Hussein's fear of the influence of Ayatollah Khomeini's charismatic revolutionary leadership on Iraq's large Shia population, which had been relentlessly victimized by his brutal regime. From the perspectives of neighbouring Arab states and the United States, however, the Iran-Iraq War was a blessing in disguise. If Saddam could defeat the Iranian forces, which were severely weakened in the aftermath of the revolution, then the Arab sheikhdoms would not have to worry about Khomeini's threats to export the revolution to their states. From the vantage point of Washington, the defeat of Iran would have been especially welcomed. The Iranian revolution was the first humiliation the lone superpower had experienced in the Middle East. Neither the Arab states nor the United States understood the real potential power of the Islamic revolution, but they were certain that it was something they could ignore at their own peril.

The Iran-Iraq War threatened to oust the Islamic rulers from power while the revolution was still in its infancy. The Iraqi invasion had to be defeated. But in addition to fighting the war with armed forces ravaged by the revolution, Iran encountered a systematic American campaign to close international markets for the purchase of military weapons. The Soviet Union, however, turned out to be willing to sell weapons to Iran, covertly at first, since it was the chief supplier of weapons to Iraq, but openly later on. The Soviet leaders were calculating the long-term benefits of having Islamic Iran – which had long been pro-American – on their side.

The Soviet supply of weapons played a crucial role in Khomeini's decision to abandon all semblance of neutrality and gain access to weapons from Moscow and all other sources that either were not under US embargo or were not complying with it. Thus the Iran-Iraq War led to the eventual major reliance of Iran on Soviet weapons. That reliance outlasted the Cold War, because American economic and military sanctions continued to deprive Iran of Western arms. Russia, the chief successor state of the Soviet Union, thus became Iran's major military supplier.

The Iran-Iraq War was settled in favour of Iraq. One reason for that outcome was the huge financial and political support for Iraq from the Persian Gulf monarchies. Only Syria and Libya sided with Iran. The second, and crucial, reason was the significant measures taken by the Reagan administration to help Iraq win. For instance, Reagan, despite opposition from Congress, removed Iraq from the list of known terrorist states. That action enabled the United States to sell Defender helicopters to Iraq. Between 1982 and 1988, the Defense Intelligence Agency (DIA) supplied Iraq with detailed information on "Iranian troop deployments, tactical planning for battles, plans for air strikes and bomb damage assessments." A national security directive made clear that "the US 'would do whatever was necessary and legal' to prevent Iraq from losing its war with Iran." The United States also initiated a global campaign to ensure the supply of hi-tech instruments, chemical and other industrial goods, and even the transfer of US weapons from Saudi Arabia, Egypt, and Jordan to Iraq. The United States not only had full knowledge of Iraq's use of chemical weapons on Iranian forces, but it also allowed Dow Chemical to supply $1.5 million worth of pesticide to Iraq, knowing that it would be used against Iran. In 1991, the *Financial Times* reported that a chemical company from Florida shipped cyanide to Iraq during the 1980s using a special CIA courier. It is a well-known fact that cyanide was used extensively during that war.[3] Through these actions, Washington left little doubt in Iran how serious it was about defeating and ousting the Islamic rulers from power.

The United States' decision to reflag Kuwaiti oil tankers and to deploy US naval vessels to escort them under the pretext of "defense of freedom of the sea" further escalated its support for Iraq in that war. In reality, that action was to deter Iran from attacking the Kuwaiti and Saudi vessels. As active supporters of Iraq, Saudi Arabia and Kuwait were de jure parties to the war and, as such, their vessels were regarded by Iran as fair game. Although Iran may have been justified in attacking those vessels, the United States was more interested in confronting the Iranian navy and punishing Iran. The United States dropped all semblance of tacitly supporting Iraq when, in 1987, its navy attacked and destroyed Iranian oil platforms. That could be construed as an all-out attempt by the United States to defeat Iran in that war. On 20 July 1988, Iran reluctantly accepted the terms of ceasefire outlined in UN Resolution 598. Nothing could have more aptly expressed Iran's dejection than the words of Ayatollah Khomeini: "Happy are those who have departed through martyrdom. Happy are those who have lost their lives in this convoy of light. Unhappy am I that I still survive and have drunk the poisoned chalice."[4]

Although Iran lost the war waged by Saddam Hussein largely because of America's aggressive maneuvers in the diplomatic arena and in equipping the Iraqi military, it was not exactly left without any countermeasures against the United States. One significant place that provided ample opportunity for taking countermeasures against the lone superpower was Lebanon.

IRAN AND THE ISLAMIZATION OF LEBANON

Lebanese politics had been highly charged since the 1970s because of the escalating violence between Israel and the Palestine Liberation Organization (PLO), which took refuge in Lebanon after King Hussein expelled it from Jordan following the civil war of 1970. With the growing power of the PLO in Lebanon and its use of Lebanese territory to launch attacks on Israel, the Jewish state increasingly considered invading Lebanon to eradicate the PLO. The Taif Agreement of 1976 legitimized Syria's military presence in Lebanon as a stabilizing Arab force. But inside Lebanon, the rising spirals of violence due to the PLO were also causing enormous resentment among the Shias, who were in the majority in the southern part of that country.

Throughout the 1980s, Iran played a crucial role in the increasingly turbulent politics of Lebanon, exercising its version of Islamism in order to influence the distribution of political power in support of its own strategic interests. For that purpose, Iran deftly utilized, if not exploited, the commonality of Shia Islam between its polity and Lebanon. It also established a powerful nexus with Syria, the dominant state in Lebanon and a country where the Alawite (a sect of Shia Islam) regime of Hafez al-Assad was in control of the government. One should never underestimate Iran's decision to establish a permanent presence and influence in Lebanon. Syria, for its part, exploited its own nexus with Hezbollah for predominantly geopolitical purposes.

The roots Hezbollah's creation go back to the groundbreaking work done by Musa al-Sadr, an Iranian cleric of Lebanese descent. Prior to Iran's Islamic revolution, he "devoted two decades to raising the political and religious consciousness and the quality of life of Lebanon's long-underprivileged Shia community."[5] Al-Sadr established the Amal movement (or Hope movement) in 1974 as an antithesis to the *zuama* (feudal lords) clientism-ridden politics of Lebanon. The Amal movement politicized the Shia populace of Lebanon. Since the Iranian revolution was also a Shia event, it infused the Shias of Lebanon with militant pride and heightened their political ambitions about what they could achieve inside Lebanon, where the 1943 National Pact had made them virtually powerless.[6] By the 1980s, they were no longer willing to suffer quietly in a class struggle that had systematically marginalized them. The Shias of Lebanon, with a mounting pride in their faith and an equally powerful resolve to change the Sunni and Christian-dominated political power structure in their favour, were ready and willing candidates for the ideological and military education provided by large contingents of Iranian agents sent to serve the strategic objectives of Iran.

Iran played a major role in creating Hezbollah, which officially came into existence on 16 February 1985 (although it may have been a distinct entity since 1982).[7] Iran's Revolutionary Guard ensured that Hezbollah emerged, first, as a potent paramilitary force and then as a major politico-military organization. Indeed, no single act of Iran was more significant in establishing its political clout and promoting its strategic presence and interests in Lebanon than its creation of Hezbollah. According to one source, "Critical Hizbollah decisions ... are said to be verified with Iran's Supreme Leader 'Ali Khamenei, considered by the party to be their ultimate source of authority."[8] Hezbollah's presence permanently altered the internal power distribution of Lebanon, enabling Iran to become a potent actor in challenging the strategic dominance of the United States and in thwarting Israel's ambitions to transform Lebanon into a vassal state.

The worldview of the Hezbollah leadership was heavily religious and imbued with the philosophies of Ayatollah Muhammad Baqir al-Sadr, Grand Ayatollah Muhsin al-Hakim of Iraq, Ayatollah Rouhollah Khomeini of Iran, and Ayatollah Hussein Fadlallah. As such, Hezbollah was initially in harmony with the proposition of establishing the rule of the clergy (*vilayat-e-faqih*) in Lebanon. Its manifesto, issued in 1985, declared it to be a representative of all oppressed Muslims in Lebanon and throughout the world. Echoing the vision of the Islamic revolution of Iran, the manifesto declared, "We are the sons of the *ummah* (Muslim community) – the party of God (Hizb Allah) the vanguard of which was made victorious by God in Iran ... We are an ummah linked to the Muslims of the whole world by the solid doctrinal and religious connection of Islam ... Our behavior is dictated to us by legal principles laid down by the light of an overall political conception defined by the leading jurist (vilayat al-faqih)." It ridiculed the United States' depiction of it as "nothing but a bunch of fanatic terrorists whose sole aim is to dynamite bars and destroy slot machines."[9] Its ideology was anti-imperialistic, and it favoured an Islamic government. Originally, it declared fidelity to Ayatollah Rouhollah Khomeini. However, Hezbollah abandoned the doctrine of *vilayat-e-faqih* in the 1990s when the party started to understand the irreconcilable conflict between its implementation and the pluralistic nature of the Lebanese polity.

Hezbollah was contemptuous of corrupt Lebanese politics and wanted no part of Amal's perspectives related to accommodation and clientelism, in which votes were bought through a complex process of meetings between heads of clans/families and party representatives in exchange for promises to supply various social services to those families. It took Hezbollah several years to finally settle down, in terms of defining its Lebanese identity, its ideology, and its modus operandi – cumulatively described as a process of Lebanonization – before it emerged both as a paramilitary and as a political organization of considerable influence inside the Lebanese political arena. It accepted the multiconfessional political posture of Lebanon, decided to participate in the elections, and declared its commitment to promoting the political rights and protecting the economic interests of the Shias – the largest and growing segment of the Lebanese population. And the Islamic Republic of Iran bankrolled Hezbollah's position.

Although Hezbollah shared Iran's antipathy toward the United States, its views of the Soviet Union were equally inflammatory. One Hezbollah commentator described the communist superpower as "not one iota different from the Americans in terms of political danger, indeed [the Soviet Union is] more dangerous than them in terms of ideological considerations."[10] Nevertheless, according to Hezbollah, "the starring role for Islam's main enemy ... went to the United States," which directly or indirectly through "its 'spearhead' Israel" has inflicted "suffering upon the Muslims of Lebanon."[11]

Hezbollah also shared Iran's uncompromising attitude toward Israel and its occupation of Palestine. It, like Iran, viewed any negotiations with the Jewish state as "only a form of compromise, which validates Israel's occupation of Palestine ... The ultimate objective is to destroy Israel and to liberate Palestine." In its fight against the Israeli occupation forces in Lebanon, Hezbollah's chief strength was its capacity to absorb casualties and resolutely carry on. Consequently, the conventional deterrence capability of Israel's military power – a power that has altered the map of the Middle East since 1967 – met its match, and Iran played a major role in creating that reality.

The Israeli invasion of Lebanon in 1982 was an attempt by the Jewish state to establish a hegemony over Lebanon that would at least match the then prevailing Syrian hegemony over that country. If Israel was successful, then it could use the Lebanese template to assert its influence, if not dominance, in other countries of the Middle East. The Israeli leadership in Jerusalem was too clever to explicitly assert that objective; however, the rulers in Damascus and Tehran were equally adroit discerning Israel's designs. They were not about to allow Lebanon to become a vassal state of Israel. Syria used its geographic proximity with Lebanon and the confluence of strategic objectives with Iran, and the latter's clout over the Shias of Lebanon, to thwart Israel's hegemonic ambitions. The Hezbollah Party played a decisive role in the fulfillment of that objective. Both Iran and Syria supported Hezbollah in making it hard for the Israeli armed forces to stay in Lebanon's so-called security zone. In response to a low-intensity guerrilla campaign carried out by Hezbollah in 2000, Israel unilaterally decided to withdraw. After that development, Iran's prestige and sphere of influence in Lebanon was to remain high for a long time. For Hezbollah, the Israeli withdrawal was regarded as merely "a prelude to its final obliteration from existence and the liberation of venerable Jerusalem from the talons of occupation."[12]

Hezbollah's Islamic perspectives and eagerness to take on the Israeli occupation forces between 1982 and 2000 enabled it to emerge as a powerful fighting and political force in Lebanon. Hezbollah also became a useful tool in the foreign policy of Syria, which could not dislodge the Israeli occupation from the Golan Heights through its own military force. Instead, Syria, during much of its own occupation of Lebanon (from 1976 to 2005), used Hezbollah to escalate or de-escalate pressure on Israeli forces to bring Israel to the negotiating table or to persuade it to withdraw from the Golan Heights. In return, Syria facilitated Iran's provision of training, finances, and military hardware to Hezbollah. Even after the Syrian withdrawal from Lebanon in 2005, Syria served as an important conduit of arms supply to Hezbollah.

The Hezbollah-Iran nexus enabled the latter to influence the Arab-Israeli conflict by providing both training and financial support to the Hamas of Palestine, especially between 2001 and 2003 when Sunni Arab leaders appeared more concerned about sustaining their autocratic rule under the short-lived but voluble criticism from the Bush administration. After Hamas captured the political control of Gaza in the elections of January 2006, it endured systematic isolation from the United States and the West for its refusal to renounce violence and negotiate with Israel. Fully exploiting the West's attempt to isolate that organization, Iran continued its role as the single most important channel of financial support for Hamas's defiance of the West, thereby earning considerable popularity for its audacious stand against the lone superpower in the Arab streets.

The most significant aspect of Iran's involvement in Lebanon is the intensification of the Islamist challenge both for US dominance in the Levant and for America's unqualified support of the Israeli occupation of Lebanon from 1982 through 2000. Equally important, while Iran's clout remained high in Lebanon, the United States struggled to maintain its own long-standing prestige in that country. The radical Shia groups that preceded Hezbollah played a major role in that challenge. When US peacekeeping forces attempted to shore up the government of Bashir Gemayal in Lebanon, a Christian-dominated government that would be subservient to Israeli occupation, the Shia groups intensified their attack on the Western forces. When US forces pulled out of Lebanon, these groups shifted their attention to targeting the Israeli occupation forces. Consequently, the decision of the Jewish state to pull out from most of Lebanon in 1983, and then from the so-called security zone in 2000, was an ultimate homage to the credibility of Hezbollah as a successful Islamist fighting force. The United States did not fare any better than Israel. It was forced to withdraw its forces from Lebanon. The US exit was nothing short of a defeat, but no US official was ready to admit it.[13]

The 1983 bombing of the US Marine barracks in Beirut, which resulted in the deaths of 241 service personnel, including 221 marines, was generally thought to have been carried out by Hezbollah's progenitor, Islamic Jihad. This incident was described as "the worst disaster for the US military since the end of the Vietnam war."[14] The "early conclusion" of Casper Weinberger, secretary of defense, was that "a lot of circumstantial evidence ... points toward Iran."[15] Regardless of the ultimate veracity of that statement, the massacre of the US marines in Lebanon became one more enduring source of hostility and rancor between Washington and Tehran.

When comparing the support of Syria and Iran to Hezbollah, the brunt of Hezbollah's success in bringing about the withdrawal of Israeli forces from its territories belongs to Iran, largely because Iran's chief motivation was to defeat the United States and Israel, to publicize its (Iran's) support of the Palestinian cause, and through those endeavours to emphasize the overall Islamic nature of its revolution. In Lebanon, Iran's focus was the conflict between the US/Israel and Shia Islam, while in occupied Palestine, it focused on the conflict between the US/Israel and Sunni Islam. Syria, on the other hand, was principally driven by its near obsession to control Lebanon and to use whatever tactics it could to bring about Israel's withdrawal from the Golan Heights. Iran and Hezbollah also shared the view that conflict between the Arabs and the Israelis was "an existential struggle," not merely "a conflict over land."[16] Such a perspective left little room for compromise. However, when Hezbollah's leader, Hassan Nasrallah, was asked if he "was prepared to live with a two-state settlement between Israel and Palestine," he replied that his organization would not sabotage what, in the final analysis, was a "Palestinian matter."[17]

In the context of the long-standing presence and influence of Iran in Lebanon, one must briefly recall the outcome of the 2006 Hezbollah-Israeli war and its implications for Iran. That war involved Israel's reneging on a deal reached between the government under Ariel Sharon and Hezbollah to release some of the latter's fighters from an Israeli jail. As a tactic to force Israel to fulfill that deal, Hezbollah kidnapped two Israeli soldiers in an audacious raid. The government of then Prime Minister Ehud Barak saw that brazen act as an opening for Israel to destroy Hezbollah as a fighting force through an intense air campaign. Israel, assuming that its military was ready for that war and that heavy air bombardment would force the Lebanese government to abandon its support of Hezbollah, anticipated a quick and decisive victory "with minimal costs in blood and resources."[18] Those assumptions, simply put, turned out to be wrong.

During the war, Hezbollah demonstrated its capabilities as a well-equipped force "trained in modern infantry and guerrilla tactics" against the Israel Defense Forces (IDF), a conventional fighting force less suited to guerilla warfare. The long-term "focus on low intensity conflicts, which was necessary for confronting Hamas and similar groups, reduced the IDF from the formidable conventional fighting force that it was in the 20th century to an organization that was best suited for stability operations."[19] The chief constraining variable for the Israeli government was that it did not want to conduct a ground operation into Lebanon for fear of large force casualties. Besides, such an operation would also have meant leaving its forces to occupy parts of Lebanon. That was not an option because the Hezbollah-sponsored suicide attacks had forced Israel out of Lebanon only a few years earlier, in 2000.

This war is generally depicted as a defeat of Israel and a victory for both Hezbollah and Iran. Despite its intense air campaign against Hezbollah, Israel succeeded only in diminishing, not destroying, that organization's fighting capabilities. And by surviving that campaign and demonstrating its military tactics against the much more formidable Israeli forces, Hezbollah put a serious dent in the previously unchallenged deterring capabilities of the IDF. Iran, as the chief supporter and trainer of Hezbollah, was considered another winner of this war. As Hezbollah successfully carried out its psychological campaign of serving the social needs of the Lebanese population during, but especially after, the cessation of hostilities, stock in that organization and that of Iran went up significantly in the Arab world. Hezbollah had succeeded in surviving the intense punishment of mostly American-armed fighting forces – an unprecedented achievement when one recalls what happened to the Arab forces in the 1967 Arab-Israeli War. Needless to say, the American war planners closely scrutinized the "lessons learned" in the context of Iran's own asymmetrical warfare capabilities.[20]

HUSSEIN FADLALLAH, HEZBOLLAH, AND IRANIAN MANEUVERS IN THE LEVANT

The intricacy of Iran's role in the turbulent and increasingly Islamized politics of Lebanon may best be understood by taking a close look at the crucial but less publicized role of Ayatollah Sayyed Mohammad

Hussein Fadlallah – an extremely sophisticated Islamist thinker of his time – in the politics of Lebanon throughout the 1970s, 1980s, and beyond. Fadlallah's political philosophy was so nuanced that, had he been an ayatollah of Iran or Iraq, his impact would have been as great, if not greater, than that of Ayatollah Rouhollah Khomeini. However, because Fadlallah spent most of his adult life attempting to create an Islamist Lebanon, his influence on the overall thinking of the global Islamist movement was not fully appreciated. Martin Kramer, an Israeli academician, has done a credible job in explaining Fadlallah's political philosophy. A detailed overview of that philosophy is in order, since it sheds considerable light on a major Islamist of the Shiite sect, yet a man who really wanted to be recognized as a noteworthy Islamic thinker.[21]

The world first took notice of Fadlallah when Hezbollah was a brand new entity on the Lebanese political scene. As Hezbollah's gunmen fought against Israel, which they perceived as America's vanguard in the region, Fadlallah translated "the rage of Hezbollah into speeches, sermons and lectures, on tape and in print." As Kramer explains, "Hezbollah's deeds amplified Fadlallah's words, carrying his voice far beyond his own pulpit to the wider world. Fadlallah's words interpreted and justified Hezbollah's deeds, transforming resentment into resistance." Although international media coverage portrayed him, rather simplistically, as the leader of Hezbollah, his place in that movement "eluded definition." Even though the Islamic revolution of Iran inspired the Shias of Lebanon to bring about a radical political transformation of their polity, the revolution itself was still a distant phenomenon whose meaning and purpose had to be interpreted for the *sui generis* political realities of Lebanon. It was Fadlallah's transformational leadership that served that role. Describing the dire need for such leadership, Bernard Lewis wrote, "Islam is a powerful but still an undirected force in politics. As a possible factor in international politics, the present prognosis is not favorable. There have been many attempts at pan-Islamic policy, none of which has made much progress. One reason for their lack of success is that those who have made the attempt have been so unconvincing. This still leaves the possibility of a more convincing leadership and there is ample evidence in virtually all Muslim countries of the deep yearning for such a leadership and a readiness to respond to it."[22] Fadlallah filled this great vacuum, making Islam relevant at a time when the world of Islam was rapidly changing and encountering alien (and often anti-Islamic) ideas.

Fadlallah had an innate ability to sense people's "deep yearning" for "convincing leadership," and he was gifted with complementary talents to hone his skills and externalize his vision. Born and educated in Iraq, Fadlallah refined his ideas through his fortuitous association with one of Shia Islam's greatest thinkers, Sayyid Muhammad Baqir al-Sadr. The meeting of two highly prolific minds must have been a feast for the flight of the imagination. In the late 1950s in Iraq, Fadlallah and al-Sadr collaborated to transform the ideas of their learned articles into a political movement – al-Dawah. Al-Dawah was perceived as a threat by the paranoiac Iraqi regime, which was willing to use all means to intimidate, imprison, or even physically harm the clerics of that movement.

The Iraqi regime's campaign to suppress al-Dawah was one of the reasons for Fadlallah's decision to return to his ancestral home in Lebanon in 1966. He settled down in the shantytown of Nabaa in east Beirut, where the Shia and the Palestinians resided. In Lebanon, Islamists were already well entrenched as a result of the political activism of Sayyid Musa al-Sadr (a distant relative of Sayyid Muhammad Baqir al-Sadr), who had publicized the exploitation of the Shia masses by the privileged class. By doing so, he made many enemies in Lebanon's privileged Shia community, which welcomed Fadlallah as a native son and promoted his introduction to Lebanon's political arena as a counter to Musa al-Sadr.[23]

When Fadlallah arrived in Lebanon, he was received as an important cleric because of his education and affiliation with Ayatollah Abul Qasim al-Khoei, one of Iraq's most influential marjas (sources of emulation). In the ongoing conflict between the Shia school in Najaf (Iraq) and the Shia school in Qom (Iran), al-Khoei upheld the former, a school that strongly adhered to the Quietist tradition that forbade Shia clerics from participating in politics. The Qom school, on the contrary, advocated the *vilayat-e-faqih* (rule or religious guardianship of the clergy) model promoted by Ayatollah Khomeini. (The current Islamic government of Iran has been promoting this model inside Iraq.) Grand Ayatollah Ali al-Sistani of Iraq, who succeeded his teacher al-Khoei as marja, was also a staunch upholder of the Quietist model.[24] Since Fadlallah was a student of al-Khoei, he could never wholeheartedly support Khomeini's *vilayat-e-faqih* model for Lebanon. Fadlallah's status in Lebanon increased in 1971 with the succession of Ayatollah al-Khoei, after the death of Ayatollah Muhsin al-Hakim. Fadlallah and al-Sadr pledged allegiance to al-Khoei, who made Fadlallah his representative in

Lebanon. That development provided him with a platform from which to build his influence.

In his sermons, Fadlallah used the language of the Qur'an to address the burning issues of the day – issues that were fervently brought to the attention of the Arab populace by President Gamal Abdel Nasser of Egypt. While Nasser promoted pan-Arabism (or the unity represented by that ideology) as a solution to Arab problems, Fadlallah remained focused on Islam, and on the plight of Muslims in Lebanon and in the greater Middle East. In this sense, he was a trailblazer. Adopting the anti-imperialistic rhetoric of pan-Arabism, Fadlallah stated that "only Islam could serve as the basis for a viable struggle against imperialism ... Imperialism cannot bear having Muslims proceed from a premise of intellectual self-reliance and it cannot bear having the Muslims act through economic and political self-sufficiency. It wants us to continue sitting at its table, *feeding ourselves with the thought and consumer products it offers us*" (emphasis added). On this issue, Fadlallah's thinking was heavily influenced by the notion of "pan-Islamic nationalism" publicized by Hasan al-Banna of Egypt (chapter 3).

Fadlallah also developed a highly nuanced perspective – and one that clearly differed from that of al-Sadr – regarding the Palestinian conflict and its significance for Arabs and Muslims at large. Al-Sadr formed the Shiite militia, Amal, to promote his revolutionary ideology according to which the Shias were not to allow themselves to be victimized. They must arm themselves just like other communities of Lebanon and learn to survive "among the wolves." Although he sympathized with the Palestinians, whom he regarded as dispossessed, he wanted the entire population of Lebanon – not just the Shias in the southern part of the country – to share the burden of suffering stemming from the presence of the Palestinians in their midst. Al-Sadr sought to help the Shias at a time when "lives in Lebanon [had] gone mad with sectarian violence." (He disappeared in 1978 while travelling in Libya, presumably murdered by Muammar al-Qaddafi's assassins.)

Fadlallah's complicated perspective on this issue was a synthesis of his background as a Shia Arab, his immersion in the political language and symbolism of pan-Arabism and Arab socialism and, above all, his vast knowledge of politicized Islam acquired through his unique association with Baqir al-Sadr. For Fadlallah, "Israel was the instrument of a wider western plot to dominate the Arab and Muslim world"; it was a "cancer" that must be "excised." He "proclaimed

Islam a theology of liberation at a moment when Arab revolutionaries and intellectuals denounced it as the paramount obstacle to an effective Arab challenge to Israel." Yet he tempered his harsh rhetoric with a cautious approach as to what should be done.

While southern Lebanon was immersed in a battle between the Christian Phalangist militia and the Palestinians, Musa al-Sadr "struck a deal with the Phalangist militia" for the safe passage of the Shiites. To al-Sadr's critics, that deal "smacked of defeatism and betrayal." Fadlallah did not air his views. However, during the furious days of the battle, he was writing his book, *Islam and the Logic of Power*, which did contain his definitive views about the "empowerment of Islam." Fadlallah believed that the "power imperialism enjoyed over Islam was temporary and could be defeated, because it rested upon unbelief and exploitation." In this context, "the armed Shiite [was] an asset of Islam in a comprehensive confrontation with unbelief." Fadlallah did not advocate "wanton violence"; in his view, violence should be "conceived as part of an overall plan of liberation." When the shockwaves of the Islamic revolution in Iran reached Lebanon, Iranian emissaries started to press the Shia clerical establishment to choose "the stirring slogan of an Islamic state." Fadlallah proclaimed his support for an "ecumenical and universal Islam." Still, he remained a cheerful supporter of the Islamic revolution of Iran.

As Iran's growing influence and presence in Lebanon in the 1980s began to affect Lebanese politics, Fadlallah found himself increasingly forced to go along with Iranian preferences, in particular, the creation of Hezbollah. Although Fadlallah "privately opposed" the party, he decided "to remain formally outside the bound of Hezbollah" and frequently denied any association with it. His dissociation with Hezbollah was carefully managed. There were constant consultations between Fadlallah and Hezbollah's chief interlocutors, the Iranian emissaries in Lebanon. Whenever they agreed, they "carefully coordinated their actions and statements." Whenever they disagreed, "they went their separate ways."

The growing battle between Israel and the Palestinian refugees residing in southern Lebanon created internal strife in southern Lebanon. The Shiite Amal party took up arms to defeat the Palestinian hegemony there. Fadlallah's own notion of solidarity with the Palestinians found few takers during the late 1970s. The Israeli invasion of Lebanon in 1982 created a fleeting hope among the Shias that they would be saved from Palestinian hegemony. However, when

Israel attempted to transform that invasion into its own hegemony, the Shias also turned against the Jewish state. Then the Shias watched the United States and France come to their rescue. However, when the United States decided to throw "its support behind the claims of Christian privilege and Israeli security," it also became the target of Shia wrath. The March 1983 attack against the US forces by Hezbollah's clandestine arm, Islamic Jihad, forever altered the state of politics in Lebanon.

Fadlallah explained the Shia's rage to the world, stating that the United States, instead of saving Lebanon from Israel, had become a party to Israel's plan "to secure political gains for the purpose of complete control over the region." He ominously concluded, "There is no alternative to a bitter and difficult jihad, borne from within by the power of effort, patience and sacrifice – and the spirit of martyrdom." Statements of this nature made him a potential endorser of violence against the American and French forces, and yet his position was deliberately ambiguous. While vehemently denying any personal role in the attacks, he also stated that "the deeds deserved to be applauded." Similarly, although he viewed suicide as a legitimate part of jihad if carried out "to have a political impact on an enemy whom it is impossible to fight by conventional means," he refused to issue a fatwa sanctioning the suicide bombing ("self-martyrdom"). This type of ambiguity served Fadlallah well, even though his critics remained dubious about his real position on Hezbollah, the use of violence, and the notion of suicide to attain political objectives.

Despite the internal rift in Lebanon between the Palestinians and the Shias, Fadlallah maintained that the Arab-Israeli conflict was a reason for unifying Muslims. He continued to insist, in his lectures, that the Jewish state was "inherently expansionist"; it was driven, first and foremost, by the desire to steal Arab land. Israel would not stop at stealing Palestinian territory; it "coveted" southern Lebanon as well. The Shiites were "next in line ... to be dispossessed by an expanding Israel, and ... no agreement could prevent it." Israel's ultimate objective, as Fadlallah envisioned it, was to expand its territory "from Euphrates to [the] Nile" and "to establish Jewish culture at the expense of Islamic culture or what some call Arab culture." In Fadlallah's judgment, therefore, peace with Israel was impossible. Through these activities, according to Fadlallah, Israel intended to serve "American imperialism." He saw this strategic link between the United States and Israel as "aimed at turning the entire region into a

US-Israeli zone of influence, as required by strategic, political, and economic interests of the United States." These two actors operated on the basis of a division of labour: "America acts diplomatically and tells Israel to move militarily." Fadlallah saw "no difference between the United States and Israel, the latter is a mere extension of the former." They are "working in complete harmony ... Thus it was a fantasy for Arabs to believe they could drive a wedge" between the two. The only way to fight Israel, according to Fadlallah, was through the strategy of jihad, whose purpose was to remove Israel "from the map completely." As Fadlallah saw it, the liberation of Palestine required "the emergence of Islamic resistance in Palestine itself," as well as a broad "Arab Islamic plan for confrontation." Even then, Israel's elimination may require "one hundred years if necessary."

Fadlallah's greatest contribution to Islamic thinking – and as a counter to the differences between the Sunnis and the Shias of Lebanon – was to minimize those differences by depicting them as "*not theological but philosophical*" (emphasis added). As such, he stated, these differences could be translated into "an intellectual problem, to be examined by researchers in a scholarly way so as to reach a solution." By so describing the Sunni-Shia differences, he earned the trust of the Sunnis of Lebanon. In this capacity, he "had the best chance of any Shiite cleric to emerge as linchpin of any coalition the two communities might form, as guide to Shiites and Sunnis alike." Such a role might also have been driven by his self-perception as a leader who worked at "the level of the Islamic world." However, because of the theological differences between the Shias and Sunnis, "Fadlallah could never be certain that any Sunnis – even those impressed by his ecumenism – would follow him down the road to an Islamic state."

Fadlallah envisioned an equitable and comprehensive "Islamic political, social, and legal order" in which "all Lebanese could live in harmony, regardless of their religious affiliation." Yet he ultimately concluded that the conditions for the rule of Islam did not exist in Lebanon in the present or immediate future. The idea of an Islamic state was problematic for Lebanon as a multiconfessional country. The Sunnis could not accept the Islamic government of Iran – comprising the Twelver Shias – as a model. Similarly, the Christians of Lebanon would "resist any attempt to substitute the rule of Islam for the tattered confessional order that guaranteed their privileges." Both Muslims and Christians viewed Fadlallah's intellectual approach – his notion that if one "asked for more than was reasonable, it was usually in order to get something reasonable" – as a "piece of deceit." Fadlallah's eventual conclusion that an Islamic state was not possible in Lebanon caused a rift with the Iranian leadership. In fact, Khomeini refused to meet with him for three years.

The presence of Syrian forces in Lebanon since 1976 enabled Syria to develop a strategy of bringing that country into its orbit. That plan was disrupted when Israel invaded Lebanon in 1982. Syria's countermeasure was to establish a powerful nexus with Iran. Iran brought its money, Revolutionary Guard, and weapons to Lebanon. The complicating factor underlying this nexus was that, while Iran wanted to establish an Islamic state, Arab nationalism dominated Syria's vision for Lebanon. The Lebanese were squeezed between either cooperating with the Israeli invaders or finding a modus vivendi with Syria.

Fadlallah, as was his forte, developed a nuanced position in which he found reasons, through his own Islamic activism, to cooperate with Syria. Both Arab nationalism and Islamism were aimed at liberating Palestine and shaking off great-power domination. In Fadlallah's view, Arabism could become an acceptable basis for identity, "provided it also inspired action against imperialism." In advocating cooperation with Syria against Israel, Fadlallah became a "paradoxical defender of Lebanese independence." Although he was in favour of cooperation with Syria, he was equally vehement about maintaining the status of his country as an independent entity.

As the administration of George H.W. Bush attempted to build a "new world order," Fadlallah pondered the potential of Islam. He talked about the characteristics that the world of Islam possessed to become powerful – for instance, the size of the Muslim global community, its potential capabilities, the strategic location of Muslim countries in the Middle East, and, above all, their natural resources. Those strengths should enable Muslims to emerge as a powerful bloc. At the same time, he was cognizant of the fact that Muslims "strive to weaken" themselves.

Fadlallah was in favour of Muslim countries' acquisition of nuclear power. He criticized the double standards of the great powers on this issue: "We see that many states have nuclear weapons, and it poses no great problem. But when it is reported that an Islamic country wants nuclear weapons to defend itself against another state that has them, the arrogant use all their pressure to prevent this state from acquiring weapons that would strengthen it." He believed that Iran would acquire nuclear weapons by either buying or stealing them. He also thought that proliferation of nuclear weapons to one or more Islamic countries would lead to "normalization," that is, to "a balance of power between Islam and the West, superseding the abnormal state in which 'global arrogance' commanded millions of times the destructive power of the combined forces of Islam." Fadlallah was most perceptive in his understanding of the dynamic nature of power among nation states. "Power is not the eternal destiny of the powerful. Weakness is not the eternal destiny of the weak." The weak would acquire power "if, deep within themselves, they kept alive the spirit of rejecting 'global arrogance.'"

By expounding his thinking on such heady issues, Fadlallah, indeed, emerged as "the foremost philosopher of power in contemporary Islam." By advocating the linkage between nuclear proliferation and normalization, he "nurtured the vision of Islam's return to its proper status as a world power." In order to save it from destruction by the great powers of the West, and "to realize its destiny," Islam has "to dominate others. The West could not be allowed to end history now, or create a 'new world order' resting on a gross disequilibrium in its favor." In these words, Fadlallah sounded as if he was spelling out the strategic future of Iran for the next several decades.

There is no palpable evidence, however, that Iran's alleged aspiration to develop nuclear weapons has been influenced by Fadlallah's vision of Islam's strategic future. Even if that were the case, Iran's rhetorical emphasis on animosity with Israel has made this goal highly unattainable. Israel, in turn, would not hesitate to destroy Iran's nuclear facilities through military action in order to prevent it from acquiring nuclear weapons. Even in the absence of Iran-Israel animosity, US-Iran antagonism was too powerful an obstacle for Iran to overcome if it wanted to become a nuclear weapons power.

FACING THE POST–9/11 AMERICAN JUGGERNAUT

For the Sunni leaders of a number of Iran's neighbours, its emergence as a major power of the Middle East was a challenge that could not be matched. For the Arab autocrats, the only game in the region was to rely on the military power of the United States. That reliance proved to be most credible when, in the aftermath of Saddam Hussein's invasion and occupation of Kuwait in 1990, the US-led international coalition brought about an end to the aggression. It appeared that, even though Saddam stayed in power in Iraq until 2003, the status quo in the Middle East was not going to be threatened by any other country. Saddam Hussein's invasion of Kuwait seemed to have validated the Iranian assessment of how dangerous the Iraqi dictator really was to the stability of the neighbourhood.

The Gulf War victory, combined with an exhaustive review of America's foreign policy in the 1980s, could have provided the basis for a US rapprochement with Iran. However, the United States did not spend any time reexamining its support of Saddam during the Iran-Iraq War. Instead, it was preoccupied in the early 1990s with the momentous developments related to the implosion of the Soviet Union and how to transform its foreign policy to deal with a unipolar global order for which it was not at all ready, but for which it was still eager to do all it could to secure. Such transformation of the global power arrangement carried enormous promise for America's unprecedented global dominance.

But the Islamist challenge inside the Persian Gulf region was also evolving. The United States' decision to remain in Saudi Arabia intensified that challenge and, as a result, US forces stationed there were attacked twice in the 1990s. According to the *9/11 Commission Report*, the bombing of the Khobar Towers complex of the Saudi military base in Dahran was carried out by the "Saudi Hezbollah, an organization that had received support from the government of Iran." It added, however, "While the evidence of Iranian involvement is strong, there are also signs that al Qaeda played some role, as yet unknown."[25] The United States was eager to find some conclusive evidence of the culprit or culprits behind the Khobar Towers attack and take retaliatory measures, especially if that culprit was Iran. However, Saudi Arabia was not interested in serving as Washington's instrument for that purpose, because it was working on its own policy of reaching a rapprochement with Tehran.

The 9/11 attacks on the United States could have radically transformed antagonistic Iran-US ties to friendly ones. After all, the lone superpower was attacked by al-Qaida, which was considered an enemy of Iran. The Taliban regime was also hostile toward its own Shia citizens (Hazaras). Iran became a strong supporter of Ahmad Shah Masood's Northern Alliance, which was at war with the Taliban. Thus, Iran had every reason to support the US invasion of Afghanistan to bring about the dismantlement of the Taliban regime toward the end of 2001. However, once again, the United States was more interested in carrying out George W. Bush's global war on terrorism (GWOT) to punish al-Qaida than it was in finding a basis for rapprochement with Iran. In fact, in the post–9/11 era, Washington assigned primacy to a highly inward-looking hubristic neoconservative ideology that was fully focused on looking for "enemies" in the Middle East. Iran and Iraq were two obvious targets for the neocons' fury. Their ideology became the main driving force behind the Bush administration's military invasion of Afghanistan.

The easy US military victory over the Taliban in 2001 became the basis for America's biggest mistake of the post–9/11 era – its invasion of Iraq. That invasion also significantly escalated Iranian clout in a country where the majority of the population (about 65 percent) practiced Shia Islam. When the United States toppled the Sunni regime of Saddam Hussein and implemented the rule of democracy – which the Bush administration claimed was the reason for its invasion of Iraq, but only as an afterthought – the Shias were destined to emerge as the new ruling force in Iraq. That reality ended the domination of the Sunnis, who had ruled Iraq despite comprising less than 35 percent of the population.

The Bush administration invaded Iraq with a number of shifting strategies and rationales. Ultimately, after failing to find weapons of mass destruction – the chief stated reason for invading Iraq – it settled on the rationale of implanting democracy and then using Iraq as a "shining" example for the rest of the Middle East. Another explanation was that the road to settlement of the PLO-Israeli conflict passed through Baghdad. Once Saddam Hussein was toppled, argued President George W. Bush and his national security officials, violence and suicide acts in occupied Palestine would subside. All of these rationales took Iran into account in one way or another, albeit indirectly in some instances.

The fifth-rate Iraqi army was not expected to give the mighty US-led coalition forces much of a fight. The Saddam regime became a quick victim of the "shock and awe" strategy. This strategy soon suffered a serious setback of its own because of the deteriorating security situation, but US aspirations to transform the shape of the political map of Iraq and the larger Middle East remained undeterred. Washington was forced to make a critical tactical shift from an overall preference for unilateralism to a selective application of multilateralism in Iraq, allowing the United Nations to play a limited role in forming an interim government. However, a potent competition between the

United States and Iran was already evolving, whose objective was not only to maintain control over the shape of events in Iraq, but also to determine whether the elected government there would have a heavy presence in and influence over the Islamic or secular forces.

Even the US outlook on implanting democracy in Iraq went through several iterations. First, there was the Pentagon's version of it, whereby the "coronation" of Ahmad Chalabi as president was to take place right after the cessation of hostilities. Since Secretary of Defense Donald Rumsfeld, his deputy, Paul Wolfowitz (the official part of the Pentagon), and Richard Perle, aka "the Prince of Darkness" (the unofficial player, who then served as president of the powerful Defense Advisory Board that counsels the Pentagon on defense matters), got most of their first-hand knowledge and a substantial part of their "intelligence" on Iraq from Ahmad Chalabi, they bought his description of the potential outcome of the US invasion lock, stock, and barrel. According to his portrayal, the invasion of Iraq would be a cakewalk; Iraqi troops would lay down their arms, and American troops would be offered sweets and rosewater, the traditional Arab welcoming gesture to those they chose to honour.

But when the US invasion was met with stiff resistance – whose intensity kept escalating with the passage of time – other haphazard measures were introduced. The option of installing Chalabi was quickly abandoned, and discussions of a secular democracy and elections surfaced within Iraq's Coalition Provisional Authority. Then the US packed the Iraqi Governing Council with expatriate Iraqis, with the clear intention of using them as leading proponents of secular democracy. Finally, a sort of "exit strategy" was settled upon in Washington whereby an interim Iraqi government composed of a number of handpicked Iraqis took charge in the lead-up to the general election in early 2005. Throughout that course, America's purpose was to implant a secular democracy that would allow the presence of US forces for an unlimited time. Iraq, under this vision, would become a friendly state that would even legitimize the regional dominance of Israel. Considering that Iraq was a major Arab state, such cowing of post-Saddam Iraq would have been the capstone, albeit unstated, achievement of the Bush administration in the Middle East.

However, Iran, the Iraqi Shia clergy, the Shia populace, and the Sunni insurgents (who emerged as a potent force starting in May 2003) had entirely different agendas inside Iraq.[26] An immediate concern for the Iraqis, as well as for the US occupation authorities, was whether a democratic Iraq would be modelled after the Islamic Republic of Iran or whether it would be a moderate Islamic democracy, with a limited role for the clergy. Iran's *vilayat-e-faqih* model appeared too much in line with the former dominance of Ayatollah Khomeini. Besides, Iraq had the overarching presence of Grand Ayatollah Ali al-Sistani, who promoted a *sui generis* Iraqi democracy where the clergy would serve as spiritual advisers on major political and religious matters without being rulers à la Khomeini. The Iraqi Shia sect opted for the Sistani model, thereby resolving all of the conflicts associated with the *vilayat-e-faqih* model. This choice of governance notwithstanding, Iran's influence on the politics of its neighbour was not likely to diminish.

Iran's role in the Shia side of the power equation in Iraq is extremely calculating and multidimensional. Iran has strong theological ties with Iraq; it served as an important source of anti-regime protest throughout the heyday of Saddam's rule, and continues to play a similar role regarding the presence of US forces in its neighbouring state. Iran's influence on Iraq's underground economy has remained substantial. As such, it is expected to influence the future course of that country's politics.

As Iraq plunged into internal chaos brought about by the activities of the insurgents and other Islamist forces, the Bush administration intensified its rhetoric about Iran's alleged role in destabilizing Iraq. Iraq's Sunni Arab neighbours, fearing Iran's growing influence, concurred with America's allegations. However, a study issued by the International Crisis Group, which conducted extensive research on the issue inside both Iran and Iraq, cast doubt on those allegations: "The evidence of attempted destabilising Iranian intervention is far less extensive and clear than is alleged; the evidence of *successful* destabilising intervention less extensive and clear still … In fact, there is no indication that Iranian electoral manipulation is anything more than speculation or that the Shiites' victory was anything other than the political translation of their demographic predominance."[27]

As an invading and occupying power, the United States faced a highly disadvantageous situation in Iraq. As much as its leaders and intelligence agencies thought that they knew the internal dynamics of the Iraqi political arena, they found out the hard way that their supposed knowledge of that country was grossly inadequate. Iranian security agencies, on the contrary, were "highly familiar with Iraq's physical and political terrain" and were "able to sustain an active intelligence presence in southern Iraq, Baghdad and Kurdistan." Iran used its many tools, including a "widespread network of paid informers," the Revolutionary Guard, petrodollars, and well-targeted social welfare campaigns to heavily influence Iraq's fledgling democratic political process by assisting its favoured political parties. Even then, its activities created "little resonance" and had "negligible impact on Iraqi society" because of the "deep suspicion and resentment on the part of many Iraqis toward their neighbour."[28]

Still, no one can deny that Iran enjoyed ample advantages over the United States by the sheer fact that it was Iraq's neighbour. As such, it was going to ensure that Iraq did not reemerge as a threat, as it had been during the dictatorial rule of Saddam Hussein. Iran was equally determined that there would not be an independent Kurdistan, which would have "huge implications for Iran's disaffected Kurdish minority." At the same time, unless US-Iran relations improved, Iran would promote manageable chaos in Iraq in order to keep the US forces preoccupied. Even if the United States got out of Iraq, Iran was most likely to continue its foreign policy of keeping the lone superpower "at bay."[29] One also can rest assured that Iran will – to the utter chagrin of the United States – continue to influence Iraqi elections. That tactic has nothing to do with the frequently mentioned charges from Washington about Iran's alleged predilections to destabilize Iraq. A destabilized Iraq is not in the interest of Iran, but a stable Iraq with a governance over which Iran has a behind-the-scenes influence and role is very much in Iran's interest.

From Iran's point of view, the post–9/11 era has proven to be most troubling for its relations with the American archenemy. When the United States decided to refocus the brunt of its attention from Afghanistan (Iran's neighbour to its east), it started a new "war of choice" in Iraq (Iran's neighbour to its west). When Iraq became a stable place, around 2009, the United States once again refocused on the Afghan front where it currently remains. The war in Afghanistan was a significant war for President Barack Obama, as the war in Iraq had been for President Bush. Consequently, to the leaders in Tehran, the world in the post–9/11 era appeared not only uncertain but also full of potentially perilous contingencies involving the United States.

To top it off, President Bush declared his intention to take the war to the doorstep of any country that sponsored terrorism. He identified Iran as a member of his infamous "axis of evil" concept. As such, taking military action against Iran (and North Korea, another member of that alleged "axis") appeared more alive than ever before.

Since the administration of President Bill Clinton, Iran had been a target of US economic sanctions that aimed to bring about regime change without necessarily taking military action. In fact, economic sanctions as a US policy tool toward Iran had emerged during the administration of President Jimmy Carter, when he froze Iranian assets in 1979 to put pressure on Iran for the release of 444 American hostages. Clinton's use of economic sanctions was merely a return to that policy.

The Iran Sanctions Act (ISA) – originally called the Iran-Libya Sanctions Act – was introduced in May 1995 during the administration of President Bill Clinton in response to Iran's support of Hezbollah and Hamas, which the US government depicted as "terrorist" organizations. The rationale underlying the ISA was to "curb strategic threat from Iran by hindering its ability to modernize its key petroleum sector, which generates 20 % of Iran's GDP [gross domestic product]." This Act was scheduled to expire in August 2001, because of relatively better US relations with Iran and Libya. Under the presidency of Iran's Mohammad Khatami, US-Iran relations somewhat improved. However, opposing US legislators argued that Iran and Libya would "view its expiration as a concession."[30] Thus, the Act was renewed in August 2001.

Iran's nuclear research program provided renewed impetus for US economic sanctions when the ISA was to sunset in August 2006. Iran stated that its nuclear program was peaceful in nature; it was to serve as a source of energy when its oil and gas reserves were depleted. The United States accused Iran of intending to use that program to eventually develop nuclear weapons. Iranian denials to the contrary failed to convince Washington. That Iran remained opaque, at best, about the actual number of nuclear plants and the full scope of their activities made for a stronger case by the United States about Iran's real intentions. Iran's highly active ballistic missile programs complemented its alleged intentions to develop nuclear weapons. The newly extended Act, which was to expire in 2011, authorized "funding for pro-democracy activities in Iran." It was more stringent in taking action against countries "whose companies have violated ISA and applied the U.S. trade ban on Iran to foreign subsidiaries of U.S. companies."[31]

President Barack Obama found it prudent to continue the policies of his predecessors by issuing an executive order in March 2010 "banning US trade and investment with Iran." The US Senate passed legislation in the same month "targeting Iran's energy sector." The United States, Canada, and the European Union also took various collective and unilateral actions to make it very difficult for Iran to modernize its energy sector. UN Resolution 1929, passed in June 2010, put "the squeeze on Iran's Revolutionary Guards-owned businesses, its shipping industry, and the country's commercial and financial service sector."[32]

The history of economic sanctions as a tool for putting pressure on a targeted country has produced mixed results. Sanctions have to be applied on a prolonged basis; they require effective coordination among various participating countries; and, most important, they have to succeed in closing most – if not all – avenues available to the targeted country for doing business. None of these criteria can be achieved unless such sanctions are passed by the UN Security Council, where any one of the five permanent members can veto them. Thus, the United States required the cooperation of China and Russia to pass a resolution. For their own strategic reasons, those countries have, more often than not, taken a jaundiced view of readily using the sanction tool to punish countries with which they must do business.

Iran falls in that category, since Russia is its chief source for the transfer of nuclear technology. Doing business with Iran is highly lucrative for Russia and feeds its voracious appetite for hard currency. Iran also serves as an important source for China's rising needs for oil and gas. Still, the Obama administration has been effective in persuading Beijing and Moscow to support UN resolutions that added further layers of sanctions on Iran. However, additional economic sanctions have not forced Iran to stop enriching uranium, a key condition for the United States to relax sanctions. What is important to note here is that the reason Iran is not willing to give up its nuclear research program has a lot to do with its own strategic calculations and security perceptions toward the United States.

Since its inception, the Islamic Republic has envisaged a world where the United States consistently threatened its existence. The US maneuvers against Iran during its war against Iraq have already been discussed. Most troubling for Iran, in the aftermath of the terrorist attacks the Bush administration appeared almost eager to take military action against countries that it depicted as "rogues," "pariahs," or sponsors of terrorism. Iran was included on all those lists. Iran also watched the destruction of the regime of its archenemy, Saddam Hussein, under the pretext that he was concealing weapons of mass destruction. Iran seemed to have concluded that the only reason the United States was able to destroy Iraq was because Iraq did not own nuclear weapons, which it could have used against the invading US forces. More to the point, had Iraq possessed nuclear weapons, the United States would not have invaded in the first place. Thus, Iran, without saying so, appeared bent on acquiring nuclear weapons, because they do indeed provide "existential deterrence."[33] Another option for Iran was to increase its arsenal of ballistic missiles, especially those possessing high accuracy and mobility, and not easily targeted. Iran could also continue to seek avenues of strategic cooperation with China and Russia.

IRAN, CHINA, AND RUSSIA: THE UNSTEADY ANTI-US NEXUS

Iran-China-Russia strategic ties have to be examined by developing a brief understanding, first, of China-Russia ties with each other, second, of the nature of their respective relations with the United States, and third, of how these two great powers view the dynamics of their respective relations with Iran.

As much as the Iran-US interactions are described as confrontational, Iran's foreign policy toward China and Russia has an entirely different face. It has been characterized by a high degree of cooperation. In the unipolar global power arrangement of the post–Cold War era, Iran found a convergence of interests with China and Russia. Like Iran, those two countries were not happy with unipolarity, which had diminished their prestige and status. Russia, the chief successor of the USSR, did not inherit the Soviet Union's mantle of superpowerdom, and the United States treated it accordingly. Toward China, one of the foremost rising powers, the United States pursued a policy of containment, despite its denials to the contrary.

China's own ambivalence toward the United States and the West in general was amplified by the arms embargo imposed after the Tiananmen Square massacre in 1989. The eager coverage of the protest movement by Western media angered the Chinese leaders, who viewed the media exposure and the Western arms sanctions as a violation of their country's sovereignty. After the implosion of the Soviet Union, the pro-American proclivities of Russia made China uncertain about the future of its ties with that country. However, Russia's foreign policy toward China improved as a result of domestic pressures for balanced ties between East and West. Consequently, between 1992 and 1996, China and Russia held seven summits. The major development resulting from those summits was the signing of the 1996 strategic partnership by President Boris Yeltsin of Russia and President Jiang Zemin of China. These developments aside, what also brought the two countries together was the general American penchant for the expansion of NATO, and the decision of that alliance in 1999 to wage war in Kosovo. The fact that NATO decided – which really meant that its dominant power, the United States, played a leading role in formulating that decision – not to seek a UN mandate for that war escalated the feelings of weakness (and related frustrations) on the part of Russia and China. It should be noted that, during that war, US war planes "accidentally" bombed the Chinese embassy in Belgrade. China was infuriated. It never believed the US explanation that the bombing was not a deliberate act.

The Sino-Russian ambivalence was temporarily set aside when the US homeland was attacked by Middle Eastern terrorists and the United States declared a global war on terrorism. Both China and Russia supported the resulting US invasion of Afghanistan. They had long viewed the Taliban-dominated Afghanistan as the training ground for the Uighur Muslims of China and the Chechen Muslims of the Chechen Republic of the Russian Federation, who were struggling to secede from those countries. China and Russia depicted these secessionist forces as "terrorists" and claimed that the separatists were aligned with al-Qaida in Afghanistan and involved in waging regional "jihads." The United States' declaration of a GWOT complemented the Chinese and Russian brutal suppression of the Uighur and the Chechen Muslims. Before the terrorist attacks on its territory, the United States had been skeptical of Chinese and Russian claims and had insisted on political resolution of the disputes. However, under the radically transformed posture after 9/11, the Bush administration discarded its highly nuanced approach toward the Chinese and Russian treatment of their religious minorities. Instead, it depicted the secessionist movements of Beijing and Moscow as part of "global terrorism."

Iran was also in favour of the US invasion of Afghanistan. The hostility between Iran and the Taliban government stemmed from the latter's brutal treatment of the Hazara Afghans (Shias), who were deemed "heretics" under the Wahhabi creed. In fact, Iran and Afghanistan came close to military conflict in 1998, when the Taliban massacred a number of Iranian diplomats who were holed up in the Iranian consulate office in Mazar-e-Sharif – a Shia-dominated city. Angry over that incident and as a warning to the Taliban, Iran conducted war games that included thousands of Revolutionary Guard soldiers.[34]

As an important aspect of invading Afghanistan, Washington sought permission from Russia to base its forces in Kyrgyzstan, Uzbekistan, and Tajikistan. It also promised to withdraw those forces at the conclusion of military actions. Russia agreed to the stationing of American forces in those Central Asian countries; however, both Moscow and Beijing remained highly skeptical of the US promise.

This convergence of interests on the issue of terrorism notwithstanding, China and Russia watched in dismay as the United States invaded Iraq in 2003 without seeking the approval of the UNSC. The invasion brought back bad memories of a similar US action – the Kosovo war of 1999. China and Russia, in opposing the US invasion of Iraq, were highly critical of the Bush doctrine and its related hubristic notions about "regime change." In their view, GWOT was just another manifestation of the US resolve to strengthen its power and prestige under a unipolar global power arrangement. Still, as great powers, the modalities of their respective strategic perspectives were such that China and Russia could not develop a straightforward template of response toward the lone superpower. Instead, they had to respond almost on an issue-by-issue basis. Depending upon the significance of the issue, they could decide to cooperate or not without necessarily taking their eyes off of the primary objective of working toward a multipolar global power arrangement. In these highly intricate strategic interactions among China, Russia, and the United States, what gives America sustained advantage over both of them is the high priority that Beijing and Moscow assign to developing a special relation (or even a strategic partnership) with Washington, even at the expense of undermining each other's strategic interests.[35] This reality also creates periods of cooperation and tensions vis-à-vis the United States. This type of relationship is not necessarily harmful to the Chinese and Russian interests, as long as they each remain in the driver's seat in terms of picking and choosing the issues of cooperation, selective cooperation, partial cooperation, or no cooperation.

Unfortunately for Iran, the preceding attitudes of China and Russia toward the United States substantially affect some of the most critical objectives of its foreign policy. As much as Iran remains an important player within the context of the distribution of power in the Middle

East, for China and Russia, it is not consistently viewed as an actor of high significance. China needs access to Iran's oil and gas reserves. However, it can also fulfill its voracious energy needs from other energy suppliers of the Middle East, Africa, or Latin America. China has to regularly calculate how far it should go to maintain access to Iran's energy sources without antagonizing the United States. Similarly, Russia needs Iran's hard currency resulting from lucrative contracts for building nuclear plants in that country. However, Russia must arrive at a similar balance as China between sustaining its trade ties with Iran and not alienating the United States. On issues paramount to Russia, it will abandon cooperation with Iran in order to preserve comity with Washington.

Iran could have improved its bargaining position vis-à-vis Russia and China when the Central Asian countries first became independent. Given their geographical proximity and predominantly Muslim population, Iran had some advantage in approaching these countries. In fact, the administration of President George H.W. Bush expected that Iran would be highly proactive in Central Asia in promoting its Islamic model of government. However, Iran either did not think such an approach was feasible or did not wish to antagonize Russia and China by promoting an Islamic model in Central Asia. But the Iranian move to stay out of Central Asia had its own payoff, in the sense that neither Moscow nor Beijing regarded Iran as a source of competition for their own objectives to dominate Central Asia.

Given that the international environment is not about to create other more promising alternatives for Iran, it continues to seek close ties with both China and Russia. As an integral aspect of pursuing such ties, Iran actively sought membership in the Shanghai Cooperation Organization (SCO), which comprises China, Russia, Kazakhstan, Kyrgyzstan, Tajikistan, and Uzbekistan.[36] (A detailed discussion of the SCO will be provided in chapter 7.) Iran was given observer status by that organization in May 2008; it could not become a new member because it was under US economic sanctions at the time. Since the lifting of the economic sanctions in January 2016, Iran has been eligible.

Joining the SCO continues to be a promising option for Iran. As proactive as Iran remains within the Middle East, it badly needs a global forum where it can coordinate its policies with like-minded nations. Despite the potential competitive nature of the strategic interests of China and Russia, and the ever-changing perspectives of those two countries toward the United States, the SCO has a strong potential to emerge as an anti-American organization. This is the most attractive aspect of the SCO for Iran. As long as the United States and Iran maintain adversarial relations, the latter is of the view that it can improve its global maneuverability by joining that organization.

Because of the US-sponsored economic and arms sanctions, Iran had no choice but to rely heavily on purchasing weapons from Russia and China. Iran knew all about the qualitative differences between Chinese and Russian arms and those of the West. It also knew that, from the perspective of military modernization, the purchase of arms from a variety of sources negatively affects interoperability-related aspects of a country's warfighting capabilities. This was a serious predicament for Iran when the economic sanctions were in place. With the lifting of those sanctions, Western arms markets may become open for Iran. In the interim, in the absence of those sanctions, both China and Russia – particularly Russia – will sell Iran some of its most advanced weapons. In fact, on 16 February 2016, Iran announced that it would purchase $8 billion worth of advanced military equipment from Russia. The long list included Russia's latest S-400 Triumph anti-aircraft missile system. Iran also wanted "to buy and possibly license for domestic production Russia's new Sukhoi Su-30SM fighter jet, which is used for air-to-air and air-to-surface combat."[37] In the immediate aftermath of the lifting of economic sanctions, both China and Russia have been eagerly seeking expanded trade ties with Iran.

The strategic horizons of Sino-Iranian and Iran-Russia cooperation remain highly complex. From Iran's perspective, the fluctuating levels of cooperation in US-China and US-Russia ties could enhance its chances of extracting support from those two countries for the development of its own highly sophisticated inventory of ballistic missiles. Aside from these on-again, off-again patterns of cooperation from China and Russia on missile production capabilities and nuclear weapons know-how, Iran has North Korea's missile and nuclear knowledge at its disposal. North Korea, as a near-failed or failed state, has nothing to offer to anyone except its missile and nuclear knowledge. Kim Jong-il's ties with the United States were so bad that he found himself under no obligation to be constrained by legal requirements of the Missile Technology Control Regime and the Non-Proliferation Treaty. Indeed, North Korea withdrew from the treaty in 1993. Under Kim Jong-il's successor, Kim Jong-un, North Korea's policy toward Iran remains unchanged.

These idiosyncrasies of Iran's strategic relations with China and Russia notwithstanding, Iran has been steadily developing its inventories of ballistic missiles.[38] Iran has wanted to develop indigenous production capabilities for ballistic missiles since the so-called War of the Cities against Iraq in the late 1980s. It purchased a few scud missiles from Libya, but was driven by the need to develop its own capabilities. In the late 1980s, Iran signed an agreement with North Korea to build a missile production facility in Sirjan. Throughout the 1990s, Iran remained focused on acquiring technological sophistication to build intercontinental ballistic missiles (ICBMs). It made some breakthroughs when it built its Serjil missile and its Safir satellite launch vehicle (SLV). In addition, "Iran's successful launch of the small communications satellite Omid in February 2009, using the two-state solid propelled Safir SLV, demonstrates its technical progress in the exploitation of solid-fuel technologies."[39] US intelligence has been interested in Iran's Safir rockets, especially because a study conducted by a group of American and Russian experts "concluded that the *Safir*'s staging technology would be critical to Iran's potential development of longer-range ballistic missiles." Specialists disagree about the capacity of Safir to carry "a nuclear warhead of roughly 1000kg weight";[40] however, overcoming these and other technical difficulties may be only a matter of time for Iran.

Iran's ballistic and other missile development capabilities provide a rationale for the United States to build a robust ballistic missile defense (BMD) system. What benefits Iran is the fact that both Russia and China regard America's unilateral pursuit of the BMD system as a threat to their own nuclear deterrence capabilities: "Both China and Russia are suspicious that the US is trying to 'encircle' them with elements of the ABM [anti-ballistic missile] system, while stating that it is directed against other states [North Korea and Iran]."[41] A second advantage for Iran is that, since BMD in the United States is "a project rather than a fixed program, the ... plans are subjected to revision, depending on assessment of missile threats and political conjuncture." And since China or Russia – or both – may see any revisions as negatively affecting their own deterrence, they are likely to take countermeasures either to overwhelm the US BMD program or to consider helping Iran to further improve its own ballistic missile inventory. Under these circumstances, the nature of the threat to Iran from China or Russia is likely to vary because of changing US relations with either or both of them. Third, as a general principle,

Russia was not persuaded by the US depiction of Iran as a "rogue state." Russia is more inclined to play the role of "mediator" between the United States and Iran. Consequently, Russia "stalls between an inefficient opposition to the US BMD program and a possibility of cooperation with the US on this issue, which would implicitly mean that Russia agrees to consider Iran a 'rogue state.'"[42] What is important to note is that Russia's waffling on the status of Iran as a rogue or nonrogue state does not work against Iran as the United States might envision.

UNIPOLARITY AND THE LAST RESORT: THE "SAMSON OPTION"?

Even though Iran does not speak about it, there is that hope that a highly developed, indigenous ballistic missile program would also equip it to develop nuclear-tipped missiles when it is able to master or purchase the capabilities to develop nuclear weapons. But why is Iran so desperate to develop these capabilities? A rather straightforward answer is that, from the very emergence as an Islamic republic, Iran felt threatened by the United States. All American presidents – from Jimmy Carter, who was in the White House at the time of the Islamic revolution, to Barack Obama – have taken measures aimed at weakening Iran's government or bringing about regime change. Iran never had a superpower willing to shield it under its nuclear umbrella. That brutal reality was never more evident than during the Iran-Iraq War. As if fighting a war with Iraq was not overwhelming enough for the Iranian leaders, they also watched the United States actively support Iraq's war-related actions with the clear purpose of defeating Iran and bringing about regime change. Iran bitterly concluded that it had to depend on its own defensive and offensive capabilities. Under these circumstances, the rulers of that state had no choice but to develop a rather rigorous doctrine of self-reliance. Developing ballistic, cruise, and anti-ship missiles are objectives that Iran has been consistently working toward, despite US restrictions that closed most avenues of global dual-use technology. Iran is seriously interested in developing nuclear technology. Even though it publicly denies any desire to acquire nuclear weapons, the rumour mill of the Internet reports that it already possesses the know-how to develop these weapons and will develop them in the future.[43] The official US position is that it will not.[44] The US invasion of Iraq, which did not have nuclear weapons, and America's fruitless endeavours to persuade Kim Jong-il and then his successor, Kim Jong-un, to give up North Korea's nuclear weapons have served as the best evidence for why Iran should develop nuclear weapons.

Iran fully understands the risks associated with its unspoken desire to develop nuclear weapons – it may be attacked by the United States or Israel. But what seems to motivate Iran is that it is entirely persuaded that the lone superpower will not abandon its covert and overt endeavours to bring about regime change unless Iran has nuclear weapons. Since Iran is doomed to operate in a unipolar global order, it will have to determine the best modus operandi under that arrangement. And developing nuclear weapons – the ultimate Samson Option – seems to be an integral part of it, sooner or later. Ironically, Israel's own calculation for having nuclear weapons was driven by the very same notion. Israel was convinced that the Arab states would do anything to destroy the nation and its "temple." Israel's nuclear weapons brought an end to those fears. In the twenty-first century, the Islamic Republic of Iran feels the same way toward the United States and Israel.

Despite having consistently tense – indeed hostile – relations with the United States, Iran never really closed the option of seeking a rapprochement. It was during the US invasion of Afghanistan that Iran approached the Bush administration to improve strategic ties. However, when President Bush, in a major speech, labelled Iran as one of the members of the "axis of evil," that hope was dashed. For the remainder of George W. Bush's two terms in office, the chance for development of a rapprochement with Iran was minimal.

When President Barack Obama entered the White House in 2009, he famously offered America's "unclenched" fist to Iran (which was more of a public relations gesture than a promise of substantive changes in America's policy toward that country), but for a price.[45] He wanted Iran to abandon its nuclear research program. But Iran figured that its stakes were much too high to oblige the new president without reaching a comprehensive rapprochement. Besides, the atmosphere between the two countries for such a bargain was not amenable. The complete absence of mutual trust and the amount of suspicion on both sides doomed the negotiations. Obama's failure to persuade Iran, which he called an "outlier" state,[46] prompted him to continue putting pressure on that country through added economic sanctions. Iran, for its part, became convinced that there never was much difference between Bush and Obama in their ulterior motives regarding Iran, which were anything but good.

One can imagine how little the United States had learned from its unilateral invasion of Iraq, and the deleterious implications for regional stability and for its own economy, when American officials continued to insist in their public statements that "all options [regarding Iran] are still on the table, including the military option."[47] That was a not-so-cryptic threat about the option of taking military action; Bush officials said this about Iraq before invading it. From the US side, issuing such not-so-veiled threats was supposed to scare Iran into giving up its desire to develop nuclear weapons. However, such threats became an additional reason for Iran to develop nuclear weapons.

The motivation underlying Iran's nuclear program was a highly rational one. It was based on deterring the United States and Israel from using the military option to bring about regime change, as the United States did against Iraq in 2003. Given the frequently uttered Israeli threats to deprive Iran of its nuclear option, leaders in Tehran envisioned having nuclear weapons of their own as an ultimate deterrence.[48]

At the same time, Iran also wanted to end the double standards the United States exercised by giving a wink and a nod to Israel's growing nuclear arsenal, while denying that very same right to Iran. Even under Obama, the United States continued its endless sanctions and turned a blind eye to Israel's periodic threats to attack Iran's nuclear facilities. India and Pakistan exposed the bias in this double standard when they brought their respective nuclear weapons programs out of the basement in 1998. India is the only country currently enjoying the fruits of that audacious decision. Today, India is America's strategic partner. Pakistan has not been able to achieve that status. However, it has been persistent about persuading the United States to grant a similar strategic partnership sometime in the future.[49]

The greatest enemy of the nuclear weapons–related double standard is the fact that the nuclear genie is out of the bottle. The knowledge of how to make a bomb is no longer a Western monopoly. North Korea has emerged as the latest gatecrasher into the nuclear club. When Iran witnesses a nuclear India being rewarded by the United States with cooperation in nuclear technology and becoming a recipient of cutting-edge technology and weapons from the Nuclear Supplier Group, it concludes that becoming a nuclear power might not be a bad thing, if not now, then, to be sure, sometime in the not-too-distant future.

Iran's concerns about its security from a potential US attack or from a combined military action of US and Israel have never lessened. Now that Saddam Hussein and his regime have been swept into the dustbin of history, Iran is the last confrontational state in the Middle East. Syria has never been much of a challenge to Israel or to the United States, since its military power does not pose even a minimal threat to nuclear-armed Israel. The continuation of civil war in Syria has increased the possibility that the Assad regime may not be around for long. Iran, on the contrary, has never accepted America's dominance in the Middle East. At the same time, it has remained highly proactive in expanding its own sphere of influence in the region, in direct competition with the United States.

Iranian leaders have always played down America's assertion that a peaceful resolution of the Palestinian conflict would emerge. In that capacity, Iran enjoys considerable sympathy inside the Arab world. To the embarrassment of a number of leading Arab states, Iran has emerged as the major supporter of Hamas's ostensibly permanent defiance of Israel, while other Arab rulers jockey to either gain or secure a favourite spot on America's list of "friends" in the Middle East.

At the same time, Iran seeks an anti-Taliban nexus with Russia and India, states that are apprehensive about the potential return of the Taliban in Afghanistan. Afghanistan offers Iran a great opportunity to escalate its clout, because Russia and India remain wary that the United States may pull its troops out of that country in 2017. Iran is worried about the acutely anti-Shia posture of the Taliban; India is determined not to allow Pakistan the upper hand in Afghanistan under a potential Taliban return to power; Russia is fearful of the promotion of regional jihads under a Taliban rule, such as it experienced during the late 1990s. Thus, Iran, India, and Russia are very much interested in developing their own options to deal with post-American Afghanistan.

Lebanon was a place where Iran demonstrated a lot of clout and influence, with the support of Syria. However, with the Syrian regime fighting a bloody war against its own citizens (à la the Qaddafi regime between February and October 2011), there is little doubt that Iran's presence and influence throughout the Levant will suffer if/when the Syrian regime falls. In August 2013, the Syrian regime was suspected of using chemical weapons on the anti-regime forces. That suspected act crossed the line drawn in the sand by President Barack Obama. Now Obama's credibility was on the line. When it appeared that the Pentagon had developed a plan of attack on Syria, US secretary of state John Kerry luckily, from the perspective of the Assad regime, came to its rescue. During a press conference in London, when asked whether there was any way Syria could avoid being attacked by the United States, Kerry replied yes, if the Assad regime were to agree to get rid of all of its chemical weapons under some international supervision. Russia, the staunchest supporter of the Syrian dictatorship, saw that statement as a golden opportunity to save Syria from a pounding by the US military. Under Moscow's advice, the Assad regime agreed to get rid of its chemical weapons under the UN's supervision. The Obama administration was amenable to that option. Syria, under the supervision of an obscure UN agency, the Organisation for the Prohibition of Chemical Weapons, completed the inventory and destroyed a large number of its chemical weapons stocks; the remainder of those weapons were to be carried by a US ship and destroyed on the high seas.

So, the Assad regime survived. And Obama's decision might have changed the future dynamics of the Syrian conflict in the following way. Russia entered the conflict as a major supporter of Syria. In that capacity, it started bombing the anti-Assad Islamist groups that were supported by the United States, Saudi Arabia, and the UAE. The US-supported groups were disadvantaged in that they were not heavily armed, because the Obama administration remained apprehensive about their loyalty – whether they were really moderate Islamists or whether they were connected with Jabhat al-Nusra, an al-Qaida affiliate. Russia's entry into that conflict with an air campaign aimed at the US-supported Islamists instead of ISIS gave the Assad regime a new lease on life. The United States, recognizing the weakness of its position, changed its objective of demanding the ouster of al-Assad. Instead, Secretary of State John Kerry stated that, while the United States remained committed to the eventual removal of al-Assad, it did not have to occur in the near future. Thus, in meetings among the United States, Saudi Arabia, Iran, and Russia in Vienna, Austria, over the future of Syria, the bone of contention was the participation of the Assad regime and that of the US-backed Islamists in the negotiations.

Iran's participation in the negotiations was much resented by Saudi Arabia; however, given that the Russian-Iranian nexus had an upper hand in the Syrian theatre of operations, Saudi Arabia was in no position to have a voice in excluding Iran. More to the point, the Obama administration fully understood how crucial Iran's role had become in the future resolution of the Syrian conflict, and wanted to include that country.

While the participants in the Syrian conflict bickered over who was or was not going to be at the negotiating table in Vienna, ISIS was targeted only by the US Air Force. Turkey's participation in that conflict was hindered by its objection to the participation of the Kurdish forces, which had become significant for the fulfillment of the United States' own objective of destroying ISIS in Syria. (More about this subject later.)

Even after Iran signed the Joint Comprehensive Plan of Action with the United States in July 2015, Iranian leaders continued to distrust the lone superpower. Iran's supreme leader, Ali Khamenei, has made a habit of referring to the lone superpower as the "Great Satan" and the "ultimate embodiment of arrogance." Suspicion of the United States is arguably endemic among Iranians of Khamenei's generation. They grew up watching how the United States, along with Great Britain, sabotaged democracy by ousting Mosaddeq and putting the Shah on the throne to ensure that Iran remained a secure source of oil and served America's strategic objectives in the Persian Gulf and the Middle East. They witnessed how the Carter administration tried to roll back the Islamic revolution by urging the Iranian Army to overthrow the regime. They saw how hard the United States strove and what tactics it applied to bring an end to the Islamic Republic during the Iran-Iraq War. Iran was a quintessential "rogue state" and an "axis of evil" in the parlance of America's top leaders. But the younger generation of Iranians are curious about the United States; they love most things Western, and they would be happy to see the reestablishment of diplomatic ties.

The United States probably loathed Iran more than it did any communist country during the heyday of the Cold War, simply because no communist country humiliated the United States as Iran did during the hostage crisis in the late 1970s and by sponsoring the Beirut bombing of 1983. More important, Iran's practice of Islamism, which ousted the Shah and brought about the hostage crisis, was seen by the United States as a clear defeat of its own practice of secular fundamentalism (as discussed in chapter 1). And the clash of these two "isms" continues in Iraq, Syria, and the global media, as well as in the political arenas of Iran and the United States.

Iran has significantly diminished its nuclear research program. However, the question remains whether it has entirely abandoned its aspirations to acquire nuclear weapons. The answer depends on whether the United States has really accepted the legitimacy of the Islamic Republic and whether it no longer envisages with suspicion or antagonism Iran's aspirations to remain a regional power. If both Iran and the United States find avenues of cooperation in the Middle East in the coming years, they may end up seeking a strategic rapprochement, which would fulfill these aforementioned preconditions on the part of the United States.

Reasons for a rapprochement are many. Both Iran and the United States are enemies of ISIS and are already fighting a war against that terrorist entity in Iraq and Syria. And both Iran and the United States remain apprehensive about the future of Afghanistan, even if the Taliban were to emerge as a governing partner with the government of President Ashraf Ghani. If the Taliban were to oust the elected government of Afghanistan through terrorist campaigns, then the United States and Iran would likely face another front where their respective forces would be fighting the Taliban and even ISIS, since the latter has escalated its presence in Afghanistan. The initiation of an era of friendship and cooperation between the United States and Iran would create an environment in which the latter would not only abandon reconsideration of nuclear weapons development, but would also say goodbye to its "Samson Option" of the pre-US-Iran nuclear deal era.

IRAN'S ACHILLES HEEL

As much as Iran has emerged as a major player in the Middle East in the past thirty years or so, at least two issues stand out as a potential Achilles heel for the long-term stability, and even survival, of the Islamic Republic. The first one is a sustained challenge to the political legitimacy of the government. The heavily conservative nature of the Islamist government has created a power play whereby Iran's deep state – its national security organizations and establishments, right-wing groups inside its *Majlis* (parliament), and the very person of Iran's supreme leader, Ali Khamenei – exercises inordinate power and influence over the population. These groups are focused on preserving and defending the legacy established by the Islamic revolution of 1979 – that is, the Shia version of Islamism. The systemic exclusion of liberal groups and ideas has caused sustained tensions and raised doubts about the legitimacy of the government. If ignored or left unattended for a long period of time, these tensions could create another social movement of the magnitude of the Islamic revolution, bringing about regime change.

Second, in a governmental system where the conservative forces are so dominant, liberal forces consistently find themselves at the fringes of the political process in terms of their ability to influence it. The conservative groups have paid little attention to the fact that more than 60 per cent of Iranians were either born after the revolution or were too young at the time to have any memory of it. A majority of these young Iranians reportedly prefer a system of government that resembles a Western-style democracy, and they would like to see their government establish friendly relations with the United States. But despite their admiration for democracy, the attitude of young Iranians toward the US government remains largely negative. The anti-Iranian media coverage in the United States, which is readily available for Iranians to read, also keeps the Iranian opinion of the United States in a state of flux.[50]

The very idea of the *vilayat-e-faqih* (rule of the clergy) created the office of the supreme leader, who exercises enormous power and is fully capable of undermining popular will whenever it does not suit his frame of reference. He appoints the six members of the all-powerful Council of the Guardian, serves as commander of the armed forces, and confirms the election of the president. The concentration of power in the office of the *faqih*, which was tailor-made for Rouhollah Khomeini, exposes the political system to frequent crises of legitimacy from within for at least two reasons. First, Ali Khamenei neither enjoys the aura of revolutionary awe that Khomeini exuded as the spiritual guide of the revolution, nor possesses credentials as a Shia scholar of a high caliber. Second, Khamenei's autocratic style has been a constant source of tension and contention inside Iran. One need only recall the controversy regarding ballot box stuffing that was alleged to have occurred during the presidential election of 2009. The subsequent political turbulence of the Green Movement and the jailing of two major presidential contenders – Mir-Hossein Mousavi and Mehdi Karroubi – spoke volumes about the perceived low legitimacy of the government headed by Ahmadinejad after the elections, both domestically and in the international arena.

Moreover, Ali Khamenei deftly used his position as commander-in-chief of the armed forces to expand his power by appointing former members of the Islamic Revolutionary Guard Corps (IRGC) as heads of Iran's National Security Council, the Expediency Council, the Bonyad-e Mostazafan va Janbazan (Foundation of the Oppressed and Disabled), and the Islamic Republic of Iran Broadcasting (a corporation in control of radio and television). Even former president Mahmoud Ahmadinejad was a member of the IRGC. Thus the IRGC became "the dominant group in not only defense policy, but in domestic political and economic affairs." As "a sort of a Praetorian army," it attempted to suppress the liberal supporters of former president Mohammad Khatami and at the same time to expand its economic power by overseeing "many sectors of the Iranian economy, including oil, construction, agriculture, mining, transport, the defence industry and import-export companies."[51] In its present capacity, the IRGC functions to preserve and promote the highly conservative perspectives of the ruling elite, leaving little-to-no room for the forces of moderation and change to maneuver.

Considering these realities, the election of President Hasan Rouhani was a pleasant surprise for a large portion of the Iranian population as well as for the West. After the dark and confrontational legacy of former president Mahmoud Ahmadinejad, it was hoped that Iran would pull itself out of a sustained posture of anti-westernism and contentious foreign policy, which had earned Iran the friendship of Venezuela, North Korea, Syria, Cuba, and other states that remained on the fringes of the international political arena. Those hopes were fulfilled when Iran successfully negotiated its nuclear agreement with the United States. Consequently, the United Nations officially lifted the economic and arms sanctions on 16 January 2016. The signing of the nuclear deal was a success for the moderates of Iran, but there remains a nagging concern that the hardliners were not happy about it.

The second major challenge for the security and abiding interests of Iran is the ongoing civil war in Syria. Syria is Iran's long-term, and presently only, Arab ally. Since the Islamic revolution, the congruity of interests between Tehran and Damascus has evolved into a powerful alliance. The outbreak of civil war in Syria was therefore a major source of apprehension for Iran. It also jeopardized its other crucial interests, which, aside from ensuring the survival of the Assad regime, are as follows: continuing its sectarian conflict with Saudi Arabia, which is dedicated to ending al-Assad's rule in Syria; pursuing its policy of defiance with the United States, notwithstanding the potential that, with the conclusion of the nuclear deal, this conflict might be measurably reduced; expanding its regional power by strengthening ties with Russia; and containing, if not destroying, ISIS.[52]

Luckily for Iran, Russia was equally adamant about the survival of the Assad regime. That reality alone prompted a great deal of maneuvering by the great powers. China was very much in agreement with Russia in supporting the Assad regime. Both Moscow and Beijing had been unhappy watching the dismantlement of the Qaddafi regime, largely through the implementation of the UN-sanctioned NATO air power, back in March/April 2011. They were in no mood to allow the passage of another UNSC resolution authorizing the use of power against Syria. The only other alternative was for the United States and Russia to negotiate the fate of Syria. And as long as the issue was under negotiations, chances of a regime change in that country would remain minimal, at least as a result of another NATO or US-only military action.

Russia's entry into the Syrian conflict not only averted a major crisis in Iran's foreign policy, it also created a huge opportunity for Iran to act strategically to save the Syrian dictatorship. After realizing that the Syrian army generals were too demoralized or too incompetent to wage counterinsurgency warfare against the anti-regime forces, Iran deftly inserted its Quds Force in order to turn the tide of the battle in the Assad regime's favour. The Quds Force is a battle-hardened force that gained an enormous amount of experience in conducting counterinsurgency operations against the US forces during the American occupation of Iraq. Iran also decided to heavily use Hezbollah fighters and the rising forces of the Shia "Special Groups" from Iraq who were originally trained by the Iranian Quds Force.[53]

Iran is aware that its capabilities to sustain the Assad regime are contingent upon the continued willingness of the United States to negotiate the future modalities of peace in Syria with Russia and other pro- and anti-regime forces. Still, Iran appears determined to make the best of its limited options. Iran also knows that the ouster of the Assad regime would expand the influence of Saudi Arabia and the UAE, both of which have already couched their antagonisms toward Iran in the context of a Sunni-Shia rivalry. Thus, Iran's foreign policy stakes in Syria are high. That reality may explain why the Shia militias, including Hezbollah, have proven to be highly driven forces. About the only other equally motivated anti-Assad force is al-Nusra, a Sunni self-styled jihadist group affiliated with al-Qaida.

In this sense, Shia Islamism is very much at war with Sunni Islamism. The United States and Russia, although important players, are not a part of this Islamism-related competition. For Russia and Iran, the ultimate prize in this competition is winning a long-term presence in the Levant. That may also prove to be a success for Shia Islamism, while a defeat of Saudi and UAE forces would mean a defeat for Sunni Islamism. If the Saudi and UAE forces are defeated, political stability in Syria will continue to face constant challenges from the Sunni jihadists.

ISIS remains the other major pursuer of Sunni Islamism. In that capacity, it will continue to challenge the Assad regime, even if it loses the Syrian portion of its "caliphate." Thus the military conflict in Syria is not likely to go away anytime soon. The question is whether Iranian and Russian commitments to safeguard the Assad regime will endure.

CLOSING OBSERVATIONS

Iran's unique brand of Islamism has been a big thorn in the side for the United States. The potency of that phenomenon grew as the United States decided to wage its "global war on terrorism" and invade Afghanistan and Iraq. What was different between the Bush and Obama presidencies was that the focus of that war shifted first from Afghanistan (from 2001 to 2003) to Iraq and then back to Afghanistan (starting in 2009). Iran had a greater influence and considerably larger potential to challenge America's interests in Iraq than in Afghanistan because Iraq is predominantly a Shia country and Afghanistan is not. The "Worldwide Threat Assessment of the US Intelligence Community" grimly reported in 2016 that the Taliban's rising capabilities were "steadily chipping away at Afghanistan's security" and that the Taliban had coalesced into a "relatively cohesive force under the new Taliban Senior Leader Mullah Akhtar Mohammad Mansour despite some early opposition."[54] A return of the Taliban to power would be at least as hostile to Iran as it would be to the regime of Mullah Omar. If anything, the anti-Shia aspect of the Wahhabi ideology has become more popular in Afghanistan and Pakistan in the twenty-first century than ever before. Thus, neither America's continued presence in nor withdrawal from Afghanistan will be of much benefit to Iran. It will have to develop its own strategy when the US force withdrawal materializes.

From Iran's perspective, the Syrian war took a turn for the better when President Obama failed to bomb Syrian forces when al-Assad allegedly used chemical weapons against his civilian population. Vladimir Putin took full advantage of Obama's reluctance and plunged his military forces into that conflict. The US hesitancy about arming the anti-Assad but "moderate" Islamist groups also worked well for Iran and Russia. To add insult to injury, Russia pursued a policy of endlessly bombing the anti-Assad Islamist forces backed by the United States, Saudi Arabia, and the UAE. As a result, ISIS's grip on the territories it occupied remained mostly intact.

From the perspective of this study, the Saudi/UAE campaign to promote Sunni Islamism by defeating the Assad regime and creating a Sunni-dominated government received a major setback when President Obama refused to send in US ground troops. Instead, the United States armed the People's Protection Units (YPG) – the military wing of the Democratic Union Party (PYD) in Syria. The PYD has close ties with the Kurdistan Workers' Party (PKK), which both Turkey and the United States regard as a terrorist group. Russia not only read Obama's "conflict-averse" stance, but also initiated an aggressive air campaign against the US-Saudi-backed Islamists who were focused on ousting al-Assad from power.[55]

Continued US reliance on the PYD has been severely criticized by Turkish president Recep Erdoğan. He publicly asked the Obama administration, "Are you on our side or the side of terrorist ... organizations?" Turkey wanted the United States to take a hard militaristic stand to oust al-Assad, instead of arming the PYD to do its fighting. It was of the view that the Obama administration remained cavalier about the prospect of the Kurds building an independent Kurdistan as their reward for helping the United States. Erdoğan frequently stated that he would not stand for such an outcome. The US position is that Turkey is letting the al-Nusra (al-Qaida affiliate in Syria) and ISIS jihadists "flow across the border."[56] In reality, both the United States and Turkey should share part of the blame for why the Assad regime has gotten the upper hand in the continuing Syrian war.

The United States was accurately criticized for its lackadaisical approach to the conflict and particularly for its preference for a political resolution. And Turkey was not alone in its criticism. French foreign minister Laurent Fabius, in his last press conference before resigning from his job, aired similar frustrations by disparaging the US policy as "ambiguous." He added that the United States was not "making a strong enough commitment to oust Assad."[57] The intra-NATO squabbling was music to the ears of both Iran and ISIS.

From the perspective of the strategic interests of Iran, its decision to conclude a nuclear deal with the United States opened up a plethora of opportunities. The US economic sanctions, although they were major impediments to Iran's long-standing policy of self-reliance, forced its domestic industries to concentrate on research and development and to diversify their sources of national revenue. As a result, an International Monetary Fund report noted that Iran's "non-oil revenues as a share of total fiscal revenues during 2012–14 were the highest among all oil-exporting Middle Eastern and North African countries at 56%."[58] Iran also manifested every intention of continuing to build its "knowledge-based economy" in the coming years. Russia, China, the European Union, and even many American companies appeared fully prepared to do business with Iran. Considering these developments, Iran's prospects for emerging as a major regional power appeared obtainable. What still was needed, however, was Iran's resolve to enter into a dialogue with major Western countries, as well its regional neighbours, to find avenues of cooperation where unconventional tactics and strategies, especially the use of terrorism, would be permanently abandoned.

7

Central Asia: Where the Islamists Challenge the Great Powers

SYNOPSIS

Central Asia is distinct and important for three reasons. First, it is there that the three great powers – the United States, Russia, and China – compete for influence and dominance. Second, this is a region where the United States does not have a dominant presence, and where the chances of its future ascendancy are slim. Finally, the Islamists and the self-styled jihadist forces in Central Asia, although they do not pose an imminent threat to the stability of any existing regime, continue to evolve in the five republics: Kazakhstan, Kyrgyzstan, Tajikistan, Turkmenistan, and Uzbekistan. That is not to say that the Islamist groups have equal prospects in these countries. Quite the contrary, they have a palpable advantage in Uzbekistan, Tajikistan, and Kyrgyzstan, but very little presence in Kazakhstan. Turkmenistan is a difficult state to make any reasonable judgment about, because it remains the hermit state of Central Asia (à la North Korea).

Russia and China are greatly interested and concerned about the nature of Islamist activism in Central Asia because it affects the Muslim minorities within their own borders: in China's Xinjiang province and in the Chechen Republic of the Russian Federation. The United States is fighting a war in Central Asia's immediate neighbourhood, Afghanistan, and it used an air force base in Kyrgyzstan as an important point of logistical support for its forces in Afghanistan until it was closed in 2014. Although Washington has not developed a coherent strategy toward the region, it has shown its resolve to make its presence in Central Asia a lasting phenomenon.

The Islamist forces in this region pose the least amount of challenge to the West because the United States, Russia, and China are committed to preventing any possibility of regime change that would bring to power either an Islamist or an Islamist-led government. However, as long as these republics are reigned by autocratic rulers and remain economically underdeveloped, Islamist and jihadist groups will remain very much alive and proactive.

The *sui generis* nature of Central Asia stems from the high-profile presence of both Russia and China. Russia is primarily concerned about ensuring that no Central Asian republic becomes a victim of Islamism (capturing of territories by a jihadist entity). Since Russia does not have the massive economic resources of China, it is concentrating on providing military assistance to those states and conducting joint military exercises aimed at defeating jihadism. China, on the contrary, being an economic giant, has launched a globally oriented Silk Road Initiative, which is also focused on Central Asia. In addition, the Central Asian republics have been reaping economic payoffs as members of the Shanghai Cooperation Organization (SCO). The United States has opted to keep its profile comparatively low in Central Asia. However, the Central Asian republics have been closely following the dynamics of American military presence in Afghanistan, hoping that the United States will be able to stabilize Afghanistan by defeating the Taliban as a jihadist force.

The next section provides an overview of the problems endemic to the Central Asian states. Instead of a country-by-country analysis, the chapter then examines the Islamist challenge in the Ferghana Valley, which is shared by Uzbekistan, Kyrgyzstan, and Tajikistan.

A PLACE WHERE MISERY RULES

The Islamist and jihadist forces in Central Asia have maintained a low profile since the US invasion of Afghanistan in 2001. They have been targeted by the autocratic rulers, who are especially fearful of them after witnessing the regime-change-related capacity of a social movement like the Arab Awakening. There also have been coordinated endeavours by Russia and China to ensure that the Central Asian dictatorships are not overthrown as a result of a cataclysmic event. However, as the Middle East, South Asia (Pakistan and Afghanistan), and North Africa remain a hotbed of Islamic radicalism, there is little doubt that the spillover effect of Islamism-related violence will show its face in one or more states of Central Asia (most probably in Tajikistan or Uzbekistan). This violence includes attempts by the jihadists and Islamists to capture political power, acquire territories, and topple regimes.

Central Asia is a Pandora's box of problems. The US director of national intelligence, Admiral Dennis Blair, described the region in a report prepared in 2009 as "ill-equipped to deal with the challenges posed by Islamic violent extremism, poor economic development, and problems associated with energy, water and food distribution."[1] In 2013, Blair's successor, General Charles Clapper, stated, "The threat of instability remains in the states of Central Asia. Central Asian leaders have prioritized regime stability over political and economic reforms that could improve long-term governance and legitimacy. Most fear any signs of Arab Spring–type uprisings and repress even small signs of discontent."[2] The threat assessment given by Clapper in 2016 remained at the same level, except that the impending reduced US force presence in Afghanistan was a source of consternation for the US security officials.[3]

Central Asia was the home of the Silk Road before the opening of sea-lanes to India, China, and the Americas. It was from here that the great Timurids and Moguls rose to put their indelible imprint on the history of this vast contiguous area. This was the region where the two great powers of the nineteenth century – Russia and Great Britain – played their now-famous "great game." The father of modern geopolitics, Sir Halford Mackinder, once said that whoever controlled Central Asia would wield enormous power in the world. Most recently, Zbigniew Brzezinski, who served as national security advisor to President Jimmy Carter, depicted Central Asia (along with the Caucasus) as "the Eurasian Balkans." The countries in this area, he observed, "are of importance from the standpoint of security and historical ambitions to at least three of their most immediate and more powerful neighbors, namely, Russia, Turkey, and Iran, with China also signaling an increasing political interest in the region." He went on to add, "The Eurasian Balkans are infinitely more important as a potential economic prize: an enormous concentration of natural gas and oil reserves is located in the region, in addition to important minerals, including gold."[4]

All five states of Central Asia have been ruled by tyrannical regimes. A quick glance at recent and current leaders will shed light on the nature of the problem and why the region is prone to potentially cataclysmic change. Of the five republics, Turkmenistan has the smallest population of a little over five million people. Its first president, Supramurad Niyazov, called himself "Turkmenbashi" (Father of all Turkmens), and spent a sizeable portion of his country's resources creating a cult of personality for himself and his deceased mother. Prominent Pakistani journalist Ahmed Rashid described Niyazov's regime as "the most repressive and dictatorial regime in the region ... The indiscriminate use of the death penalty, the torture of prisoners in the overflowing prisons (which frequently erupt in riots), and the disappearance of dissenters without a trace all point to a regime that is paranoid about staying in power." Rashid added, "Niyazov banned the teaching of English and other foreign languages in schools to isolate the population from Western trends, and Turkmen students were forbidden to take up scholarships abroad."[5] Niyazov died in 2006 and was replaced by Kurbanguly Berdymuhammadov. His ruling style was equally repressive, but without the cult of personality of his predecessor. Amnesty International's 2013 report, *Turkmenistan: An "Era of Happiness" or More of the Same Repression?*, describes a highly repressive regime that uses "systematic harassment of any kind of opposition or dissent ... People expressing views that are different from the government's are treated as enemies of the state."[6] Two very positive features of Turkmenistan are that it is blessed with ample gas and oil reserves, and it has the most homogeneous population of all of the Central Asian republics.

In Kazakhstan, President Nursultan Nazerbayev's regime is also known for brutalizing its citizens. An opposition member of parliament described his rule as a "super-presidential republic – the president decides everything."[7] Opposition parties and newspapers are banned, opposition leaders are chased out of the country, and corruption is widespread "at every level of government." Nazerbayev coerced the rubber-stamp parliament into passing a bill "that conferred political and legal rights to him and his entire family granting blanket immunity against any charges that had already been made or that would be made in the future."[8] A report from Human Rights Watch issued in January 2013 states, "Kazakhstan initiated a harsh and unprecedented crackdown on freedom of expression and political plurality, imprisoning outspoken opposition and civil society activists and shutting down an opposition group and key independent media outlets."[9]

President Islam Karimov of Uzbekistan is yet another autocratic and brutal ruler, perhaps the most brutal of them all. He banned all political parties in 1992. Rashid writes, "In a series of crackdowns in 1992, 1993, and after 1997, Karimov arrested hundreds of ordinary Muslims for alleged links with Islamic fundamentalists, accusing them of being Wahhabis, and closing down mosques and madrasas, and forcing mullahs into jail or exile."[10] An Amnesty International report on Uzbekistan notes that "authorities intensified their crackdown on civil society. They placed rights activists under house arrest and incommunicado detention for peaceful civic activism, extended the prison sentences of opposition figures without due process, and deported international journalists attempting to visit the country."[11] The paranoiac nature of the Karimov regime was highlighted in a report that his regime banned the teaching of political science in the universities "on the grounds that it is a western pseudo-science that does not take the 'Uzbek model' of development into account." The subject of political science was changed to "The Theory and Practice of Building a Democratic Society in Uzbekistan."[12]

Of all the Central Asian republics, Kyrgyzstan holds the most promise of becoming a democracy. It has already experienced two regime changes, first as a result of a coup (often referred to as the "Tulip Revolution") in March 2005 that ousted President Askar Akayev. Akayev was replaced by Kurmanbek Bakiyev; however, he was just as repressive, inept, and nepotistic as his predecessor. Bakiyev was ousted as a result of a violent protest in April 2010, and former foreign minister, Roza Otunbayeva, became interim president. She promised to hold new elections the following year. The November 2011 elections brought to presidency the former prime minister, Almazbek Atambayev.

Tajikistan is a state whose weakness is its own worst enemy. It was a victim of a bloody civil war that lasted from 1991 to 1997. The sovereignty of the government has been barely discernable. According to Rashid, "Tajikistan remains the most disadvantaged of the Central Asian nations. The economy is in ruins, the government has no control over large tracts of territory, and the drug smuggling from Afghanistan for onward journey to Europe has become a major factor in the continued destabilization of the country."[13] A report published in May 2010 described Tajikistan as "poorer than most of sub-Saharan Africa or the poorest countries of Asia."[14] Its president, Emamoli Rahmon (who officially dropped his Russian-style surname, Rakhmonov, in 2007), is also an autocrat. However, until August 2015, when the Islamic Renaissance

Party of Tajikistan (IRPT) was banned and given only ten days to suspend all activities, Tajikistan was the only country that had not banned Islamic parties.[15]

All of these repressive regimes hold power in a region plagued by poverty, extremely low standards of living, and disease, and they stay in power by suppressing human rights and civil liberties. In every single state, the "national leaders cemented their personal power by creating super-presidential regimes, in which the balance of power between executive and legislatures was overwhelmingly weighted toward the former." Uzbekistan and Turkmenistan, along with Belarus, are regarded as "the least-reforming of the Soviet successor states."[16] The Freedom House Report of 2006 evaluated "the state of freedom" during the calendar year 2005 on a scale of 1 to 7, with 1 being the best score and 7 the worst. For political rights and civil liberties, respectively, Kyrgyzstan scored 5 and 4; Kazakhstan 6 and 5; Tajikistan 6 and 5; Turkmenistan 7 and 7; and Uzbekistan 7 and 7.[17] The Human Rights Watch World Report 2015 stated, "Central Asia's already poor human rights record deteriorated further in 2014 … The governments of Kazakhstan, Kyrgyzstan, Tajikistan, Turkmenistan, and Uzbekistan failed to uphold and in some cases further undermined their core human rights commitments."[18] In both Tajikistan and Kyrgyzstan, torture is a "widespread concern." The Human Rights Watch report of January 2013 stated, "There were some small, positive steps on human rights in Kyrgyzstan and Tajikistan. But overall, their poor human rights records have not improved despite, for example, government pledges to tackle the problem of torture … during visits to each by the UN's Special Rapporteur on Torture."[19]

How did Central Asian countries sink to such levels of poverty and related despair? As colonies of the Soviet Union, they were exploited by Moscow for their natural resources and purposely kept dependent on "Mother Russia" as a guarantee against secession. Joseph Stalin, Nikita Khrushchev, as well as Leonid Brezhnev, purposely created multi-ethnicity by deporting "various peoples to Central Asia," thereby "changing the region from relatively homogeneous to multi-ethnic and multi-religious." These policies led to the "crystallization of ethnic and clan groups"; Russians often acquired the "best positions, while the titular nations (e.g., the Kazakhs in Kazakhstan and Kyrgyz in Kyrgyzstan) of the republics were kept in lower positions." Another highly deleterious outcome of the policies of Soviet leaders was ethnic fragmentation "between Russians and Ukrainians and indigenous people, between indigenous peoples, such as Tajik and Turkic speakers, and within ethnic groups, such as divisions between North and South (in Kyrgyzstan) or hordes (in Kazakhstan) or different tribes (in Turkmenistan)."[20] To this day, Central Asian countries conduct 40–50 per cent of their trade with Russia. This economic dependence is also a horrible fact of their existence, since it keeps them from developing a pluralistic economy with the capability and keenness for global trade. As long as the communist regime lasted, citizens of these countries were deprived of their Muslim identity and labelled Soviet citizens, as if that were a badge of honour. When the Soviet Union collapsed, these countries found themselves seriously lacking a corps of civilian leaders, except for the communist apparatchiks who served as heads of the Communist Party or were handpicked presidents from Moscow. Not surprisingly, with the collapse of the Soviet Union, these countries only reluctantly became independent republics.

The region's tainted colonial history aside, current political elites of all Central Asian countries bear much of the blame for the region's problems. They have been accused of funnelling tens of millions of dollars abroad to private bank accounts, while their populations become increasingly impoverished.[21] The primary motivation of the Central Asian dictators is to ensure that the longevity of their respective brutal rules is not seriously challenged from a variety of internal threats related to political, social, and economic instability, high levels of unemployment, ethnic tensions, confrontations between various elites, high rates of corruption, ineffective governance, and high rates of drug trafficking coming from Afghanistan.[22] Nevertheless, in at least three republics – Kazakhstan, Uzbekistan, and Turkmenistan – the rulers face opposition.

Tajikistan and Kyrgyzstan, as previously noted, remain unstable polities. Tajikistan is so fragile that no one can be certain when the next civil war or other such calamitous event might bring about a regime change. A 2016 report issued by the International Crisis Group stated, "Tajikistan, Central Asia's poorest state, is under dangerous pressure both internally and externally. President Emomali Rahmon's 23-year rule is marred by violence, lack of accountability, corruption and mass migration. Remittances and drug trafficking are key sources of income... Controls on religion and political opposition, including a ban on the moderate Islamic Renaissance Party of

Tajikistan (IRPT), foster resentment. Security along the 1,400-km border with Afghanistan is inconsistent at best, and increasing instability in northern Afghanistan, where Central Asian militants are allied with the Taliban, poses a threat to Tajikistan, Kyrgyzstan and Uzbekistan alike."[23] Kyrgyzstan has been especially unstable since the outbreak of major ethnic riots between the Kyrgyz majority and the Uzbek minority in 2010. "Bishkek remains occupied by threats to its internal security, which emanate in part from forces beyond Kyrgyzstan's borders. These include religious extremism and terrorism, narcotics trafficking, and ethnic tensions that threaten to undermine its efforts to create a sense of civic identity."[24]

In general, Central Asia remains a ticking time bomb. These countries face multiple intractable problems: economic stagnation, falling standards of living, high unemployment rates, corruption and drug-trafficking, growing dependence on neighbouring states "for energy, water, raw materials and goods," and "increasing intergenerational conflict, expressed in clashes over traditional versus modern values, customs, and beliefs."[25] The chief concern of the autocratic rulers is to stay in power. Three of these countries – Uzbekistan, Kyrgyzstan, and Tajikistan – are either failing or failed states.

THE NATURE OF THE ISLAMIST CHALLENGE IN THE FERGHANA VALLEY

Because all five states are predominantly Muslim, there is a general fear that all of them – some sooner rather than later – will face challenges to their stability from Islamist or even jihadist forces. The Islamist challenge was serious in the pre–9/11 era, especially in the Ferghana Valley – areas shared by Uzbekistan, Kyrgyzstan, and Tajikistan.[26] The US invasion of Afghanistan in 2001 brought about a severe weakening of the power, visibility, and presence of Islamist parties like the Islamic Movement of Uzbekistan (IMU). However, because of the scarcity of correct information coming out of these Central Asian countries, there is no way of knowing how influential or powerful the IMU or other Islamist groups have become in Central Asia toward the conclusion of the second decade of the twenty-first century. When the Islamist challenge does escalate in Central Asia, the general understanding is that the foremost target will be the government of Uzbekistan. That country is ruled by the most ruthless dictator in the region, Islam Karimov. But Kyrgyzstan and

Tajikistan are equally vulnerable because they are the poorest of the Central Asian republics.

The Ferghana Valley is where the battle of Talas was fought between the Arab warriors of the Abbasid Caliphate and those of the Chinese Tang Dynasty. This battle marked the victory of Islam. During the Soviet days, it was purposely divided in such a way "that Tajiks, Uzbeks, and Kyrgyz were found on all sides." This policy also enabled the Soviet authorities to be continuously "called upon by the people in the region to help them manage conflicts that were bound to emerge as a result of these artificial divisions."[27] Since the implosion of the Soviet Union into five independent states in Central Asia, this valley straddles three countries, Uzbekistan, Kyrgyzstan, and Tajikistan. Today, the Ferghana Valley comprises seven administration provinces: three Uzbek (Andijan, Ferghana, and Namangan), three Kyrgyz (Batkan, Osh, and Jalalabad), and one Tajik (Sugh, which was formerly known as Leningrad). The best way to understand the profile of the Ferghana Valley is to develop a cumulative picture of three countries that share it.[28] The Ferghana Valley is one of the potential hotspots of Central Asia. What happens there, "for better or worse – has widespread ramifications for the region as a whole." Because of their "ethnic diversity, the highly concentrated and growing population including a high percentage of youth, high rates of unemployment and widespread economic stress, complex borders in a region occupied by parts of three newly sovereign states, and [their] recent history of tensions," the countries in the Ferghana Valley are source of regional instability.[29] The domestic politics are fragile and incendiary. The civil war in Tajikistan from 1992 to 1997 seems to have permanently weakened that country, making it vulnerable to unanticipated developments. Uzbekistan faced political violence in the Andijan in May 2005, which Karimov's security apparatus brutally suppressed, resulting in hundreds of deaths. The interethnic conflict of Kyrgyzstan in June 2010 was only the latest reminder of this reality. That country had ousted its president (Bakiyev) in April 2010 through internal turmoil. The political passions of that event had barely cooled down before the outburst of ethnic violence against the Uzbeks, who were economically disadvantaged.

The Ferghana Valley has the largest population in Central Asia (up to 250 inhabitants per square kilometre, as compared to an average of 14 inhabitants per square kilometre in the rest of Central Asia).[30] And the political consciousness of the general population toward

Islam is on the rise. And yet somehow the Central Asians maintain their Islamic and ethnic identities in separate boxes. Although they share a common identity as Muslims, there have been violent ethnic riots over economic issues that affect the rights and privileges of ethnic minorities. There have also been several outbreaks of conflict between different ethnic groups and the IMU. Regarding the mounting political fermentation of the Ferghana Valley, a Central Asian specialist wrote, it "exhibits the most vivid example of the Islamic revolution taking place throughout the region and exposes Afghanistan's ideological impact on Central Asia. This is a hard, rural place, with cotton fields worked with sweat and picked by hand. The people are desperately poor. They see little that the new national governments have done to help their lives. Dissatisfaction is high, the lure of Islam as an answer to their dreary existence is strong."[31]

Islamist political groups in Central Asia base their perspectives of political change on Islam. Like Islamist groups throughout the Muslim world, they regard the existing regimes as "anti-Islamic," and thus a legitimate target for dismantlement by violent means. They regard the West, and especially the United States, as the "enemy" of Islam, and so Western targets should be treated with similar acts of violence. The work of at least four previously discussed Islamic thinkers stands out as highly relevant in the context of Central Asia. The first is Sayyid Qutb of Egypt, whose notion of the battle against *Jahiliyya* (state of ignorance) is at the heart of the stated rationale for global jihad of al-Qaida, and all Islamist and especially jihadist groups that emulate it. Any political system not based on the Qur'an and hadith (statements of the Prophet of Islam), said Qutb, is not operating in accordance with the Shariah (laws of Islam) and is based on Jahiliyya. Jahili societies, he argued, intend to crush true Islam; they should be annihilated by *jihad bil saif* (holy war by sword) and be replaced by true Islamic regimes. He reinterpreted jihad to mean the permanent conflict between the Islamic system and all contemporary political systems. Two South Asian Islamic scholars, Abul A'la Maududi and Abul Hasan Ali Nadwi, also describe Islam as a perpetually revolutionary ideology, with the power to change contemporary societies and rebuild them to conform to its own tenets and ideals. Another Egyptian Islamist, Muhammad Abd al-Salam Faraj, the founder and the theorist of Egyptian Al-Jihad, raised the status of militant jihad to the sixth pillar of Islam. What emerges from the preceding are the notions of militancy, absence of compromise and flexibility, and an insistence on creating a society of Islamic puritanism by radically altering the extant power structure – which is essentially the pursuit of Islamism. Thus the basic strategy of all Islamist groups is to alter the political status quo in the Ferghana Valley. The two pan-Islamist and self-styled jihadist groups determined to bring about political change are the Hizb ut-Tahrir (HT) and the Islamic Movement of Uzbekistan (IMU).

THE HIZB UT-TAHRIR

The founder of the HT (also referred to as the Hizb al-Tahrir) was a Palestinian named Taqi-Uddin Al-Nabhani. The party was initially established in Jordan in the early 1950s in East Jerusalem. Today, its branches and supporters are present in Central Asia, the Middle East, Europe, Australia, and North America. Although it has invited Shias to join, it is predominantly a Sunni organization.

Like all *salafi* movements (i.e., movements that adhere to the traditions of the Salaf, the pious ancestors of the days immediately following the death of the Prophet of Islam), the HT staunchly believes that the sanctity of Islam has been shattered by the general tendency in the world of Islam to deviate from the practices of the Prophet of Islam and his companions. Thus, its strategic objective is to revitalize that glory by returning to the purest form of Islam. For this reason, the HT advocates the establishment of a caliphate. As explained in one of its press releases, "The Khilafah is the global leadership for all the Muslims in the world. Its role is to establish the laws of the Islamic Shari'ah and to carry the call of Islam to the world. It is a model completely distinguished from any other ruling style such as democracy, theocracy or monarchy. The Shari'ah that is applied in founding the ruling, in caring for the citizen's affairs, and in the external affairs is from Allah. It is a system of unity not a system of union. The system of government in Islam, which is the system of Khilafat [caliphate], is a unitary system of one state and not a federal system. Muslims all over the world are not allowed to have more than one Islamic State."[32] Thus, "the HT has a vision of uniting Central Asia, Xinjiang Province in China, and eventually the entire umma (Islamic world community) under a *khilafat* (caliphate)."[33]

At least in Central Asia, the HT is very secretive, largely as a result of highly repressive practices of the Uzbek regime of Islam Karimov and other autocrats of the region. Thus, it is hard to determine the nature of its popularity. Still, according to one study, around 6,000 members or sympathizers are serving time in the prisons of Kazakhstan, Uzbekistan, Kyrgyzstan, and Tajikistan. The US State Department's assessment of this number is approximately 4,500 in Uzbekistan alone.[34] However, at no given time should such numbers be taken as authentic. Pakistani journalist Ahmed Rashid, who is considered one of the most authentic sources on the HT and other matters regarding Central Asia, states that this movement "is so secretive and decentralized that its leaders haven't revealed themselves even to their own supporters, and only one member of each of the organization's five-man cells is in contact with a member of another cell."[35] In his book, *Jihad*, Rashid explains that, at the local level, members of the HT are organized in small *daira* (Arabic for cells; the Uzbek word is *halqa*). "Each daira comprises five to seven members and is headed by a *mushrif*. Members of each daira only know each other. The mushrif is the person who knows or can contact individuals at the higher level of the organization. Each city or district may have one or more organizations, whose leaders are called *musond*. *Musonds* are under regional leaders, *masul* (person in charge). *Masuls* are directly under the country leader, *mutamad*."[36]

The HT operates on the basis of a three-stage strategy. In order to form the party group, the first stage focuses on culturing or educating people to believe in the ideas and methods of the party. In the second stage, the party members interact with the ummah, encouraging members of the community to embrace and fully incorporate Islam in their private and public affairs. The third stages focuses on establishing an Islamic government, "which will carry the message of Islam to the whole world."[37]

The party could possibly acquire a large following in Muslim polities if it was allowed to operate openly and without any obstruction from government. The HT seeks an educated following and eschews appealling to the uneducated and rural masses of Central Asia. Hence it is often described as an elitist organization. Its literature discusses various aspects of Islamic theology in a rather straightforward and thoughtful fashion. It does mention the doctrine of jihad, but not as a strategy to capture political power. Instead, the party discusses in detail the notion of *ijtihad* (renewal and reinterpretation). In the context of Islamic theology, ijtihad is a concept that promotes peaceful change.[38]

Whether the HT has remained a nonviolent entity is difficult to judge because it has been driven into hiding. In principle, all governments would have problems dealing with political organizations that promote radical change of the magnitude of establishing a caliphate. The highly authoritarian republics of Central Asia know no other way of dealing with the HT except to outlaw it and brutally suppress anyone who is even remotely suspected of supporting that organization. Consequently, the HT has no alternative but to remain highly secretive.

In the highly charged post–9/11 era, however, it appears that the party may no longer be dedicated to the principle of peaceful change. The HT envisages the governments of the Ferghana Valley countries as illegitimate, misguided, and anti-Islamic in orientation. It is hard to imagine that replacing the existing governments with a caliphate will be a peaceful process. Furthermore, given the proclivity of the governments of Uzbekistan, Tajikistan, and Kyrgyzstan to suppress the activities of the HT through violent tactics, it is hard to fathom that the functionaries of that organization will rely indefinitely on nonviolent responses. Indeed, despite the HT's insistence that it favours peaceful change, its rhetoric has become increasingly shrill and vitriolic. In a leaflet entitled "Annihilate the Fourth Crusade," the HT states,

> O Noble Islamic Ummah! Undoubtedly, George Bush's declaration of war against the Muslims of Iraq is a declaration of war against the entire Islamic Ummah, because the Muslims of Iraq are an inseparable part of the single Islamic Ummah. The rulers of the Muslims have betrayed the Ummah and deceived the Muslims by claiming that they are against the war on Iraq. The people did not believe their false speeches as the reality of their actions were plain to see. Despite their alliance with America, America despises the rulers of the Muslims and has no regard for them. Thus she ignored their pleas for a United Nations' resolution, no matter how flimsy, to cover their compromised position and protect themselves from the wrath of the Muslims, revengeful against America and her allies. Despite all of this, America neither paid heed to their pleas nor made allowances for their compromised position. They collaborated with America, Britain and the enemies of Islam, thinking that these forces will defend for them their thrones and save them from this Ummah's

> retribution. They have forgotten the inevitable doom that awaits them just as it awaits all of the traitors who preceded them in allying with the kuffar [nonbelievers] and the enemies of Islam.[39]

The HT perceives itself as a party that is on the right path of establishing a worldwide Islamic caliphate, a goal that it has been pursuing since 1953.[40] As Rashid notes, "Indeed, the group's aim to create a single, worldwide Islamic government can best be described as Islamic radicalism's closest equivalent to the Western concept of globalization."[41]

On a worldwide scale, the HT communicates with its audience through a heavy use of modern technology. The Internet serves as the main channel for the distribution of its propaganda, literature, and messages. Even within Central Asia, it relies heavily on social media and email for propagating its messages to those who have access to such technologies. It communicates with the masses, who by and large do not have access to technology, by distributing leaflets. Its "favorite form of propaganda is the *shabnama* (night letter), which is printed at night and pushed under people's doors like a newspaper ... Posters are also slapped up on village walls at night – appearing even on the walls of police stations."[42] In addition, it relies on social and secretive networks in the Ferghana Valley to distribute its messages. According to one source, "Activists distribute leaflets and books that often contain scathing criticisms of regional governments. They also rely on underground meetings rather than public speeches. These techniques make the Hizb-ut-Tahrir operatives hard to find and to silence. They also let the Hizb-ut-Tahrir members send messages more quickly than the government can suppress or discredit them."[43]

With the global availability of social media, HT is reported to be using the Internet for propaganda purposes especially in those Muslim countries where the party has been banned. These include not only the Central Asian republics but also countries like Bangladesh. The HT's tactics include using local volunteers and activists to paste posters in different communities announcing the dates and times of various sponsored events on the Internet. The local populace gets that information and visits the announced websites at the appointed time. This tactic is frustrating to the law enforcement officials, because they cannot invade private homes at will to prevent people from watching those programs or reading the new propaganda material.[44] The HT posts articles on an array of weighty political, social, and economic issues that are of great interest to young Muslims all over the world. These articles discuss, from an Islamic perspective, how issues affect the ummah (Islamic community at large). Since most traditional imams (leaders in mosques) are trained only in religious matters and have little-to-no knowledge of the serious issues of the globalized world, websites like that of HT and other modern Islamic entities attract a large audience.[45]

According to a British source, "The organisation is entirely financed by its activists and we do not accept any financial assistance whatsoever from any government authority. Since the Hizb ut-Tahrir work relies upon the dissemination of thoughts, the costs of operating are minimal, as thoughts cost nothing."[46] Still, it is also suspected of receiving funds from South Asian and other Gulf and Muslim charities and even from some Muslim governments.

Assessing the Popularity of Hizb ut-Tahrir

Given the highly closed nature of the region, it is difficult to independently assess the nature and the extent of the popularity of the HT in the Ferghana Valley. Media reports on the issue have their own obvious and latent biases. Keeping this in mind, according to reports by Radio Free Europe/Radio Liberty, there is limited support for the HT in Central Asia.[47] But the increased authoritarianism in the region and the brutal style of government is helping that organization. According to David Lewis of the International Crisis Group, in the Kyrgyz city of Osh, the HT is feeding on discontent, especially among the young who are attracted to it as an alternative form of political expression. He cautions that the HT's influence "should not be exaggerated as it has little public support in Central Asia."[48] Its core constituency is the Uzbek territory. On the other hand, another report describes increased activism of the HT in Tajikistan: "Hizb ut-Tahrir, the nonviolent but banned Islamic movement that Central Asian presidents often invoke as a 'terrorist' threat, is increasingly active in Tajikistan, especially in the capital, Dushanbe. Tajik authorities are taking steps to counter the movement's efforts to expand its appeal. The rise of Hizb ut-Tahrir's profile is also a source of concern for mainstream Islamic political leaders, including Islamic Renaissance Party (IRP) leader Said Abdullo Nuri, who on September 4 [2002] portrayed the movement as a threat to Tajikistan's stability."[49]

According to Kyrgyz journalist Alisher Khamidov, efforts by Central Asian governments to counter the HT's messages through the use of local media and "state-controlled clergy" have not persuaded the party's followers or the general public: "Both the state-supported clergy and the media lack credibility among the wider public ... Unlike state supported clergy members and government officials, the HT activists enjoy a reputation as highly honest, incorruptible, and determined individuals."[50]

Beyond conflicting news reports, a more meaningful way to comprehend how the HT is being received by the population is to examine the level of support for the separation of religion and politics, and Islamic governance, in the Ferghana Valley. According to one study, "Opinions on the feasibility of the separation of Islam from governance vary throughout the region. The basis for differentiation lies primarily in how people define their identity. Muslim identities are stronger in Tajikistan and Uzbekistan and the south of Kyrgyzstan, and less so in the north, where nomadism has been much more significant. The stronger the Muslim identity, the smaller the space tends to be between religion and the state. In all three countries, both government officials and the official Islamic establishments routinely express their support for a separation of Islam from the state."[51] On the issue of Islamic governance, which is one of the chief objectives of the HT, the same study notes, "There is a lack of popular support for Islamic governance in Central Asia, but support for secular liberal democracy also seems fragile."[52]

Based on the preceding, although there are mixed reports about the popularity of and support for the HT, the organization has effectively brought its message to the populace by pursuing different tactics to cope with the strategic environment in each Central Asian country where it is active. For instance, in Uzbekistan, it "spreads its message clandestinely." In Kyrgyzstan, where the political environment is comparatively liberal, it launches "public relations campaigns." In Kazakhstan, it does its best to avoid confrontation, since it is still growing its cadres. In Tajikistan, the HT pursues a complex strategy of confronting both the government and the Islamic Renaissance Party, which remains "its main political competitor."[53] The notion of Islamic governance has a good chance of finding a sympathetic ear as long as the existing governments fail to improve the political and economic quality of life for their citizens.

Strengths and Weaknesses of the HT

The chief source of the HT's strength is its firm belief that it is on the right path. One of its leaflets states, "Hizb ut-Tahrir will never be destroyed, by Allah's Leave ... It should be known that it never happened in the past, nor will it happen now, or happen in [the] future that Hizb ut-Tahrir will be destroyed ... Despite campaigns of oppression, intimidation, and arrests, and attempts to destroy the Hizb undertaken by the [Muslim] regimes, Hizb [ut-]Tahrir derives its strength from Allah ... and the Ummah, which increases in strength and popularity day after day."[54] The HT has gained whatever popularity it has in the Ferghana Valley by keeping its audience focused on political oppression in the region. Its current popularity will likely diminish once political pluralism starts to evolve there. Until that happens, the HT is likely to operate in an environment that is not at all hostile from the viewpoint of its audience.

In assessing the popularity of this organization, its critics tend to ignore an important fact. The Ferghana Valley, indeed, the whole of Central Asia, is a region where the orientation toward and knowledge of Islam was systematically suppressed under the former Soviet Union, and where current governments systematically ensure that a controlled version of Islamic education (derisively described as "official Islam") is offered to the general populace.

In such a controlled milieu, the HT has assigned itself the task of enhancing the knowledge of Islam. The Islamic knowledge and orientation offered by the religious scholars affiliated with the HT have been judged by independent sources as decidedly superior to the teaching provided by half-educated "official imams."[55] The HT's rationale is that, once Muslims become increasingly aware of their religious heritage and become practitioners, its chances of establishing the caliphate will also increase. This expectation is wishful thinking, at best, perhaps even naive. The increased knowledge and commitment on the part of the residents of the Ferghana Valley, or even Central Asia, provide no guarantee that they will support the establishment of the caliphate.

Another source of strength for the HT in the Ferghana Valley is its anti-Americanism. Even though Central Asia has not been traditionally known for its anti-Americanism, that has changed owing to the general unpopularity in the Muslim world of the US occupation of Iraq and Afghanistan. And the HT has capitalized on that reality. A leaflet issued in June 2003, for example, voices its hostility toward the United States:

> America has been seduced by the illusion of power. She gives no credence to anything other than her interests, however much harm she causes to others. She rejects any international agreement, whatever it is, if it does not put her above everyone else. That is why she has refused to sign up to the international court for war crimes, fearing that this may be extended to her soldiers ... The United States, encouraged by the unexpected ease in occupying Afghanistan and Iraq, has begun talking openly about reshaping the Muslim world according to her criteria and design. She has begun to draw up plans to break up the Muslims' lands along federal or decentralist forms, which will shake and weaken the unity of the state. What is taking place in Afghanistan and Iraq attests to this. Also talk by politicians in the Arabian Peninsula is paving the way for this, under the pretext of preserving security, fighting terrorism, women's rights and extremist (thoughts) stemming from the education curriculum.[56]

Needless to say, this statement is hyperbolic and is not a correct depiction of reality. However, among a large number of Muslim readers, both inside and outside Central Asia, these anti-American views may have many sympathizers.

When viewed from its perspective, the HT's decision to exploit anti-Americanism to build its own base of support in the region is a highly tenable tactic. It is convinced that the United States will not radically alter its policy of supporting the current governments of the Ferghana Valley anytime soon. Thus, its adoption of contentious anti-American rhetoric is not likely to hurt its cause. President Obama remained too busy with the Middle East and other heady global issues to pay much attention to Central Asia, and therefore the anti-American rhetoric of organizations like the HT has not received much media coverage.

ISIS's declaration of a caliphate in June 2014 was rejected by the HT. The HT's spokesman in Jordan, Mamdooh Qatishaat, labelled ISIS a militia and said that its so-called caliphate has no sultan (authority), that it cannot provide external and internal security to its citizens, and that, following the methodology of the Prophet of Islam, it cannot send emissaries to foreign governments: "So how can the place be the Khilafah [Caliphate] State if it is not even a state in origin and if it does not possess the components that make up a state?"[57] Whether the HT accepts or rejects an ISIS caliphate will neither add to nor subtract from the value or prestige of that caliphate in the eyes of those who are fighting and dying for it; nevertheless, the HT's loud rejection of it means that these two organizations are likely to face enormous conflict when ISIS finally enters the political environment of Central Asia.

THE ISLAMIC MOVEMENT OF UZBEKISTAN (IMU)

The Islamic Movement of Uzbekistan (Harakat ul Islamiyyah Özbekistan) is a pan-Islamist jihadist party formed in 1998. Reports of its membership state that it contains Chechens and Uighurs, in addition to Uzbeks, Pakistanis, Kyrgyz, Tajiks, and Afghan Arabs (i.e., Arabs who fought in the US-sponsored war in Afghanistan against the former Soviet Union). The political leader and cofounder of this party, Mullah Tahir Yuldashev, was previously affiliated with the Islamic Renaissance Party of Tajikistan (IRPT); however, he broke from it around 1998 when that party, after the conclusion of a civil war, agreed to become part of the conventional political process. The pan-jihadist predilections of the IMU were apparent when Yuldashev travelled to Saudi Arabia in the late 1990s and picked a Saudi of Uzbek origin, Zubayr ibn Abdul Raheem, as head of the religious leadership of the IMU.[58] Yuldashev also played a crucial role in establishing a link between the IMU and al-Qaida in 1999, when the Taliban were in power in Afghanistan. The United States declared the IMU a terrorist organization in 2000.

The military strategist, cofounder, and commander of the IMU was Jumaboi Ahmadzhanovitch Khojaev, also known as Juma Namangani. He is described in the Western lexicon as a "born-again Muslim." What he lacked in years of practicing Islam he made up for in his commitment to jihad, carrying out numerous guerrilla attacks in Uzbekistan and Kyrgyzstan. In May 2001, Namangani reportedly launched a political party called the Hizb-e-Islami of Turkestan (Islamic Movement of Turkestan, IMT), which was expected to serve as an umbrella organization, subsuming all self-styled jihadist parties of Uzbekistan, Tajikistan, and Kyrgyzstan. It was reported to be behind several violent attacks in Afghanistan, Indian-administered Kashmir, Tajikistan, and Kyrgyzstan.[59]

The IMU, like the HT, is fully committed to the Wahhabi doctrine of Islamic puritanism. The IMU's goal of establishing a Wahhabi-style Islamic government would not likely attract much popular support if the Ferghana Valley came under democratic rule. However, since it was being ruled by autocratic regimes, people tended to view the IMU as a force for change. Even then, it was hard to imagine that Muslims of the Ferghana Valley would want to replace political repression under secular regimes with the tyranny of a Wahhabi autocratic rule that the IMU persistently promotes.[60] In an environment of political repression, the IMU's message of political change was positively received, but this was no guarantee that the IMU would be able to translate that reception into support for its advocacy of militant jihad. A 2003 report by the International Crisis Group found that the majority of Muslims were either unfamiliar with the concept of jihad or unwilling to discuss it (table 7.1). It also noted, "More people in Tajikistan think that *jihad* should not be used against the government than in Uzbekistan or Kyrgyzstan, possibly because of the associations of the Islamist factor in the country's civil war."[61]

Namangani's strong jihadist views were developed in the madrassa run by Jamiat-ul-Ulama of Pakistan (JUM), which also provided financial assistance to his group in the late 1990s. The leadership of the Taliban-governed Afghanistan "encouraged the IMU in its 'holy war' against the Uzbek regime." The Taliban's supreme leader, Mullah Omar, reportedly "allowed the Uzbek Islamists to launch attacks into Central Asia and use a military training camp in Afghanistan."[62] Al-Qaida and the Arab jihadists "had been developing links with the IMU since the end of 1990s, particularly with Namangani." Al-Qaida's prominent jihadist theorist, Abu Mus'ab al-Suri, reportedly had an "even stronger influence on the IMU." Al-Suri regarded Central Asia as "one of the main fronts for the international jihadist fight and a natural battlefield for the Taliban's future emirate." The IMU seemed to have adopted al-Suri's views on jihad and envisioned "its fight as a clash of civilizations not only with 'near enemy' – Karimov and the Central Asian Republics – but also with the 'far enemy' – the United States, Russia, Israel, and the Jews."[63]

By developing strong ties with al-Qaida and the Taliban regime in Afghanistan, the IMU became an important player in carrying out regional jihad in Central Asia, Chechnya, and the Xinjiang province of China. Tahir Yuldashev was reported to have travelled extensively in Pakistan, Afghanistan, and the Persian Gulf region in order to

Table 7.1 Attitudes toward jihad in Uzbekistan, Tajikistan, and Krygzstan

	The percentage (%) of Muslims who believe that:			
	Jihad is permissible in critical situations or against nonbelievers	*It is not acceptable to use force to protect Islam*	*Force should never be used against the government*	*Not familiar with the concept of jihad or reluctant to discuss it*
Uzbekistan	8.5	12.9	9.2	60.1
Tajikistan	32.5	8.4	14.8	37.8
Kyrgyzstan	10.1	30.0	Not reported	47.9

Source: International Crisis Group, "Is Radical Islam Inevitable in Central Asia?"

establish networks with al-Qaida and other Islamists and jihadists and to have received funding from all friendly sources in countries of that region. Between 1998 and 2001, the IMU also worked assiduously to establish its operating base inside Central Asia.

As a result of these developments, the IMU acquired such a reputation in the ranks of the global security community that, in the aftermath of the 9/11 attacks, President George W. Bush publicly added the names of IMU and Namangani to the "financial hit list of 27 terrorist organizations and individuals allied with Usama Bin Laden." IMU assets were to be frozen or confiscated. However, as a "low-tech" jihadist group, it was unaffected by that announcement. It had no bank account and it received all of its financial assistance through "its involvement in the huge regional trade in Afghan heroin."[64]

Namangani was reportedly killed during the US invasion of Afghanistan in November 2001. His death was a major setback for the IMU. It was pretty much destroyed in that war; however, its reputation as "a group with a genuine strike force and proven professionalism" remained long after the demise of Namangani.[65] Pakistan's noted specialist on the jihadist groups of Pakistan, Afghanistan, and Central Asia, Ahmed Rashid, writes, "Namangani was one of the most important 'foreign Taliban' commanders in northern Afghanistan during the recent fighting there. He led a pan-Islamic force of Uzbeks, Tajiks, Pakistanis, Chechens, and Uighurs from Xinjiang province in China. They fought on the side of the Taliban in Afghanistan, but their long-range goal was to establish an Islamic state throughout Central Asia."[66] The remainder of that tattered organization moved to southern Waziristan (Pakistan) in late 2001 or early 2002. Around the same time, there were rumours that an unknown number of members had splintered from the mother organization and formed an entity called the Islamic Jihad Union.

In October 2009, Yuldashev was reported to have been killed by a US drone attack in Waziristan, Pakistan, where he was hiding. Usmon Odil, his deputy commander, succeeded him. Odil was reported to have been killed in August 2012.[67] He was replaced by Usman Ghazi. The migration to Afghanistan, the death of Namangani and countless other members in the US invasion of Afghanistan (Operation Enduring Freedom, OEF), and then the death of Yuldashev brought about several radical changes in the IMU's outlook and objectives. Matthew Stein writes, "The IMU's original leadership had a precise goal of establishing an Islamic caliphate in the Fergana Valley. Circumstances forced Yuldashev to set aside this goal while the IMU settled and regrouped in Pakistan. After his death the IMU's goals seemed to vanish altogether. A current lack of consistent leadership and subsequent goals has meant that the IMU is difficult to differentiate from other militant or terrorist groups operating in Afghanistan or Pakistan, particularly when the remnants of the IMU rely on others to stay operational."[68]

Although IMU forces suffered a major setback during military clashes with the US and the Northern Alliance in 2001, its forces were reported to have gathered strength toward the conclusion of the second decade of the twenty-first century. But there were also reports of tensions between the IMU and the Taliban. The IMU's current leader, Usman Ghazi, was reported to have pledged his allegiance to ISIS in September 2014. Since then, the IMU's status in Afghanistan has been unclear. However, the strategic objective of the IMU seems to have remained "more dependent" on jihadists groups in Pakistan and Afghanistan – where the IMU is reportedly staying – than on ISIS. "For the United States, the IMU remains a threat while the country's forces remain in Afghanistan, although the threat is more from associated groups with better capabilities." For the Central Asian governments, "the IMU remains a threat, but a minor one compared to the capabilities of the group in 1999–2000."[69]

By 2015, however, ISIS's calls for jihad and support for it were becoming considerably popular in Central Asia at large. According to a report published in January 2015 by the International Crisis Group, between "2,000 and 4,000" Central Asian citizens "have left for IS-held territory to fight or otherwise support the Islamic State cause ... [IMU] members have been active recruiters for IS in the Ferghana Valley and have taken advantage of what in Central Asia is seen as a glamorous association to reinvigorate their own group. The IMU also appears to have acted as a bridge for a wider variety of Central Asian fighters, including Uighurs from western China."[70] That was indeed a foreboding omen for the future stability of Central Asia as a region as well as China's Xinjiang province.

THE CENTRAL ASIAN ISLAMIST CHALLENGE AND THE GREAT POWERS

China

Although the Islamist challenge to the security and stability of the Central Asian republics was neither imminent nor grave, the confluence of economic underdevelopment, repressive autocratic rule, and lack of transparency in the region made the indigenous governments, along with Russia and China, apprehensive.

China's security concerns about the growing activism of the secessionist forces of Xinjiang and their related aspirations to cooperate with the Central Asian jihadist groups – who were busy developing their own nexus with the Taliban and al-Qaida groups of Afghanistan – forced the leaders in Beijing to develop a complex counter strategy. As an important international aspect of that strategy, China decided to create powerful linkages between counterterrorism activities inside Xinjiang and those pursued by its Central Asian neighbours. The proclivities of the jihadist groups of Central Asia, Chechnya, and Afghanistan to seek regional cooperation had to be matched by similar countermeasures by those regional governments. To exert similar pressures on the jihadists of Central Asia, China direly needed the cooperation of its neighbours, who were equally, if not more, apprehensive about the growing challenge from jihadist groups inside their own borders. Another important feature of that strategy was China's drive to suppress (through cooperation with the Central Asian states) the Uighur groups, an estimated 500,000 people who resided across the porous border of Xinjiang and Central Asia.

The creation of the Shanghai Five in 1996 was driven by this quest for cooperation, even though its original raison d'être was to seek the settlement of territorial disputes among China, Russia, Kazakhstan,

Tajikistan, and Kyrgyzstan. It started focusing on counterterrorism in 1999. It should be remembered that 1996 was the year when the Taliban consolidated their rule in Afghanistan. At the time of the 1999 Taliban summit in the Kyrgyz capital, Bishkek, "Kyrgyz forces were fighting Islamic militants in the southern part of the country. China was conducting a crackdown on Muslim Uyghur separatists in the Western Xinjiang region and Russia was on the eve of starting the second Chechnya war of the 1990s."[71] The Shanghai Five was transformed into the Shanghai Cooperation Organization (SCO) on 15 June 2001, only three months before the 9/11 terrorist attacks on the United States.

Furthermore, China has been deftly pursuing "the most ambitious infrastructure projects ... linking Central Asia to China and East Asia, rather than to South Asia or to Europe." Such projects, including "roads, railways, and pipelines," underscore "China's growing economic and cultural presence in the region ... [and] are likely to have a more enduring impact on Central Asia's long-term development than either the war in Afghanistan or Russia's push for regional integration."[72]

Finally, and as a measure complementing the aforementioned strategy, China decided to cooperate with the United States in the aftermath of the 9/11 attacks on America's homeland. However, that aspect of China's international strategy turned out to be complicated and vexing. In order to facilitate its invasion of Afghanistan, the United States sought basing facilities in a number of Central Asian countries. Despite the fact that the American invasion of Afghanistan was aimed at eradicating, as much as possible, the jihadist groups from that country, China's reading of that move was variegated and multidimensional. Leaders in Beijing took no time to conclude that, once the United States introduced its military forces into Central Asia, it would do everything to prolong their presence indefinitely. Chinese leaders watched how enthusiastically the United States offered NATO membership to a number of members of the former Warsaw Pact alliance. They also watched with concern the sustained engagement of four Central Asian countries – Kazakhstan, Kyrgyzstan, Uzbekistan, and Tajikistan – in the NATO Partnership for Peace program. That development had much potential for America's ability to entice those countries into closer military ties in the future. These US maneuverings to maximize its strategic advantage were variables that China knew it not only had to watch with great care, but against which it must create its own prompt countermeasures. Because of these intricate concerns, China's policy regarding the growing Islamist challenge inside Central Asia was heavily coloured by the balance of power–related complexities regarding America's growing presence in Afghanistan and Central Asia. Consequently, on the one hand, China clearly wanted to cooperate with the United States in its then military invasion of Afghanistan, but on the other hand, it remained apprehensive about the long-term implications of that cooperation on its own profound aspirations to dominate the strategic affairs of Central Asia.

The United States' initiation of the so-called global war on terrorism commenced a phase when the administration of President George W. Bush needed the cooperation of both China and Russia. Since both of these countries had been experiencing escalated violence from their own jihadist groups, such cooperation was not hard to come by. In December 2001, China allowed the United States to open an office of the Federal Bureau of Investigation (FBI) in Beijing to coordinate the war on terrorism. However, "significant differences soon emerged between the two sides on the Uyghur issue" when Washington refused to "repatriate to China any Uyghurs who had been captured in Afghanistan during the anti-Taliban campaign." The United States also continued to disagree with "China's labeling of terrorists in the Muslim Northwest." Washington "did not deem the Uyghur nationalists to be terrorists."[73] All of that changed in favour of China when, in August 2002, the US Department of State designated an almost obscure Uighur entity, the Eastern Turkistan Islamic Movement (ETIM), as a "terrorist group." The United States claimed that the ETIM was affiliated with al-Qaida and that it was planning an attack on the US embassy in Kyrgyzstan. The Uighur case for independence suffered a major setback, and the US labelling of the ETIM provided the direly sought legitimacy for China's highly suspicious oppressive campaign of the Uighurs inside Xinjiang.

As much as China appreciated the United States' sanctioning of the ETIM as a "terrorist" group, its own campaign to fight against "splittism and separatism" (euphemism for the secessionist movement of Xinjiang) continued with utmost fervour, using the forum of the SCO. China heavily relied on joint military exercises conducted with the members of that organization. The first bilateral antiterrorism exercise was held in October 2002 by China and Kyrgyzstan. In August 2003, all the members of the SCO (with the exception of

Uzbekistan) conducted "Cooperation 2003" to support a variety of counterterrorism scenarios in Eastern Kazakhstan and China's Xinjiang province. In August 2005, the SCO initiated the first Peace Mission exercise. Only Chinese and Russian forces participated, with China providing most of the troops and Russia providing "the most sophisticated equipment including Russian Tu-160 and Tu-95 strategic bombers as well as some 140 warships."

Peace Missions 2009 and 2010 were exercises in which Chinese and Russian forces participated, while the rest of the SCO members were invited to send military observers.[74] Peace Mission 2010 introduced "nighttime maneuvers" and aerial refuelling as practices for future joint SCO exercises, and the Chinese air force conducted its first cross-border flight from China to Kazakhstan. Since Tajikistan had experienced violent attacks from radical Islamists only months preceding the Peace Mission 2010, and Kyrgyzstan had also experienced domestic turmoil resulting in the ousting of its president, these members attached urgency to their participation in this exercise from their respective threat perceptions.[75] Uzbekistan pulled out of the 2010 exercise at the last minute.

The aim of these military exercises was to assure the Central Asian states that "China and Russia will help them manage their security challenges."[76] The larger purpose was to keep those countries from seeking the help of the United States or the EU in emergencies. However, the failure of the SCO to intervene in the ethnic riots of Kyrgyzstan in June 2010 raised serious questions about that organization's credibility in providing security against future outbursts. What also was working against the SCO's future functioning in this capacity was that domestic turbulence in any Central Asian country involved the issue of sovereignty, which should not be violated. No country was more sensitive about that issue than the People's Republic of China (PRC). Moreover, even if a Central Asian country requested the intervention of the SCO, both China and Russia (its dominant members) would have to be highly mindful of the reaction of the global community.

China had been impressed by the United States' military capabilities in dismantling the Taliban regime in Afghanistan and, in the process, significantly diminishing the size and fighting capabilities of the jihadist groups of Central Asia residing there. So, the Sino-American cooperation to counter terrorism should have easily materialized. The chief obstacle in the way of its development was the clashing strategic perspectives of these two major powers about the ultimate purpose underlying America's presence in Central Asia. The fact of the matter is that China had to decide whether it would accept the long-term strategic presence of the United States in Central Asia as a price for Washington's cooperation with Beijing on counterterrorism. China's calculation was that the US presence there in the future would not only grow in size but also in scope, thereby directly clashing with China's own strategic aspirations in the region. Thus, a decision was made in Beijing that the best course for China would be to pursue a policy of self-reliance and, with the participation of Russia and the Central Asian countries, to build institutions that would directly deal with the counterterrorism-related challenges and threats from Central Asia. Another major benefit of creating such institutions would be that China could link the counterterrorism-related activities outside its borders with those inside Xinjiang. Such thinking drove China's involvement in the creation of the SCO.

China's preference for a policy of self-reliance was also driven by the antipathy that its leadership shared with the leaders of Central Asia regarding America's predilection for promoting democracy by actively encouraging the "color revolutions," primarily through US-based nongovernmental organizations (NGOs). The color revolutions, so called because their promoters adopted a colour or flower as a symbol, occurred in a number of states of the former Soviet Union in early 2000. Examples include Georgia's "Rose Revolution," Ukraine's "Orange Revolution," and Kyrgyzstan's "Tulip Revolution." Invariably (with the exception of Kyrgyzstan), these states became democratic after the revolution. For China, the spread of democracy in one or more Central Asian countries was cause for concern, since it would likely be repeated in other countries ruled by iron-fisted autocrats.

The March 2005 "Tulip Revolution" in Kyrgyzstan, despite all expectations, did not result immediately in a democracy. President Askar Akayev's successor, Kurmanbek Bakiyev, established another corrupt and autocratic regime. Consequently, Bakiyev suffered the fate of his predecessor when rising political protest and violence – also referred to as the "people power revolution" – brought an end to his rule on 7 April 2010. He fled to the south of Kyrgyzstan and then to Belarus. The presidency of Roza Otunbayeva played a crucial role in the emergence of democracy in that country. The presidential elections of October 2011 brought to office Almazbek Atambayev, who had previously served as prime minister. Despite Kyrgyzstan's march toward democracy, China did not feel threatened because of its continued cooperation with Kyrgyzstan on what they call cross-border terrorism. Kyrgyzstan does not want to be "labeled by Beijing as a base for militants, specifically ones from the East Turkistan Islamic Movement (ETIM), who China claims have been trained in jihadi camps in northwest Pakistan."[77] The two countries have elaborate agreements governing border security hotlines and cooperation between their law enforcement forces.

In the context of keeping its control over Xinjiang (and Tibet), China has remained apprehensive about the color revolutions. In response to those revolutions in the former states of the Soviet Union, China increased its control and vigilance over the so-called liberal and critical media as well as civil rights activists. President Hu Jintao ordered a systematic inquiry into the causes of the color revolutions in order to develop the PRC's countermeasures. Interestingly, the majority of Chinese scholars involved in that inquiry were "affiliated with the propaganda/censorship sector, the official ideology system, and security bureaucracies of the party-state."[78] These scholars found that the color revolutions occurred for three reasons: "intense domestic grievances, electoral politics exploited by the opposition, and interventions by Western powers for their geostrategic interests." Having identified the causes, they recommended that China's leaders, to prevent the occurrence of color revolutions inside the country, pursue their stated priority of "economic expansion over systematic political reform" and deal with "vices such as official corruption and growing inequality." In addition, they recommended that the government escalate "effective control over the activities of non-CCP [non-USSR] political and rights activists, the contents and outlets of the press and media, and Sino-Western civil society networks."[79]

The analysis of Chinese scholars regarding the changed nature of post–9/11 American strategic interests in the former socialist countries (of which China's chief concern was America's importance in Central Asia) was significant because it was sponsored by the government. As such, it was highly likely that China's leaders would not only study it carefully but also adopt its recommendations. According to that analysis, bringing about regime change (a phrase frequently used by the Bush administration) through the use of color revolutions – which had become a very important feature of America's exercise of "soft power" by then – would also characterize US strategy toward Central Asia. This was a region with vast energy reserves (aka strategic material). As such, China anticipated that the Central Asian states would become an important focus of US attention in the coming years. According to the Chinese analysis, the Bush administration envisaged Central Asia as a key region in which to seek allies. However, because the United States had already been involved in two regional wars, in Afghanistan and Iraq, the most prudent way to bring about regime change in Central Asia was through the use of color revolutions (an exercise of soft power). To promote democratization, the United States injected a vast amount of money into Central Asia and used American-based NGOs to spread the "ideology and institutions of the liberal democracy and market economy in the region." Through a mixture of open and clandestine activities, the US government was educating the Central Asian elite to promote democracy inside their countries. "Local opposition parties, networked and empowered, then used the U.S.-provided funding and learned skills to run and manipulate mass media, instigate popular discontent, disrupt political order, and eventually seize power." Thus, the Chinese scholars concluded that "democratization was only a smokescreen for Washington's ulterior agenda: further Westernizing Eurasia for a perpetual American hegemony."[80]

As the United States became increasingly bogged down in the "Iraqi quagmire," China found it easier to be critical of Washington's decision to invade that country. China also realized that the nature of its strategic relations with the United States was such that it had little choice but to pursue a highly independent policy toward terrorism and especially toward its involvement in Central Asia.

China has become more important to the economic development of Central Asia than has the United States, which has reduced its economic assistance to countries in this region. China, on the other hand, has increased its investment in infrastructural development projects such as energy pipelines, road and railroad construction, and oil, gas, and uranium production.[81] Consequently, the aggregate trade value of Central Asia to China "has risen from $1 billion to almost $50 billion since 1990."[82] Recognizing "that Middle Eastern supplies remain vulnerable to disruption due to terrorism, military conflicts and other instability, ... [the Chinese] government has been promoting the development of land-based oil and gas pipelines that would direct Central Asian energy resources eastward toward China." For China, the oil from Central Asia is highly valuable because the oil "can reach China overland rather than through vulnerable maritime routes susceptible to interception by the U.S. Navy."[83]

While pursuing its economic interests in Central Asia through the SCO, China "has refrained from establishing military bases and negotiating bilateral defense treaties in the region, and it has never sold major weapons systems to Central Asian militaries ... Beijing has also never sought to advance the SCO as a potential rival to Moscow's main regional security institution, the Collective Security Treaty Organization (CSTO), which includes all the same Central Asian members as the SCO, but not China."

A brief mention should be made here of China's Silk Road Initiative, which was first presented to the world during President Xi Jinping's trip to Kazakhstan in 2013. Through the declaration of this strategy, China certainly has come a long way from the days of Deng Xiaoping, who advised future Chinese leaders to "keep a low profile." The ultimate purpose of the Silk Road Initiative is to transform China into a power centre of global trade by 2049. As such, the initiative has been aptly described as "the largest programme of economic diplomacy since the US-led Marshall Plan for post-war construction of Europe."[84] Indeed, it is considerably larger in scope, in that it involves several continents. This strategy focuses on "two roads, or rather 'One Belt, One Road' (OBOR). The 'belt' refers to the Eurasian land route between China and Europe, while the 'road' is a maritime trade route linking Chinese ports with the African coast and European Mediterranean nations."[85]

Despite the highly ambitious aspects of the Silk Road Initiative, China remains fearful that its Xinjiang province could become a "conduit for importing the 'three evil forces' of regional terrorism, religious extremism, and ethnic separatism into the rest of China."[86] Still, China does not wish to deploy its security forces to Central Asia and "is comfortable relying on good intelligence, law enforcement, development assistance, and other non-military tools augmented with some low-level Chinese security assistance to the local governments."[87]

Russia

Russia, like China, is fully aware of the potentially volatile linkage of Central Asian strategic affairs to its North Caucasus Muslim challenge, but it does not know how to control, influence, or even manage that challenge. The implosion of the Soviet Union in 1991, the consequent emergence of a number of Central Asian states, and the development of jihadist groups in Central Asian countries and North Caucasus altered Russia's perception of these groups. The attitude of Russian leaders changed from unadulterated contempt to mixed feelings of awe and respect for the resiliency of and cooperation among those groups in challenging the established governments of Central Asia, China, and Russia itself. The establishment of the Taliban regime in Afghanistan in 1996 and the increasing visibility and influence of al-Qaida in Afghanistan were also developments that both China and Russia watched with great trepidation. As much as Russia labelled the Central Asian states "near abroad" and a region where it could flex its muscle, it placed Afghanistan in an entirely different category. Since the Soviet Union had been militarily defeated in Afghanistan, post-Soviet Russia held no designs to reassert itself there. Fearing the growing influence of the Taliban regime of Afghanistan in neighbouring Central Asia, Russia did get involved in providing economic and military assistance to the Northern Alliance – the anti-Taliban military organization under the commandership of Ahmad Shah Masood. However, the Northern Alliance was unable to emerge as a major threat or even as a challenge to the Taliban regime between 1998 and 2001. In the interim, Sino-Russian propaganda continued to harp on the growing nexus among the jihadist groups of the North Caucasus and Xinjiang, al-Qaida, and similarly oriented Central Asian groups. Although Russia cofounded the SCO in part to fight religious extremism and splitism, that organization did not emerge as an effective tool for taking on the jihadists.

The United States' decision to declare a global war on terrorism in the aftermath of the 9/11 attacks on its territory and to invade Afghanistan was seen by both Russia and China as a blessing in disguise. The type of globally oriented militancy that George W. Bush's rhetoric carried in his vociferous sloganeering speech of "Either you are with us or you are with the terrorists" sounded like music to the ears of Putin and the Chinese leaders. They correctly anticipated that the mounting militancy of the Bush administration would become an important basis for cooperation among the three great powers. Putin was adroit not only in recognizing the window of opportunity that the 9/11 attacks on the US territory presented for Russia, but in commencing a systematic campaign to exploit it. Before those attacks, a "major bone of contention between the U.S. and Russian Federation was the burning issue of Chechnya." Although President Bush "had muted" his "criticism of Russia's brutal war against the Chechens" after entering the White House, a number of US officials "continued to define the Chechens as Afghan-style *mujahedeen* 'freedom fighters' engaged in a David versus Goliath struggle against a transcontinental neo-Soviet imperium."[88]

The pre–9/11 conspiratorial perspectives nurtured by President Vladimir Putin – who imagined that the United States and other Western countries were using the Russian and Chinese jihadist groups to weaken those two countries[89] – quickly disappeared after the terrorist attacks on the US homeland. Putin was the first foreign leader to call Bush after the 9/11 attacks to offer condolences. Then, in a follow-up to that call, he made a televised speech addressing the American people: "I would like to say that we are with you," he said. "We entirely and fully share and experience your pain. We support you."[90] Putin was eager to cooperate with the United States in its invasion of Afghanistan by providing intelligence and by opening Russian air space for US aircraft in their search and rescue operations.

Despite the fact that the 9/11 attacks promised to alter US foreign policy in a significant way, and despite the palpable convergence of the Russian and American interests related to terrorism, Russia was not about to forget or even to overlook the competitive reality of US-Russian strategic affairs. Post-Soviet Russia was dismayed that, as the major succeeding state of the Soviet Union, it was not being treated as a superpower. Between the presidencies of Boris Yeltsin and Vladimir Putin, Russia also had grown to resent what it perceived as America's obsession with NATO expansion and eagerness in encouraging the member states of the former Warsaw Pact to join the alliance. Although both post–Cold War American presidents, Bill Clinton and George W. Bush, continued to publicly assure Russia of America's friendship and altered perspective – which no longer perceived Russia as a competitor or an adversary – American foreign policy under those presidents was contrary to their assurances. Consequently, Russia, along with the PRC, developed highly suspicious perceptions about the lone superpower. When the 9/11 attacks almost instantly triggered acute proactivism in Washington, neither Moscow nor Beijing could afford to ignore the inherently competitive nature of their ties with the United States. Despite their willingness to cooperate with Washington on the issue of global terrorism, they knew that, in the long run, the United States would not ignore the temptation to take advantage of whatever strategic openings places like the Central Asian region had to offer.

This prospect loomed large in Russian and Chinese involvement in Central Asia – a region of high foreign policy interest to both of them. Russia and China had already created the SCO, which was to focus on the strategic affairs affecting Central Asia. Russia also proceeded to establish the Collective Security Treaty Organization (CSTO) as a military alliance. Since an analysis of the Sino-Russian involvement in the SCO was provided earlier in this chapter, a review of Russia's interests in the CSTO is in order here.

The CSTO – comprising Armenia, Belarus, Kazakhstan, Kyrgyzstan, Russia, Tajikistan, and Uzbekistan – was formed in 2002. It grew out of the old Collective Security Treaty, which was a military alliance between the former states of the Soviet Union. The CSTO had two overarching objectives. The first was to monitor and weaken the linkage between jihadist groups in the North Caucasus and Central Asia. The jihadist groups of North Caucasus had acquired a high level of activism and militancy in response to bad governance and Russia's use of intense repression as a policy tool; the Russian perspective, however, was that the militant activism of those groups was encouraged and promoted by the similarly inclined forces of Central Asia. Second, the CSTO was created to ensure that the Central Asian states remained within the orbit of Moscow and were not enticed away by the United States. The United States' attention to the enlargement of NATO throughout the 1990s was a characteristic that Moscow expected to be emulated in Central Asia sooner or later. In that sense, the CSTO's high interests in creating a strong military bond with the Central Asian states was an exercise of strategic proactivism on the part of Moscow.

Although Russia remains, along with China, a dominant player in the SCO, it is through the CSTO that it has been "creating dependency in Central Asian governments" and building a major presence in the region through its military officer training programs, sale of Russian military weapons at concessional prices, and drug interception operations. Under the auspices of this organization, Russia has also maintained the Anti-Terrorism Centre in Tashkent, the Kant Air Base in Kyrgyzstan, and the Russian 201st Motor Rifle Division in Kulyab, Tajikistan. Like the raison d'être of the SCO, the founding document of the CSTO stated that member states realize that "terrorism, separatism and extremism represent a threat against international peace and security."[91] One analyst notes that "Tajikistan and Kyrgyzstan in particular are beholden to Russia because of their heavy reliance on Russian military equipment and because of the large Russian troop deployments" within their borders.

In addition, Russia adopted a number of maneuvers to enhance its influence in Central Asia. For instance, while the Anti-Terrorism Centre (ATC) in Bishkek proposes and plans military exercises, the Russian Federal Security Service supervises them. Since Russian security officials hold personal loyalty to Putin, "clear formal and informal links exist between the ATC and the highest members of the Russian government."[92] Furthermore, Russia's proposal for close coordination between the CSTO staff and Russian general staff favoured that country, and more so after the CSTO formed the Collective Rapid Reaction Force (CRRF) in 2009. The young Central Asian military officers who were trained in Russia to fill the slots allocated for their countries were expected to share Russia's vision of security when they acquired senior positions in their military. The secretary general of the secretariat of the CSTO has also played a crucial role in enhancing Russia's influence and implementing the preferences of its top leadership in that organization.[93]

Ideally speaking, Moscow wants the CSTO to emerge as a military alliance of the calibre of NATO. As a collection of authoritarian states, the CSTO has some advantages but also a number of disadvantages. One advantage is that, as authoritarian states, the heads of the CSTO member states alone are at liberty to decide whether their country will join, or not join, any military exercise under the organization's auspices. They do not have to be concerned about domestic public opinion or opposition from their legislatures. Moreover, should the alliance intervene to restore order when a member state faces domestic turbulence, it will not likely meet with international opprobrium, as was the case when Putin unilaterally and illegally decided to annex Crimea into the Russian Federation in March 2014 and continued a policy of militarism in Ukraine from 2014 on.

On the other hand, the Central Asian states are suspicious of Russia's real intentions in their region. The member states can never be free from the fear that Russia might arrange to oust a president whose policies negatively affect its interests. In fact, Moscow was reported to have played such a role in ousting President Kurmanbek Bakiyev of Kyrgyzstan in 2010. Bakiyev's "crime" was that he promised the Russians that he would expel the Americans from his Manas Air Base and, in return, would receive financial assistance from Russia. However, he made an about-face and raised his rental fees to the Americans and let them stay, infuriating Moscow. Consequently, a general understanding was that Russia played a crucial role in the massive outbreak of the anti-Bakiyev protest in Kyrgyzstan in April 2010, which Russia denied.[94] (In June 2014, the United States closed the Manas Air Base in Kyrgyzstan, which was its only Central Asian air base.[95]) The CSTO's potential for sustaining Russia's political clout in Central Asia, and the legacy of Russia's predecessors (Czarist Russia as well as the Soviet Union) of colonizing that region, have fostered suspicion among Central Asian heads of state. Despite this suspicion, or maybe because of it, Russia continues to implement policies aimed at increasing the role of the CSTO.

The CSTO's intervention in the internal affairs of member states is controversial, but less controversial than intervention by Russia alone. The weaker states, especially Kyrgyzstan and Tajikistan, may want the CSTO or Russia to come to their aid in times of domestic turbulence, but that would be depicted as intervention by other member states, especially given Russia's record of imperialism in Central Asia. As a result, Russia refrained from intervening in Kyrgyzstan during the political turbulence of 2004. In June 2010, when Kyrgyzstan was hit by a violent ethnic conflict, Bishkek pleaded for Russian intervention. Russia wisely decided against it and, instead, suggested a multilateral response under the auspices of the CSTO.[96] Uzbekistan has remained a constant critic of the CSTO's paper resolve to intervene in the internal turbulence of a member state through the use of its Collective Rapid Reaction Force. President Islam Karimov has consistently argued that, since the Commonwealth of Independent States has plenty of "frozen" conflicts, any options for resolution should exclude the CRRF. Uzbekistan prefers that the CRRF "exclusively confront external threats" involving CSTO's member states.[97]

The Russo-Uzbek conflict related to CSTO came to a head in June 2012 when Uzbekistan suspended its membership in the organization. That was a major jolt to Putin's aspirations to develop the CSTO along the lines of NATO. Since US-Pakistan relations were already strained, Uzbekistan's exit from CSTO triggered rumours that Washington was considering that country as an exit route for military supplies to Afghanistan, given that Uzbekistan "has the best railway network links in the region."[98] Since that country also has had the worst human rights record, its anticipated negotiation with the United States was expected to be far from smooth. It was also speculated that Karimov's decision to quit the CSTO was driven by his desire to establish military ties with the United States. Karimov knew that he would have "to co-ordinate any potential plans to host Western military with the CIS military bloc," but he preferred to have "a free hand in deciding on the US base." The abrupt departure of Uzbekistan from CSTO also highlighted that country's "reputation for unilateral actions" and proved once again Karimov's reputation as a "difficult partner."[99]

Even though the People's Republic of China is not competing with Russia in the realm of military presence in Central Asia, Russia continues to face an uphill battle. Its economy has been constrained by economic sanctions imposed by the United States and the EU. Low oil prices in the global market have presented an almost insurmountable challenge for Vladimir Putin's hegemonic ambitions involving Ukraine. Putin's decision to enter the Syrian conflict was not only enormously pricey, but also equally risky for him. According to the figure provided by the usually reliable IHS Jane's Intelligence Review, "the minimum cost of keeping this operation going is $2.4 million per day."[100] Even if Russia and its Iranian forces succeed in temporarily turning the tide of war in favour of the Assad regime, the overall Sunni Islamist challenge inside Syria will most likely linger. Putin is likely to find out the hard way how easy it is to enter into a conflict in the Middle East and how difficult it is to retreat from it without permanently wearing the albatross of shame around his neck. His predecessors in the former Soviet Union learned that lesson; however, Putin is too obsessive about procuring the glory of a superpower to realize what awaits his forces in Syria.

Putin's militarism in Ukraine and his annexation of Crimea have made him a highly capricious mentor from the perspective of Central Asian dictators. Thus, they will do their best to keep their distance from Russia. Central Asia's weakest states, Tajikistan and Kyrgyzstan, are more dependent on Russian economic and military assistance than the others. However, if either of them was to destabilize from within, Putin, despite his infamous proclivities for military adventurism in Ukraine and Georgia (where his forces apportioned territory in a war against that country in 2008), may have a hard time rationalizing insertion of his troops to stabilize them.

Russia's resolve to win the strategic competition with the United States (and even with China) for dominance drives the Kremlin to preserve the political status quo in Central Asia at all costs. If or when one or more autocrats of Central Asia are overthrown as a result of a social movement à la the Arab Awakening, Russia is afraid that its hegemony will come to an end (a Central Asian version of the domino effect!). Thus, it is hard to make a conclusive statement as to whether Russia is more motivated about sustaining its sphere of influence in Central Asia because of its heightened strategic competition with the United States, or because of its conviction that its presence in the region is intrinsically linked with its continued ability to maintain its rule over the North Caucasus republics.

In summary, the future of China's involvement in Central Asia appears bright. China's spectacular ascent in the global arena perhaps accounts for its optimistic attitude toward the future of Central Asia, a region where economic decay and acute corruption keep the potential of cataclysmic regime change very much alive. Chances are high that an enormous financial investment in China's Silk Road Initiative may bring about noticeable economic development and political stability in that region. Moreover, China "has not claimed neighboring countries as a Chinese sphere of privileged interests, which is how Russia has framed its relationship with countries on its border."[101] Despite the potential for positive developments, escalating radicalization of Muslims in Xinjiang and its potential spillover effects into Central Asia (or the reverse effects of that trend into Xinjiang) are causing ample consternation among Chinese leaders. There is no doubt that, if China were to conclude at some point that its security interests were threatened, especially by jihadist forces, "it could develop capabilities to play a security role."[102] China is also raptly watching the dynamics of the Taliban-related conflict in Afghanistan and has wisely opted to rely on Pakistan and the United States to find a political solution.

On the contrary, Russia, as a major power contiguous to Central Asia, has little reason to be optimistic about the future of its sphere of influence in the region. Just to keep up with China's accelerated economic activities and its related mega-investments, Russia must also make large economic investments in the region. However, its economy has been under considerable pressure related to the constant slump in oil prices in the global market. To further complicate matters, Putin has not only annexed Crimea, but he continues to threaten Ukraine's sovereignty. The reaction to his adventuristic policies by the West has been equally severe, in the form of economic sanctions. As if these events were not disconcerting enough, Putin plunged his country into another obdurate crisis – the one in Syria. These developments are likely to force Russia to abandon its militarism in Ukraine and start negotiations for the lifting of Western economic sanctions, and perhaps even cut its losses and get out of Syria. Otherwise, Russia's strategic interests in Central Asia could erode to disastrous proportions.

The United States

After the implosion of the Soviet Union and the emergence of Central Asian countries as independent states, the United States' involvement in Central Asia lacked any systematic strategic thinking. Washington got involved in the region principally to make sure that Iran did not succeed in implanting its own model of Islamic government. The United States supported the entry of Central Asian states into Western organizations and became somewhat involved in eliciting Turkish support in countering Iranian influence and in promoting the Turkish model of secular democracy. Since Russia did not show much enthusiasm for dominating the strategic affairs of Central Asia in the early 1990s, the United States' involvement in the region was not driven by any urgency to make its own presence felt.

The nexus between the Taliban and al-Qaida, and the resultant activities of the jihadist groups in Central Asia and its contiguous areas in the late 1990s, slightly altered the picture for the United States. The top decision makers paid some attention to Central Asia, but without taking many visible steps to get involved. Even when China and Russia established the Shanghai Five and then the Shanghai Cooperation Organization, the United States largely remained on the sidelines. The exception, of course, was Washington's involvement in the pipeline issue related to the Caspian Sea oil reserves.[103]

The United States' direct involvement in Central Asia emerged as a secondary, but still an important, addendum to its invasion of Afghanistan in 2001. The United States needed Central Asian military bases. Knowing the ambivalence of Moscow and Beijing to America's decision to seek these military bases, the Bush administration tried to soften the shock by assuring those countries that it would withdraw its forces at the end of Operation Enduring Freedom. Neither Russia nor China found that assurance credible; however, they understood that the United States' invasion of Afghanistan would significantly enhance their own respective capabilities to defeat the jihadist forces inside their borders. Thus, they went along with the US request. However, they never felt comfortable about having even a temporary presence of US forces in Central Asia.

Tajikistan and Kyrgyzstan were only too eager to provide military facilities to the United States. As one study points out, the Central Asian states accepted the Sino-Russian domination of the SCO more out of need than desire.[104] They viewed the United States' overtures as opening new vistas of military and economic assistance. More important, President George W. Bush's clarion call in September 2001 – "Either you are with us or you are with the terrorists" – was interpreted by the Central Asian states as an unambiguous signal that America would use its military might to eradicate the "terrorist" forces in their region.

The effectiveness and speed with which the United States dismantled the Taliban regime in 2001 created a genuine fear amid all jihadist forces in that region, and especially in Central Asia. One of the chief outcomes of US military operations in Afghanistan was that the Islamic Movement of Uzbekistan was pretty much destroyed and its leader, Juma Namangani, killed. The remaining IMU fighters took part in one or more battles, alongside the Taliban, against NATO forces. But they largely moved to the Pakistani tribal areas, where they participated in terrorist attacks alongside the TTP and, consequently, came under numerous drone attacks by the United States. The Pakistani Army's Operation Zarb-e-Azb, starting in June 2014 (see chapter 5), made the IMU its top priority target and forced the IMU to take refuge back in Afghanistan. Its presence in that country was a factor in the escalation of conflict between the Afghan National Army and the Taliban.

By the second decade of the twenty-first century, it was difficult to make a reasonable judgment about the future presence of the IMU in Afghanistan or its potential return to Uzbekistan. There have been reports of ideological differences between the current IMU leader, Usman Ghazi, and the Taliban. As a fighting group profoundly committed to carrying out global jihad, the IMU was critical of the Taliban, whom it accused of becoming more nationalistic than jihadist. There have also been reports that a faction of the IMU pledged allegiance to ISIS.[105]

The threat of ISIS's mounting presence in Afghanistan and its potential spillover effects in Central Asia raised the significance of that region to the United States, as well as to China and Russia. However, because the United States was fighting wars against ISIS and al-Qaida–related groups in Iraq and Syria, and the Taliban of Afghanistan, Central Asia remained an area of ancillary interest.

In the waning months of his second term, President Obama started a new round of dialogue with the Central Asian states, under the rubric "C5+1 Initiative" (Kyrgyzstan, Uzbekistan, Kazakhstan, Turkmenistan, Tajikistan, plus the United States), by dispatching secretary of state John Kerry to the region.[106] The format of that initiative was to open bilateral dialogues with each of the five countries. Despite the good intentions underlying this approach, Central Asia did not capture much of Obama's time or attention. Perhaps the best option for the United States would have been to persuade China to incorporate Afghanistan into its Silk Road Initiative in a major way. The rationale is that if Afghanistan continued to sink in the Taliban-created volatility, the very stability of the Central Asian republics would be threatened. Unfortunately, the current Chinese Silk Road Initiative bypasses Afghanistan. Only China can change that, and the United States is best positioned to persuade China in that direction. China, along with the United States, was already involved in facilitating peace negotiations between the Taliban and the Afghan government. Pakistan also played a major role in the successful conclusion of those negotiations. Since peace in Afghanistan is so intrinsically linked with the peace and stability of Central Asia, there is no reason for the United States and China not to pursue an initiative along the lines described here. It may turn out to be a win-win situation for all parties involved.

DYNAMIC POLITICAL MANEUVERINGS BETWEEN THE CENTRAL ASIAN REPUBLICS AND THE GREAT POWERS

Of the three great powers, Russia and China offer the Central Asian states the prospect of strengthening the status quo. Before the April 2010 "Roza Revolution" in Kyrgyzstan, which brought to office Roza Otunbayeva, there was a general understanding that at least Russia would come to the rescue of the Central Asian autocrats if they were swept aside by internal political change. However, given Russia's reluctance to send troops to reestablish law and order in the wake of ethnic riots between the Kyrgyz and the Uzbeks in southern

Kyrgyzstan, one wonders how other leaders of Central Asia – especially Islam Karimov and Emomali Rahmon – would assess their reliance on Russian security guarantees. China's role in Central Asia is primarily to provide economic assistance and to conclude trade, oil, and gas deals with the Central Asian republics without openly or publicly discussing the military aspect of its ties to them. However, because China and Russia are the founding and dominant members of the SCO – which has been conducting joint exercises against the jihadist threat in that area – the Central Asian republics view China as playing a significant role in their security.

The autocratic rulers are reluctant to pursue Western trade avenues, fearing that those alternatives would lead to political demands from the West for democracy and political and economic pluralism. Yet they may not want to limit their options by relying excessively on Russia or China for trade, either. With the launch of the Silk Road Initiative, China further strengthened its economic role in Central Asia. This development, along with the lingering effects on both the United States and Europe of the 2008 global economic meltdown, may incline the Central Asian states to accept more economic dependency on China.

Although the lone superpower has had the least presence in Central Asia since the independent creation of those countries, it has the greatest potential to increase its footprint in the coming years, if for no other reason than to stabilize Afghanistan. That issue is of considerable significance to the Central Asian countries, as well as China and Russia. From the Central Asian perspective, some of the jihadist forces fighting in Afghanistan are of Central Asian origin. The Central Asian countries know that if, by a long shot, the United States is ousted from Afghanistan, it will only be a matter of time before the Islamist forces escalate their presence and intensify their struggle to topple the existing regime. So, they are watching the ups-and-downs of America's war in Afghanistan with rapt attention. China is equally interested in (if not concerned about) the outcome of the war in Afghanistan, because a jihadist victory would intensify the activities of the secessionist forces in its Xinjiang province. Russia is aware that the outcome of this war will affect the Muslim minorities within its own borders. The worst-case scenario would be a full-fledged jihadist attack on Russian security forces stationed in a number of North Caucasian states.

Political developments in Kyrgyzstan and Uzbekistan in 2005 significantly favoured Chinese and Russian strategic interests. When Askar Akayev was ousted as a result of a political coup in March 2005, the other Central Asian autocrats, especially Islam Karimov of Uzbekistan, were visibly shaken, largely because Kyrgyzstan's domestic political arena was more vibrant than that of the other Central Asian countries. Those in official circles inside the Central Asian states felt that, somehow, the United States was behind the coup, with an objective of introducing democracy to Kyrgyzstan and its neighbouring Central Asian states. Only two months later, in May 2005, there was a major political demonstration in the city of Andijan of Uzbekistan, which Karimov's government brutally suppressed. According to unconfirmed reports, security forces fired on unarmed civilians and killed hundreds of people. The Bush administration was vocal in advocating an international inquiry, thereby convincing the already paranoid Karimov that Washington was behind attempts to democratize his country. The Uzbek president had been suspicious of the United States' role in the "Orange Revolution," which had taken place between November 2004 and January 2005. The so-called Tulip Revolution that ousted Akayev further convinced Karimov that the "color revolutions" were being used by Washington to bring about democratic political change. Even before the Andijan incident, Karimov had started his political maneuvering to favour Moscow and Beijing. After the turbulence in Andijan, he demanded withdrawal of US forces stationed at Uzbekistan's Karshi-Khanabad (K2) Air Base.[107]

Although that development was a blow to the US presence and interests in Central Asia, its effects did not promise to be enduring, mainly because the lone superpower continued to serve as a major alternative to Central Asian countries if or when their strategic ties with China or Russia soured. In this sense, the political maneuverings involving the three great powers and the Central Asian countries remain dynamic. The Islamist groups in the region are very much aware of this reality. While they bide their time about facilitating violent political change, they remain highly active in promoting their message. Thus Central Asia is a region of considerable significance for every actor in this "great game."

The United States' return to defeat and dismantle the Taliban and al-Qaida in 2009, under President Barack Obama, started a different phase in that country's involvement in Central Asia. The link between the security of Afghanistan and Central Asia was always fully comprehended by all great powers. The Central Asian leaders recognized how significant the US invasion of 2001 really was in reducing the Islamist-related security threats to their regimes. When the United States promised to fully focus on Afghanistan under Obama starting in 2009, there were hopes that Central Asian security would also improve, especially if the United States stayed for a long time and fulfilled its previously unfinished mission.

However, when President Obama entered into office, the chief problem faced by the new administration was the global economic meltdown of 2008 and its deleterious effects on the United States. Thus, the new administration was forced to drastically switch the modalities of its involvement in Afghanistan from long-term nation building to short-term presence, reducing its force presence and training the Afghan Army to take charge of the security of their country. What also motivated Obama was that the goal of nation building, which required massive capital investment, had little-to-no support inside the United States. In general, the Taliban of Afghanistan and the Central Asian regimes perceived this strategy as a euphemism for "cut and run." The cumulative effects of these developments compelled the Central Asian republics to rely more heavily than before on China and Russia for their security-related threats. From the point of view of the Islamists (i.e., the HT) and the jihadists (i.e., the IMU), the promised US withdrawal from Afghanistan, whenever it occurs, has to be good news. They can always develop operational plans to maximize their Islamism-oriented activities – to acquire territory for a particular motive and based on a particular ideological understanding of Islam. Neither group is likely to succeed at bringing about regime change, but their increased proactivism in conjunction with the sustained bad governance of the Central Asian autocrats will continue to keep the entire region turbulent and highly prone to cataclysmic political changes.

As it turned out, the United States kept postponing plans to withdraw its forces from Afghanistan because of the worsening security situation in that country. Luckily, from the vantage point of the Central Asian republics, no self-styled jihadist group was able to bring about regime change. However, those republics remain wary about the slow but steady influence and presence of ISIS in Afghanistan. In the interim, the process of radicalization continues to gather momentum as the repressive capabilities of all governments in the region intensify.

THE LOOMING MENACE OF RADICALIZATION OF CENTRAL ASIA

In the context of one of the main themes of this book – the Islamic challenge – the Central Asian countries are unique in that the challenge posed by Islamist and jihadist groups to the political status quo in this region is far less threatening than it has been, say, in Pakistan and Afghanistan, and in some countries of the Middle East and Africa. The chief reason is the short history of these republics – they became independent when the USSR imploded in December 1991. Although Central Asian countries – like those in South Asia and the Middle East – also withstood the ignominy of colonialism, the current rulers have not manifested much resentment toward Russia, their chief occupier during the czarist and communist eras. However, because of the closed nature of those countries, it is hard to make an informed judgment as to whether there is any profound antipathy among the Central Asian masses toward Russia. Under autocratic rule, people likely do not have access to historical accounts of brutalities committed by czarist Russia and the Soviet Union. Regarding current modalities of those respective countries' ties with Russia, the Central Asian people are exposed only to the official accounts published in the heavily controlled mass media of their countries. In this sense, an accurate assessment about the popularity or unpopularity of Russia in Central Asia will have to wait until one or more Central Asian countries become democratic. However, at least regarding the United States, the Pew Research Center found that US policies under President George W. Bush – especially his "war on terrorism" – were very unpopular, receiving high-to-very-high negative ratings in public opinion polls.[108] Uzbekistan was a rare exception; 85 per cent of Uzbeks gave the United States a positive rating, and about 35 per cent held "a very favorable view of the U.S."[109]

Regarding future chances for growth of the Islamist challenge, the most worrying part of Central Asia is the Ferghana Valley, which is shared by Uzbekistan, Tajikistan, and Kyrgyzstan. In these three countries, Islamic awareness is either already high or on the rise as a result of religious education provided in underground religious schools, and because of the people's own curiosity and interest regarding Islam.

Still, since there is no systematic Islamization of the polities of these Central Asian countries by their governments – as was the case in Pakistan – religious extremism has not yet become a dominant force. However, because of the long presence of Central Asian jihadist groups in the FATA region of Pakistan and their education in the Deobandi schools of that country, these groups are increasingly committed to extremist and radical interpretations of Islam. As they return to Central Asia, and especially as they have ample opportunity to intermingle and socialize with their fellow citizens, the chances are high that they will succeed in radicalizing a large number of people in their respective countries. In this regard, Uzbekistan, Kyrgyzstan, and Tajikistan are likely to be places where the jihadist groups will intensify their activities in the coming years. In fact, according to one 2009 report, such realities have already emerged in the three countries of the Ferghana Valley.[110]

But all is not gloom and doom in Central Asia. If one is looking for at least some evidence of how an open political system in the region has the capability to dampen the influence of Islamist and jihadist groups, then the ouster of Bakiyev and the resultant opening up of the Kyrgyz political system should suffice. According to one report, Bakiyev's ouster "removed a lightning rod of discontent for pious Muslims, thus reducing the radicalization tendency." He had alienated a large number of Muslims by implementing policies that "restricted freedom of worship." His 2008 repression in Nookat of Muslims "who were seeking to hold a public celebration of the Muslim holiday of Eid al-Fitr, proved a useful recruiting tool for militants." Indeed, a representative of the HT in Kyrgyzstan admitted in an interview that "the more tolerant approach of Kyrgyzstan's provisional government was making recruiting efforts more difficult for Hizb." He added, "Under democracy, when there is freedom of speech, when nobody beats you, it will be difficult to deliver my thoughts to the people, to persuade them. It takes at least two years for us to recruit a person. If there is democracy, it will take a longer time, maybe three years or more."[111] The downside of the relatively democratic Kyrgyzstan is that it has remained an immensely corrupt and nepotistic state. President Akayev, President Bakiyev, and (since 2011) President Almazbek Atambayev have left shameful legacies of high corruption, clientelism, cronyism, and nepotism.[112] So, despite the presence of democracy, Kyrgyzstan seems to await yet another chaotic change. And every time an elected president is ousted because of massive protest and breakdown of law and order, the Islamists and jihadists envision it as another opportunity to push the country in the direction of Islamism.

In the context of great power relations, however, Atambayev caused consternation in Washington by announcing just a few days after his reelection that he would soon ask the United States either to leave the Transit Centre at Manas (formerly known as the Manas Air Base) by 2014 or to reach some sort of an agreement with Russia and other countries to establish a civil transit centre there. The United States closed that facility on 3 June 2014.[113]

In tracking potential turbulence in Central Asian countries, one has to be careful about cross-checking the official bulletin describing those events with other non–Central Asian sources before arriving at any definite conclusions. As one report points out, political violence may result because of the prevalence of ethnic tension in Central Asia (e.g., the Kyrgyz-Uzbek ethnic hatred of Kyrgyzstan, and the Tajik and Uzbek antipathy of Tajikistan).[114] However, "the main drivers of the current conflict are clashing economic and power interests that are the unresolved legacy of the Tajik Civil War."[115] Political turbulence may also be caused by ongoing succession-related conflicts taking place in Kazakhstan and Uzbekistan.[116]

CLOSING OBSERVATIONS

Central Asia is a unique region for a number of reasons. First, it has been given high significance by China and Russia. These countries are determined to increase their respective presence and sphere of influence, while keeping that of the United States to a minimum. The United States, while it does not have a strong or widespread presence, has not at all given up on escalating it in the coming years. The future shape of the US presence and interest in this region greatly depends on what happens to the political stability in Afghanistan and how that stability (or the lack thereof) affects Central Asia.

Second, as a result of sustained interest and activism on the part of the great powers, the Central Asian countries know that their maneuverability vis-à-vis those actors promises to remain visible in the coming years. At least for now, they are members of the SCO, an alliance created by China and Russia, and the Partnership for Peace, an arrangement that is part of NATO. As members of these entities, the Central Asian states have the best of both worlds.

Third, the Islamist challenge in Central Asia experienced a serious setback because of the US invasion of Afghanistan in 2001. But because at least three of the five states in the region – Uzbekistan, Kyrgyzstan, and Tajikistan – are regarded as fragile, weak, or "flimsy,"[117] the jihadists are likely to bounce back and to escalate their popularity and maneuverability there if the governments in those countries do not improve their performance in the next few years.

Fourth, as long as brutal and autocratic regimes continue to exist in Central Asia, the jihadist forces know very well that chances for their future success remain very much alive.

Fifth, the HT, which has not been depicted as a "terrorist organization" anywhere in the world, has palpable potential for success because it has been systematically heightening the Islamic knowledge and orientation of the masses in almost all Central Asian countries. In that capacity, it could pose a potent challenge to autocratic rule and instigate change in the region.

As much as all three great powers have a presence in Central Asia, Russia and China have an advantage over the United States because of their geographical proximity to the region. However, that advantage is not of great value because the Central Asian states remain highly skeptical (indeed suspicious) of Russian maneuvers in the name of providing them with security against jihadist forces. By the same token, even though the People's Republic of China has been successful in linking its strategic presence to a number of infrastructure-related projects in Central Asia, the republics will be closely watching China's mounting assertiveness in East Asia and wondering whether or when such behaviour will also be demonstrated in their region. In that sense, China, too, remains a source of concern to the Central Asian dictators.[118]

Russia and China are gravely apprehensive of the Islamist challenge, which forces them not only to remain allies but also to ensure that the SCO as an alliance remains enticing enough for Central Asian countries not to abandon it. China's Silk Road Initiative in 2015 promises enormous economic benefits to the Central Asian republics, and Russia's focus on the military aspect of the alliance may offer security and stability against the jihadist forces. In these respects, the SCO is an advantageous alliance for the Central Asian republics.

Of all the Central Asian leaders, Islam Karimov has demonstrated the highest degree of Machiavellianism toward Russia, China, and the United States. Even though he closed the K2 air base to the US forces, he has kept very much open the option of inviting them back if seriously threatened by jihadist attacks. What is keeping him on the side of Moscow and Beijing is that he is genuinely afraid of the United States' capabilities to bring about a democratic change through the use of nongovernmental organizations (NGOs), as it is alleged to have done in Kyrgyzstan prior to March 2005. At the same time, his fear of increased jihadist incursion in his country remains very much alive, especially considering the escalated military operations of the Taliban of Afghanistan, in which the IMU is an active participant. Other Central Asian leaders are also afraid of that potential US role; however, they are pragmatic and realistic enough to remain on the side of Russia and China, while not ruling out the option of improving their strategic ties with the United States in the coming years. For Kyrgyzstan and Tajikistan, there is a profusion of fear related to bad governance, sustained presence of Islamists within their borders, and the potential deleterious spillover effects of the ongoing war in Afghanistan. So, the Central Asian autocrats are constantly indulging in a great game in which they envision a clear-cut threat from the jihadists but also remain wary of a potential implosion of their regimes through the introduction of democracy. Under these circumstances, they appear to have judged their connections with Russia and China to be less threatening to their preferred status quo than overtures toward the United States. In this sense, a great game of high stakes based on pragmatism and realism is being played out by the great powers and the countries of Central Asia.

While the United States has less presence in Central Asia than Russia and China, its presence in Afghanistan for the purpose of stabilizing that country promised to raise its stock among the Central Asian countries. These countries were of the view that "because the U.S. is not a regional power capable of exerting hegemony, an active U.S. role helps them maintain a regional balance and preserves their own room to maneuver."[119] However, the worsening security in Afghanistan has kept their levels of concern high. They continue to hope that the United States stays engaged in Afghanistan. Such US presence, along with Russian security commitments in countries like Tajikistan and Kyrgyzstan, still contains abundant promise of stability in those countries, even in Turkmenistan.

In the second decade of the twenty-first century, the United States is so preoccupied with uncertainties and turbulence in the Middle East and with Obama's Asia Pivot strategy that Central Asia holds little of President Obama's attention, although he recognizes the intrinsic linkages between the rising power and influence of the Taliban in post-US Afghanistan and the potential escalation of pro-activism among jihadist forces in Central Asia. Because of this unfortunate reality, the United States will be forced to act reactively and episodically if or when political explosions happen in one or more countries in the region, whereas the most prudent way of dealing with the security situation in Central Asia is to develop a strategy to facilitate long-term economic development and good governance.

8

Conclusions

In this chapter we return to some of the theses and themes that were articulated in the introductory chapter. The chief focus of this book has been the nature and dynamics of the Islamic challenge to the United States. This conflict is between the liberal philosophy that is at the heart of the American state and certain perspectives that militant Islamists say that Islam demands. To recall the discussion from chapter 1, in the American outlook, as enunciated by William T. Cavanaugh, life is divided "into separate religious and secular spheres." The Islamists, on the other hand, categorically reject that position. In fact, they regard secularism (and any opinion that it propounds) as fundamentally "un-Islamic." Americans, writes Cavanaugh, are habituated to envisage "that devotion to one's religion is fine within limits, while public patriotic devotion to one's nation is generally a good thing." Americans "are appalled at violence on behalf of religion," but they "generally accept the necessity and even the virtue of killing for one's country."[1] One reason for their disgust at any manifestation of religious violence is their view that religion has a strong tendency to push the believer toward absolutism, which "makes obedience blind and causes the believer to subjugate all means to a transcendent end."[2] This American conviction about the moral superiority of their own secular belief, also labelled as secular fundamentalism, condescendingly regards the religious perspective of the Islamists and self-styled jihadists as the "irrational other."

At least from the American point of view, the intended or conscious purpose of secular fundamentalism is not to vilify or disparage Islam. However, the end result is the same: to Muslims the world over, and particularly to the Islamists and jihadists, secular fundamentalists seem to have no problem in going to war and killing the "irrational" ones. For secular fundamentalists, such killing for their country is "virtuous." What the United States does in responding to the jihadists in the name of secularism, promotion of democracy, and glorification of the country, so do the jihadists (perpetrate violence and go to war) for the glory of Allah and Islam. Couched in this framework, an end to this conflict appears inconceivable, or at least unfeasible, for the foreseeable future. We will return to this issue later in this chapter.

The conflict between the Islamists and the West predates the United States' entry into the affairs of the Muslim world – especially in South Asia, the Arab world, and Iran. Great Britain and France were the hegemons in those regions during the period between the two World Wars, with the exception of Iran, which was not yet colonized. However, the Western powers ensured that it was reigned by a pro-Western ruler. As was discussed in chapter 2, the Islamists' focus was on the conflict with their native regimes. The issues of intense contention – Islamic government, sovereignty of God, secularism, and the Western version of modernization – were not part of Islam's theological doctrines.[3] But the Islamists and the jihadists developed articulate positions on these issues, and the repetition of these views through the decades has assigned them a quasi-theological status. These positions require reinterpretation in the twenty-first century, more now than ever before, to understand why the conflict between the Islamists and the United States has intensified since the middle of the last century. Islamists (not the self-styled jihadists) constitute a large section of the Muslim population; they play a visible role in setting the parameters of public debate between Islam and the West, and they enjoy support from a noticeable section of the populace in any country. In many instances, Islamists also propose solutions to a number of problems faced by the world of Islam.

This book began by describing the modalities of the conflict between the Islamists and the Western-backed autocratic regimes of the Middle East, North Africa, and South Asia. The Islamists were anti-regime groups who by and large pursued peaceful ways to change the governing style of the regimes. However, they did not propose any nuanced models (or outlines) of governance relevant for the contemporary era, nor did they proffer feasible programs for economic and social development. All they advocated was some type of Islamist government that would restore seventh-century Islamic puritanism. The Islamists also blamed the West and the concepts of political and economic development that it promoted – democracy, popular sovereignty, secularism, and Western-style modernization under which religion had no role – and categorically rejected these "un-Islamic" proclivities. No matter how unfair the Islamists' views of the West might have been, what mattered was that their antipathy stuck. As we move from the generations of Islamists of the nineteenth century through to the twenty-first century, if anything, this characterization of the West as anti-Islamic remains equally entrenched and harsh. The current generation of Islamists responds with hostility to the Western promotion of democracy, secularization, and modernization.

The chief argument of chapter 2 was that it was the failure of the Islamists to change the political nature and economic status of their polities that paved the way for the emergence of the self-styled jihadists. The age-old question of "What went wrong?" – why the Muslim civilization has not seen its glory days since the degeneration of the Ottoman Empire into the "sick man of Europe" and its dismantlement in the aftermath of the 1916 Sykes-Picot Agreement – has never been persuasively answered.[4] The argument that the Ottoman Empire's failure to secularize the polity accounted for the lack of modernization and industrialization in the world of Islam is the most controversial and least acceptable explanation to Muslims because it assumes the separation of religion and the state. Simplistic explanations – such as Muslims are weak and backward because they moved away from the practice of "true" Islam – also remain contentious, albeit popular inside a number of Muslim countries.

Part of the Muslim problem – a minor one but still important enough to identify – is that Muslims have spent a major portion of their energy blaming the West and their own autocrats for their problems, not themselves. True, the turbulent nature of autocratic rule seeped into all aspects of the Muslim polity. The highly status quo–oriented educational policies of the autocratic rulers made it effectively impossible for Muslim youths to become top-notch scientists or Islamic scholars equipped with erudite knowledge of Islamic *fiqh* and its application to the problems of an increasingly intricate globalized world.[5] In its place, the systematic promotion of obscurantism and mediocrity – hallmarks of the autocratic regimes – turned almost all Muslim countries into places where conspiracy theories and blame games mushroomed (chapter 2).

When the Islamists failed to pull their polities from the interminable eras of backwardness and mediocrity, the jihadists became the vanguard of the Muslim struggle to terminate their backwardness. However, they were even less sophisticated than the Islamists, and equally clueless about crafting models of economic development and political stability. They promoted the militant doctrine of jihad to overthrow the autocratic rulers from their respective countries and to establish a caliphate along the pattern of the one that prevailed under the Prophet of Islam in the seventh century (chapter 3).

The self-styled jihadists committed a gross injustice against Islam by adopting only the military version of jihad and excluding other interpretations of that doctrine – hence the modifier "self-styled." Arguably, they adopted militant jihad because they witnessed what it was capable of achieving when used against a superpower – it brought about the defeat and ouster of the Soviet Union from Afghanistan in the late 1980s. What they either deliberately overlooked or truly failed to understand, in their zealous haste to credit that prodigious development to Islam, was that victory was only possible because another superpower – the United States – wholeheartedly sponsored and supported the mujahedeen fighters. The jihadists' profound belief that their vigorously contested jihad resulted in the defeat of the Soviet Union in Afghanistan has driven two ensuing generations to try to emulate that victory by terminating autocratic rule in their respective countries. Although no jihadist group succeeded in overthrowing any government, their declaration of jihad certainly has become a profound and sustained source of apprehension for the United States and all Muslim countries.

In this context, we should revisit another major theme of this book – Islamism. As previously noted, Islamism involves an effort to acquire territory for a particular motive and based on a particular ideological understanding of Islam (chapter 1). As such, it is stridently anti-US, aims to bring about an end to the autocratic political status quo that prevails in most Muslim countries, and intends to establish a Muslim caliphate. Its Sunni practitioners are driven by the Takfiri doctrine (chapter 3).

Ironically, the United States – the devout practitioner of secular fundamentalism – became an unwitting founder and promoter of Islamism in Afghanistan in the 1980s when its jihad defeated the Soviet Union. But it was the mujahedeen's long war of the early 1990s – and their exercise of Islamism – that briefly brought them to power in that country. The jihadists perceived that development as further evidence of the power potential of militant jihad. However, the Islamic Republic of Pakistan played a crucial role in making that a reality. When the mujahedeen government conclusively demonstrated its ineptness to rule Afghanistan, Pakistan once again provided crucial support, which enabled the Taliban to emerge as the next rulers of Afghanistan in 1996.[6] By then, the concept of Islamism had been successful three times just in Afghanistan.

The jihadists were ready to enact their version of Islam elsewhere in the world of Islam, but without success. A paramount reason for that was America's powerful resolve to ensure the defeat of Islamism, especially after the success of the Shia version of Islamism that ousted a staunch US ally and brought to power a truculently anti-American Islamist regime. The Islamic Republic of Iran's threats to export the Islamic revolution to neighbouring Persian Gulf states convinced Washington how potentially threatening Islamism could be for other Muslim states (chapter 6). Witnessing what the mujahedeen and then the Taliban did to Afghanistan in the 1990s only strengthened the US resolve.

In the context of Islamism, there is another great irony. Pakistan, which had the most visible record of success in being a major player during the American-sponsored jihad in April 1980 and then the sole promoter of two successful campaigns of Islamism in Afghanistan in 1992 and 1996, itself became a target of the Tehrik-e-Taliban-e-Pakistan's (TTP) exercise of Islamism. The TTP attempted to destabilize the country to bring about a regime change, which, though impossible to achieve, has remained its objective since 2007. As was discussed in chapter 5, Pakistan is the only country where the extreme form of Islamization was a state policy. Initiated under Zulfiqar Ali Bhutto, the Islamic agenda intensified under the dictatorship of Zia-ul-Haq. A crucial feature of Zia's Islamization was the use of jihadists to wage periodic terrorist attacks in Indian-administered Kashmir. That policy stemmed from Pakistan's irrational refusal to accept the Line of Control, which divides Indian- and Pakistan-administered Kashmir, as a de facto international border. The use of jihadist groups to carry out campaigns of terror never proved to be an effective tactic for Pakistan. Particularly when the jihadists turned against the government during heightened hostilities under Musharraf (a supporter of George W. Bush's global war on terrorism [GWOT], which Pakistani jihadists, in turn, perceived as America's war against Islam),

Pakistan should have revisited its use of these groups as a tool of foreign policy. Such reexamination also would have enabled Pakistan to develop an effective domestic strategy to eradicate the growing presence and influence of the TTP and other terrorist groups. In 2014, the government of Prime Minister Nawaz Sharif – elected into office in March 2013 – could not make up its mind whether to fight or to negotiate with the TTP, knowing full well that the TTP's "negotiating agenda" would be too farfetched and outlandish to serve as the basis for discussion. A quick glance at the draft of the TTP's original demands to the government of Pakistan underscores their preposterous nature.[7]

- stop drone attacks
- introduce Shariah law in courts
- introduce an Islamic system of education in both public and private educational institutions
- free Pakistani and foreign Taliban from jails
- remunerate people for damage to property during drone attacks and rebuild those properties
- hand over control of tribal areas to local forces
- withdraw the army from tribal areas and close down check posts
- drop all criminal allegations against the Taliban
- release prisoners from both sides
- guarantee equal rights for all, poor and rich
- offer jobs to families of drone attack victims
- end the interest-based banking system
- stop supporting the US war on terrorism
- replace the democratic system of governance with an Islamic system
- break all relations with the United States

The TPP's demands that the very nature of the Pakistani government be changed from a democratic state to a hardline Islamist state (which is an exercise of Islamism) and that Pakistan suspend its ties with the United States were too bizarre for any consideration.

The Pakistan Army's Operation Zarb-e-Azb was developed to defeat the Islamism of the TTP. Through this operation, the Pak Army unequivocally signalled to the TTP that regime change was not going to happen. The operation destroyed the strongholds of the jihadists and enfeebled their presence in a number of major Pakistani cities (chapter 5). However, in carrying out Zarb-e-Azb, the Pak

Army did not go far enough. It had yet to make a clean break from its policy of differentiating between the "good" and the "bad" terrorists, letting the "good" ones survive. Through this policy, the Pak Army continued to signal its willingness to use domestic terrorist groups like the Lashkar-e-Taiba (LeT) and the Lashkar-e-Jhangvi ("good" terrorists) against Indian-administered Kashmir. Similarly, by not destroying the Haqqani group (another "good" terrorist group) residing on the Pak-Afghan border, Pakistan has indicated its willingness to intermittently use it against Indian diplomatic personnel in Afghanistan. In a larger sense, Pakistan's refusal to destroy this group also underscores its anxiety regarding the US policy of facilitating India's role in stabilizing Afghanistan. Although Pakistan has been unable to persuade the United States to abandon that policy, it has discouraged India from playing that role without being overt about it. While Pakistan continues this duplicitous policy, its fight against the TTP is far from over. Pakistan also continues to exert its influence over the Taliban of Afghanistan. Mullah Akhtar Mansour, successor to the late Mullah Omar, resides in Pakistan, which provides that country palpable influence over the off-again, on-again negotiations between the Taliban and the Afghan government. However, because the ranks of the Afghan Taliban are riddled with internal strife, Pakistan's influence over the modalities of those negotiations remains spasmodic. At the same time, as long as the United States continues to recognize the significance of Pakistan in the negotiations, Pakistan is likely to reap considerable benefit through economic assistance, the sale of advanced military technology, and most notably, the continuation of a US-Pak strategic dialogue.

Iran's exercise of Islamism (chapter 6) had a profound effect on the thinking and attitudes of Islamists and jihadists all over the world, as well as the United States, for at least two reasons. First and foremost, for the Islamists and the jihadists, the establishment of an Islamist government in the twentieth century was persuasive evidence that it could be emulated elsewhere in the world of Islam. Second, the United States was shocked that even Iran's well-armed military could not save its ruler from the humiliating collapse of his regime at the hands of revolutionary groups led by a firebrand Islamist.

Consequently, Washington's response was to create the US Central Command (CENTCOM), a regional military command (aka unified command) specifically aimed at squelching the prospects of regime change in the Middle East as a result of another Islamic revolution.

The United States was in no mood to witness the abrupt transformation of another regime from its close ally, and even a gendarme, into a regime that not only challenged its strategic dominance in the Middle East but also developed countermeasures to further erode it. The United States kept firmly in mind its objective of unravelling the Islamic Republic. The Iran-Iraq War served as an excellent opportunity to do just that. Washington did its best to dismantle the Islamic Republic during that war, providing intelligence to Iraqi forces on Iranian troop movement and even supplying chemicals for Iraq's development of chemical weapons, which Iraq used mercilessly on Iran.[8] The US Navy was involved in skirmishes with the Iranian Navy, and Iran claimed "that American helicopters were aiding Iraq in the Fao Peninsula attack," which the then secretary of defense, Frank C. Carlucci, denied as untrue.[9] American secular fundamentalism failed miserably in dismantling the Islamic Republic, but it has not yet forsaken that endeavour.

The earnestness of America's resolve to defend the status quo in both the Persian Gulf and the Middle East was confirmed, once and for all, when the United States used CENTCOM as the chief vehicle to conduct the 1991 Gulf War. That event was the first exercise of American secular fundamentalism at war with the world of Islam.

Iran would neither forget nor forgive America's support of its archenemy, Iraq, during the worst challenge to the survival of its regime. Iran responded with effective countermeasures in the Levant, creating Hezbollah and helping Syria to prolong its occupation of Lebanon until 2005. The Iranian military supplies to Hezbollah fuelled that organization's impressive performance against a militarily superior Israel in the 2006 Hezbollah-Israeli war. Syria served as a highly dependable supply channel for Iranian arms and missiles to Hezbollah before and after that war.

Iran fully exploited the US military invasion of Iraq and the resultant demise of its worst enemy, Saddam Hussein. Iran's immediate response was to do its utmost to bring an end to the US occupation of Iraq, because it correctly concluded that the long-term American occupation of Iraq would enable the lone superpower, once again, to maneuver a regime change in Iran. After US troops withdrew from Iraq, Iran's influence there flourished. However, the transformation of al-Qaida in Iraq (AQI) into ISIS, its defeat of the Iraqi Army in Mosul, its participation in the Syrian civil war and capture of territory there, and its declaration of an Islamic caliphate in the captured territories in Iraq and Syria posed major challenges to the rising influence of Iran in Iraq. ISIS's declaration of a caliphate was another significant exercise of Islamism, as defined in this book. Given that the rise of ISIS was a direct outcome of the highly myopic anti-Sunni policies of the then prime minister of Iraq, Nouri al-Maliki, Iran recognized that the resultant outburst of Sunni rage would engulf Iraq in a sectarian war. Iran's response was to send the Shia militias and its Quds Force to the rescue.

Iran's participation in the Syrian civil war, from its very inception in 2011, was an integral aspect of the Iran-Syria strategic alliance (formed in 1979), which was both anti-US and anti-Israel. The continuing civil war in Syria, in which ISIS was also a major player, meant that Iran was forced to give heightened import and urgency to its participation in that war. A weighty feature of that war was that the Saudi-UAE-backed Sunni Islamists were seeking to oust the Alawite (a small sect of Shia Islam)-dominated Assad regime and establish a Sunni-dominated Islamist regime (a supposedly moderate Islamist regime), while ISIS wanted to expand the territorial size of its already-declared caliphate. From the point of view of this book, this was a war between two versions of Islamism through the capture of territories: Sunni Islamism versus Shia Islamism. Another crucial aspect of the civil wars in Syria and Iraq was that, while the United States fought ISIS through the use of its Air Force and Special Forces, Iran was also busy fighting ISIS in both countries as well. The chief difference was that Iran wanted to defeat and eradicate ISIS in order to firmly implant the Assad regime, while the Obama administration's position on ousting the Assad regime remained in a state of flux.

In the second decade of the twenty-first century, Iran's Islamic regime appeared to be conducting an effective foreign policy. Its influence in Iraq was high, while the United States could not even negotiate a status of forces agreement (SOFA) with the government of Nouri al-Maliki in order to continue stationing its forces in Iraq in 2001. Iran concluded the nuclear deal with the United States and other members of the Perm 5+ Germany on 14 July 2015 and started the lengthy but welcomed process of emerging as a "normal" member of the global community of nations. Iran and the United States were fighting ISIS in Iraq and were pushing for the same objective: stabilizing the Shia-dominated democratic government of Iraq.

These positive developments notwithstanding, there still remained a number of issues of considerable dissension between Washington and Tehran. Most significant was Iran's wholehearted support of the Assad regime's attempt to stay in power. Iran's continued role as chief supporter and source of military supplies to Hezbollah was another issue of major divergence, since the United States depicted Hezbollah as a terrorist organization. Iran's role in Syria and Lebanon went to the heart of the Iranian strategic maneuvers to sustain its presence and clout in the Levant. Unless these issues were resolved, chances of a major rapprochement with the United States were minimal.

The third issue of major contention between Washington and Tehran was the Islamic Republic's emergence as a major player in Russia's endeavours to compete with the United States for influence. Russian president Vladimir Putin advised the Assad regime to destroy its arsenal of chemical weapons in order to forestall US military attack. Syria complied under the supervision of the Hague-based Organisation for the Prohibition of Chemical Weapons.[10] Putin exploited that opening by entering the civil war in Syria as one of the major defenders of the Assad regime. This development only boosted Iran's role in Syria.

Finally, in the long-standing strategic tug-and-pull between Iran and the Persian Gulf countries, the United States has been unequivocally on the side of the latter. In the second decade of the twenty-first century, the Iran–Gulf State conflict, in addition to sustaining its erstwhile competitive characteristics on a variety of strategic issues, acquired a potentially explosive sectarian distinctiveness. As the largest Shia state, Iran regarded itself as the leader and voice of Shia Muslims everywhere. The Saudis made a similar claim regarding Sunni Islam. In that capacity, the latter, after accusing Iran of supporting the 2011 protest movement in Bahrain, brutally intervened, with virtually no objection from the Obama administration. As a *New York Times* dispatch noted, "Though the United States eventually sided with the demonstrators in Egypt, in Bahrain it has instead supported the leadership while calling for restraint and democratic change." A Saudi government official, in an apparent indirect reference to the lack of objection (or even a tacit endorsement) from the Obama administration, stated that "the United States was informed Sunday that the Saudi troops would enter Bahrain on Monday."[11]

The most dangerous aspect of Saudi-Iranian animosity is the ongoing civil war in Yemen. As such, this war has become a conflict between the Saudi-backed Sunnis, Iran-backed Houthi-Zaidi Shias, and al-Qaida in the Arabian Peninsula (AQAP), which is also Sunni but is opposed to both the Houthis and the Saudis. Saudi Arabia wants to establish Sunni Islamism in Yemen, while Iran desires the establishment of Houthi-dominated Islamism, even though it denies participation in that conflict. AQAP wants a version of Islamism very similar to the one that ISIS has established under its so-called caliphate. Lately, there have been reports of the increasing presence of ISIS in Yemen, which is anything but good news for all parties to Yemen's civil war. The intensity of this conflict is underscored by the fact that even that country's "security forces have split loyalties." Some units are backing the current president, Abdrabbuh Mansour Hadi, while others are backing his predecessor, the politically influential Ali Abdullah Saleh.[12]

The sectarian/strategic animosity between Iran and Saudi Arabia is also evident in Lebanon, where the "proxy war" between those two countries is being fought by the Saudi-backed Hariri group (named after the late Lebanese prime minister, Rafiq Hariri, whose assassination was suspected to have been carried out by Iranian-backed Hezbollah, which it denied).[13] Consequently, the global community witnessed a number of terrorist attacks and assassinations in Lebanon suspected to have been carried out by pro-Saudi groups in retaliation for Hezbollah's military participation to support the besieged Assad regime.[14]

Chapter 7 analyzed the maneuvers of the great powers – the United States, Russia, and China – in dealing with the Islamic challenge in Central Asia. This is the only region where the United States not only faced competition from China and Russia, but also encountered a palpable disadvantage in that it has remained marginalized and is not a visible player in the Sino-Russian strategic maneuvers. For now, the challenge to Central Asian regimes from the Islamists and jihadists is minimal. However, given the gross economic backwardness and brutal autocratic rule in Central Asian countries, the tide of events is likely to turn in favour of the Islamists/ jihadists sooner rather than later. If or when that happens, the United States will have to revisit its erstwhile benign neglect of the region and develop a strategy to counter the Islamism-oriented activities of the jihadists. In the meantime, growing instability in Afghanistan remains an issue of primary concern for both China and Russia, since it is most likely to destabilize one or more Central Asian countries.

ALL IS NOT GLOOM AND DOOM BETWEEN ISLAM AND THE UNITED STATES

The conflict between Islamists and the United States has a tremendous potential for resolution when one inquires whether Muslims at large wish to live in a democracy. Muslim perspectives on democracy are unique. John Esposito and Dalia Mogahed, after analyzing the Gallup Poll's massive multiyear research study on Muslim attitudes toward a number of issues affecting their religion, global terrorism, and the United States' role in tackling it, report that Muslim attitudes toward democracy are highly nuanced. While a majority of Muslims admire a number of features of Western democracy, "those surveyed do not favor wholesale adoption of Western models of democracy." Since "overwhelming numbers of Muslims continue to identify religion as a primary marker of their identity, a source of guidance and strength, and crucial to their progress," they "appear to want their own democratic model that incorporates Sharia – and not one that is simply dependent on Western values." While "Muslims see no contradiction between democratic values and religious principles," they do not manifest a preference for a theocracy or a secular democracy.[15] What Muslims really want is "Islamic democracy." In that model, the Islamic Shariah should serve at least as "a source of legislation." The significance of this point is underscored by the fact that, according to Esposito and Mogahed, "In only a few countries did a majority say that *Sharia* should have no role in society; yet in most countries, only a minority want *Sharia* as 'the only source' of law."[16]

Even regarding secularism, one clearly discerns the emergence of a nuanced interpretation among Islamist scholars. Secularism – generally described as a doctrine or a concept separating religion and politics – has generated intense controversy in the world of Islam and remains a source of conflict with the United States. In a seminal volume, *Al-Islam Wa Usul Al-Hukm*, Ali Abd al-Raziq, an Egyptian judge regarded as the intellectual father of the notion of Islamic secularism, questioned the necessity of having a caliphate – an Islamic concept of state that combines religion and politics.[17] Al-Raziq argued that "the caliphate is not a religious regime, that it is not required by Islam, and that, despite the pretensions of the caliphs, they could not possibly have been the successors or caliphs of the Prophet because the Prophet 'was never a king, and he never tried to establish a government or a state; he was a messenger sent by Allah, and he was not a political leader.'"[18] Needless to say, few Muslims, if any, accept al-Raziq's position on the role of the Prophet of Islam, who is regarded by the overwhelming majority of believers as both a messenger of Allah and the head of a state. In the latter capacity, he is also regarded as a politician.

One of the most famous poets in the world of Islam, Allama Muhammad Iqbal of Pakistan, represents a majority of Muslim scholars in an oft-quoted couplet (*sher*) in which he condemns secularism:

> *Jalale padshahi ho ki jamhoori tamasha ho*
> *Juda ho Deen Siyasat say to reh jatee hai Changayzi*
> (Whether the system of government is a dictatorship, monarchy, or a circus by democracy
> If that system of government is devoid of religion,
> then you are left with tyranny).[19]

By the same token, many Islamists "cast secularism as a completely foreign doctrine imposed on the Islamic world by colonial powers. They hold up traditional Islamic society, particularly during the first century or so of Islam, as an ideal model reflecting religious principles guiding the community in all areas of life, including politics."[20] Abu Muhammad Asim al-Maqdisi, renowned Palestinian-Jordanian Islamist, writes, "The democracy is the evil result of secularism and its illegitimate daughter, because secularism is a fake doctrine that aims at separating the religion from the governance."[21]

Prominent Islamists who have lived only in Muslim countries tend to be more critical of secularism than those who have resided in the West. Yusuf al-Qaradawi, one the most respected Egyptian scholars, states that secularism and Islam "are incompatible in a country in which the majority of the population is Muslim."[22] Given his limited experience of living in only Egypt or Qatar, in reproving secularism, he might also have been expressing his strong aversion for the secular, despotic rule of Hosni Mubarak, president of Egypt from 1980 to 2011. Mubarak (and other despots including Bin Ali of Tunisia, the military rulers of Algeria, and Bashar al-Assad of Syria) used the practices and, in some cases, the veneer of secularism to wheedle support from major Western countries. Mubarak made it clear to the United States that his rule was the only alternative to a chaotic Islamic takeover. Al-Qaradawi rejected the notion that Islamic rule is inherently unstable, asserting that Islam "represents an inseparable unity in a life ruled by God alone, God who is Lord over both the heavens and the earth."[23]

Another major Islamist, Rachid al-Ghannouchi of Tunisia, holds a markedly different position on this issue. Although he condemned the form of secularism practiced by the regime of Zine-El-Abideen Ben Ali and by the governments of Arab Maghreb, he endorsed the mode of secularism in Turkey. He labelled Bin Ali's regime as "pseudo-secular" and depicted the ultra-secularism of the Maghreb governments as "no more than 'pre-modern European-style regimes from the age of theocracy and absolutism.'" He added, "Secularism in the Muslim world and despotism almost always go hand in hand. Authoritarian governments take the worst of secularist doctrine and use it as a weapon against Islamists by equating Islam with fundamentalism and extremism and setting secularism as a prerequisite to democracy."[24] However, for al-Ghannouchi, the practice of secularism in Turkey is a preferred state of affairs and is worthy of emulation in post-Ali Tunisia.

As much as the critiques of al-Qaradawi and al-Ghannouchi regarding secularism reflect their personal experiences of living in only Muslim countries (although al-Ghannouchi spent over two decades living in exile in London, an experience that considerably moderated his views), the views of European Islamic scholars reflect their own *sui generis* experiences of living in regions where Muslims are in the minority. As such, they have learned to adapt and to integrate their views on secularism by emphasizing religious pluralism, integration, assimilation, and tolerance.

Mustafa Ceric, the Grand Mufti of Bosnia-Herzegovina, and Tariq Ramadan, a noted scholar at Oxford University and the grandson of Hasan al-Banna, are two such individuals. Ceric, who was educated at al-Azhar University of Egypt and the University of Chicago – two elite educational institutions of the Islamic world and the West, respectively – rejects the notion of "a clash between Islam and Western values and secularism." Instead, he advocates "a synthesis, an identity based on common values as a basis for citizenship [for European Muslims]." He believes that "to live in a secular Europe" or in any European country "does not negate religiosity ... 'I am proud that Islam defines my European patriotism.'" As a result of a fusion between Islamic and European cultures, Islam synthesized and "developed its unique traditions." Ceric is most prescient in suggesting "that the successful encounter of Europe and Islam has two interconnected prerequisites: Muslims must embrace their European identity and European governments must facilitate Muslims' integration by accommodating and institutionalizing their religious needs." Such rapprochement would lead to European acceptance of Islam as one of the religions of Europe. Ceric affirms that issues like democracy, rule of law, human rights, and individual freedom are also Islamic values. "If European-born Muslims look inside their faith for what are presented as Western notions of human rights and individual freedom, they will find them." He believes that European governments should facilitate Muslim integration through education and the training of imams, a suggestion that is controversial because, as critics point out, it would lead to "a new hybrid: government-sponsored Islam – American Islam, French Islam, British Islam etc."[25]

Tariq Ramadan explicitly advocates secularism on the part of European Muslims. He is of the view that "embracing secularism and an open society is not a betrayal of Muslim principles for it enables all citizens to live together and [creates] the necessary condition for religious freedom – for Muslims and others." Thus, he exhorts Western Muslims to spread the following message at home and abroad: "We live in democracy, we respect the state of law, we respect open political dialogue and we want this for all Muslims." To be sure, Ramadan does not advocate complete assimilation of Muslims. Instead, he suggests the following: "Muslims must be allowed to develop their own European Muslim identity and culture just as other faiths and ethnic groups have done before them." He strongly urges European Muslims to accept "the constitution, laws and framework of any European country in which he/she lives."[26]

These were the beginnings of important debates over issues that, in the past, Muslims had rejected as un-Islamic or even as anti-Islamic. Such debates promise to open new vistas and interpretations that are direly needed in order to transform the world of Islam from within. This significant development has the potential to become the basis for a rapprochement between Islam and the United States in the coming years. However, the emergence of ISIS, the massive migration of Syrian, Iraqi, and even Afghan refugees, and ISIS's global social media calls for Muslims to perpetrate violence on individuals in the West were all serious setbacks for the promise of a rapprochement between the West and the world of Islam.

THE FUTURE OF THE ISLAMIC CHALLENGE

The United States and the Sunni Islamism of ISIS

Toward the middle of the second decade of the twenty-first century, jihadists may be viewing different regions of the Muslim world with a blend of optimism and pessimism. One of the chief reasons underlying their optimism is that the Sunni Islamism of ISIS acquired a swathe of territories in Syria and Iraq and declared it a Sunni caliphate on 29 June 2014. Toward the end of 2015, support for and allegiance to ISIS was reported to be growing. Although a United Nations announcement on 7 February 2016 stated that ISIS has thirty-four affiliates worldwide, the IntelCenter reports that number as forty-three (table 8.1).[27]

The same UN announcement stated, "The recent expansion of the Daesh [i.e., ISIS] sphere of influence across west and north Africa, the Middle East and south and southeast Asia demonstrates the speed and scale at which the gravity of the threat has evolved in just 18 months."[28] Another report, which is periodically updated by CNN, noted, "Since declaring its caliphate in June 2014, the self-proclaimed Islamic State has conducted or inspired more than 70 terrorist attacks in 20 countries other than Iraq and Syria, where its carnage has taken a much deadlier toll; those attacks outside Iraq and Syria have killed at least 1,200 people and injured more than 1,700 others ... The deadly tentacles of ISIS have spread quickly, from the terrorist group's epicenter in Iraq and Syria to points around the globe."[29]

ISIS's global visibility stems from its mandate and its multifaceted cyber strategy. From the beginning, it portrayed itself "as restoring idealized eras of earlier Islamic history in a way that resonates with many of the region's Muslims." It has deftly used global social media to highlight historical Muslim grievances related to Western colonization and the delineation of artificial borders to create "independent" states in Muslim regions. According to one dispatch, "ISIS media frames its campaign in epochal terms, mounting a frontal assault on the national divisions and boundaries in the Middle East drawn by Western powers after World War I. These 'Crusader partitions' and their modern Arab leaders, ISIS argues in its English-language magazine, were a divide-and-conquer strategy intended to prevent Muslims from unifying 'under one imam carrying the banner of truth.'"[30]

Table 8.1 Support and allegiance pledged to ISIS

Country	*Support*	*Allegiance*
Afghanistan		al-Tawheed Brigade in Khorasan, 23 Sep 2014 Heroes of Islam Brigade in Khorasan, 30 Sep 2014
Algeria		al-Huda Battalion in Maghreb of Islam, 30 Jun 2014 The Soldiers of the Caliphate in Algeria, 30 Sep 2014 al-Ghurabaa, 7 Jul 2015 Djamaat Houmat ad-Da'wa as-Salafiya, 19 Sep 2015 al-Ansar Battalion, 4 Sep 2015
Egypt	Mujahideen Shura Council in the Environs of Jerusalem, 1 Oct 2014	Jamaat Ansar Bait al-Maqdis, 30 Jun 2014 Jund al-Khilafah in Egypt, 23 Sep 2014
India		Ansar al-Tawhid in India, 4 Oct 2014
Indonesia		Jemaah Anshorut Tauhid, Aug 2014 Mujahideen Indonesia Timor, 1 Jul 2014
Iraq		Ansar al-Islam, 8 Jan 2015
Lebanon		Liwa Ahrar al-Sunna in Baalbek, 30 Jun 2014
Libya*	Islamic Youth Shura Council, 22 Jun 2014	Islamic State Libya (Darnah), 9 Nov 2014 Lions of Libya (unconfirmed), 24 Sep 2014 Shura Council of Shabab al-Islam Darnah, 6 Oct 2014
Nigeria		Boko Haram, 7 Mar 2015
Pakistan	Jundullah, 17 Nov 2014	Tehreek-e-Khilafat, 9 Jul 2014 Leaders of the Mujahid in Khorasan (ten former TTP commanders), 10 Jan 2015
Pakistan/ Uzbekistan		Islamic Movement of Uzbekistan (video), 31 Jul 2015
Philippines	Abu Sayyaf Group, 25 June 2014 Bangsamoro Islamic Freedom Fighters, 13 Aug 2014 Bangsamoro Justice Movement, 11 Sep 2014	Ansar al-Khilafah, 14 Aug 2014 Jemaah Islamiyah, 27 Apr 2015

Table 8.1 Support and allegiance pledged to ISIS (*Continued*)

Country	*Support*	*Allegiance*
Russia		Central Sector of Kabardino-Balakria of the Caucasus Emirate, 26 April 2015 The Nokhchico Wilayat of the Caucasus Emirate, 15 Jun 2015
Saudi Arabia	Supporters of the Islamic State in the Land of the Two Holy Mosques, 2 Dec 2014	
Somalia		al-Shabaab Jubba Region Cell Bashir Abu Numan, 7 Dec 2015
Sudan	al-I'tisam of the Koran and Sunnah, 1 Aug 2014	
Syria		Jaish al-Sahabah in the Levant, 1 Jul 2014 Faction of Katibat al-Imam Bukhari, 29 Oct 2014 Martyrs of al-Yarmouk Brigade (part of IS), Dec 2014
Tunisia	Okba Ibn Nafaa Battalion, 20 Sep 2014	Jund al-Khilafah in Tunisia, 31 Mar 2015 Mujahideen of Tunisia of Kairouan, 18 May 2015
Yemen		Mujahideen of Yemen, 10 Nov 2014 Supporters for the Islamic State in Yemen, 4 Sep 2014

* The support or allegiance of the Lions of Libya, 24 September 2014, is unconfirmed.

Source: IntelCenter, "Islamic State's Global Affiliates."

ISIS has perfected many ways to accomplish its cyber strategy. First, it used cyber-propaganda campaigns to globalize its grievances and to push for the overthrow of the "near enemies" of Islam – existing governments in all Muslim states. Second, it carefully tailored "its recruiting pitch, sending starkly different messages to Muslims in the West and to those closer to home. But the image of unstoppable, implacable power animates all of its messaging."[31] Third, it publicized the brutal killings of its "enemies," including Western journalists and others who were unfortunate enough to be caught, as well as religious minorities like the Yazidis and the Shias. Posting the horrid decapitations of these individuals on global media was clearly aimed at creating terror in neighbouring states and throughout the West. Fourth – and a crucial trait – it drew heavily on native English speakers from the United

States, the UK, and Australia to promote its message. One of its star jihadists was the US-born Anwar al-Awlaki, who frequently recorded his messages in colloquial English and posted them on YouTube, where they were viewed by millions. Al-Awlaki also had a Facebook page for propaganda purposes, and he "helped produce a full-color, English-language magazine called *Inspire*."[32] Even though he was killed as a result of a drone attack (under a highly controversial law known as Authorization to Use Military Force) in 2011 before ISIS came into existence, using native English speakers remained a compelling part of ISIS's cyberwar strategy.[33] To this feature, ISIS added the use of "disseminators" to propagate its jihadist campaign. These are "unaffiliated but broadly sympathetic individuals who sometimes appear to offer moral and intellectual support to jihadist opposition groups."[34] Commenting on the import of disseminators, Peter Neumann, director of the International Centre for the Study of Radicalisation, said, "The thing about the disseminators is they are not necessarily people in Iraq or Syria, they might be based in London or the north of England and have appointed themselves as an official spokesman of Isis. The really novel thing about this conflict is the role of social media, the recruitment of foreign fighters."[35] Their messages are virtually impossible to control by intelligence agencies; disseminators spring up on their own, entirely self-motivated to "serve" ISIS's jihadist objectives. The fifth feature of ISIS's global cyber strategy was to provide considerable publicity to the mass murder attacks carried out by independent or semi-independent operators, as in the case of the 2015 attacks in Paris, France. The lone-wolf assassination, carried out in San Bernardino, California, by a married couple of Pakistani origin, also falls into this category. Both of these attacks were part of ISIS's campaign against the "far enemy." The scariest part of these types of attacks is the potential for catching Western law enforcement off guard, no matter how vigilant it may be.

It is a tribute to the overwhelming power of the information age, not to ISIS, that its cyber strategy could not be countered effectively by the United States, whose mastery of information warfare is legendary. As young jihadists from all over the world started to respond to ISIS's call for jihad, the United States, along with a number of its Western allies, found themselves facing an increasingly uphill battle in their attempts to discourage them. Even when ISIS's social media accounts were blocked by Western governments, "new ones appear[ed] immediately."[36]

The United States was also losing the massive "tweet war" against ISIS. The US Department of State's Center for Strategic Communication, which has had a great deal of experience conducting a Twitter campaign against al-Qaida, turned its attention to counter-messaging tweets from ISIS members and from sympathizers all over the globe. A senior member of the center admitted that "because the group's [ISIS's] social media messaging contains an 'element of truth,' it is hard to combat its online campaign."[37] As one journalist observed,

> A core component of ISIS' social media messaging is that tens of thousands of innocent people have been suffering and dying in Syria at the hands of Syrian leader Bashar al-Assad, that ISIS is a powerful counter-force opposing the Assad regime, and that it has racked up multiple successes in this endeavor, such as the radical group's capture of a major Syrian military air base in August. These assertions have the benefit of being accurate. That makes it harder for the State Department to push a different narrative about ISIS and reach people who may be on the fence about joining its cause.[38]

However, jihadists have at least two reasons to be wary, if not pessimistic. First was the United States' determination to establish a coalition of Western and Muslim nations to counter ISIS, not only on the battlefields of Iraq and Syria but also in cyberspace. Second was the likelihood of a growing "war" between ISIS and al-Qaida, especially since the former continued to widen its presence in territories that were regarded by the latter as part of its erstwhile stronghold. An examination of these two issues follows.

As part of countering ISIS in Iraq and Syria, in January 2016 the United States and France hosted a joint meeting of seven Western countries (including Australia, Germany, Great Britain, Italy, and the Netherlands) that were most heavily involved in fighting that entity. The meeting explored ways to target ISIS more aggressively. The second phase of that conference was to invite twenty-six other nations "involved in the military side of the campaign against the Islamic State, along with Iraq to meet … and detail how they may be able to offer more resources." As a supplement to these diplomatic activities, the Obama administration intensified use of its "elite expeditionary targeting force" to include up to 200 Special Operation troops in Iraq. France also deployed 3,500 troops to "the frontlines of the battle."[39] The military component of the US cyber strategy entailed "commissioning more aggressive attacks" on ISIS in Iraq and Syria to erode "the group's abilities to use social media and the Internet to recruit fighters and inspire followers."

In February 2016, the US Cyber Command (established in 2009) "ramp[ed] up the fight against ISIS on the cyber front." Its focus was to disrupt ISIS's online activities "to prevent the group from distributing propaganda, videos, or other types of recruiting and messaging on social media sites such as Twitter, and across the Internet in general."[40] The Pentagon's focus on cyberspace sabotage was expected to seriously damage the offensive capabilities of ISIS's electronic and computer experts.[41] However, it was not determined how the cyber strategy would impede the technical, web-related capabilities of the terrorists or prevent them from "going dark" by encrypting their messages. ISIS's two-part strategy was simple: "Connect from afar, then plot in private." Following is an example of how it works:

> An Islamic State jihadist schemes a plot from inside captured territory in Syria or Iraq. Using public social media networks, he finds possible partners in Europe or the Americas. Then they move into direct person-to-person chatting apps that encrypt conversations. WhatsApp and Telegram encrypt text. Signal encrypts phone calls. Wickr sends self-destructing messages. FaceTime, the video chatting app for iPhone, is encrypted too. For email, there's a tool called PGP. The popular, legal options are numerous. All of these programs turn words into jumbled computer code. Government spies can't break that code fast enough.[42]

The actual success (or lack thereof) of US cyberwar endeavours is likely to emerge in a year or so. In the meantime, both sides – ISIS and the United States – will continue to add more sophistication to their respective countermeasures to win.

In the aftermath of the murderous November 2015 attacks in Paris, the cyber-revenge group, Anonymous, declared its own war on ISIS. The seriousness that ISIS attached to that threat was evident when, according to one post on the Internet, ISIS warned its members to take the following precautionary measures:[43]

- beware of links from unusual senders
- constantly change IP addresses

- do not accept messages from unknown users on Telegram
- avoid Twitter direct messages
- use different usernames for emails and social media

No one really knows who is behind this group. It could be a Europe-based group with a tacit wink and nod, if not support, from its government, or a US-based group with links to one or more of its secret government agencies. However, the principle of having more than one group conducting cyberwarfare against the ostensibly invincible cyber capabilities of ISIS will likely bring about its downfall.

The second reason for pessimism among jihadists is the likelihood of a "war" between al-Qaida and ISIS. Al-Qaida witnessed its heyday after its attacks on the US homeland on 11 September 2001. However, thanks to the United States' decision to invade Afghanistan and dismantle al-Qaida, it would never be whole again. Its leadership was killed off one by one. Its top two leaders became fugitives, and one of them, Bin Laden, was killed by US Special Forces in 2011. His successor, Ayman al-Zawahiri, is hiding somewhere in the Pakistan-Afghanistan area. The Arab Awakening and its astounding success in ousting three of the longest-reigning tyrants of the Arab world – in Tunisia, Egypt, and Libya – further marginalized al-Qaida.

The conflict between al-Qaida and AQI has been ongoing since the US forces occupied Iraq, when AQI's Musab al-Zarqawi ignored al-Zawahiri's advice to stop killing Sunni Muslims and butchering Iraqi Shias. al-Zarqawi regarded his operational experience against the US forces in Iraq and his leadership of jihad in that country as abundantly superior to the advice of "armchair jihadis" like Bin Laden and al-Zawahiri. Besides, his commitment to the Takfiri doctrine was more unalloyed and uncompromising than that of his al-Qaida counterparts (chapter 3). These differences continued to prevail long after the death of al-Zarqawi. When ISIS became economically independent from al-Qaida, "largely through revenue from commandeered oil fields, border tolls, extortion and granary sales," it became fully capable of thriving on its own "without links to Qaeda leaders in Pakistan."[44] The seething rift between al-Qaida and ISIS was dramatized when al-Qaida's General Command announced in February 2014 that ISIS "is not a branch of the al-Qaeda group ... does not have an organizational relationship with it and [al-Qaida] is not the group responsible for their actions."[45] That announcement further marginalized al-Qaida's already ebbed status in the jihadist community. Jabhat al-Nusra became its affiliate in Syria and a nemesis to ISIS.

The capture of territory in Iraq and Syria catapulted ISIS onto the world stage. Its next step – which it carried out skillfully – was to start its own franchises throughout the world of Islam. That included Muslim Indonesia and Malaysia, and even countries with Muslim minorities like the Philippines and Thailand. Of course, challenging al-Qaida in its strongholds like Pakistan and Afghanistan was pretty much a declaration of "war" (if not an intra-jihadist jihad). ISIS jihadists also targeted the North African countries of Libya and Egypt in their persistent effort to marginalize al-Qaida. This intra-jihadist jihad between ISIS and al-Qaida was also a war between two leaders: Abu Bakr al-Baghdadi and Ayman al-Zawahiri, both of whom belonged to a different generation of jihadists. Both were lifelong jihadists, but the former grew up confronting US forces in Iraq and was arrested by the US military and imprisoned in Camp Buca, Iraq.

There are no precise reasons available for al-Baghdadi's arrest, nor are there any authentic reports of his behaviour while in that prison. However, commentators have speculated that he was radicalized during his incarceration.[46] Al-Baghdadi's entire post-incarceration career has been spent on the battlefields of Iraq and Syria. And the fact that he has a doctorate in Islamic Studies from the Islamic University of Baghdad gave him solid religious credentials to argue issues of theology with al-Zawahiri.

Ayman al-Zawahiri, an eye surgeon by profession, also grew up in a highly tumultuous politico-religious environment – that of Egypt in the 1950s and 1960s. He developed a jihadist outlook by studying the writings of a fellow Egyptian and one of the doyens on that subject in the Arab world, Sayyid Qutb. His youth was spent fighting the security forces of Egypt and in the company of various jihadists who also wanted to overthrow the Egyptian government. He moved on to Saudi Arabia and then to the Pakistan-Afghanistan area at a highly opportune time, when the US-sponsored jihad was very much in progress. Al-Zawahiri met Bin Laden in 1986 and eventually emerged as his deputy of the then newly formed terrorist group, al-Qaida.[47]

After the US invasion of Afghanistan in November 2001, both al-Zawahiri and Bin Laden escaped to Pakistan via Tora Bora. Al-Zawahiri not only eluded the intense search by the United States but also outlived Bin Laden and became the head of al-Qaida after Bin Laden's death in 2011. But the fact that al-Zawahiri was hiding somewhere in the remote reaches of the Pakistan-Afghanistan border, while the then al-Zarqawi-led AQIP fought the US forces from 2004 to 2009, stole the jihadist limelight from al-Zawahiri. The resurgence and transformation of AQI into ISIS/ISIL/IS, and the eventual declaration of a caliphate by Abu Bakr al-Baghdadi in 2014, made al-Zarqawi a jihadist superstar in global jihadist circles. As an entity that institutionalized the Takfiri/jihadist ideology of al-Zarqawi, ISIS and its leader, al-Baghdadi, found al-Zawahiri's admonitions for moderation impertinent and irrelevant.

By and large, the conflict between these two jihadist entities is about seeking supremacy and expanding their respective influence in different regions of the world through acquisition of affiliates. The conflict between al-Zawahiri and Abu Bakr al-Baghdadi is also about which operational and expansionary perspective of jihad has a future. Judging from the way ISIS is expanding in Asia, Africa, and the Middle East, and the way its lone-wolf attacks have escalated fear in the streets of Europe and even in the United States, the "war" between these two terrorist entities is not likely to be over any time soon. One possible scenario for a truce between them could come if either or both leaders were eliminated or captured, with a resultant downward slide in the expansionist pace of ISIS. The way things are in the middle of 2016, ISIS's expansion is very much on the rise. Its presence in Libya is mounting with such speed that President Obama departed from his much-ballyhooed reluctance to take on another military action against Libya and, in February 2016, ordered the bombing of ISIS strongholds in the western part of that country.[48]

The Unembellished Face of Conflict between Global Jihadists and the United States: Islamism versus Secular Fundamentalism

The ultimate challenge for jihadist forces is the primacy of the United States, whose presence in the Muslim regions and support of pro-American regimes is considered a threat to Islam. Thus, the jihadists aspire to oust those "un-Islamic" regimes, and they consider themselves to be promoters of Islamic government. The establishment of the caliphate is the ultimate objective of their fight with the United States. As discussed in chapter 1, the United States is the promoter, par excellence, of liberal democracy and secular fundamentalism, an ideology that envisions Islam as "dangerous and volatile because it mixes religion and politics."[49] From the jihadist perspective, therefore, the conduct of jihad against the United States and the West is better understood as a cosmic, religious war. The battle is "not between armies or nations but between the angels of light and the demons of darkness ... a conflict in which God is believed to be directly engaged on behalf of one side over the other."[50] And jihadists believe that God is on their side. Their struggle has "the imprimatur of the divine; hence the outcome of their fight is preordained: Islam in its pristine purity will prevail."[51] Their Takfiri outlook allows no compromise with anyone, much less with the ultimate enemy, the United States – the mega-crusader hell-bent on defeating them and changing the face of their religion to make it look more like Christianity. Such a depiction of the United States makes jihad obligatory, crucial, and urgent; it is a must-win battle. This is their struggle to sustain and promote the glory of Islam. Fighting to the death is not only a requirement but also the epitome of saving one's soul and going to heaven.

Secular fundamentalism similarly glorifies war in the name of nationalism, secularism, and democracy. According to Mark Juergensmeyer, many American politicians and commentators have elevated the war on terrorism "above the mundane – 'like all images of cosmic war, all-encompassing, absolutizing and dehumanizing.'"[52] *Most important, since secular fundamentalism is based on the belief that religion causes violence, this ideology may blind the United States (and the West) to its form of fanaticism.* Heroes are given medals of honour; their statutes are erected in public places; ships and aircraft carriers are named after them. These are secular embodiments of glorifying the nation by sacrificing lives. While there is no doubt that the jihadist lexicon does not include the words *compromise*, *cooperation*, or *consensus-building*, the question remains whether the priests of secular fundamentalism have any inclination to question their own beliefs or to moderate their views of the jihadists in order to reach a compromise with those who envision a compromise as "un-Islamic." If this struggle between them is indeed a religious as well as a secular version of cosmic war, then the solution is the complete obliteration of the other side.

Keeping this brief discussion in mind, no war between the United States and the jihadists has ended in the declaration of a truce. The March 2016 ceasefire (truce) being observed in the Syrian theatre of operation had no participation by, or endorsement from, any jihadist group. It was a negotiated ceasefire among the United States, its allies, and Russia, Iran, and Syria. Similarly, the jihadist groups being targeted by American drone attacks in Iraq, Syria, and Yemen, and in North, West, and East Africa have given no indication that they were either leaning toward a negotiated end to their respective conflicts or, more to the point, expected any of these conflicts to end in the foreseeable future.

Only Afghanistan emerged as a place where the United States was pushing the government of President Ashraf Ghani to negotiate a peace deal with the Taliban, and was persuading Pakistan to facilitate those negotiations. The Ghani administration was ready and willing. Even Pakistan was prepared to play a positive role, as long as the outcome of the negotiations would not lead to the lessening of its influence in Afghanistan or to the escalation of India's presence and influence in that country. However, the Taliban had shown a mix of episodic willingness and unwillingness to pursue a dialogue for a peaceful resolution of that conflict. Most likely, the Taliban had concluded that the ultimate victory belonged to them. They knew how corrupt and inept the government headed by Ashraf Ghani really was. Besides, every time the Taliban forces confronted the Afghan Army, the latter's ability to repulse the Taliban attack had been unimpressive. More importantly, the Taliban knew that the US military was not likely to remain in their country for long. Even if it were to remain there, its role would likely be limited for fear of absorbing high casualties. So, the best strategy for the Taliban was to outwait the United States' presence in their country and, in the interim, to keep chipping away at the government forces. It would be the height of naïveté on the part of President Obama's successor to believe that the Taliban would allow a pro-US government to remain in their country in any way, shape, or form.

By the same token, the way the civil war was continuing in Yemen, the only discernible outcome seemed to be the defeat of the Saudi forces therein. Those forces came from a country whose dollar reserves were fast depleting because of the continuing depressed global oil prices and the huge expense of financing the Yemeni and Syrian wars. More to the point, the Saudi forces had never been known for their fighting excellence or proficiency. The Saudi monarchy had been utterly spoiled by decades-long American security guarantees that the United States would come to its rescue by emulating the 1991 Gulf War, as long as the Saudi kingdom was willing to foot the bill and allow the stationing of US forces inside the birthplace of

Islam. Unfortunately, from the Saudi vantage point, the chance of similar American intervention in the future were slim, unless Saudi Arabia experienced massive internal turbulence. Even then, American intervening forces would be walking on eggshells in attempting to differentiate the "good" Saudis from the "bad" ones. Besides, a potential outbreak of domestic rebellion also would mean the abrogation of the pact of 1744 between the Saudi government and Muhammad ibn 'Abd al-Wahhāb. The very legitimacy of the Saudi kingdom rests on that pact. Any conflict resulting in its abrogation could not be resolved in a short time span. Consequently, any long-term stationing of US troops in Saudi Arabia would guarantee an unprecedented series of jihadist attacks on those forces.

But what about the almost inexorable future decision of Saudi Arabia to withdraw its forces from the escalating violence of the Yemeni civil war, which was being fuelled by a mix of sectarian and jihadist hatred? Again, the US response would likely be a continued reliance on its drone attacks, which would provide no prospect of ending that civil war, but would create a semblance of "doing something" in the form of periodically killing one or more so-called high-value jihadist leaders. That is precisely what the Obama administration has been doing since 2009. Rightly concluding that the deteriorating conflict in Yemen may be even more difficult to resolve than the one in Afghanistan, the United States most likely will stay out of it and insist that the conflict be resolved by Muslim countries.[53]

As if the preceding description of the escalation of regional jihad is not foreboding enough, the situation in Africa looks even more desperate and chilling. This is a region that was aptly labelled by the *Economist* as "Jhafrica."[54] Even Sudan's eminent Islamist, Dr Hassan al-Turabi, whose claim to fame was that he invited Osama Bin Laden to his country in 1992, expressed alarm about "the rise of militant Islam in Africa" just a few days prior to his death on 5 March 2016.[55]

President Obama's decision to bomb ISIS forces in western Libya in February 2016 might have signalled the intensification of militarism on a front where the US and Western forces were already fighting the jihadists. One must keep in mind that termination of the Qaddafi regime in Libya on 20 October 2011 and the degeneration of post-Qaddafi Libya into a near-failed stated demonstrated how the good intentions of the NATO forces could turn sour. However, the US bombing of ISIS in Libya in 2016 is likely to intensify the ongoing military conflict between the Egyptian Army and the Ansar Bait al-Maqdis. The fledgling secular democracy of Tunisia is most likely to fall as a result, and Algeria and Morocco are likely to be the other two "falling dominos" of North Africa.[56] The serious deterioration of Africa in the jihadist quicksand was fittingly highlighted by a South African specialist on radical Islam, Hussain Soloman:

> To compound matters further still, Islamic State and Al Qaeda are both vying for influence and recruits on the African continent. Islamic State has sleeper cells in Mauritania, Morocco and Sudan whilst it has armed groups in a further seven countries. These include Egypt, Libya, Algeria, Tunisia, Nigeria, Mali and Niger. Meanwhile Al Qaeda is active in Somalia, Algeria, Mali, Niger, Mauritania and Libya. In their bloody competition, each terrorist group seeks to outdo the other in acts of barbarity to serve as a magnet to more recruits and to emphasize their potency and relevance.[57]

Given these deteriorating conditions in the Middle East, South Asia, and Africa, America's top secular fundamentalists, as much as they may not want to, will be forced to seek alternatives to lower the infernos of the jihadist wars, even more so because US policies of the past decade have failed to bring stability to the region. For example, President George W. Bush, after menacingly declaring in 2001 that "either you are with us or you are with the terrorists," set out to reshape the lands of Islam in the Middle East in the image of American pluralistic democracy. In other words, he wanted to remake the jihadist "irrational other," as depicted by Roxanne Euben (chapter 1) into the image of American rational secular fundamentalists.[58] However, when the first democratic elections of 2005 brought Islamists to the Iraqi parliament – turning Iraq into a Shia-dominated Islamist democracy – Bush had serious second thoughts about his resolve to reshape the Arab autocrat-governed world into American-style democracy. The Islamist democratic Iraq also became a friend of Iran (or least came under Iran's visible influence). When the Sunni Arab states witnessed the dismantlement of the Sunni Taliban government in Afghanistan and the ouster of Saddam Hussein's Sunni regime in Iraq, which escalated Iran's influence in the region, they started transmitting their alarm to Washington. King Abdullah of Jordan declared that a "Shia crescent ... went from Damascus to Tehran, passing through Baghdad, where a Shia-dominated government had taken power and was dictating a sectarian brand of politics that was radiating outwards from Iraq across the whole region," a statement that grabbed Bush's attention.[59] Besides, the secular fundamentalism of George W. Bush was already markedly chastened by the beating that the US forces took from AQIP, pro-Iran militias, and simply irate Ba'athist Iraqi insurgents. Bush's secular fundamentalism was forced to eat a large portion of "humble pie."

Consequently, there were no more deployments of ground troops to invade and occupy any Muslim country. Bush's successor, President Barack Obama, quickly decided to withdraw American troops from Iraq. Even when Obama agreed to increase the size of US forces in Afghanistan upon the recommendation of the then commander of US forces, General Stanley McChrystal, he also set a date for the potential withdrawal of troops from Afghanistan.[60] Obama's signature approach to GWOT was to increase the pace of drone attacks in various Muslim countries fighting the regional or global jihadists. In response to the upward spiralling of ISIS-sponsored wars in Iraq and Syria, Obama decided to use America's mighty air force. Thus, jihadist warfare brought about a remarkable mutation in America's GWOT: an escalated "drone war," no more massive deployment of ground troops, the use of Special Forces for limited expeditionary operations wherever required, and the use of the Air Force.

Another mutation in Obama's GWOT was that the United States and its Western allies increasingly started to advocate for the involvement of military forces (preferably ground troops) from Muslim countries to fight ISIS. Saudi Arabia established the precedent of becoming a belligerent in the ongoing civil war in Yemen. Four other Arab members – Bahrain, Morocco, Qatar, and the UAE – were part of the Saudi-led coalition, while Somalia agreed to provide its air space to the jets from Saudi Arabia and its partners in that war. The United States established another precedent by providing intelligence as well as search and rescue facilities for downed Saudi pilots. US and UK military personnel were deployed to the Saudi Command and Control Center to support Saudi air strikes in Yemen. In addition to fighting the civil war in Yemen, Saudi Arabia surprised a number of Muslim countries by issuing a list of participating countries without first acquiring their permission. No wonder that the list was referred to in some circles as a "coalition of the surprised" to fight terrorism in Afghanistan, Egypt, Syria, and Iraq.[61] As unimpressive and uninvolved as that coalition was in 2016, at least it pointed to the beginning of an era when Muslim/Arab countries would be more inclined to commit their own forces to fight the jihadists rather than relying heavily (or solely) on the United States, the United Kingdom, or any other Western country.

Despite these mutations, the most immutable aspect of America's GWOT was that it relied primarily on the use of its military, even after knowing that that apparatus had miserably failed to show any promising results in democratizing even one Muslim country. The US Department of State's Office of Public Diplomacy and Public Affairs has been known for its clumsy and simplistic campaign to "win the hearts and minds of Muslims," which is not going anywhere. No one seems to realize that the chief problem is with American secular fundamentalism, which requires wholesale changes in America's view of Islam. Historically, the United States has carried out hegemonic policies that were clearly immoral, even if some gobbledygook argument was proffered to allege that they were not in violation of international law. For instance, America participated in an illegal regime change in Iran in 1953 to bring to power a sycophant ruler who was willing to serve as a lapdog for Anglo-American hegemony; the United States, as a manifestation of its unbridled hostility toward the Islamic Republic of Iran, remained fixated on bringing about illegal regime change in that country; America invaded Iraq in 2003, based on cherry-picking intelligence, to deprive the Iraqi dictator of nuclear weapons that he never possessed to begin with; and America manufactured another farcical justification that Saddam's ouster would not only democratize Iraq, but also become the harbinger of a democratic Middle East. An unstable Iraq, with the powerful presence of ISIS and al-Qaida, is reprehensible evidence of the recent failure of America's foreign policy, whose chief motivating force may just be its secular fundamentalism.

Having asked themselves why Muslims hate America, the secular fundamentalist priests of American democracy started parroting a contrived answer: "because they hate our value system and our way of life." The real answer was proffered in a study done by the Pentagon in 2004:

> American direct intervention in the Muslim World has paradoxically elevated the stature of and support for radical Islamists, while diminishing support for the United States to single-digits in some Arab societies.

- Muslims do not "hate our freedom," but rather, they hate our policies. The overwhelming majority voice their objections to what they see as one-sided support in favor of Israel and against Palestinian rights, and the longstanding, even increasing support for what Muslims collectively see as tyrannies, most notably Egypt, Saudi Arabia, Jordan, Pakistan, and the Gulf states.
- Thus when American public diplomacy talks about bringing democracy to Islamic societies, this is seen as no more than self-serving hypocrisy. Moreover, saying that "freedom is the future of the Middle East" is seen as patronizing, suggesting that Arabs are like the enslaved peoples of the old Communist World – but Muslims do not feel this way: they feel oppressed, but not enslaved.
- Furthermore, *in the eyes of Muslims*, American occupation of Afghanistan and Iraq has not led to democracy there, but only more chaos and suffering. U.S. actions appear in contrast to be motivated by ulterior motives, and deliberately controlled in order to best serve American national interests at the expense of truly Muslim self-determination.
- Therefore, the dramatic narrative since 9/11 has essentially borne out the entire radical Islamist bill of particulars. American actions and the flow of events have elevated the authority of the Jihadi insurgents and tended to ratify their legitimacy among Muslims. Fighting groups portray themselves as the true defenders of an Ummah (the entire Muslim community) invaded and under attack – to broad public support.
- What was a marginal network is now an Ummah-wide movement of fighting groups. Not only has there been a proliferation of "terrorist" groups: the unifying context of a shared cause creates a sense of affiliation across the many cultural and sectarian boundaries that divide Islam.
- Finally, Muslims see Americans as strangely narcissistic – namely, that the war is all about us. As the Muslims see it, everything about the war is – for Americans – really no more than an extension of American domestic politics and its great game. This perception is of course necessarily heightened by election-year atmospherics, but nonetheless sustains their impression that when Americans talk to Muslims they are really just talking to themselves.

> … Thus the critical problem in American public diplomacy directed toward the Muslim World is not one of "dissemination of information," or even one of crafting and delivering the "right" message. *Rather, it is a fundamental problem of credibility. Simply, there is none – the United States today is without a working channel of communication to the world of Muslims and of Islam* [emphasis added]. Inevitably therefore, whatever Americans do and say only serves the party that has both the message and the "loud and clear" channel: the enemy.[62]

The serious lack of credibility highlighted in this report *still very much persists*. The official community of Washington has either neglected or refused to take remedial action, even though America is struggling to create a counternarrative to ISIS, which has a more sophisticated strategy to propagate its own perspective in the world of Islam.

Despite a rare moment of truth in the aforementioned report – that anti-American feelings in the Muslim world have a direct relationship to America's policies toward Muslim countries – the United States' campaign to "win the hearts and minds of Muslims" continues to envisage Arab and Muslim grievances with the United States as purely a Muslim problem. The US administration appears to believe that these grievances have no relationship to what America has been doing in the Middle East and the Muslim world since its ascendance as a superpower.

Thus, the Bush administration's "hearts and minds" campaign and the Obama administration's campaign to find a counternarrative to ISIS have remained fixated on finding a Hollywood version of a "solution" that would counter the glossy simplicity of ISIS propaganda with equally glossy and simplistic American propaganda. As recently as February 2016, US secretary of state John Kerry made a trip to Hollywood asking its image-makers "to take a more active role in the propaganda battle against Daesh [another name for ISIS]."[63] Writing about how futile Kerry's endeavour was likely to be, Jake Anderson of *Anti-Media* noted that Kerry's meeting with Hollywood media experts "had more in common with past Hollywood-fueled propaganda than Kerry might like to admit." He added, "One might think the government would try to conceal such blatant efforts to influence public opinion on matters related to the military-industrial complex; instead, Kerry takes to social media to flaunt the federal government's symbiotic working relationship with Hollywood." A former CIA deputy director, Michael Morell, was exactly right in casting doubts on Kerry's efforts, when he said, "The reason the United States can't be the brand behind the counter-narrative is because we have no credibility when we're talking about Islam."[64] No one seems willing to recognize that ISIS propaganda contains elements of truth that must be countered with truth, not with Hollywood gloss.

THE UNITED STATES AND THE ISLAMIC REPUBLIC: IS THE IRANIAN VERSION OF THE ISLAMIST CHALLENGE RESOLVABLE?

The Shia Islamism of Iran is markedly different from its Sunni counterpart in that, after bringing about regime change in Iran, it was not exported to any other country. The Islamic Republic, at times, threatened to export its revolution to Persian Gulf regimes, but those threats were hollow for one very important reason: the Islamic revolution of Iran was potentially implementable only in other Shia-dominated states like Iraq. That might have been one reason that Saddam Hussein decided to trigger a war with Iran in 1980. Even after the ouster of the Saddam regime in 2003, however, Iran did not seriously consider implanting the Iranian model – the *vilayat-e-faqih* (rule of the clergy) – mainly because Iraq's grand ayatollah, Sayed Ali al-Sistani, even though Persian by birth and ethnicity, opposed it. He was a practitioner of the "quietist" role for clerics in affairs of the state. Iran did export its Islamism to the Shias of Lebanon, which had the intended or inadvertent effect of heightening their political activism and militancy, which in turn led to improvements in their social and economic lot. Since Lebanon is a multiconfessional country, the implantation of the *vilayat-e-faqih* model of government was not conceivable.

In the early to mid-1980s, Shia Islamism was used by Iran against the United States and Israel through the use of Hezbollah, a creation of Iran (chapter 6). Shia Islamism also heightened and even emboldened the political activism of the Shias of Saudi Arabia and Bahrain. However, it posed no threat to Saudi stability, despite the Saudi paranoiac spins to the contrary. The 2011 Shia uprising against the Sunni autocracy in Bahrain was brutally crushed by Saudi Arabia, while the Obama administration issued only a muted protest of that outrageous act.

However, Iranian Islamism was highly resolute and successful in mounting that country's political influence and presence in post-Saddam Iraq. Iran's militias also played a highly tangible role in expediting the departure of US forces from Iraq, since it was apprehensive that Bush might use those forces to bring about regime change in Iran.

After withdrawal of US forces from Iraq, Iran had only one serious obstacle left in the unrelenting pursuit of its emergence as a major regional power: the resolution of conflict with the United States over its nuclear research program. That program was the subject of intense conflict negotiations between 2002 and 2015.[65] The United States, along with Israel, never believed that Iran had no intention of using that program to develop nuclear weapons. Therefore, it kept assiduously imposing a variety of economic sanctions to break Iran's will to continue its program. It was the effectiveness of those sanction regimes – in which Russia, China, and the EU sided with the United States – that swayed Iran to bring about a drastic reduction in the scope and pace of that program without totally terminating it (a demand that Israel volubly advocated). The signing of the US-Iran nuclear deal, the Joint Comprehensive Plan of Action, in July 2015 opened a new era of economic prosperity for Iran. It was determined to utilize the lifting of those economic sanctions to gain full access to Western technology to rebuild its oil and gas sectors and its civil-industrial technological base.

The most promising feature of Iranian Islamism is its flexible and pragmatic approach to raising its strategic profile in the world. Despite the frequent insistence of its supreme leader, Ali Khamenei, that "hostility between the Islamic republic and the 'arrogant' United States will not abate after a landmark nuclear agreement and that Iran will keep supporting regional groups and governments that the West opposes,"[66] Iran continued to cooperate with the US in the Iraqi theatre of operation. Both countries pursued the same objective: defeating ISIS. However, they were on opposing sides of the war in Syria. Iran's forces were fighting ISIS to sustain the Assad regime, while the US/Saudi-backed Islamists were principally in the fray to oust al-Assad and (secondarily) to defeat ISIS's caliphate. Iran's decision to quickly release ten US sailors who were captured when their boats, for some unexplained reason, "deviated" from international waters into Iranian territorial waters, was clearly a sign of the warming of US-Iran ties. The timing of that capture was particularly delicate from Iran's vantage point, since the United States and Iran were "negotiating a [separate] prisoner swap" and the government of Iran "was also taking its last measures to comply with the nuclear deal, which allowed economic sanctions against the country to be lifted."[67]

What favoured Iran in Syria was the Obama administration's assertion that it was "not seeking so-called regime change … in Syria." Instead, the United States' top priority was to reach a "cease-fire and humanitarian access."[68] The United States knew that there was no realistic alternative to the Assad regime. Obama did not want the post-Assad Syria to become another jihadist-infested failed state à la post-Qaddafi Libya.

Regarding the much publicized Iran-Saudi sectarianism-driven strategic rivalry, the United States was not a player. While the theological basis of the Saudi-Iranian rivalry may not be resolvable, its strategic aspects certainly are, and the United States has an important prospective role in facilitating a future rapprochement between them.

In that Saudi-Iranian rivalry, Iran definitely had the upper-hand in Iraq and Syria in 2016. Even in Yemen, if Iran remained only tangentially involved while Saudi Arabia steadily sinks, Iran would have very little to lose. Iran knew that whoever had the upper hand in that civil war would also be faced with the unenviable challenge of investing enormous amounts of capital to build the poorest country in the Arab world. Yemen was the Afghanistan of the Arabian Peninsula – another "black hole" where billions of dollars disappeared without showing any improved economic development and political stability; Iran did not want to become a cash cow to build Yemen's political stability, which, as in the case of Afghanistan, appeared a chimera.[69]

Aside from the bitter historical legacy of US support for Reza Shah's highly corrupt regime, for which the Islamic Republic had loathed America, the United States and Iran may be able to find a basis of cooperation in the coming years. As mentioned, the Iran-US nuclear deal has opened up avenues of cooperation. The United States' long-standing and intermittent accusation regarding Iran's alleged support and sponsorship of terrorism is a subject that may be resolved, as long as both sides continue to cooperate in the post-nuclear-deal era. Similarly, Iran's military support of Hamas is potentially resolvable. But Iran's support of Hezbollah is not resolvable, at least in the near future, because it is tied to Iran's larger strategic interest of sustaining its presence and sphere of influence in the Levant. Still, considering the mounting ominousness of the global jihadists' threat to peace and stability in the Middle East, the highly pragmatic Iranian Shia Islamism and the secular fundamentalism of the United States may be able to find a basis for rapprochement.

Unlike the Sunni jihadist Islamism of al-Qaida and ISIS and their respective affiliates – which is primarily driven by their ferocious and unyielding commitment to Salafism, Takfirism, and caliphate-centrism – Iranian Islamism came into existence as a nationalistic, militant response to that country's bitter historical experience with the hegemonies of the United States and Great Britain. As Iran begins to enjoy the fruits of the post-US economic sanctions era, it is likely to be less bitter and unbending and more cooperative with the lone superpower, but only if their respective strategic interests in the Middle East (particularly in West Asia) do not collide. In that sense, the Iranian Islamist challenge to the United Stated is resolvable.

ISLAMISM VERSUS SECULAR FUNDAMENTALISM: IS THERE A WAY OUT?

This study would not be complete without a discussion of the way out regarding the jihadists' challenge to the United States. Since that challenge is to bring about an end to American primacy in the Muslim world and to topple various governments in South Asia, the Arabian Peninsula, the Levant, and Africa, it should be examined in the regional context. Additionally, the conflict is not of the same intensity or potency in all Muslim regions. For instance, in Central Asia, the Islamic challenge is smoldering but has not yet exploded. Besides, in that region, it is focused on Russia and China. Because of their contiguity with Central Asia and their own respective Muslim insurgencies, both Russia and China have remained proactive by conducting periodic military exercises and by introducing mega-programs of economic development under the rubric of the Silk Road Initiative (chapter 7).

In South Asia, Africa, and the Middle East, the jihadist challenge remains both active and highly volatile and is also focused on the United States and the West. So, the first question is, how should that challenge be dealt with in those regions? The second, and most important, question is whether there is a solution to this challenge: in other words, whether the secular fundamentalists and regional/global jihadists will be able to find a modus vivendi for their respective clashing objectives, or whether the United States will find solutions to global jihadism by bringing about radical changes in its secular fundamentalism and then developing radically different policies, in cooperation with its Western and, most important, Muslim allies and partners. For that purpose, the ostensibly immutable interests of both sides must be examined to see whether there is a way out.

For a brief but meaningful discussion of the way out on this issue, we need to revisit the thesis presented in chapter 1 and reconsidered earlier in this chapter. The jihadist groups' challenge to the supremacy of the United States in the Muslim regions and inside various Muslim states through the conduct of regional and global jihad is essentially a cosmic war. According to the arguments presented by Cavanaugh and Juergensmeyer, secular fundamentalists of the United States are conducting their own version of a cosmic war. Of these actors, the jihadists are immutable; there is no chance for a compromise from their side. They are ready and determined to fight for the glory of Islam to the death, and they are doing so by spreading this cosmic war – the destruction, mayhem, carnage, slaughter, and resultant instability – to regions of the Arab world, South Asia, and Africa. The 2016 Saudi-sponsored war in Yemen has perceptibly increased terrorist and suicide bombing incidents inside the kingdom. These episodes are the most persuasive examples of how senseless cosmic wars really are. Since the United States is a rational actor, it must first face the music by recognizing that its own cosmic war is no different from that carried out by the jihadists. Second, it should consider how to stop fighting its own cosmic wars and start looking for other realistic alternatives. Adoption of such an attitude would make America's cosmic wars mutable.

Assuming that the United States may be willing to find a way out, it will have to think about taking a number of critical steps based on pragmatic realism. Pragmatism is the philosophy that "the truth of an idea is dependent on its workability; ideas or principles is [*sic*] true so far as they work."[70] Realism recognizes that "all nation-states are motivated by national interest, or, at best, national interests disguised as moral concerns."[71] Interpreting and integrating these definitions for the purpose of discussion here, the usefulness or utility of secular fundamentalism is dependent upon its feasibility to promote or sustain America's strategic interests in different regions of the world. So, in the context of this study, the litmus test of secular fundamentalism through the lens of pragmatic realism is to determine whether it can bring about a number of revolutionary changes aimed at promoting the strategic interests of the United States in the Muslim world at large, or at least preventing serious erosion of those interests.

In order to find a way out, the United States must be willing to implement some or all of the following steps. First, it must consider "backing away from a messianic liberalism that seeks to spread Western-style social order throughout the world, by force if necessary." Second, it must consider "deconstructing the liberal ideology about the religious/secular divide that obscures so much of the current debate." Third, it must contemplate "confessing ... [its] own sins in the Middle East." Fourth, it must consider "adopting some humility about ... [its] ability to know what is best for every other country." Finally, and most important, it must try "to build bridges with all reasonable factions of an Islamic society, not only with those who promote U.S. interests."[72] Only by adopting one or more of these measures can the United States begin to move toward peace.

Admittedly, these are drastic (or even iconoclastic) suggestions for the United States to consider adopting. However, given how unyielding, fearless, and audacious the jihadist challenge has become to the strategic interests of the lone superpower, America's remedial and curative measures have to be nothing short of correspondingly iconoclastic. On the basis of the aforementioned measures, the United States, with the full participation of Muslim governments, should develop new comprehensive antiterrorism strategies, as opposed to counterterrorism tactics, which have not stabilized even one country being threatened by regional jihadist forces. The burden of crafting antiterrorism strategies has to be borne by the United States, the West, and, above all, Muslim countries. Eradicating the jihadist challenge is certainly not the problem of the United States and the West alone. Muslim governments have played a large role in its creation through corrupt and inept governance and autocratic practices, to mention only a few. Thus, they must also play a major role in participating with the West in defeating and eradicating it.

For the United States, to pretend that it could win the GWOT by carrying out endless bombing sorties, conducting shortsighted tactical drone attacks on various jihadist-infested countries, and fashioning naively crude and simplistic campaigns to "win the hearts and minds of Muslims" is nothing but an endless exercise of sheer stupidity. The bombing campaigns in conflict-ridden Muslim countries are only creating more unswerving and brutal young jihadists, who are not only more committed to violence but also willing to take the fight to erstwhile serene and peaceful Western cities. In the process, larger and larger sections of the Arab and Muslim world are looking like battlefields. Paris, London, and Brussels are increasingly being victimized by terrorist attacks.

There is no more resounding evidence of the unreserved failure of US counterterrorism tactics, and those of its Western and Arab partners, than the creation of a young generation committed to extreme violence. Today's jihadists are developing increasingly sophisticated strategies to "win the hearts and minds of Muslims." And their campaign is based upon sophisticated knowledge and understanding of the causes for the decline of the Muslim civilization at the hands of the West. Thus, their campaigns are producing more sympathizers and West-haters in the Muslim world.

Of all of the issues identified as reasons for the sustained anti-Americanism in Muslim countries, it is the United States' consistent and "blind" support of Israel and the autocratic rulers that stand out as most significant. Realistically, no US president, whether Democratic or Republican, will change this policy of supporting Israel in the foreseeable future. However, it should be clearly understood that the Palestinians are becoming more desperate with each passing day. The unresolved state of this conflict – in conjunction with the intense activism of ISIS – promises to push incidents of violence and instability in the Levant to an insurmountable level, even inside the militarily formidable Israel.

Whereas the United States may not be willing to stop supporting Israel, it should stop supporting the autocrats. They create only a semblance of stability by relying heavily on their US-supported (and in a number of cases US-trained) security apparatus, and by suppressing even minor instances of criticism of their rule. The ouster of three long-reigning dictators in the aftermath of the Arab Awakening has proven that autocratic rule is by nature unstable and lacking in durability. Some of the current despots – especially al-Sisi of Egypt and the Algerian military junta – are sitting on powder kegs.[73] Others, like the autocrats of Bahrain and Jordan, are presiding over regimes that appear to be likely targets of incipient instability in the near future.[74] So, the best policy for the United States is to encourage those potentates to gradually democratize their polities.

Second, the United States should put an end to drone attacks that – despite persistent denials – are causing seemingly endless civilian casualties, thereby escalating anti-American rage among Muslims and producing growing numbers of jihadists.[75] Third, the United States should drastically reduce its military presence in the Arab world. The post–9/11 era has convincingly proven that the enhanced US military presence has never intimidated the jihadists into lowering the scope or intensity of their activities. On the contrary, it has deepened the perception that the United States is committed to prolonging the rule of highly corrupt regimes over the Arab masses and perpetuating the occupation by Israel of Muslim Palestine. Fourth, a massive program of good governance must be introduced to train Middle Eastern bureaucrats how to reduce inefficiencies and increase governmental transparency. Cynics would argue that even the US government is not known for bureaucratic efficiency. Maybe so. But considering the notorious levels of corruption, the ineptness of the Arab bureaucrats, and the frequency of governmental inertia, logjams, and backlogs, there is much that US administrators can do to teach their Arab counterparts. The United States could be of great service to the Arab world by making the functioning of its own government more transparent.

The damage done to the US presence and influence in the Middle East through the continued clash of jihadism and secular fundamentalism may only be managed (or even lessened) by focusing on what is in the best interests of the Muslim/Arab countries *and* the United States. Present US support of Israel and Middle Eastern dictators, as well as America's heightened military presence and continued drone war, has done nothing to lower jihadist violence or to stabilize the Arab world. A negotiated solution to the Afghan conflict should be pursued by the United States with the uninterrupted support and participation of China and Pakistan. China is fully conscious of the relationship between the stability of Afghanistan and the Central Asian states. Another concurrent step should be the creation of massive nation-building programs and good governance in Afghanistan, with full cooperation between the United States, the European Union, and oil-producing Arab states. Pakistan must play an active role in the resolution of the Afghan conflict by abandoning, once and for all, its duplicitous policies regarding its support of its own domestic jihadists, whose raison d'être has been to carry out terrorist attacks inside Afghanistan and in Indian-administered Kashmir. Adoption of the aforementioned suggestions by the United States would go a long way toward ensuring prospects for peace and stability in the Muslim world.

Notes

CHAPTER ONE

1 Cavanaugh, "Root of Evil."
2 Cavanaugh, "Does Religion Cause Violence?"
3 Euben, *Enemy in the Mirror*, 44.
4 Cavanaugh, "Root of Evil."
5 Juergensmeyer, *The New Cold War?*, 15. Also quoted in Cavanaugh, *Myth of Religious Violence*, 199. One of the best definitions of "cosmic war" is provided by Reza Aslan as promotional copy for his book *How to Win a Cosmic War*: "A cosmic war is a religious war. It is a battle not between armies or nations, but between the forces of good and evil, a war in which God is believed to be directly engaged on behalf of one side against the other." http://www.amazon.com/How-Win-Cosmic-War-Globalization/dp/B0027A3FZ8.
6 Euben, *Enemy in the Mirror*, 44.
7 For instance, see Dekmejian, *Islam in Revolution*, especially chapters 1 and 2.
8 Technically, the originator of this doctrine was reported to be Hurqus ibn Zuhair, who questioned the Prophet of Islam's distribution of spoils after the Battle of Hunain (630). See Kenny, *Muslim Rebels*.
9 Emmanuel Sivan makes this excellent point in *Radical Islam: Medieval Theology and Modern Politics*, 90.
10 Algar, *Wahhabism*; Sayyid Qutb's magnum opus is *Fi Zilal al-Qu'ran* [In the shade of the Qu'ran].
11 Lewis, "Revolt of Islam."
12 Ibid.
13 Lewis, *What Went Wrong?*, 7.

14 Fromkin, *A Peace to End All Peace.*
15 "Indian Mutiny," *Encyclopedia Britannica*, last modified 5 September 2014, http://www.britannica.com/event/Indian-Mutiny.
16 Maududi, *Khilafat o Malookeyat* [The caliphate and governance].
17 "Eisenhower Doctrine," *Encyclopedia Britannica*, 5 January 1957.
18 Technically, Osama Bin Laden declared jihad on the United States in August 1996; see "Call to Arms."
19 Cavanaugh, *Myth of Religious Violence*, 204.
20 Sullivan, "Religious War."
21 Cavanaugh, *Myth of Religious Violence*, 205.
22 An excellent discussion on the Muslim opposition to secularism is presented by Leonard Binder in his analysis of the writings of Ali Abd al-Raziq. Binder, *Islamic Liberalism*, 131.
23 Kranz, "The Tunisian Miracle"; Diamond, "Tunisia Is Still a Success."
24 Al-Banna labelled Israel as America's "device to establish commercial hegemony over the Middle East." Quoted in R. Mitchell, *Society of the Muslim Brothers* (1969), 228–9. Bin Laden's November 2002 "Letter to America" stated, "The creation and continuation of Israel is one of the greatest crimes, and you are the leaders of its criminals. And of course there is no need to explain and prove the degree of American support for Israel. The creation of Israel is a crime which must be erased. Each and every person whose hands have become polluted in the contribution towards this crime must pay its price, and pay for it heavily."
25 The United States' participation, along with Great Britain, in ousting the government of Dr Mohammad Mosaddeq of Iran in 1953 may be viewed as one of the major events in the history of the US involvement in the Middle East; however, for a long time, the United States did not admit its role in that antidemocratic coup.
26 Kerr, *Arab Cold War.*
27 el-Sadat, *In Search of Identity.*
28 Anka, "RAW."
29 Roggio and Joscelyn, "Central Asian Groups."
30 Garthoff, *Detente and Confrontation.*
31 "Historic Deal"; see also Broad and Peçanha, "Iran Nuclear Deal."
32 "Struggle for Iran's Soul."
33 The fact that the government of President Mohammad Morsi of the Muslim Brotherhood was ousted by the military barely a year after it won the first-ever democratic elections did not prove whether US apprehensions regarding an Islamist government were indeed based

on reality or on mere military paranoia and fear of losing its vast economic interests. See Kholaif, "The Egyptian Army's Economic Juggernaut."

34 Diamond, "Tunisia Is Still a Success."

35 "Infinite Justice."

36 Ford, "Europe Cringes."

37 Mayer, "Predator War"; see also "What Obama's Predator-Strike Policy Tells Us."

38 The reference is to the following statement: "But while all Islamic groups were puritan, Salafi and Wahhabi, not all puritan groups were militant." El Fadl, *The Great Theft*, 86.

39 Maulana Abul A'la Maududi was interested in the Islamization of modernization. See Nasr, *Mawdudi*, especially section 2, "Islam Reinterpreted," 49–140.

40 Mozaffari, "What Is Islamism?," 21.

41 Ibid., 23.

42 I am grateful to an anonymous reviewer for this perceptive observation, which I have quoted directly.

CHAPTER TWO

1 Samuel P. Huntington, an eminent American political scientist, presents the controversial argument of civilizational decline in his now classic book, *The Clash of Civilizations and the Remaking of World Order*.

2 "Ayat al Kursi (Verse of the Throne)," Qur'an 2:255.

3 Rustow, "Ataturk."

4 Inalcik, "Traditional Society."

5 "White Revolution," *Encyclopedia Britannica*.

6 Qur'an 3:110.

7 Voll, "Foreword," viii.

8 Ibid.

9 Ibid., ix.

10 Khadduri, *Political Trends*, 55.

11 El Fadl, *The Great Theft*, 35–7.

12 Ibid., 37.

13 Ibid., 37–9; emphasis added.

14 Ibid., 40.

15 al-Banna, qtd in Mitchell, *Society of the Muslim Brothers* (1993), 228; see also chapter 8 in its entirety.

16 Ibid., 229.

17 Ibid., 232; see also chapter 9 in its entirety.
18 Nasr, *Mawdudi*, 4 and 20, passim.
19 Ibid., 54.
20 Nasr, *International Relations*, 13.
21 In fact, his insistence on the Islamization of Pakistan, when combined with the official version of Islamization under the dictatorship of General Zia-ul-Haq, contributed inordinately to that country's emergence as a volatile Islamist entity.
22 Al-Maqdisi, *Millat Ibrahim*.
23 This point has been made in at least two books; see Clarke, *Against All Enemies*; and Woodward, *State of Denial*.
24 Interestingly enough, the Office of the Historian of the US Department of State has been using this phrase to describe global terrorism. See "Introduction to Curriculum Packet."
25 For an erudite discussion of "hard power" and "soft power," see Nye, "Decline of America's Soft Power."
26 Riedel, "Al Qaeda Strikes Back."
27 Al-Naji, *Management of Savagery*.
28 Kennedy, *Rise and the Fall of the Great Powers*, xvi.
29 Belasco, *The Cost of Iraq*. According to a study done in 2013, "the U.S. war in Iraq has cost $1.7 trillion with an additional $490 billion in benefits owed to war veterans, expenses that could grow to more than $6 trillion over the next four decades counting interest." See Trotta, "Iraq War."
30 Jervis, *Meaning of the Nuclear Revolution*.
31 Moghadam, "Motives for Martyrdom."
32 Qur'an 4:29–30.
33 Malka, "Must Innocents Die?"; Holtmann, *Martyrdom, Not Suicide*.
34 Pape, *Dying to Win*. See also Pedahzur, *Root Causes of Suicide Terrorism*; Khosrokhavar, *Suicide Bombers;* Tahir-ul-Qadri, *Introduction to the Fatwa*; "Inside the Mind of a 'Black Widow.'"
35 Paulson, "Does Islam Stand against Science?"
36 The Trucial States system created by Great Britain is one example. It lasted from 1820 through 1971; see Onley, "Britain's Informal Empire."

CHAPTER THREE

1 CNN Wire, "ISIS Has Inspired over 70 Terrorist Attacks."
2 For examples, see the Qur'an, Sahih Bukhari 1:2:24, 3:46:649, 4:52:65, 4:52:196, 9:93:550; Sahih Muslim 1:31, 1:32, 1:33, 1:130, 1:149, 20:4645, 20:4684, 20:4685, 20:4687; and Abu Dawud, 14:2635.

3 Some other verses in the Qur'an that either mention the phrase *jahidu* or *qatilu* are 2:190–2, 2:216, 8:38–9, 8:65–7, 9:5 aka ayat al-saif "sword verse," 9:29, 9:73, 9:123, 25:52, 29:68–9, 47:4, and 66:9.
4 Ibn Taymiyya, *Majmu'at al-Rasa'il al-Kubra.*
5 Qadri, "What Is Jihad?" Interpretations differ as to the number of verses in the Qur'an that refer to jihad. Tahir-ul-Qadri's interpretation demonstrates the multiplicity of interpretations of this complex issue.
6 Algar, *Wahhabism*; Sayyid Qutb's magnum opus is *Fi Zilal al-Qu'ran* [In the shade of the Qu'ran].
7 Algar, *Wahhabism*, 19–20.
8 Philips, *Fundamentals of Tawheed*, 17–18.
9 Algar, *Wahhabism*, 34.
10 al-Banna, "His Political Thought."
11 Mitchell, *Society of the Muslim Brothers* (1969), 30.
12 Maududi, *Jihad in Islam*, 28.
13 Ibid., 5–6.
14 *Encyclopedia of the Middle East*, s.v. "Sayyid Qutb."
15 Smurr, "Power of Ideas," 8.
16 Qutb, "Foreword," v–x.
17 Qutb's commentary on Sura V, 5:44–48, as qtd in Shepard, "Sayyid Qutb's Doctrine of Jahiliyya," 524.
18 Kerr, *Arab Cold War.*
19 Faraj, qtd in Jansen, *Neglected Duty,* 151.
20 Azzam, *Defense of the Muslim Lands.*
21 Ibid.
22 Ibid.
23 Azzam, qtd in Musallam, *From Secularism to Jihad*, 191.
24 For a discussion of this point, see Nasr, *Shia Revival.*, especially chapter 4, "Khomeini Moment," 119–45.
25 Halliday, "Iran's Revolution."
26 Raghavan, "Strategic Depth in Afghanistan"; see also Gujral, "Musharraf Must Discard Zia Legacy."
27 Huntington, *Clash of Civilizations*, 1.
28 Fukuyama, "The End of History?"
29 Krauthammer, "Unipolar Moment," 1.
30 Pfaff, "Redefining World Power," 1.
31 Bush, *National Security Strategy*, 2.
32 al-Maqdisi, *Democracy: A Religion!*, 10.
33 Atwan, *Secret History of al Qaeda*, 45.

34 This topic has been covered by a variety of writers: Gerges, *Far Enemy*, 12 and 44, passim; Brooke, "Strategic Fissures"; Steinberg and Werenfels, "Between the 'Near' and the 'Far' Enemy."
35 Osama Bin Laden, interview by Peter Arnett, CNN, March 1977.
36 "Jihad against Jews and Crusaders."
37 Bin Laden, "Text of Fatwah."
38 Qtd in Lia, *Architect of Global Jihad*, 368.
39 Brooke, "Strategic Fissures," 51.
40 Lia, "Abu Mus'ab Al-Suri's Critique."
41 Fishman, "After Zarqawi," 21.
42 Moghadam and Fishman, *Self-Inflicted Wounds*, 128, 124.
43 Ibid., 38, 125.
44 Kean et al., *9/11 Commission Report*, 17.
45 Sly, "Al-Qaeda Disavows Any Ties."
46 After a number of al-Qaida leaders were successfully targeted in 2010 and 2011 along the Afghanistan-Pakistan borders, and especially after the assassination of Osama Bin Laden in May 2011, al-Qaida faced a bleak future. This reality underscores how prescient al-Suri really was in proposing the notion of "leaderless jihad." See Wright, *Looming Tower*; Wright, "Master Plan."
47 For a detailed biography of al-Suri, see Lia, *Architect of Global Jihad*.
48 Foley, "Cost of Wars." According to a report published in 2013, the cost of war in Iraq and Afghanistan for the United States was to reach $4 to $6 trillion. Londoño, "Iraq, Afghan War Costs."
49 Lemieux, "A Cyber Strategy."
50 Liang, "Cyber Jihad."
51 "Zarqawi Letter."
52 Arango and Schmidt, "Last Convoy."
53 al-Kadhimi, "Terrorism in Iraq."
54 Cordesman, "Salvaging the War in Afghanistan."
55 Waraich, "Pakistan Cuts Off Nato's Supply Line."
56 "How the Andijan Killings Unfolded."
57 President Zine El Abideen Ben Ali of Tunisia was ousted on 14 January 2011, President Hosni Mubarak of Egypt was brought down on 11 February 2011, and Muammar Qaddafi of Libya was thrown out of power and killed on 20 October 2011.

CHAPTER FOUR

1 I am grateful to an anonymous reviewer for this definition. Also see Mozaffari, "What Is Islamism?"

2 Stoessinger, *Crusaders and Pragmatists*, chap. 4, 107–31. Surprisingly enough, the Western rhetoric of describing Middle Eastern leaders has not changed at all. US public officials made similar comparisons in the case of Saddam Hussein, especially during the US invasion of Iraq.

3 Ba'athist (or renaissance) parties aspired to enlighten Arab culture in Iraq and Syria under their guidance. Although they emphasized the notion of enlightenment in their rhetoric and propaganda, in reality they established the dictatorship of two strongmen – Saddam Hussein in Iraq and Hafiz al-Assad (father of Bashara al-Assad) in Syria. "Ba'athism," *Wikipedia*, https://en.wikipedia.org/wiki/Ba%27athism.

4 Tyler, *World of Trouble*, 41.

5 Atherton, "The Soviet Role in the Middle East." See also Dawisha and Dawisha, *The Soviet Union and the Middle East.*

6 For a detailed background of this war, in which Egypt and Syria attacked Israel, see Peretz, "Arab-Israel War of 1973."

7 Kissinger, *Years of Upheaval*, chap. 18, 21, and 23.

8 Graubard, *Kissinger*, 18.

9 Tyler, *World of Trouble*, chap. 4.

10 Ahrari, OPEC.

11 Lerner, *The Passing of Traditional Society*; Apter, *Modernization*; Huntington, *Political Order in Changing Societies.*

12 Shafiq, "Secularism and the Arab-Muslim Condition," 139.

13 Ibid., 148–9.

14 Center for Homeland Defense and Security, "Persian Gulf Security Framework."

15 For instance, see Clarke, *Against All Enemies.*

16 Shin, "A Critical Review."

17 For instance, see de Borchgrave, "Bin Laden and Mullah Omar."

18 Atwan, *Secret History of al-Qaida*, 45.

19 Jerusalem Center for Public Affairs, "Maintaining Israel's Qualitative Military Edge."

20 "Eight Point Fahd Plan"; Global Policy Forum, "Saudi-Initiated Peace Plan."

21 These communist countries are China, Cuba, Laos, North Korea, and Vietnam.

22 "Sunni Rebels."

23 "No-Fly Zone."

24 According to the Information Clearing House website, "The Project for the New American Century, or PNAC, is a Washington-based think tank created in 1997. Above all else, PNAC desires and demands one thing:

The establishment of a global American empire to bend the will of all nations. They chafe at the idea that the United States, the last remaining superpower, does not do more by way of economic and military force to bring the rest of the world under the umbrella of a new socio-economic Pax Americana." Pitt, "Project for the New American Century."

25 "State Department Experts."
26 Beehner, "Coalition of the Willing."
27 For the deadly role of the IEDs in the death of American forces in Iraq, see Barry, Hastings, and Thomas, "Iraq's Real WMD."
28 Baker and Hamilton, *Iraq Study Group Report*.
29 McCary, "Anbar Awakening."
30 Allawi, "How Iraq Can Define Its Destiny."
31 Abedin, "The Muslim Brotherhood."
32 "Libya: The Next Failed State."
33 Bruno, "Yemen."
34 Lynch, "War Crime Concerns."
35 Clapper, "Worldwide Threat Assessment" (2016).

CHAPTER FIVE

1 Cohen, *Idea of Pakistan*, 168.
2 Khan, *Friends Not Masters*, 203.
3 International Crisis Group, "Pakistan: Madrasas," 7. Ayub's ideas were later adopted by General Zia-ul-Haq.
4 Isani, "Rise and Fall of the Jamaat-e-Islami."
5 Ahmed, *Bangladesh*, 188.
6 Ibid.
7 A community founded by Mirza Ghulam Ahmad, who claimed to be the "Promised One." The Muslims' main fight with that community is the same as with anyone, after the Prophet of Islam, who claims to be a prophet. Those who follow such a claimant are not considered Muslims.
8 Bhutto, *Awakening the People*, 6.
9 Ahle Hadith/Salafi, a Sunni school of thought (sometimes referred to as a "sect"), claims to represent the "true" Islam of Prophet Muhammad and his companions. Any deviation from the "ways of the Salaf" (pious ancestors), in their view, is not acceptable, and is akin to *shirk* (the sin of associationism). They regard the Shias as *kafirs* (nonbelievers) and reject Sufism as polytheism. The only sources of true Islam, according to their interpretations, are the holy Qur'an and Hadith (sayings of the

Prophet). The Jamiat Ahle Hadith follows an extremely literal understanding of those two primary sources of Islamic law.

10 Cohen, *Idea of Pakistan*, 170.
11 Paraphrased from ibid., 169.
12 After Bhutto's hanging, India's well-known journalist Khushwant Singh interviewed General Zia-ul-Haq. When asked why he rejected worldwide appeals for pardoning Bhutto, Zia said, "'Two bodies, one coffin,' … meaning it was either Bhutto or him. So Zulfikar Ali Bhutto was hanged in 1979." Singh, "Burnt Inside of Pakistan's House."
13 Weaver, "Bhutto's Fateful Moment."
14 Z. Hussain, *Scorpion's Tail.*
15 Esposito, "Islamization."
16 Ibid., 214–16.
17 Cohen, *Idea of Pakistan*, 112–13.
18 International Crisis Group, "Pakistan: Madrasas."
19 Ibid., 5.
20 Dossani and Rowan, *Prospects for Peace*, 23.
21 Ibid., 24.
22 Yousaf and Adkin, *Bear Trap*, 25–6.
23 "Reagan Doctrine, 1985."
24 Coll, *Ghost Wars*, 93.
25 As Olivier Roy notes, "Saudi strategy throughout the 1980s was to strengthen a radical Sunni fundamentalist camp in order to counterbalance the impact of the Iranian Revolution among the Muslim masses." Roy, *Afghanistan*, 87.
26 "Every religious, political and opinion leader interviewed [in April 2002] by ICG concurred with this view." International Crisis Group, "Pakistan: Madrasas," 12.
27 For a discussion of "shell state" see Napoleoni, *Terror Incorporated*, especially chapter 5, "Birth of the Terror State-Shell."
28 Musharraf, *Line of Fire*, 201.
29 Rashid, *Descent into Chaos*, 159, 160.
30 Ibid., 382.
31 The Hanafi school, named after Imam Abu Hanifa an-Numan ibn Thabit, is one of the largest schools of Islamic jurisprudence.
32 International Crisis Group, "State of Sectarianism in Pakistan," 23.
33 Roy, *Afghanistan*, 91.
34 Miller and Woodward, "Secret Memos."
35 Waraich, "U.S. Aid Package."
36 Ryan and Cornwell, "Kabul Embassy Attack."

37 Joscelyn, "Admiral Mullen."
38 Landler, "U.S. and Pakistan Agree to Reinforce Strategic Ties."
39 Associated Press of Pakistan, "Time for World to Recognize Pakistan."
40 For detailed coverage of A.Q. Khan and his nuclear Kmart, see Sanger, *Inheritance.*
41 Haass, "Double Standards."
42 J. Hussain, "Where Things Stand."
43 The first such instance was in 1929, when Habibullah Kalakani, a Tajik, captured power for several months.
44 Rashid, *The Taliban*, 87–8.
45 Ibid., 2.
46 Ibid.
47 Ibid., 93.
48 "Afghan-Arabs Part One"; see also "Afghan-Arabs Part Three."
49 *Tora Bora Revisited*, 3.
50 Pew Research Center, "A Year after Iraq War."
51 Sanger, "Biblical Quotes."
52 Page, "Declare Victory."
53 Ahrari, "Lessons in Disaster."
54 "White Paper."
55 Hastings, "Runaway General."
56 Cordesman, "Afghanistan at the End of 2011," 1.
57 Mahr, "Karzai Refuses to Budge."
58 Nordland and Rubin, "Karzai's Bet."
59 "Stop 'Baseless Propaganda.'"
60 Jamal and Hadi, "Beyond the Blame Game."
61 Small, "What Now for China's Afghanistan Strategy?"
62 A. Ahmed, "Combating Opium."
63 Browne, "Top U.S. General in Afghanistan."
64 Fair, Malhotra, and Shapiro, "Politics in Pakistan."
65 Pew Research Center, "Osama Bin Laden Largely Discredited."

CHAPTER SIX

1 Mneimneh, "Arab Reception of Vilayat-e-Faqih."
2 Ibid.
3 King, "Arming Iraq."
4 Bulloch and Morris, *The Gulf War*, 1.
5 Norton, "The Role of Hezbollah."

6 As a result of the National Pact of 1934, Lebanon emerged as a multi-confessional state. The three dominant religious groups made the following commitments.

- The Maronite Christians committed themselves to "an Arab-affiliated Lebanon, instead of a Western one" and promised not to seek foreign intervention.
- Similarly, Muslims forsook any desire "to unite with Syria."
- The president of the republic is always to be a Maronite Catholic; the prime minister, a Sunni Muslim; and the speaker of parliament, a Shia Muslim.
- Distribution of lower offices was based on the following rules: the deputy speaker and deputy prime minister is always to be a Greek Orthodox Christian; the chief of general staff, a Maronite Catholic; and the chief of army staff, a Druze. Members of parliament are to be on the ratio of 6:5 in favour of Christians to Muslims.

See "National Pact," https://en.wikipedia.org/wiki/National_Pact.

7 Sousa, "Three Phases of Resistance."

8 International Crisis Group, "Hezbollah."

9 "Open Letter."

10 *JPRS Report.*

11 Norton, *Hezbollah*, 37.

12 Ibid., 38–9.

13 Zenko, "When Reagan Cut and Run."

14 R. Wright, *Sacred Rage*, 72.

15 Ibid.

16 Saad-Ghorayeb, *Hizbu'llah.*

17 Shatz, "In Search of Hezbollah."

18 Chadwick, "2006 Lebanon War"; Cordesman, "Preliminary 'Lessons' of the Israeli-Hezbollah War."

19 Chadwick, "2006 Lebanon War."

20 Rienzi, "Iran's Response."

21 The discussion of Fadlallah's worldview is drawn entirely from Kramer, "Oracle of Hizbullah," http://www.martinkramer.org/.

22 Lewis, *Islam and the West*, 154.

23 For a detailed look at the life and political philosophy of Musa al-Sadr, see Ajami, *Vanished Imam.*

24 Mamouri, "Competition Heats Up between Qom, Najaf"; Latif, "Difference between Sistani and Khomeini."

25 Kean et al., *9/11 Commission Report*, 60.

26 "Rumsfeld Blames Iraq Problems on 'Pockets of Dead-Enders.'"
27 International Crisis Group, "Iran in Iraq."
28 Ibid.
29 Ibid.
30 Katzman, "CRS Report for Congress." Also see a recent update of this report, Katzman, "Iran Sanctions."
31 Katzman, "CRS Report for Congress."
32 Bruno, "Lengthening List of Iran Sanctions."
33 Marc Trachtenberg described "existential deterrence" as follows: "The mere existence of nuclear forces means that, whatever we say or do, there is a certain irreducible risk that an armed conflict might escalate into a nuclear war. The fear of escalation is thus factored into political calculations: faced with this risk, states are more cautious and more prudent than they would otherwise be." Trachtenberg, "Influence of Nuclear Weapons," 139.
34 MacLeod, Fischer, and McGirk, "Tehran vs. the Taliban."
35 Lukin, *The Bear Watches the Dragon*; D. Mitchell, "China and Russia."
36 Bailes et al., "Shanghai Cooperation Organization."
37 Kredo, "Iran to Spend $8 Billion."
38 "Design Characteristics of Iran's Ballistic and Cruise Missiles" (table).
39 Nuclear Threat Initiative, "Iran."
40 Ibid.
41 Ruck et al., "US Plans for Ballistic Missile Defense."
42 Ibid.
43 When this author typed in "Does Iran already have nuclear weapons?" there were more than 3,100 responses to that query. A number were of the view that it does.
44 General James Clapper, the director of National Intelligence, and General David Petraeus, the director of Central Intelligence, reported to the Senate Select Intelligence Committee on 31 January 2012 that Iran has not yet crossed the "red line" of concern for triggering a forceful US response. They defined the red line as the time when Iran's enrichment of uranium reaches 90 per cent. See Benson, Crawford, and Sterling, "Iran Nuclear Program."
45 Reals, "Iran."
46 Litwak, "From 'Rogues' to 'Outliers.'"
47 "Mullen to Ashkenazi on Iran."
48 This issue is quite complicated. Israel does not want to see a nuclear-armed Iran. But that desire has less to do with the stated fear of existential threat from a nuclear Iran, when, according to unofficial estimates, Israel possesses between 75 and 130 nuclear weapons. Any

country that intends to launch a nuclear attack of any magnitude on Israel has to consider the retaliatory responses not only from the Jewish state but also from the United States. Israel's assertion of existential threat from Iran therefore sounds disingenuous. The real reason has to be that Israel does not want its nuclear monopoly in the Middle East broken. This condition applies to all Arab states and may even apply to Turkey, if it were ever to try to become a nuclear weapons power. For numbers of estimated nuclear weapons possessed by Israel, see Federation of American Scientists, "Nuclear Weapons: Israel."

49 Fair, "Should Pakistan Get a Nuke Deal?"
50 Stimson Center, "Public Opinion in Iran."
51 Mottale, "Birth of a New Class."
52 Fitch, "5 Things to Know."
53 For background, see Fassihi, Solomon, and Dagher, "Iranians Dial Up Presence in Syria"; Fulton, Holliday, and Wyer, "Iranian Strategy in Syria"; Smyth, "Hizballah Cavalcade"; Morris and Salim, "Iran Backs Syria's Battle for Aleppo."
54 Clapper, "Worldwide Threat Assessment" (2016).
55 Mead, "NATO Must Have Turkey's Back."
56 Sokan, "Erdogan Feels the US Left Turkey in the Lurch."
57 Ibid.
58 Pargoo, "How Sanctions Helped."

CHAPTER SEVEN

1 Blair, "Annual Threat Assessment," 27.
2 Clapper, "Worldwide Threat Assessment" (2013), 24.
3 Clapper, "Worldwide Threat Assessment" (2016).
4 Brzezinski, *Grand Chessboard*, 124.
5 Rashid, *Jihad*, 73–4.
6 Amnesty International, *Turkmenistan: An "Era of Happiness?*; "Total repression."
7 Kaiser, "Kazakhs' Season."
8 Rashid, *Jihad*, 64.
9 Human Rights Watch, "Widespread Rights Abuse."
10 Ibid., 84.
11 Ibid.
12 "Uzbek President Bans Teaching."
13 Rashid, *Jihad*, 92.
14 Pomfret, "Central Asia."

15 "Tajik Islamic Party Banned."
16 Human Rights Watch, "Widespread Rights Abuse," 2, 5.
17 Freedom House, "Director of Programs Testifies."
18 Human Rights Watch, "Worsening Rights Record."
19 Human Rights Watch, "Widespread Rights Abuse."
20 Tabyshalieva, "Central Asia Struggles."
21 Stodghill, "Kazakhstan: Oil, Cash and Corruption."
22 Daneykin et al., "Threats and Challenges."
23 International Crisis Group, "Tajikistan."
24 Kuchins, Mankoff, and Backes, "Central Asia."
25 Tabyshalieva, "Central Asia Struggles."
26 Most of the discussion here is based on Ahrari, "Countering the Ideological Support."
27 Slim, "Central Asia."
28 For an overview of Central Asian politico-economic conditions, see Ahrari, *New Great Game*; Ahrari, "Strategic Future."
29 "UN Ferghana Valley Development Programme."
30 Ahrari, "Countering the Ideological Support."
31 Rasizade, "New 'Great Game' in Central Asia."
32 Qtd in Ahrari, "Countering the Ideological Support," 7.
33 Rashid, "Hizb ut-Tahrir," 115.
34 Karagiannis, "Political Islam."
35 Rashid, "Central Asia Asking for Holy War."
36 Qtd in Ahrari, "Countering the Ideological Support," 7.
37 an-Nabhani, *Concepts of Hizb ut-Tahrir*, 5 and 8 passim, 76.
38 Ibid., 46.
39 Qtd in Ahrari, "Countering the Ideological Support," 11.
40 "Hizb ut-Tahrir Rejects ISIS' Declaration."
41 Rashid, *Jihad*, 121.
42 Ibid.
43 Vali, "Banned Islamic Movement."
44 Illius, "Hizb ut-Tahrir Focuses on Social Media."
45 Tremblay, "Calling for a Caliphate in Turkey"; see also Komara, "Capitalism Exploits Youth's Consumerism."
46 "Transnational and Organised Crime."
47 Blua, "Central Asia."
48 Ibid.
49 Vali, "Banned Islamic Movement."
50 Khamidov, "Countering the Call," 11.
51 International Crisis Group, "Is Radical Islam Inevitable?," 12.

52 Ibid., 11.
53 Karagiannis, "Political Islam."
54 Ahrari, "Countering the Ideological Support," 10.
55 International Crisis Group, "Is Radical Islam Inevitable?"; see also International Crisis Group, "Central Asia."
56 Qtd in "America's Domination."
57 "Hizb ut-Tahrir Rejects ISIS' Declaration."
58 Rashid, *Jihad*, 145–8.
59 Smith, "The IMU: Alive and Kicking?"
60 Also recall the low level of support for Islamic governance discussed earlier in this study.
61 International Crisis Group, "Is Radical Islam Inevitable," 15–16.
62 Balci and Chaudet, "Jihadism in Central Asia."
63 Ibid.
64 Caryl, "In the Hot Zone."
65 Balci and Chaudet, "Jihadism in Central Asia."
66 Rashid, "They're Only Sleeping."
67 Stein, "Goals of the Islamic Movement."
68 Ibid.
69 Ibid.
70 International Crisis Group, "Syria Calling."
71 Pannier, "Central Asia."
72 Mankoff, *United States and Central Asia*, 21–2.
73 Fuller and Lipman, "Islam in Xinjiang."
74 The discussion of the SCO's military exercise is extracted from Weitz, "Military Exercises."
75 Boland, '"Peace Mission-2010' Exercise."
76 Weitz, "Military Exercises."
77 Miller, "China, Kyrgyzstan Ties Warm."
78 Chen, "China's Reaction," 10.
79 Ibid., 11–12.
80 Ibid., 24, 25, 26.
81 Weitz, "Beijing and Washington."
82 Ibid.
83 Weitz, "For U.S., Dividing China, Russia."
84 Clover and Hornby, "China's Great Game."
85 "China's Ambitious Silk Road."
86 Ibid.
87 Ibid.
88 Williams, "From 'Secessionist Rebels,'" 20.

89 For instance, in a televised State of the Union address after the terrorist takeover of the school in Beslan, Putin stated that some nations were trying to weaken Russia by supporting the terrorists. "We showed weakness and the weak are trampled upon," he said. "Some want to cut off a juicy morsel from us while others are helping them. They are helping because they believe that, as one of the world's major nuclear powers, Russia is still posing a threat to someone, and therefore this threat must be removed. And terrorism is, of course, only a tool for achieving these goals." Qtd in Beene, Kubiak, and Colton, *U.S., Russia and the Global War*, 142. Another example of this belief comes to us from the head of the Duma Foreign Affairs Committee, Konstantin Kosachev, when he claimed that "Beslan should be understood in the 'dogma' that 'a good Russia is a weak Russia.'" Therefore, any terrorist act that is international in its orientation "remains an instrument of the Great Game." Ibid.
90 Azizian, "Marriage of Convenience."
91 Frost, "Collective Security Treaty Organization," 84.
92 Ibid., 86.
93 Ibid., 88–89.
94 "Kyrgyzstan's New Leadership."
95 Pillalamarri, "Last Base in Central Asia."
96 Whitmore, "Sphere of Reluctance."
97 Tolipov, "CSTO."
98 Kilner, "Uzbekistan."
99 Ibid.
100 Qtd in Ellyatt, "Russia's 'War' in Syria."
101 Rumer, Sokolsky, and Stronski, "US Policy toward Central Asia 3.0."
102 Ibid., 8.
103 Yazdani, "Caspian Oil Routes."
104 Ibid.
105 Pannier, "What Next?"
106 Mutlu, "C5+1."
107 Saidazimova, "Central Asia."
108 "American Public Diplomacy."
109 Ibid.
110 Levy, "Central Asia Sounds Alarm."
111 Trilling, "Evaluating Kyrgyzstan's Impact."
112 Collado, "Corruption and Revolution."
113 "Key US Air Base."
114 Chausovsky, "Militancy in Central Asia."

115 Coalson, "Violence."
116 Farchy, "After the Strongmen."
117 Markowitz, "When Flimsy States Don't Fail."
118 Sands, "China Seeks Hegemony."
119 Mankoff, *United States and Central Asia*, 2.

CHAPTER EIGHT

1 Cavanaugh, "Root of Evil."
2 Cavanaugh, "Does Religion Cause Violence?"
3 There is no theological doctrine in the Holy Qur'an about the establishment of Islamic government; the entire earth is God's kingdom. A famous verse of the Holy Qur'an states, "To Him belong the earth and the entire universe." When the Islamists talk about establishing an Islamic government, they have the example of the city of Medina in mind where the Prophet of Islam established a small state. The Islamist position on the sovereignty of God is that He is the sovereign of each Islamic government, and that sovereignty belongs only to God. However, this issue remains controversial among Muslims at large, especially about how to operationalize that sovereignty.
4 Muslims also point to the Kemalist legacy of secularization of the Republic of Turkey, which has created a permanent schism in the body politic of that country. Turkey's decision to institutionalize the notion of secularism was never envisaged as a "path to take" by any Muslim country. Indonesia has been practicing a version of it only since the fall of General Suharto's regime, and it is too early to conclude that secularism has become a *sine qua non* of that polity.
5 Shah, review of *Islam and Science*.
6 I am purposely not using the term "governing," which is too nuanced and sophisticated to judge the performance of the largely uneducated and inexperienced mujahedeen. If they had ruled effectively, then the Pakistani government would have neither felt the need to intervene nor succeeded in enabling the Taliban to become a major force and capture power from the mujahedeen in 1996.
7 Sherazi, "TTP Finalises 15 Point Draft."
8 Harris and Aid, "Exclusive: CIA Files."
9 See J. Solomon, "U.S., Russia Agree."
10 Cushman, "U.S. Strikes 2 Iranian Oil Rigs."
11 Bronner and Slackman, "Saudi Troops Enter Bahrain."
12 "Yemen Crisis."

13 Khouri, "Saudi-Iranian Rivalry."
14 "Al-Qaeda-Linked Groups Expand."
15 Esposito and Mogahed, *Who Speaks for Islam?*, 63.
16 Ibid., 48.
17 Raziq, *Al-Islam Wa Usul Al-Hukm.*
18 Qtd in Binder, *Islamic Liberalism*, 131.
19 Civil Service of Pakistan, "The Most Misquoted Verse of Iqbal." Iqbal also wrote, roughly translated, "It is a must to avoid democracy as even two thousand donkeys cannot reach the wisdom of a single wise man!"
20 Esposito, "Rethinking Islam," 5.
21 al-Maqdisi, *Democracy: A Religion!*
22 al-Qaradaw, qtd in Esposito, "Rethinking Islam," 6.
23 Ibid., 7.
24 al-Ghannouchi, qtd in ibid., 8.
25 Ceric, qtd in ibid., 11.
26 Ramadan, qtd in ibid.
27 IntelCenter, "Islamic State's Global Affiliates" (map).
28 Clarion Project, "ISIS Has 34 Affiliates."
29 Sanchez et al., "ISIS Goes Global."
30 Shane and Hubbard, "ISIS Displaying a Deft Command."
31 Ibid.
32 Ibid.
33 "US Cited Controversial Law."
34 Carter, Maher, and Neumann, "ICSR Report."
35 Townsend and Helm, "Jihad in a Social Media Age."
36 Shane, "ISIS Displaying a Deft Command."
37 McLaughlin, "Counter-Terrorism Tweeters."
38 Ibid.
39 Lamothe, "Fight against ISIS."
40 Associated Press, "U.S. Military Launches Aggressive Cyberwar."
41 Hennigan, "Pentagon Wages Cyberwar."
42 Pagliery, "Terrorists Hide Plans."
43 O'Neill, "Anonymous vs. ISIS."
44 Hubbard, "Al-Qaida Breaks with Jihadist Group."
45 Sly, "Al-Qaeda Disavows Any Ties."
46 McLaughlin, "Was Iraq's Top Terrorist Radicalized?"
47 For an account of the jihadist life of Ayman al-Zawahiri, see Wright, "The Man behind Bin Laden."

48 Walsh, Hubbard, and Schmitt, "U.S. Bombing in Libya."
49 Cavanaugh, *Myth of Religious Violence*, 205.
50 Aslan, *How to Win a Cosmic War*, 5.
51 Treverton et al., *Exploring Religious Conflict*, xii.
52 Qtd in Cavanaugh, *Myth of Religious Violence*, 199.
53 al-Rasheed, "Saudi War in Yemen."
54 "Africa's Jhafrica."
55 H. Solomon, "Islamism on the Rise."
56 The reference here is to the infamous phrase "falling dominos" used during the US war in Vietnam in the late 1960s.
57 H. Solomon, "Islamism on the Rise."
58 Euben, *Enemy in the Mirror*, 44.
59 Black, "Fear of a Shia Full Moon."
60 Schmitz, "Afghanistan Speech at West Point."
61 BBC News listed the following thirty-four countries as Saudi Arabia alliance members: Bahrain, Bangladesh, Benin, Chad, Comoros, Djibouti, Egypt, Gabon, Guinea, Ivory Coast, Jordan, Kuwait, Lebanon, Libya, Malaysia, Maldives, Mali, Mauritania, Morocco, Niger, Nigeria, Pakistan, the Palestinians, Qatar, Saudi Arabia, Senegal, Sierra Leone, Somalia, Sudan, Togo, Tunisia, Turkey, United Arab Emirates, and Yemen. "'Members' Surprised by Saudi Anti-terror Coalition Plan."
62 Defense Science Board, *Strategic Communication*, 48–9.
63 "Lights, Camera, Propaganda."
64 Ibid.
65 Nuclear Threat Initiative, "Iran."
66 Morello, "Nuclear Deal."
67 Schmidt, "Navy Releases Timeline."
68 Rough, "Obama's Crumbling Syria Strategy."
69 Heineman, "Afghan Black Hole."
70 "Pragmatism and Realism."
71 Ferraro, "Political Realism."
72 William T. Cavanaugh, email to author, 29 January 2016.
73 For a description of the demented techniques of torture used by the Algerian military on political dissidents and Islamists, see Fisk, "Algeria's Military."
74 Sattlof and Schenker, "Political Instability in Jordan"; see also Moore-Gilbert, "Sectarian Divide."
75 Abbas, "How Drones Create More Terrorists"; see also "Top U.S. Warfighting Experts."

Bibliography

Abbas, Hasan. "How Drones Create More Terrorists." *Atlantic*, 23 August 2013.

Abedin, Mahan. "Islamic Movements: The Muslim Brotherhood – in Eclipse or in Transformation." *Religioscope*, 8 November 2013.

"The Afghan-Arabs Part One." *Asharq Al-Awsat*, 29 June 2005.

"The Afghan-Arabs Part Three." *Asharq Al-Awsat*, 9 July 2005.

"Africa's Jhafrica: The Biggest Threat to African Peace and Prosperity Comes from a Dangerous Idea." *Economist*, 18 July 2015.

Ahmed, Azam. "Tasked with Combating Opium, Afghan Officials Profit from It." *New York Times*, 15 February 2016.

Ahmed, Moudud. *Bangladesh: Constitutional Quest for Autonomy 1950–1971*. Dhaka, Bangladesh: University Press, 1979.

Ahrari, Ehsan. "Countering the Ideological Support for HT and the IMU: The Case of the Ferghana Valley." Occasional Paper Series No. 3. George C. Marshall European Center for Security Studies, 3 October 2006.

– *The New Great Game in Muslim Central Asia*. Washington, DC: National Defense University, 1996.

– "Obama's Impending 'Lessons in Disaster'?" *Strategic Paradigms*, 29 December 2009. http://www.ehsanahrari.com/tag/mcgeorge-bundy/.

– "The Strategic Future of Central Asia: A View from Washington." *Journal of International Affairs* 56, no. 2 (2003): 157–66.

Ahrari, Mohammed E. *OPEC: The Failing Giant*. Lexington: University Press of Kentucky, 1986.

Ajami, Fouad. *The Vanished Imam: Musa al Sadr and the Shia of Lebanon*. New York: Cornell University Press, 1987.

al-Banna, Hasan. "Hasan al-Banna and His Political Thought of Islamic Brotherhood." *IkhwanWeb*, 13 MAY 2008.

Algar, Hamid. *Wahhabism: A Critical Essay*. Oneonta, NY: Islamic Publications International, 2002.
al-Kadhimi, Mustafa. "Maliki Says Terrorism in Iraq 'Directly Related' to Syria." *Al-Monitor*, 7 October 2013.
Allawi, Ali A. "How Iraq Can Define Its Destiny." *New York Times*, 1 January 2012.
al-Maqdisi, Abu Muhammad 'Aasim. *Democracy: A Religion*! Translated by Abu Muhammad al-Maleki. https://azelin.files.wordpress.com/2010/08/democracy-a-relegoin.pdf.
– *Millat Ibrahim: The Religion of Ibrahim*. At-Tibyan Publications, 1984.
"Al-Qaeda-Linked Groups Expand into Lebanon." *Al-Jazeera*, 20 January 2014.
al-Naji, Abu Bakr. *The Management of Savagery: The Most Critical Stage through Which the Umma Will Pass*. Translated by William McCants. Cambridge, MA: John M. Olin Institute for Strategic Studies at Harvard University, 2006.
al-Rasheed, Madawi. "Saudi War in Yemen Impossible to Win." *Al-Monitor*, 2 October 2015.
"America's Domination of the International Situation Is a Danger to the World and Only the Khilafah Can Save It." Network54.com, 2 June 2003.
"American Public Diplomacy in the Islamic World: Remarks of Andrew Kohut to the Senate Foreign Relations Committee Hearing." Pew Research Center, 27 February 2003.
Amnesty International. *Turkmenistan: An "Era of Happiness" or More of the Same Repression?* London: Amnesty International Publications, 2013.
– "Turkmenistan: Total Repression ahead of Elections." www.amnesty.org, 12 December 2013.
Anka, Qammer Abbas. "RAW, Afghan Soil and Pakistan-I." *The News*, 26 April 2016.
an-Nabhani, Taqiuddan. *The Concepts of Hizb ut-Tahrir*. London: Khilafah, 1953.
Apter, David E. *Some Conceptual Approaches to the Study of Modernization*. Englewood Cliffs, NJ: Prentice-Hall, 1968.
Arango, Tim, and Michael S. Schmidt. "Last Convoy of American Troops Leaves Iraq." *New York Times*, 8 December 2011.
Aslan, Reza. *How to Win a Cosmic War: God, Globalization, and the End of the War on Terror*. New York: Random House, 2009.
Associated Press. "U.S. Military Launches Aggressive Cyberwar on ISIS." *CBS News*, 26 February 2016.

Associated Press of Pakistan. "Time for World to Recognize Pakistan as de jure Nuclear Power with Equal Rights!" *World Defence Pakistan*, 8 May 2010.

Atherton, Alfred L., Jr. "The Soviet Role in the Middle East: An American View." *Middle East Journal* 39, no. 4 (1985): 708–15.

Atwan, Abdel Bari. *The Secret History of al-Qaeda*. London: Saqi Books, 2006.

Azizian, Rouben. "A Marriage of Convenience: Russia's Response to U.S. Security Policies." Asia Pacific Center for Security Studies, March 2003.

Azzam, Abdullah Yusuf. *Defense of the Muslim Lands: The First Obligation after Iman*. http://thegorkabriefing.com.

Bailes, Alyson J.K., Pál Dunay, Pan Guang, and Mikhail Troitskiy. "The Shanghai Cooperation Organization." SIPRI Policy Paper No. 17. Stockholm International Peace Research Institute, May 2007.

Baker III, James, and Lee H. Hamilton. *The Iraq Study Group Report*. New York: Vintage Books, 2006.

Balci, Bayram, and Didier Chaudet. "Jihadism in Central Asia: A Credible Threat after the Western Withdrawal from Afghanistan?" Carnegie Endowment for International Peace, 13 August 2014.

Barry, John, Michael Hastings, and Evan Thomas. "Iraq's Real WMD; Deadly Puzzle: IEDs Are Killing U.S. Soldiers at a Scary Clip at War with an Insidious Weapon." *Newsweek*, 27 March 2006.

Beehner, Lionel. "The Coalition of the Willing." Council on Foreign Relations, 22 February 2007.

Beene, Eric A., Jeffrey J. Kubiak, and Kyle J. Colton. *U.S., Russia and the Global War on Terror: 'Shoulder-to-Shoulder' into Battle?* Research report submitted to Air Force Fellows, Air University, Alabama, March 2005.

Belasco, Amy. *The Cost of Iraq, Afghanistan, and Other Global War on Terror Operations since 9/11*. Congressional Research Service, 29 March 2011.

Benson, Pam, Jamie Crawford, and Joe Sterling. "Iran Nuclear Program Stokes US Concern." CNN, 31 January 2012.

Bhutto, Zulfiqar Ali. *Awakening the People: A Collection of Articles, Statements and Speeches 1966–1969*. Reproduced by Sani Panhwar Member Sindh Council PPP, 2006.

Binder, Leonard. *Islamic Liberalism: A Critique of Development Ideologies*. Chicago: University of Chicago Press, 1988.

Bin Laden, Osama. "A Call to Arms against Infidels 'Occupying the Land of the Two Holy Sanctuaries.'" About.com, 23 August 1996.

– "Declaration of Jihad against Americans Occupying the Land of the Two Holy Mosques." http://college.cengage.com/history/primary_sources/world/two_holy_mosques.htm.

– "Full Text: Bin Laden's 'Letter to America.'" *The Guardian*, 24 November 2002.

– "Text of Fatwah Urging Jihad against Americans – 1998." *Al-Quds l-'Arabi*, 23 February 1998.

Black, Ian. "Fear of a Shia Full Moon." *The Guardian*, 26 January 2007.

Blair, Dennis C. "Annual Threat Assessment of the Intelligence Community." Senate Select Committee on Intelligence, 12 February 2009.

Blua, Antoine. "Central Asia: Is Hizb ut-Tahrir a Threat to Stability?" *Radio Free Europe/Radio Liberty*, 23 August 2004.

Boland, Julie. "Learning from the Shanghai Cooperation Organization's 'Peace Mission-2010' Exercise." Brookings, 29 October 2010.

Broad, William J., and Sergio Peçanha. "The Iran Nuclear Deal – A Simple Guide." *New York Times*, 15 January 2015.

Bronner, Ethan, and Michael Slackman. "Saudi Troops Enter Bahrain to Help Put Down Unrest." *New York Times*, 14 March 2011.

Brooke, Steven. "Strategic Fissures: The Near and Far Enemy Debate." In *Self-Inflicted Wounds: Debates and Divisions within Al-Qa'ida and Its Periphery*, edited by Assaf Moghadam and Brian Fishman, 45–68. New York: Combating Terrorism Center at West Point, 2010.

Browne, Ryan. "Top U.S. General in Afghanistan: 2016 'Possibly Worse Than 2015.'" CNN, 4 February 2016.

Bruno, Alessandro. "Yemen: The World's Newest Failed State." *Geopolitical Monitor*, 12 February 2015.

Bruno, Greg. "The Lengthening List of Iran Sanctions." Council on Foreign Relations, 22 November 2011.

Brzezinski, Zbigniew. *The Grand Chessboard, American Primacy and Its Geostrategic Imperatives*. New York: Basic Books, 1997.

Bulloch, John, and Harvey Morris. *The Gulf War: Its Origins, History and Consequences*. London: Methuen, 1989.

Bush, George H.W. *National Security Strategy of the United States*. Washington, DC: White House, 1991. http://nssarchive.us/NSSR/1991.pdf.

Calvert, John C. *Islamism: A Documentary and Reference Guide*. Westport, CT: Greenwood Press, 2007.

Carter, Joseph A., Shiraz Maher, and Peter R. Neumann. "ICSR Report: Who Inspires the Syrian Foreign Fighters?" International Centre for the Study of Radicalisation, 22 April 2014.

Caryl, Christian. "In the Hot Zone." *Newsweek*, 7 October 2001.

Cavanaugh, William T. "Does Religion Cause Violence?" *Harvard Divinity School* 35 (Spring/Summer 2007). http://bulletin.hds.harvard.edu/articles/springsummer2007/does-religion-cause-violence.

– *The Myth of Religious Violence*. New York: Oxford University Press, 2009.
– "The Root of Evil." *America Magazine*, 29 July–5 August 2013.
Center for Homeland Defense and Security. "Persian Gulf Security Framework (PD / NSC-63)." White House Office, 15 January 1981.
Chadwick, Andrew. "The 2006 Lebanon War: A Short History." *Small Wars Journal* (11 September 2012).
Chausovsky, Eugene. "Militancy in Central Asia: More Than Religious Extremism." Stratfor Global Intelligence, 9 August 2012.
Chen, Titus C. "China's Reaction to the Color Revolutions: Adaptive Authoritarianism in Full Swing." *Asian Perspective* 34, no. 2 (2010): 5–51.
"China's Ambitious Silk Road Strategy." *Deutsche Welle*, 21 December 2015.
Chrisafis, Angelique. "Algeria Braces for More Protests." *The Guardian*, 18 February 2011.
Civil Service of Pakistan. "The Most Misquoted Verse of Iqbal." *CSS Forum*, 3 June 2010.
Clapper, James R. "Statement for the Record: Worldwide Threat Assessment of the US Intelligence Community." House Permanent Select Committee on Intelligence, 11 April 2013.
– "Statement for the Record, Worldwide Threat Assessment of the US Intelligence Community." Senate Select Committee on Intelligence, 9 February 2016.
Clarion Project. "United Nations: ISIS Has 34 Affiliates Worldwide." 7 February 2016. http://www.clarionproject.org.
Clarke, Richard A. *Against All Enemies: Inside America's War on Terror*. New York: Free Press, 2004.
Clover, Charles, and Lucy Hornby. "China's Great Game: Road to a New Empire." *Financial Times*, 12 October 2015.
CNN Wire. "ISIS Has Inspired over 70 Terrorist Attacks in 20 Countries." 22 March 2013. http://wgno.com.
Coalson, Robert. "Violence in Tajikistan's Badakhshan Province a Legacy of Civil War." *Radio Free Europe/Radio Liberty*, 26 July 2012.
Cohen, Stephen Philip. *The Idea of Pakistan*. Washington, DC: Brookings, 2004.
Coll, Steve. *Ghost Wars: The Secret Story of the CIA, Afghanistan, and Bin Laden, from the Soviet Invasion to September 10, 2001*. New York: Penguin Books, 2004.
Collado, Ramon E. "Corruption and Revolution: The Coming Turmoil in Kyrgyzstan." *Geopolitical Monitor*, January 2016.

Cordesman, Anthony H. "Afghanistan at the End of 2011: Part One – Trends in the War." Center for Strategic and International Studies, 3 January 2012.

– "Preliminary 'Lessons' of the Israeli-Hezbollah War." Center for Strategic and International Studies, 17 August 2006.

– "Salvaging the War in Afghanistan." Center for Strategic and International Studies, 23 July 2013.

Cushman, John S., Jr. "U.S. Strikes 2 Iranian Oil Rigs and Hits 6 Warships in Battles over Mining Sea Lanes in Gulf." *International New York Times*, 19 April 1988.

Daneykin, Yury, Elisey Andreevsky, Mikhail Roozhin, and Oleg Sernetsky. "Threats and Challenges to the Regional Security in Central Asian Region (the Example of the Republic of Kyrgyzstan)." *Procedia – Social and Behavioral Sciences* 166 (2015): 86–91.

Dawisha, Adeed, and Karen Dawisha, eds. *The Soviet Union and the Middle East*. New York: Holmes & Meier, 1982.

de Borchgrave, Arnaud. "Bin Laden and Mullah Omar: No Brothers in Arms." *Globalist*, 24 February 2010.

Defense Science Board. *Report of the Defense Science Board Task Force on Strategic Communication*. Washington, DC: Office of the Under Secretary of Defense for Acquisition, Technology, and Logistics, 2004.

Dekmejian, R. Hrair. *Islam in Revolution: Fundamentalism in the Arab World*. Syracuse, NY: Syracuse University Press, 1995.

"Design Characteristics of Iran's Ballistic and Cruise Missile" (table). Produced for the Nuclear Threat Initiative by the James Martin Center for Nonproliferation Studies. Last modified January 2013.

Diamond, Larry. "Tunisia Is Still a Success." *Atlantic*, 23 March 2015.

Dossani, Rafiq, and Henry Rowan, eds. *Prospects for Peace in South Asia*. Palo Alto, CA: Stanford University Press, 2005.

"Eight Point Fahd Plan, 1981: What Was the Fahd Plan of 1981 and the Fez Initiative of 1982?" http://www.palestinefacts.org/pf_1967to1991_fahd_1981.php.

"Eisenhower Doctrine." *Encyclopedia Britannica*, 5 January 1957.

El Fadl, Khaled Abou. *The Great Theft: Wrestling Islam from the Extremists*. New York: HarperCollins, 2005.

Ellyatt, Holly. "This Is How Much Russia's 'War' in Syria Costs." CNBC.com, 21 October 2015.

el-Sadat, Anwar. *In Search of Identity: An Autobiography*. New York: Harper & Row, 1977.

Esposito, John. "Islamization: Religion and Politics in Pakistan." *The Muslim World* 72, no. 3–4 (1982): 197–223.

– "Rethinking Islam and Secularism." ARDA Guiding Paper Series. Association of Religion Data Archives at Pennsylvania State University, 2010. http://www.thearda.com/rrh/papers/guidingpapers.asp.

Esposito, John L., and Dalia Mogahed. *Who Speaks for Islam? What a Billion Muslims Really Think*. New York: Gallup Press, 2007.

Euben, Roxanne L. *Enemy in the Mirror: Islamic Fundamentalism and the Limits of Modern Rationalism*. Princeton, NJ: Princeton University Press, 1999.

Fair, C. Christine. "Should Pakistan Get a Nuke Deal?" *Foreign Policy*, 23 March 2010.

Fair, C. Christine, Neil Malhotra, and Jacob N. Shapiro. "Islam, Militancy, and Politics in Pakistan: Insights from a National Sample." *Terrorism and Political Violence* 17, no. 3 (2005).

Faraj, Muhammad Abd al-Salam. *Al-Farida al-Gha'iba* [The neglected duty]. 1981.

Farchy, Jack. "Central Asia: After the Strongmen." *Financial Times*, 13 May 2015.

Fassihi, Farnaz, Jay Solomon, and Sam Dagher. "Iranians Dial Up Presence in Syria." *Wall Street Journal*, 16 September 2013.

Federation of American Scientists. "Nuclear Weapons: Israel." 8 January 2007. http://fas.org/nuke/guide/israel/nuke/.

Ferraro, Vincent. "Political Realism." Mount Holyoke College, 14 March 2012.

Fishman, Brian. "After Zarqawi: The Dilemmas and Future of Al Qaeda in Iraq." *Washington Quarterly* 29, no. 4 (2006): 19–32.

Fisk, Robert. "Is Algeria's Military Making Its Move on Ageing President Bouteflika?" *Independent*, 24 January 2016.

Fitch, Asa. "5 Things to Know about Iran's Syria Strategy." *Wall Street Journal*, 1 October 2015.

Foley, Elise. "Cost of Wars in Iraq, Afghanistan, Pakistan to Reach $3.7 Trillion: Report." *Huffington Post*, 29 August 2011.

Ford, Peter. "Europe Cringes at Bush's 'Crusade' against Terrorist." *Christian Science Monitor*, 19 September 2001.

Freedom House. "Freedom House Director of Programs Testifies on Freedom in Central Asia." Washington, DC, 26 April 2006.

Fromkin, David. *A Peace to End All Peace: The Fall of the Ottoman Empire and the Creation of the Modern Middle East*. New York: Henry Holt, 1989.

Frost, Alexander. "The Collective Security Treaty Organization, the Shanghai Cooperation Organization, and Russia's Strategic Goals in Central Asia." *China and Eurasia Forum Quarterly* 7, no. 3 (2009): 83–102.

Fukuyama, Francis. "The End of History?" *National Interest* (Summer 1989).

Fuller, Graham E., and Jonathan N. Lipman. "Islam in Xinjiang." In *Xinjiang: China's Muslim Borderland*, edited by S. Frederick Star, 320–52. Armonk, NY: M.E. Sharpe, 2004.

Fulton, Will, Joseph Holliday, and Sam Wyer. "Iranian Strategy in Syria." Institute for the Study of War, May 2013.

Garthoff, Raymond L. *Detente and Confrontation: American-Soviet Relations from Nixon to Reagan*, rev. ed. Washington, DC: Brookings Institution Press, 1994.

Gerges, Fawaz A. *The Far Enemy: Why Jihad Went Global*. New York: Cambridge University Press, 2005.

Global Policy Forum. "Saudi-Initiated Peace Plan Document." *Reuters*, 25 March 2002.

Goldstein, Gordon M. *Lessons in Disaster: McGeorge Bundy and the Path to War in Vietnam*. New York: Henry Holt, 2008.

Graubard, Stephen R. *Kissinger: Portrait of a Mind*. New York: W.W. Norton, 1973.

Gujral, I.K. "Musharraf Must Discard Zia Legacy." *Frontline* 19, no. 2 (1 February 2001).

Haass, Richard N. "India, Iran, and the Case for Double Standards." Council on Foreign Relations, 14 May 2006.

Halliday, Fred. "Iran's Revolution: The First Year." *MERIP Reports* 10 (May/June 1980). Middle East Research and Information Project.

Harris, Shane, and Matthew M. Aid. "Exclusive: CIA Files Prove America Helped Saddam as He Gassed Iran." *Foreign Policy*, 26 August 2013.

Hastings, Michael. "The Runaway General." *Rolling Stone*, 25 June 2010.

Heineman, Ben W., Jr. "The Afghan Black Hole: Governance and Corruption." *Atlantic*, 24 October 2010.

Hennigan, W.J. "Pentagon Wages Cyberwar against Islamic State." *Los Angeles Times*, 29 February 2016.

"The Historic Deal That Will Prevent Iran from Acquiring a Nuclear Weapon." White House, January 2016. https://www.whitehouse.gov/issues/foreign-policy/iran-deal.

"Hizb ut-Tahrir Rejects ISIS' Declaration of Khilafah." 5Pillarsuk.com, 2 July 2014.

Holtmann, Philipp. *Martyrdom, Not Suicide: The Legality of Hamas' Bombings in the Mid-1990s in Modern Islamic Jurisprudence.* Norderstedt, Germany: GRIN Verlag, 2009.

"How the Andijan Killings Unfolded." *BBC News*, 12 May 2005.

Hubbard, Ben. "Al-Qaida Breaks with Jihadist Group in Syria Involved in Rebel Infighting." *New York Times*, 3 February 2014.

Human Rights Watch. "Central Asia: Widespread Rights Abuse, Repression." 31 January 2013.

– "Central Asia: Worsening Rights Record." 29 January 2015.

Huntington, Samuel P. *The Clash of Civilizations and the Remaking of World Order*. New York: Simon & Schuster, 1996.

– *Political Order in Changing Societies*. Cambridge, MA: Yale University, 1968.

Hussain, Jahanzeb. "Where Things Stand One Year after Pakistan's Operation against the Taliban." *Muftah*, 6 October 2015.

Hussain, Zahid. *The Scorpion's Tail: The Relentless Rise of Islamic Militants in Pakistan – And How It Threatens America*. New York: Free Press, 2013.

ibn Taymiyah, Ahmad ibn Abd al-Halim. *Majmu'at al-Rasa'il al-Kubra.* Cairo, 1323/1925.

Illius, Shamsuddin. "Hizb ut-Tahrir Focuses on Social Media." *The Independent*, 4 September 2015.

Inalcik, Halil. "The Nature of Traditional Society: Turkey." In *Political Modernization in Japan and Turkey*, edited by Robert E. Ward and Dankwart A. Rustow. Princeton, NJ: Princeton University Press, 1964.

"Infinite Justice, Out – Enduring Freedom, In." *BBC News*, 25 September 2001.

"Inside the Mind of a 'Black Widow.'" *BBC News*, 4 September 2003.

IntelCenter. "Islamic State's Global Affiliates: Interactive World Map." http://intelcenter.com.

International Crisis Group. "Central Asia: Islam and the State." Asia Report No. 59, 10 July 2003.

– "Hezbollah: Rebel without a Cause?" Middle East Briefing, 30 July 2003.

– "Iran in Iraq: How Much Influence?" Middle East Report No. 38, 21 March 2005.

– "Is Radical Islam Inevitable in Central Asia? Priorities for Engagement." Asia Report No. 72, 22 December 2003.

– "Pakistan: Madrasas, Extremism and the Military." Asia Report No. 36, 29 July 2002.

– "The State of Sectarianism in Pakistan." Asia Report No. 95, 18 April 2005.

– "Syria Calling: Radicalisation in Central Asia." Media release, Bishkek/Brussels, 20 January 2015.
– "Tajikistan Early Warning: Internal Pressures, External Threat." Europe and Central Asia Briefing No. 78, 11 January 2016.
"Introduction to Curriculum Packet on 'Terrorism: A War without Borders.'" US Department of State. n.d.
Isani, Mujtaba. "The Rise and Fall of the Jamaat-e-Islami in the Light of Social Movement Theory." *Virginia Review of Asian Studies* (2011).
Jamal, Umair, and Hafeez-ur-Rehman Hadi. "It's Time for Afghanistan and Pakistan to Move beyond the Blame Game." *The Diplomat*, 13 September 2015.
Jansen, Johannes, J.G. *The Neglected Duty: The Creed of Sadat's Assassins.* New York: Macmillan, 2013.
Jerusalem Center for Public Affairs. "Maintaining Israel's Qualitative Military Edge: Dilemmas for the Bush Administration." *Jerusalem Issue Briefs* 1, no. 12 (16 December 2001).
Jervis, Robert. *The Meaning of the Nuclear Revolution: Statecraft and the Prospect of Armageddon.* Ithaca, NY: Cornell University Press, 1989.
"Jihad against Jews and Crusaders." World Islamic Front Statement, 23 February 1998.
Joscelyn, Thomas. "Admiral Mullen: Pakistan ISI Sponsoring Haqqani Attacks." *Long War Journal*, 22 September 2011.
JPRS Report: Near East and South Asia. Issue 87074. Washington, DC: Foreign Broadcast Information Service, 1987.
Juergensmeyer, Mark. *The New Cold War? Religious Nationalism Confronts the Secular State.* Berkeley: University of California Press, 1993.
Kaiser, Robert G. "Kazakh's Season of Repression: President of Key U.S. Ally Puts Critics on Trial, in Jail." *Washington Post*, 22 July 2002.
Karagiannis, Emmanuel. "Political Islam in Central Asia: The Role of Hizb Al-Tahrir." *CTC Sentinel*, 3 February 2010.
Katzman, Kenneth. "CRS Report for Congress: The Iran Sanctions Act (ISA)." Congressional Research Service, 12 October 2007.
– "Iran Sanctions." Congressional Research Service, 21 January 2016.
Kean, Thomas H., et al. *The 9/11 Commission Report: Final Report of the National Commission on Terrorist Attacks upon the United States.* New York: W.W. Norton, 2004.
Kennedy, Paul. *The Rise and Fall of the Great Powers: Economic Change and Military Conflict from 1500 to 2000.* New York: Random House, 1987.

Kenny, Jeffrey T. *Muslim Rebels: Kharijites and the Politics of Extremism in Egypt*. New York: Oxford University Press, 2006.

Kerr, Malcolm H. *The Arab Cold War: Gamal 'Abd al-Nasir and His Rivals, 1958–1970*, 3rd ed. London: Oxford University Press, 1971.

"Key US Air Base Supplying Afghanistan Closes." *RT America*, 3 June 2014.

Khadduri, Majid. *Political Trends in the Arab World: The Role of Ideas and Ideals in Politics*. Baltimore, MD: Johns Hopkins University Press, 1970.

Khamidov, Alisher. "Countering the Call: The U.S., Hizb-ut-Tahrir, and Religious Extremism in Central Asia." Analysis Paper No. 4. Saban Center for Middle East Policy at the Brookings Institution, July 2003.

Khan, Mohammad Ayub. *Friends Not Masters: A Political Autobiography*. London: Oxford University Press, 1967.

Kholaif, Dahlia. "The Egyptian Army's Economic Juggernaut." *Al-Jazeera*, 5 August 2013.

Khosrokhavar, Farhad. *Suicide Bombers: Allah's New Martyrs*. Translated by David Macey. London: Pluto Press, 2005.

Khouri, Rami G. "The Saudi-Iranian Rivalry Threatens the Entire Middle East." *Al-Jazeera America*, 5 January 2016.

Kilner, James. "Uzbekistan Withdraws from Russia-Led Military Alliance." *Telegraph*, 2 July 2012.

King, John. "Arming Iraq: A Chronology of U.S. Involvement." Iran Chamber Society, March 2003. http://www.iranchamber.com/history/articles/arming_iraq.php.

Kissinger, Henry. *Years of Upheaval*. Boston: Little, Brown, 1982.

Komara, Fika. "Capitalism Exploits Youth's Consumerism in the Social Media." 25 April 2016. https://hizbut-tahrir.org.

Kramer, Marti. "The Oracle of Hizbullah: Sayyid Muhammad Husayn Fadlallah." http://www.martinkramer.org/.

Kranz, Michal. "The Tunisian Miracle: A Marriage of Moderate Islam and Secular Democracy." *Gate*, 20 January 2015.

Krauthammer, Charles. "The Unipolar Moment." *Foreign Affairs* 70, no. 1 (1990): 23–33.

Kredo, Adam. "Iran to Spend $8 Billion on Russian Weapons and Warplanes." *Washington Free Beacon*, 16 February 2016.

Kuchins, Andrew C., Jeffrey Mankoff, and Oliver Backes. "Central Asia in a Reconnecting Eurasia." Center for Strategic and International Studies, June 2015.

"Kyrgyzstan's New Leadership Thanks Russia 'for Helping Oust President.'" *Telegraph*, 9 April 2010.

Lamothe, Dan. "7 Countries Have Entered the Fight against ISIS." *Washington Post*, 20 January 2016.

Landler, Mark. "U.S. and Pakistan Agree to Reinforce Strategic Ties." *New York Times*, 25 March 2010.

Latif, Iqbal. "What Is the Difference between Sistani and Khomeini?" *Newsvine*, March 2007.

Lemieux, Frederic. "A Cyber Strategy." *The Cipher Brief*, 24 December 2015.

Lerner, Daniel. *The Passing of Traditional Society: Modernizing the Middle East*. Glencoe, IL: Free Press of Glencoe, 1964.

Levy, Clifford J. "Central Asia Sounds Alarm on Islamic Radicalism." *New York Times*, 17 August 2009.

Lewis, Bernard. *Islam and the West*. New York: Oxford University Press, 1994.

– "The Revolt of Islam." *The New Yorker*, 9 November 2001.

– *What Went Wrong? Western Impact and Middle Eastern Response*. New York: Oxford University Press, 2002.

Lia, Brynjar. "Abu Mus'ab Al-Suri's Critique of Hard Line Salafists in the Jihadist Current." Combating Terrorism Center, 15 December 2007.

– *Architect of Global Jihad: The Life of Al-Qaida Strategist Abu Mus'ab al-Suri*. New York: Columbia University Press, 2008.

Liang, Christina Schori. "Cyber Jihad: Understanding and Countering Islamic State Propaganda." Policy Paper 2015/2. Geneva Center for Security Policy, February 2015.

"Libya: The Next Failed State." *Economist*, 10 January 2015.

"Lights, Camera, Propaganda: Kerry Taps Hollywood for Help Countering ISIS' Media War." *MintPress News*, 22 February 2016.

Litwak, Robert S. "From 'Rogues' to 'Outliers.'" *Globalist*, 4 May 2010.

Londoño, Ernesto. "Study: Iraq, Afghan War Costs to Top $4 Trillion." *Washington Post*, 28 March 2013.

Lukin, Alexander. *The Bear Watches the Dragon: Russia's Perception of China and the Evolution of the Russian-Chinese Relations since the Eighteenth Century*. New York: M.E. Sharp, 2003.

Lynch, Colum. "U.S. Support for Saudi Strikes in Yemen Raises War Crime Concerns." *Foreign Policy*, 15 October 2015.

MacLeod, Scott, Dean Fischer, and Tim McGirk. "Iran: Tehran vs. the Taliban." *Time*, 28 September 1998.

Mahr, Krista. "Karzai Refuses to Budge on Security Pact." *Time*, 14 December 2013.

Malka, Haim. "Must Innocents Die? The Islamic Debate over Suicide Attack." *Middle East Quarterly* 10, no. 2 (2003): 19–28.

Mamouri, Ali. "Competition Heats Up between Qom, Najaf." *Al-Monitor*, 22 May 2013.

Mankoff, Jeffrey. *The United States and Central Asia after 2014*. Washington, DC: Center for Strategic and International Studies, 2013.

Markowitz, Lawrence P. "When Flimsy States Don't Fail." *Foreign Affairs*, 25 April 2014.

Maududi, Abul A'la. *Jihad in Islam*. Beirut: Holy Koran Publishing House, 2006.

– *Khilafat o Malookeyat* [The caliphate and governance]. Lahore, Pakistan: Idara Tarjuman-ul-Quran, n.d.

Mayer, Jane. "The Predator War: What Are the Risks of the C.I.A.'s Covert Drone Program?" *New Yorker*, 26 October 2009.

McCary, John A. "The Anbar Awaking: An Alliance of Incentives." *Washington Quarterly* 32, no. 1 (2009): 43–59.

McLaughlin, Jenna. "Was Iraq's Top Terrorist Radicalized at a US Run Prison?" *Mother Jones*, 11 July 2014.

– "Why the US Government's Counter-Terrorism Tweeters Are Finding It Tough to Fight ISIS Online." *Mother Jones*, 10 September 2014.

Mead, Walter Russell. "NATO Must Have Turkey's Back." *American Interest*, 24 November 2015.

"'Members' Surprised by Saudi Anti-Terror Coalition Plan." *BBC News*, 16 December 2015.

Miller, Greg, and Bob Woodward. "Secret Memos Reveal Explicit Nature of U.S., Pakistan Agreement on Drones." *Washington Post*, 23 October 2013.

Miller, J. Berkshire. "China, Kyrgyzstan Ties Warm." *Diplomat Blogs*, 9 September 2011.

Mitchell, Derek J. "China and Russia." In *The China Balance Sheet in 2007 and Beyond*, edited by C. Fred Bergsten, Bates Gill, Nicholas R. Lardy, and Derek J. Mitchell, 133–50. Washington, DC: Center for Strategic and International Studies, 2007.

Mitchell, Richard P. *The Society of the Muslim Brothers*. New York: Oxford University Press, 1969.

– *The Society of the Muslim Brothers*. Reprint with new introduction. New York: Oxford University Press, 1993.

Mneimneh, Hassan. "The Arab Reception of Vilayat-e-Faqih: The Counter-Model of Muhammad Mahdi Shams al-Din." *Current Trends in Islamic Ideology* 8 (21 May 2009).

Moghadam, Assaf. "Motives for Martyrdom: Al-Qaida, Salafi Jihad, and the Spread of Suicide Attacks." *International Security* 33, no. 3 (2008/09): 46–78.

Moghadam, Assaf, and Brian Fishman, eds. *Self-Inflicted Wounds: Debates and Divisions within al-Qa'ida and Its Periphery*. Harmony Project, Combating Terrorism Center at West Point, 16 December 2010.

Moore-Gilbert, Kylie. "Sectarian Divide and Rule in Bahrain: A Self-Fulfilling Prophecy?" Middle East Institute, 19 January 2016.

Morello, Carol. "Ayatollah Says Nuclear Deal Will Not Change Iran's Relations with U.S." *Washington Post*, 18 July 2015.

Morris, Loveday, and Mustafa Salim. "Iran Backs Syria's Battle for Aleppo with Proxies, Ground Troops." *Washington Post*, 19 October 2015.

Mottale, Morris M. "The Birth of a New Class." *Al-Jazeera*, 22 April 2010.

Mozaffari, Mehdi. "What Is Islamism? History and Definition of a Concept." *Totalitarian Religions and Political Movements* 8, no. 1 (2007): 17–33.

"Mullen to Ashkenazi on Iran: All Options on the Table." *Jerusalem Post*, 17 November 2010.

Musallam, Adnan A. *From Secularism to Jihad: Sayyid Qutb and the Foundations of Radical Islam*. Westport, CT: Praeger, 2005.

Musharraf, Pervez. *In the Line of Fire: A Memoir*. New York: Free Press, 2006.

Mutlu, Gülay. "Is the C5+1 a Long-Awaited Initiative for Central Asia?" *Turkish Weekly*, 27 November 2015.

Nadwi, Sayyed Abul Hasan Ali. *Islam and the World: The Rise and Decline of Muslims and Its Effect on Mankind*. Translated by Muhammad Asif Kidwa. Leicester: UK Islamic Academy, 2005.

Napoleoni, Loretta. *Terror Incorporated: Tracing the Dollars behind the Terror Networks*. New York: Seven Stories Press, 2005.

Nasr, Seyyed Vali Reza. *Mawdudi and the Making of Islamic Revivalism*. New York: Oxford University Press, 1996.

Nasr, Vali. *International Relations of an Islamic Movement: The Case of the Jama 'at-i Islami of Pakistan*. New York: Council of Foreign Relations, 2000.

– *The Shia Revival: How Conflicts within Islam Will Shape the Future*. New York: W.W. Norton, 2006.

"'The No-Fly Zone War' (U.S./U.K.-Iraq Conflict) 1991–2003." *Historyguy.com*, 22 March 2003.

Nordland, Rod, and Alissa J. Rubin. "Karzai's Bet: US Is Bluffing in Warning on Security Pact." *New York Times*, 26 November 2013.

Norton, Augustus Richard. *Hezbollah: A Short History*. Princeton, NJ: Princeton University Press, 2007.

– "The Role of Hezbollah in Lebanese Domestic Politics." *International Spectator* 42, no. 2 (2007): 475–91.

Nuclear Threat Initiative. "Iran." Country profile, last updated March 2016. http://www.nti.org/learn/countries/iran/.

Nye, Joseph S., Jr. "The Decline of America's Soft Power." *Foreign Affairs*, May/June 2004.

O'Neill, Tim. "Anonymous vs. ISIS – A New Dimension of Cyber Warfare" (blog post). www.garlandtechnology.com, 8 December 2015.

Onley, James. "Britain's Informal Empire in the Gulf, 1820–1971." *Journal of Social Affairs* 22, no. 87 (2005).

"An Open Letter: The Hizballah Program." *Jerusalem Quarterly* 48 (Fall 1988).

Page, Clarence. "Declare Victory and Get Out of the Way." *RealClearPolitics*, 19 October 2006.

Pagliery, Jose. "Terrorists Hide Plans by 'Going Dark.'" CNN, 16 November 2015.

Pannier, Bruce. "Central Asia: SCO to Hold Largest Military Exercises to Date." *Radio Free Europe/Radio Liberty*, 8 August 2007.

– "What Next for the Islamic Movement of Uzbekistan?" *Qishloq Ovozi* (blog), 23 August 2015.

Pape, Robert. *Dying to Win: The Strategic Logic of Suicide Terrorism*. New York: Random House, 2005.

Pargoo, Mahmoud. "How Sanctions Helped Iranian Tech Industry." *Al-Monitor*, 4 February 2016.

Paulson, Steve. "Does Islam Stand against Science?" *Chronicle of Higher Education*, 19 June 2011.

Pedahzur, Ami, ed. *Root Causes of Suicide Terrorism: The Globalization of Martyrdom*. New York: Routledge, 2006.

Peretz, Don. "Arab-Israel War of 1973." *Encyclopedia.com* (2004).

Pew Research Center. "Osama Bin Laden Largely Discredited among Muslim Publics in Recent Years." 2 May 2011. www.pewglobal.org.

– "Tolerance and Tension: Islam and Christianity in Sub-Saharan Africa." 15 April 2010. www.pewforum.org.

– "The World's Muslims: Religion, Politics and Society." 30 April 2013. www.pewforum.org.

– "A Year after Iraq War: Mistrust of America in Europe Ever Higher, Muslim Anger Persists." 16 March 2004. http://www.people-press.org.

Pfaff, William. "Redefining World Power." *Foreign Affairs* 70, no. 1 (1990).

Philips, Abu Ameenah Bilal. *The Fundamentals of Tawheed*. Riyadh: International Publishing House, 2005.

Pillalamarri, Akhilesh. "The United States Just Closed Its Last Base in Central Asia." *Diplomat*, 10 June 2014.

Pitt, William Rivers. "The Project for the New American Century." Information Clearing House, 25 February 2003.

Pomfret, Richard. "Central Asia after Two Decades of Independence." Working Paper No. 2010/53. United Nations University, May 2010.

"Pragmatism and Realism." *LinkedIn SlideShare*, 9 December 2008.

Qur'an, Tafseer Ibn-e- Kathir. Islamabad: Maktaba Darul-Islam, n.d.

Qutb, Sayyid. *Fi Zilal al-Qu'ran* [In the shade of the Qu'ran]. Delhi, India: Kitab Bhavan, 2000.

– "Foreword." In *Islam and the World: The Rise and Decline of Muslims and Its Effect on Mankind*, by Sayyed Abul Hasan Ali Nadwi. Translated by Muhammad Asif Kidwa. Leicester: UK Islamic Academy, 2005.

Raghavan, V.R. "Strategic Depth in Afghanistan." *Hindu*, 7 November 2001.

Rashid, Ahmed. "Central Asia Asking for Holy War." *Far Eastern Economic Review*, November 2000.

– *Descent into Chaos: The United States and the Failure of Nation Building in Pakistan, Afghanistan, and Central Asia*. New York: Penguin Group, 2008.

– "The Hizb ut-Tahrir: Reviving the Caliphate." In *Jihad: The Rise of Militant Islam in Central Asia*. New Haven, CT: Yale University Press, 2002.

– *Jihad: The Rise of Militant Islam in Central Asia*. New Haven, CT: Yale University Press, 2002.

– *The Taliban: Militant Islam, Oil and Fundamentalism in Central Asia*. New Haven, CT: Yale University Press, 2000.

– "They're Only Sleeping: Why Militant Islamists in Central Asia Aren't Going to Go Away." *New Yorker*, 14 January 2001.

Rasizade, Alec. "The New 'Great Game' in Central Asia after Afghanistan." *Alternatives* 1, no. 2 (2002).

Raziq, Ali Abdel. *Al-Islam Wa Usul Al-Hukm: Bahth Fi-l Khilafa Wa-l Hukuma Fi-l Islam* [Islam and the foundations of governance: Research on the caliphate and governance in Islam]. Critique and commentary by Mamdooh Haqqi. Beirut, 1978.

"Reagan Doctrine, 1985." U.S. Department of State Archive (2001–2009). http://2001-2009.state.gov/r/pa/ho/time/rd/17741.htm.

Reals, Tucker. "Iran: Obama Must 'Unclench' America's Fist." *CBS News*, 28 January 2009.

Riedel, Bruce. "Al Qaeda Strikes Back." *Foreign Affairs* (May/June 2007).

Rienzi, Michael V. "Iran's Response to a U.S. Attack." *Small Wars Journal*, 17 February 2012.

Roggio, Bill, and Thomas Joscelyn. "Central Asian Groups Split over Leadership of Global Jihad." *Long War Journal*, 24 August 2015.

Rough, Peter. "Obama's Crumbling Syria Strategy." *Real Clear Defense*, 11 February 2016.

Roy, Olivier. *Afghanistan: From Holy War to Civil War*. Princeton, NJ: Darwin Press, 1995.

Ruck, Jimmy A., Anna Saakyan, Igor Tomashov, and William Treseder. "The US Plans for Ballistic Missile Defense: Impact on International Security and US-Russia Relations." *Stanford US-Russia Forum [SURF] Journal* 1 (2009/10).

Rumer, Eugene, Richard Sokolsky, and Paul Stronski. "US Policy toward Central Asia 3.0." Carnegie Endowment for International Peace, 25 January 2016.

"Rumsfeld Blames Iraq Problems on 'Pockets of Dead-Enders.'" *USA Today*, 18 June 2003.

Rustow, Dankwart A. "Ataturk as a Founder of a State." In *Philosophers and Kings: Studies in Leadership*, edited by Dankwart A. Rustow. New York: George Braziller, 1970.

Ryan, Missy, and Susan Cornwell. "U.S. Says Pakistan's ISI Supported Kabul Embassy Attack." *Reuters*, 22 September 2011.

Saad-Ghorayeb, Amal. *Hizbu'llah: Politics and Religion*. Sterling, VA: Pluto Press, 2002.

Saidazimova, Gulnoza. "Central Asia: What Does Closure of US Military Base in Uzbekistan Mean?" *Radio Free Europe/Radio Liberty*, 1 August 2005.

Sanchez, Ray, Tim Lister, Mark Bixler, Sean O'Key, Michael Hogenmiller, and Mohammed Tawfeeq. "ISIS Goes Global: Over 70 Attacks in 20 Countries." *CNN*, 17 February 2016.

Sands, Gary. "China Seeks Hegemony in East Asia." *Foreign Policy Blogs Network*, 16 February 2016.

Sanger, David E. "Biblical Quotes Said to Adorn Pentagon Reports." *New York Times*, 17 May 2009.

– *The Inheritance: The World Obama Confronts and the Challenges to American Power*. New York: Harmony Books, 2009.

Sattlof, Robert, and David Schenker. "Political Instability in Jordan." Contingency Planning Memorandum No. 19. Council of Foreign Relations, May 2013.

Schmidt, Michael S. "Navy Releases Timeline of Iran's Capture of U.S. Sailors." *International New York Times*, 18 January 2016.

Schmitz, Gregor Peter. "Afghanistan Speech at West Point: Obama's Half-Hearted Surge." *Spiegel Online*, 2 December 2009.

Shafiq, Munir. "Secularism and the Arab-Muslim Condition." In *Islam and Secularism in the Middle East*, edited by Azzam Tamimi and John L. Esposito. New York: New York University Press, 2000.

Shah, Zia H. Review of *Islam and Science: Religious Orthodoxy and Battle for Rationality*, by Pervez Amirali Hoodbhoy. *Al Islam eGazette*, 3 July 2009.

Shane, Scott, and Ben Hubbard. "ISIS Displaying a Deft Command of Varied Media." *New York Times*, 30 August 2014.

Shatz, Adam. "In Search of Hezbollah." *New York Review of Books*, 29 April 2004.

Shepard, William E. "Sayyid Qutb's Doctrine of Jahiliyya." *International Journal of Middle East Studies* 35, no. 4 (2003): 521–45.

Sherazi, Zahir Shah. "TTP Finalises 15 Point Draft for Talks: Sources." *Dawn*, 10 February 2014.

Shin, Dong-min. "A Critical Review of the Concept of Middle Power." *E-International Relations*, 4 December 2015.

Singh, Khushwant. "The Burnt Inside of Pakistan's House of Atreus." *Outlook*, 26 April 2010.

Sivan, Emmanuel. *Radical Islam: Medieval Theology and Modern Politics*. New Haven, CT: Yale University Press, 1990.

Slim, Randa M. "Central Asia: The Ferghana Valley: In the Midst of a Host of Crises." In *Searching for Peace in Europe and Eurasia: An Overview of Conflict Prevention and Peacebuilding Activities*, edited by Paul van Tongeren, Hans van de Veen, and Juliette Verhoeven. Boulder, CO: Lynne Rienner Publishers, 2004.

Sly, Liz. "Al-Qaeda Disavows Any Ties with Radical Islamist ISIS Group in Syria, Iraq." *Washington Post*, 3 February 2014.

Small, Andrew. "What Now for China's Afghanistan Strategy?" *Diplomat*, 1 September 2015.

Smith, James Purcell. "The IMU: Alive and Kicking?" *Central Asia-Caucasus Analyst,* 23 September 2003.

Smurr, Virginia. "The Power of Ideas: Sayyid Qutb and Islamism." Rockford College summer research project, 2004.

Smyth, Phillip. "Hizballah Cavalcade; What Is the *Liwa'a Abu Fadl al-Abbas* (LAFA)? Assessing Syria's Shia 'International Brigade' through Their Social Media Presence." *Jihadology*, 15 May 2013.

Sokan, Kenny. "Erdogan Feels the US Left Turkey in the Lurch with Syrian Conflict." *Public Radio International*, 11 February 2016.

Solomon, Hussein. "Islamism on the Rise in Africa." RIMA Occasional Papers 4, no. 3 (March 2016). Research on Islam in Muslim Africa.

Solomon, Jay. "U.S., Russia Agree on Plan on Syrian Chemical Weapons." *Wall Street Journal*, 14 September 2013.

Sousa, David. "Three Phases of Resistance: How Hezbollah Pushed Israel out of Lebanon." *E-International Relations*, 28 April 2014.

"State Department Experts Warned CENTCOM before Iraq War about Lack of Plans for Post-War Iraq Security." National Security Archive Electronic Briefing Book No. 163, 17 August 2005.

Stein, Matthew. "The Goals of the Islamic Movement of Uzbekistan and Its Impact on Central Asia and the United States." Foreign Military Studies Office, 27 February 2016.

Steinberg, Guido, and Isabelle Werenfels. "Between the 'Near' and the 'Far' Enemy: Al-Qaeda in the Islamic Maghreb." *Mediterranean Politics* 12, no. 3 (2007): 407–13.

Stimson Center. "Public Opinion in Iran." 20 February 2009. http://www.stimson.org/content/public-opinion-iran.

Stodghill, Ron. "Kazakhstan: Oil, Cash and Corruption." *New York Times*, 5 November 2006. http://www.corpwatch.org.

Stoessinger, John G. *Crusaders and Pragmatists: Movers of Modern American Foreign Policy,* 2nd ed. New York: W.W. Norton, 1985.

"Stop 'Baseless Propaganda,' Pakistan Tells Afghanistan." *Daily Times*, 4 September 2015.

"The Struggle for Iran's Soul." *Foreign Policy*, 12 October 2015.

Sullivan, Andrew. "This Is a Religious War." *New York Times*, 7 October 2001.

"Sunni Rebels Declare New 'Islamic Caliphate.'" *Al-Jazeera*, 30 June 2014.

Tabyshalieva, Anara. "Central Asia Struggles to Keep Tensions in Check." *Surviving Together* (a quarterly on grassroots cooperation in Eurasia) 15, no. 2 (1997).

Tahir-ul-Qadri, Muhammad. *Introduction to the Fatwa on Suicide Bombings and Terrorism*. Translated by Shaykh Abdul Aziz Dabbagh. London: Minhaj-ul-Quran International, 2010.

– "What Is Jihad?" Lecture presented at the United States Institute of Peace, November 2010.

"Tajik Islamic Party Banned, Given Deadline to Stop Activities." *Radio Free Europe/Radio Liberty*, 28 August 2015.

Tolipov, Farkhod. "CSTO: Collective Security or Collective Confusion?" *Central Asia-Caucasus Institute Analyst*, 1 September 2009.

"Top U.S. Warfighting Experts: Drones Increase Terrorism." *Washington's Blog*, 19 July 2015.

Tora Bora Revisited: How We Failed to Get Bin Laden and Why It Matters Today. A report to members of the Committee on Foreign Relations, United States Senate. Washington, DC: U.S. Government Printing Office, 2009.

Townsend, Mark, and Toby Helm. "Jihad in a Social Media Age: How Can the West Win an Online War?" *The Guardian*, 23 August 2014.

Trachtenberg, Marc. "The Influence of Nuclear Weapons in the Cuban Missile Crisis." *International Security* 10, no. 1 (1985).

"Transnational and Organised Crime and Terrorism." Theology Religion Essay. 23 March 2015. https://www.ukessays.com.

Tremblay, Pinar. "Islamic State Isn't the Only One Calling for a Caliphate in Turkey." *Al-Monitor*, 2 May 2016.

Treverton, Gregory F., Heather S. Gregg, Daniel Gibran, and Charles W. Yost. *Exploring Religious Conflict.* Santa Monica, CA: RAND Corporation, 2005.

Trilling, David. "Evaluating Kyrgyzstan's Impact on the Islamic Militant Threat in Central Asia." EurasiaNet.org, 10 June 2010.

Trotta, Daniel. "Iraq War Costs U.S. More Than $2 Trillion: Study." *Reuters*, 14 March 2013.

Tyler, Patrick. *A World of Trouble: The White House and the Middle East – from the Cold War to the War on Terror*. New York: Farrar, Straus & Giroux, 2009.

"The UN Ferghana Valley Development Programme." World History Archives, 1999.

"US Cited Controversial Law in Decision to Kill American Citizen by Drone." *The Guardian*, 23 June 2013.

"Uzbek President Bans Teaching of Political Science." *The Guardian*, September 5, 2015.

Vali, Davron. "Banned Islamic Movement Increasingly Active in Tajikistan." EurasiaNet.org, 4 September 2002.

Voll, John O. "Foreword." In *The Society of the Muslim Brothers*, by Richard P. Mitchell. New York: Oxford University Press, 1993.

Walsh, Declan, Ben Hubbard, and Eric Schmitt. "U.S. Bombing in Libya Reveals Limits of Strategy against ISIS." *New York Times*, 19 February 2016.

Waraich, Omar. "How a U.S. Aid Package to Pakistan Could Threaten Zardari." *Time*, 8 October 2009.
– "Pakistan Cuts Off Nato's Supply Line after 25 Troops Killed." *Independent*, 27 November 2011.
Weaver, Mary Ann. "Bhutto's Fateful Moment." *New Yorker*, 4 October 1993.
Weitz, Richard. "Beijing and Washington Brace for Central Asia 2016." *China and US Focus*, 16 December 2015.
– "For U.S., Dividing China, Russia in Central Asia Easier Said Than Done." *World Politics Review*, 7 April 2015.
– "Military Exercises Underscore the SCO's Character." *Central Asia Newswire*, 2 June 2011.
"What Obama's Predator-Strike Policy Tells Us about Bush's Covert Attacks." *Newsweek*, 30 March 2010.
"White Paper of the Interagency Policy Group's Report on U.S. Policy toward Afghanistan and Pakistan." *White House*, March 2009.
Whitmore, Brian. "Sphere of Reluctance: Russia Hesitant about Kyrgyz Intervention." *Radio Free Europe/Radio Liberty*, 15 June 2010.
Williams, Brian Glyn. "From 'Secessionist Rebels' to 'Al-Qaeda Shock Brigades': Assessing Russia's Efforts to Extend the Post-September 11th War on Terror to Chechnya." *Comparative Studies of South Asia, Africa and the Middle East* 24, no. 1 (2004).
Woodward, Bob. *State of Denial: Bush at War, Part III*. New York: Simon & Schuster, 2006.
Wright, Lawrence. *The Looming Tower: Al-Qaeda and the Road to 9/11*. New York: Vintage Books, 2006.
– "The Man behind Bin Laden." *New Yorker*, 16 September 2002.
– "The Master Plan." *New Yorker*, 11 September 2006.
Wright, Robin. *Sacred Rage: The Wrath of Militant Islam*. New York: Touchstone, 1985.
Yazdani, Enayatollah. "Competition over the Caspian Oil Routes: Oilers and Gamers Perspective." *Alternatives: Turkish Journal of International Relations* 5 (Spring/Summer 2006).
"Yemen Crisis: Who Is Fighting Whom?" BBC *News*, 25 March 2015.
Yousaf, Mohammad, and Mark Adkin. *The Bear Trap: Afghanistan's Untold Story*. London: Leo Cooper, 1992.
"Zarqawi Letter. February 2004 Coalition Provisional Authority English Translation of Terrorist Musab al Zarqawi Letter Obtained by United States Government in Iraq." US Department of State Archive, 20 January 2001–20 January 2009.
Zenko, Micah. "When Reagan Cut and Run." *Foreign Policy*, 7 February 2014.

Index